A History

of

the United States

A History of the United States

C. P. HILL, M.A.
Senior Lecturer in Education, University of Exeter

THIRD EDITION
REVISED AND ENLARGED

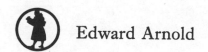 Edward Arnold

© C. P. Hill, 1974

First published 1942
by Edward Arnold (Publishers) Ltd.
25 Hill Street, London W1X 8LL

Second Edition 1966
Reprinted 1968, 1969, 1971
Third Edition 1974
Reprinted 1976, 1977

ISBN: 0 7131 1829 6

Printed in Great Britain by
The Camelot Press Ltd., Southampton

Preface to First Edition

The study of American history has been much neglected in England. This is unfortunate, as well for the intrinsic interest of the subject as for the fact that we can so easily get a misleading impression of the Americans from other sources. Hollywood is the chief of these, and Hollywood already has much to answer for. As we sit back in our seats at the cinema and marvel at its latest triumphs, we forget that behind this fantastic shop-window there is a nation with a history and traditions of its own.

This book is about the growth of that nation. I have attempted to provide for boys and girls of about fifteen to sixteen years of age a narrative history of the United States, beginning the story with the voyage of Christopher Columbus, and carrying it up to the second re-election of Franklin Roosevelt in November, 1940. The central theme is the political and economic development of the American people. If the book interests pupils younger or older, or attracts the adult reader, I shall be the more pleased. Whatever form the society of mankind takes after the catastrophe through which it is now passing, the American people must play a decisive part in the world's reconstruction, and it is therefore urgent that we should know more about them. We can scarcely know them or form a right judgment upon them without knowing their history, for that has made them what they are.

The book is based almost wholly upon secondary authorities, and it can make no claim to be a work of original research. The responsibility for my statements is my own: but I should like to thank all those who in various ways have helped me. Among them are Miss Hilda Parker, who bore nobly with an awkward guest; my colleagues, Mr. S. C. Evernden and Mr. E. L. G. Warren, and Mr. R. J. Church of St. Christopher School, Letchworth; and the publishers, who have gone to an infinity of trouble. Most of all, I must thank my wife, for her typing, her mapping, and her patience.

C. P. HILL

WARWICK,
February, 1942

Preface to Second Edition

It is a great pleasure to be able to begin the preface to a second edition of this book by observing that the opening sentence of the preface to the first edition is now quite untrue. The study of the history of the United States is no longer neglected in this country. It is the subject both of teaching and of research in the majority of British universities. In this development the British Association for American Studies, founded in 1955 by a group of lively and enthusiastic scholars, has played a central role, and its stimulating influence has spread to most of those who teach American history in universities, training colleges, and schools. If it were customary to dedicate second editions of school textbooks, this one would certainly be dedicated to B.A.A.S.

This edition differs substantially from the previous one, in two ways. First, scholars both American and British have during the last twenty-three years revised many established interpretations in the history of the United States. To incorporate the main results of this revision has involved considerable changes even in a relatively elementary book. Secondly, the book now extends to 1963 instead of to 1940: this additional material covers the period which has seen the clear emergence of the United States as the leader of the western world. I hope it is now a better book as well as a longer one. Certainly I have had much agreeable and friendly help in preparing this edition. In particular I should like to thank Professor Maldwyn Jones of the Department of American Studies in the University of Manchester and Dr. Angus J. Johnston, Head of the Social Studies Department, New Trier High School, Winnetka, Illinois, both of whom gave immense assistance by their thorough and constructive detailed criticism of the previous edition; Professor Esmond Wright of the University of Glasgow, who generously read and improved the post-1940 material; and Mr. Peter Watkins, Senior History Master at Bristol Grammar School, who was kind enough to read the proofs. Between them they got rid of many errors and misinterpretations, and they must not be held responsible for the faults that remain.

C. P. HILL

Exeter,
  March, 1965

Preface to Third Edition

This edition brings the account of American history to 1973. In order to cover the additional ten years I have divided the final chapter of the second edition into two, revised and reorganised the material it contained, and added substantial new sections. I have also taken the opportunity to make a small number of minor corrections and alterations in the body of the book. Professors Ray Billington of the Huntington Library in California and Herbert Nicholas of the University of Oxford and my former student Mr. John R. Hoover have kindly read the new material for me. I am most grateful to them for the improvements they have made in it; but they must not be held responsible for any mistakes that remain or for the view of recent history which the book suggests.

C. P. HILL

EXETER
December, 1973

Contents

Plates

ACKNOWLEDGEMENTS

We would like to thank the following for permission to reproduce the photographs used in this book:
The Mansell Collection (opposite pages 16, 80, 208); The United States Information Service (opposite pages 17, 48, 112 (bottom), 113, 145, 209); The Radio Times Hulton Picture Library (opposite pages 81, 112 (top), 144, 176); Planet News (opposite pages 177, 240, 241), Associated Press (opposite pages 252, 253).

Maps

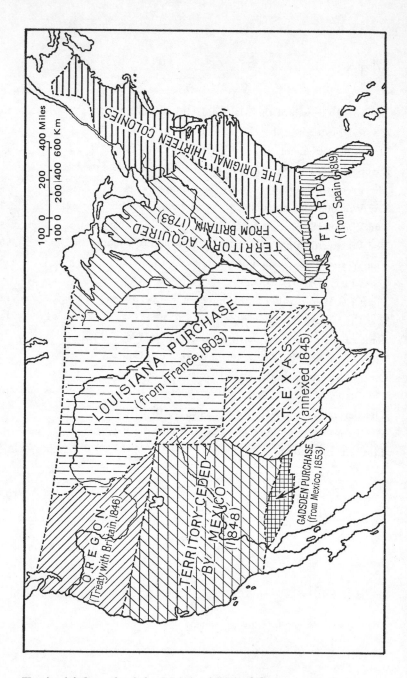

Territorial Growth of the Mainland United States

1   The Land

Most people in the United States to-day speak English, and many of them speak it as their native tongue. Yet they speak it with a marked nasal twang and they use idioms and figures of speech which many English people find hard to understand. It is the same language, but with a difference. Many American ideas and institutions are like those of England, and yet different from them. For example, Congress in the U.S.A. is the equivalent of Parliament, a vital part of the machinery of government. Like the British House of Commons, it represents the people: its members are elected by votes of the people, and they belong to political parties. Yet there are very great differences between the way Congress works and the way the House of Commons works: for example, the members of the American Cabinet are not allowed to sit in Congress, and the aims of American and British political parties are very different.

English is the language of the U.S.A. because most of its settlers, particularly in the early days, were British, and for the same reason many of its ideas and institutions are like those of Britain. The differences between them have arisen for two reasons. First, many other peoples have contributed to the growth of the U.S.A. Spaniards and Frenchmen were among the earliest explorers of North America. Thousands of African Negroes were brought in as slaves in the 17th and 18th centuries. The great flood of immigrants which poured from Europe into the U.S.A. in the 19th century contained Irish, Germans, Scandinavians, Italians and Slavs. All have left some mark. So it has come about—to give two familiar but significant examples—that the two greatest cities of California are called by Spanish names, and that one of the great cities of the Middle West is called St. Louis.

The second, and more important, reason why American civilisation is not a mere copy of English civilisation lies in the geography of the U.S.A. The land which the immigrants from Europe and their descendants have occupied has shaped and moulded their fortunes. The natural features and climate of North America have not only determined where settlers should live and what sort of occupations they should follow, attracting them to some regions and repelling them from others: they have also changed the immigrants' outlook upon life, giving to them new ways of thought and new habits. It is the geography of the U.S.A. which has changed the immigrant from English, German, Italian, Irish, Russian or whatever he was into American. American geography is the background of American history.

I. SIZE, RELIEF, CLIMATE AND VEGETATION, NATURAL RESOURCES

The most striking fact of American geography is the size of the country in comparison with the size of those lands from which most of its settlers came. The area of the U.S.A., including Alaska and Hawaii, is 3,554,000 square miles: the area of Europe without Soviet Russia is rather over half of this. The single state of Texas is five times as big as England. The eastern and western coasts of the mainland U.S.A. are each over 1500 miles long, while its Canadian boundary is over 3000 miles. Yet size alone cannot attract people to a new land. Australia with nearly 3,000,000 square miles has less than 13,000,000 inhabitants, about 6 per cent. of the population of the U.S.A. It is rather the temperate yet varied climate and the rich natural resources of the U.S.A. that have attracted settlers and made its growth possible.

Three broad features of the relief of the U.S.A. must be noted. First, the line of the Appalachian Mountains[1] runs most of the length of the eastern seaboard at a distance never greater than 250 miles from the sea. In the north the distance is often less. Secondly, to the west of these mountains lies the vast area of the Mississippi Valley, drained by the giant Mississippi River system. Thirdly, between the Valley and the west coast runs the tangled mass of the Rockies, a mountainous area nearly twice as wide as the Valley, with a general level of over 3000 feet, rising in many peaks to over 14,000 feet. (See map on page 3.)

The U.S.A.—apart from its two newest states, Alaska and Hawaii—lies wholly in the north temperate zone. But the size of the land, a latitude range of some 24 degrees and a longitude range of 58 degrees, and the presence of a great mountain barrier on the Pacific coast help to create a great variety of climate. Hence comes the difference between the snows of the Rockies and the steaming summer heat of the Mississippi lowlands: hence too the fantastic extremes of summer heat and winter cold which occur in the north of the Great Plains. So too there is a rich variety of natural vegetation, ranging from the mediterranean crops of California to the pine-forests of New England, and from the barren desert of New Mexico to the grassland of the prairies.

The country possesses a splendid variety of natural resources. The rich cotton-growing lands of the Mississippi Basin, the cornlands, the grazing areas of the Great Plains, and the orange-groves of California are among the most striking examples of the agricultural wealth of the U.S.A.; and so until the later 19th century the great mass of immigrants settled on the

---

[1] Frequently known as the Alleghenies, which is the older name, and is still used for part of the range.

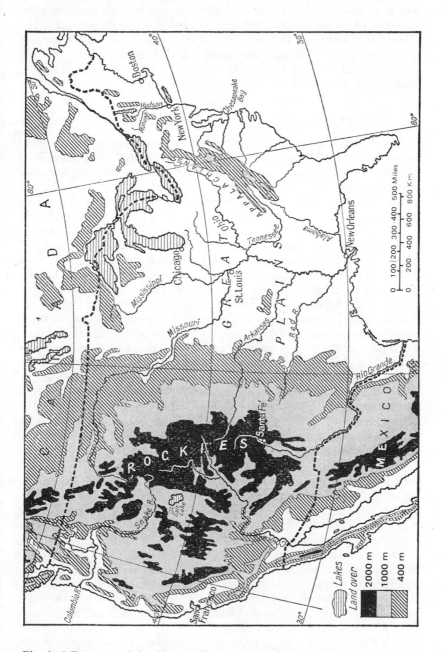

Physical Features of the United States

land. The industrial resources of the U.S.A. are very great, and enabled her to overtake Britain's industrial development in spite of a late start. She has had considerable resources of coal (e.g. in Pennsylvania and Alabama) and iron (e.g. in Minnesota); of oil (e.g. in Texas and California); of gold (e.g. in California) and other minerals (e.g. in Colorado and Nevada); and, on the whole, as generous a distribution of the basic materials of modern industry as any land in the world.

2. AMERICAN GEOGRAPHY IN AMERICAN HISTORY

These facts do much in a general way to explain the rapid and astonishing growth of the United States. There was land enough with possibilities enough to attract settlers who were, as we shall see, anxious for other reasons to quit Europe. Once these immigrants were in America, the natural resources of the land were enough to change their outlook very greatly. Let us consider now how these geographical facts have worked out in American history. All that is said in the next few paragraphs is sketchy and will need to be filled out as we read the rest of the book: but they will suggest some of the main factors that have influenced the history of the U.S.A. We are on the edge of the wood. It will be well to pause before we plunge right into it, and to take a good look at some of the greater trees.

The pride which many Americans take in mere size or bigness has become a kind of stock joke, like the Scotsman's proverbial caution about money. Many Americans 'talk big': they are proud of their skyscrapers, of the size of the Niagara Falls, of the vast industrial production of their country, of their colossal engineering feats like the Hoover Dam, of the fact that the U.S.A. has more millionaires than any other country in the world. This sort of outlook is not an accident: it reflects the great material achievements which the size of their land makes possible. This is a rather obvious result of the size of the U.S.A. There are two others, much more important, which must be mentioned here—Immigration, and the idea of the Frontier.

In 1607 104 white people landed on the coast of Virginia. This was the first British settlement, the nucleus around which the U.S.A. has grown. In 1970 there were over 203 millions of people in the United States. This almost incredible growth of population has been the result of a vast migration of human beings to this new land—a land which was large enough to hold them all, to enable them to live and to rear families. The figures of immigration, especially in the years before the First World War, are remarkable. Between 1820 and 1910 nearly 28,000,000 immigrants entered the U.S.A., 8,790,000 of them between 1900 and 1910. This last figure means an average of over three immigrants for every two minutes of the ten years. No doubt most of these people came to the New World because they were sick of the Old, where they were persecuted or unemployed, and because America offered freedom or work or the chance of getting rich quickly. But it was the mere size of the land that made immigration on so colossal a scale possible.

Many of the great multitude, especially during the second half of the 19th century, helped to swell the population of the swiftly-growing industrial cities of the eastern U.S.A. Yet many of the immigrants went straight through to break new land further west in the great spaces of the interior. And there were countless others, American-born as well as recent settlers in the eastern states, who 'went west' because they were tired of working for a boss, or because they were tired of the town in which they lived, or because the itch to wander was part of them. This call of the west has been a factor of immense importance in American history. The frontier—remember that to Americans the word 'frontier' means not only a boundary between two countries, but also the western limit of civilisation in the U.S.A., that shifting undefined line where white settlement ended and the wilderness began—was steadily pushed westward. This 'ever-moving frontier' has influenced American life in innumerable ways. Later in this book we shall look into these in more detail: here two are worth noting. First, the frontier has made American life far more genuinely democratic. The frontiersman, a typical figure in American literature, with his direct speech, sturdy self-reliance and simple ways of life, was far too independent a person to respect others just because they were rich or educated or well-dressed. On the frontier life was hard, and it was what a man was, not his wealth or his pedigree, that mattered and that other frontiersmen respected. This independence of outlook became a part of American life. The two most sincerely democratic of American Presidents in the 19th century were westerners, born and brought up in frontier households—Andrew Jackson and Abraham Lincoln. Secondly, the problems of frontier settlement provoked some of the most serious crises of American history. In particular, several times when new western states were to be admitted to the Union (e.g. Missouri in 1819–20 and Kansas after 1854) a bitter question arose—should slavery be permitted in them or not? This question of slavery in the western lands eventually helped to split the union and to lead to the American Civil War (see Chap. 13).

The relief of America has influenced its history. The eastern mountain range, the Appalachians, has played an important part in American history. Settlement of North America came from the east, and until about 1750 the Appalachians were a barrier to further penetration of the land. The early settlements were on the coastal plain east of the Appalachians, and along this plain the thirteen original colonies grew. When, by about 1800, many thousands had settled in the rich lands which lie to the west of the mountains, another difficulty arose. Just as the Appalachian barrier had hindered the movement of pioneers westwards, so it hindered the transpor of the farm produce from the western settlements eastward. Not until the building of railroads—from about 1840 onwards—was communication across the Appalachians easy, although the canals and roads built earlier in the 19th century had lessened the difficulty. This fact is one illustration of the obstacles which relief has put in the way of American transport. Settlement has been from east to west: the main natural routeways, the great river valleys, run mainly from north to south. This is particularly true of the greatest river-system, that of the Mississippi, which drains the central regions of the country southwards to the Gulf of Mexico. During the 19th century these became the great agricultural area of the country, with their prairies, their grazing-lands, and, in the south, their vast cotton-fields. In this development, 'Ol' Man River' played an immense part. His influence and that of his tributaries, notably of the Ohio, in American history has been immeasurable. The Mississippi was the great highway of the early days of settlement on the west of the Appalachians, carrying the farm produce of these western lands down to the sea at New Orleans, whence it was shipped to Europe and to the West Indies. Thus it linked the West with the southern states, while the Appalachians, until the rail-road age, cut the West off from the northern states.

Beyond the Great Plains, the Rockies, the third major feature of relief, have acted as another and a vaster barrier. When settlement, towards the end of the 19th century, reached the Rockies it slowed, for the eastern side of the mountain chain is generally dry and barren. The states of this region are sparsely populated even to-day. It was the last American area to be settled, and people came to it from the west as well as from the east. The Rockies marked the end of the frontier. Many of the settlers of those few states which lie across the Rockies came not overland but by sea: this was particularly true of California, which owed its rapid and early growth to the gold rush of 1849.

It is obvious that it is variety of climate and natural resources that have created the agricultural and industrial greatness of the United States. In American history one result of this variety has been most important— what Americans call 'sectionalism'. People in different regions differ very much from one another in their ways of life: for example, there is a great contrast between the ways in which a New York business man and a Kentucky farmer live, between the ways in which a New England fisher-man and a Louisiana cotton-planter live. Because their ways of living are different, so, to some extent, are their ways of looking at life. This is so even to-day, when standardised factory-made goods have spread every-where, when Americans can go easily by train or motor-car or aeroplane from one part of the country to another, and when press, radio, television, and advertisements spread the same ideas throughout the U.S.A. This difference is an important fact in 20th-century America, and it was infinitely more important when there were few machines or factory-made goods, and no trains or motor-cars or television to make people live and think alike and to draw them together.

Americans in the early days of the republic tended to think of themselves very often not so much as Americans, but as southerners, or westerners, or northerners—inhabitants of certain great parts or 'sections' of the U.S.A. The people of each of these three sections were bound together by some common economic interest, and most of them shared common ways of living which differed from those of other sections. For example, the people of the West—the lands across the Appalachian Mountains—were mostly pioneering farmers, living the rough lives of frontiersmen. Those of the South—that is, roughly, the states south of Chesapeake Bay[1]—became dependent on the growing of plantation crops such as tobacco and, after 1800, cotton, and owned many Negro slaves. The northern states, whose people were at first fishermen, farmers and merchants, became in the 19th century the industrial and manufacturing region of the U.S.A. And the interests of these sections began to clash. Westerners and northerners soon began to disagree, because western farmers had borrowed money from northern bankers and did not want to repay their debts. Sectional feeling between West and North ran high, and showed itself, for example, in the bitter presidential election of 1828, won by a great westerner, Andrew Jackson (see Chap. 10). But the most severe clash of sectional feeling arose between North and South over the issue of slavery. This clash nearly destroyed the Union, and produced the Civil War of 1861–5. So sectionalism, the result of the geographical differences between certain parts of the U.S.A., was a highly important factor in American history.

In these various ways—notably by way of immigration, by the growth of the frontier, and by the rise of sectionalism—American geography has shaped the history of those people who have built the U.S.A., the millions of settlers and their descendants. The remainder of this book tells the story of those people, the history of the United States of America.

2   Discovery and Colonisation, 1492-1763

On an October day in 1492 Christopher Columbus, a Genoese sea-captain in the service of Spain, landed on a small island, which is one of the group now called the Bahamas. The history of the United States began on that day: for the history of the United States is the history of the European settlement of a large part of the North American continent, and Columbus' discovery began the opening-up of America by Europeans. There is

---

[1] The area usually described as the South is that lying south of a line drawn in 1763 by two English surveyors, Mason and Dixon, as a boundary between Pennsylvania and Maryland and Delaware. (See map on page 114.) Mason and Dixon's line became the boundary between slave and free states.

evidence which suggests that in the 10th or 11th century a band of Vikings from Greenland, led by one Eric the Red, landed on the coast of North America. What we know of the Vikings and of their astonishing feats of seamanship around the coasts of Europe shows that such a voyage was well within their powers. But their lasting influence in America has been nil, while Columbus' voyage, on the other hand, began the permanent connection between Europe and America. Before Columbus the Atlantic Ocean was a barrier. Since Columbus it has been a means of communication: always perilous and at first little used, it has gradually become one of the great highways of the world.

1. THE INDIANS

This chapter will give an account of the European settlement and colonisation of North America between Columbus' day and the end of the Seven Years' War in 1763. First we must briefly consider the people whom Columbus and the later European explorers found there. In 1492 America was inhabited by a brown-skinned (usually light brown, certainly not black) people whom Columbus and his successors, because of a mistaken belief that they had found lands off or near the coasts of India, called Indians. These people were scattered fairly sparsely through the continent. In certain areas in Central and South America—the regions of Mexico and Peru to-day—they had developed what was in some respects a high level of civilisation. They had settled in fertile areas and established towns, built temples, houses and palaces, and developed an elaborate organisation of government, in addition to creating numerous objects of high artistic worth. Outside these areas, and especially in North America, the Indians lived in a far more primitive way. Permanent settlements were rarer and more scattered. The North American Indians—the Redskins—lived mainly by hunting, ranging over wide areas, each of which some Indian tribe or 'nation' claimed as its own property. Many features of Indian life have become a part of American story and legend, and are very familiar to us—the squaw and the wigwam, the canoe and tomahawk and totem-pole. Yet romantic accounts of the Red Indian's life must not blind us to the unhappy part he has been made to play in American history. He has been one of the major casualties of the advance of European civilisation across North America. He was unable to resist the superior weapons and growing numbers of the new settlers. Deprived by force or fraud of his lands, driven steadily westwards; swindled of his furs, slaughtered by the paleface's guns, demoralised by his whisky, or killed off by his diseases; he has lost the continent which once was his. Now the U.S.A. contains only about 792,000 Indians (comparatively few of whom are of pure Redskin blood), living mainly in special reserves allotted to them by the government. The one notable mark the Indians have made upon the U.S.A. lies in the innumerable Indian place-names.

2. THE SPANIARDS

Spain, at the height of her European power in the early part of the 16th century, quickly followed up Columbus' discovery. Columbus himself went on three more voyages to America, and other Spanish navigators followed him. Traders, soldiers, missionaries and civil servants soon followed the navigators. Spain had undertaken the conquest of a continent. But it was the central and southern parts of America to which the Spaniards went, not the north. This was so for two reasons. Spanish seamen, when they sailed from Spain into the open Atlantic, went southwards, to get into the track of the trade winds which would carry them across to the New World. The trades carried them not to the northern part of the new continent, but to the lands round the Caribbean Sea. Further, in central and southern America, in the West Indian islands and in Mexico and, most important of all, in Peru, they found wealth which was theirs for the taking. The Indian civilisations, those of the Aztecs in Mexico and of the Incas in Peru, offered untold loot, in gold and silver and precious stones. The discovery of the mines from which the precious metals came finally fastened a Spanish Empire on Central and most of South America. In 1521 Spanish forces under Cortez overran Mexico: between 1531 and 1535 Pizarro conquered Peru. Potosi, the richest of South American silver mines, was revealed in 1545.

By contrast with this known wealth to the south there was little to tempt the Spaniards northwards. There were, too, formidable geographical obstacles to any advance in that direction. Northern Mexico is mountainous: between southern Mexico, where the Spanish settlements were, and California lies a belt of land whose rainfall is very small and some of which is desert: this made overland advance difficult. It was no easier by sea since the prevailing winds along the Californian coast are northerly and fogs are frequent. Therefore the Spanish settlements to the north of the Tropic of Cancer were never as numerous or as important as those to the south of that line.

Yet discoveries and settlements were made. First, along the east coast, Florida (so named because it was first discovered in 1513 by the Spanish explorer Ponce de Léon on Pascua Florida, or Palm Sunday) was colonised, after earlier failures, by an expedition under de Soto in 1539. De Soto was one of several Spaniards who explored the Mississippi Basin in the first half of the 16th century: he died on the river's bank in 1541. Secondly, the Spanish conquest of Mexico (which they named New Spain) involved vague claims to a huge area extending from the Isthmus of Panama to what is now the southern boundary of Canada, and virtually from the Mississippi to the Pacific Ocean. This area, over which Spanish control was at no time complete and in which Spanish settlements were very thin, included not only the present-day territories of Mexico and the other Central American republics, but also those of several states of the U.S.A.—for example, Texas, Arizona, New Mexico, California. The ownership of Texas and the Mississippi lands was disputed with France during the 17th and 18th centuries.

Spanish colonisation was mainly the work of those tireless and courageous pioneers, the Jesuit missionaries. In spite of huge difficulties of climate and transport, and of Indian attacks, they gradually spread their mission stations farther northwards during the 17th and 18th centuries. A number of Spanish landowners also established themselves in California, building their haciendas, or farm-mansions, in the fertile lands of that region. There was little traffic by sea. The magnificent harbour of San Francisco Bay was not discovered until 1769, and then only by accident and overland! The whole process of Spanish colonisation was extremely slow, partly because of the decline of Spanish power in Europe after the end of the 16th century, and this early Spanish settlement of the far western and southwestern parts of the U.S.A. has left little permanent impression. Few traces of it remain, apart from many place-names and a romantic background for film scenarios: in this the Spanish legacy to the U.S.A. is not unlike that of the Red Indians. But we shall find the relics of Spanish power and Spanish claims important in the territorial advance of the United States later in this story.

3. THE FRENCH

The second European power to interest herself in discovery and settlement of North America was France. While Pizarro was carrying fire and sword into Peru, a French sailor named Jacques Cartier was exploring the Gulf of St. Lawrence, the greatest inlet upon the east coast of North America. In 1535 he sailed up the river as far as what is now the site of Quebec. No immediate French settlement followed Cartier's voyages, but in 1603–4 another and a greater Frenchman, Samuel Champlain, reached the same point: and in 1608 Champlain founded Quebec as the first permanent French colony in North America. Montreal, on a site also visited by Champlain in 1603, was founded in 1642, and these two settlements remained the chief towns of the French colony of Canada. Champlain, who also penetrated far into the region of the Great Lakes, discovering Lake Huron in 1615, and defeated the Iroquois Indians in a battle fought in 1609 near Lake Champlain, was the founder of French power in North America. He gave France the St. Lawrence region as a foothold for further advance. For long the French settlements here remained very small. Their inhabitants were peasants, fur-traders and fishermen, living in isolated groups and trading with the Indians, with whom they kept on good terms.

The second stage in the advance of French power in North America came during the second half of the 17th century, long after the earliest British colonies had been established. The Ohio, the greatest of the rivers which flow into the Mississippi from its left bank, rises in the Appalachian

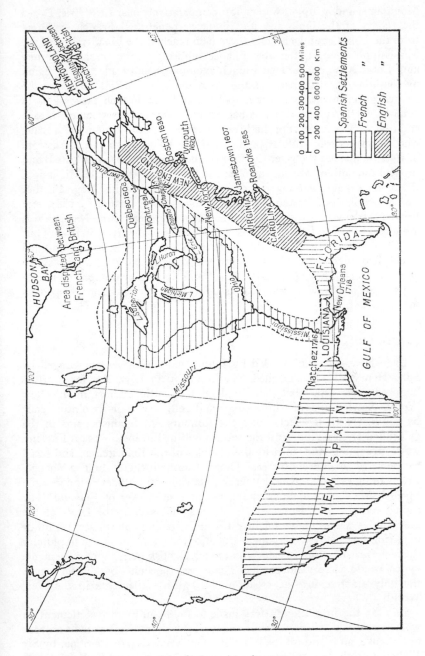

European Settlements in North America about 1700

Mountains, and its upper waters flow comparatively near Lake Erie. Down the valleys of the Ohio and its tributaries penetrated French explorers from the Lakes, and eventually these men reached the broad valley of the Mississippi. Colbert, the able finance minister of the reigning French king Louis XIV, encouraged French exploration and trade in this region by founding the Company of the West in 1664. To this company the French government gave a monopoly of trade in French possessions in America for forty years: it was backed by government assistance in cash and troops. The greatest of the French explorers of this time was La Salle, who discovered the Ohio River in 1669. He sailed down the Mississippi in 1681 (he named the river the Colbert, but the name has not lasted) and reached the Gulf of Mexico in 1682; and he claimed the whole Mississippi Basin for France, naming it Louisiana in honour of his king. Further French explorers followed La Salle, who was assassinated in 1687, and French settlements grew along the banks of the great river. Natchez was founded in 1716 and New Orleans, at the mouth of the river, in 1718. Thus the French had spread from the St. Lawrence to the Mississippi, and had established their settlements along the banks of North America's two greatest rivers. They appeared to have gained a firm grip upon the northern half of the New World, just as Spain and Portugal had grasped its southern half.

4. THE ENGLISH

English vessels, commanded by John Cabot, who was encouraged by King Henry VII, had reached Newfoundland in 1497. But for nearly a hundred years after that date England took little interest in the New World. Newfoundland, with its fogs and cold, was a disappointing start by contrast with the facts—and the rumours—of Spanish gains in the gold-filled Indies. And until the second half of Elizabeth's reign England was a struggling land, torn by the troubles of the Reformation and faced by powerful enemies overseas. Under Elizabeth there came a change. Freebooting expeditions under Drake, Hawkins and others plundered the Spanish Main, thus demonstrating the new sea-power of England. The capital released by Henry VIII's plunder and sale of the lands of the monasteries was available for investment in trading enterprises, lawful or unlawful. Gradually freebooting turned to trade, and the desire to plunder Spanish treasure-ships became an urge to establish permanent settlements which would yield good profits. Trade was the first—but by no means the only—motive for the creation of English settlements in the New World.

In 1585 the first attempt was made to found an English settlement on what is now United States soil: this was the short-lived expedition sent to Roanoke, an island off the coast of what is now North Carolina, by Sir Walter Raleigh. Several attempts at settlement, promoted by Raleigh and

Sir Richard Grenville among others, were made in the next few years, but all these failed. Early in James I's reign a number of wealthy London merchants formed a company, called the London Company (later the Virginia Company) to engage in trade with North America. It was given a charter by the King, empowering it to settle a vast territory, covering the whole of Virginia and a great deal more. Rumours of the gold which all America was still supposed to contain attracted investors to put their money in the London Company, and in 1606 the Company fitted out three ships to sail to America carrying 120 men. 104 of these landed in Virginia in April, 1607, and built a settlement which they called Jamestown. This settlement survived after its members had undergone terrible hardships. Many of them had died, either from disease or in strife with the Indians: many others were riddled with malaria: all were desperately short of food and were eating anything they could catch or find in the woods. The strength and force of character of one of the early settlers, Captain John Smith, stopped an early collapse, and in 1608 and 1609 more settlers came out. In 1610 only the opportune arrival of the first officially-appointed governor of the colony, Lord Delaware, with extra food supplies, prevented all the colonists returning home. From that time onward Virginia developed. Tobacco soon became an important crop, finding a market in England in spite of James I's views about the evils of smoking. At first the colony was governed, under the terms of the charter, by the Company from London. This was not very satisfactory, since the Company's directors knew little about life in a primitive American settlement, and since it took between five and six weeks for a vessel to carry any instructions across the Atlantic even when the weather was favourable. So in 1619 a representative assembly—the first in American history—called the House of Burgesses met in Jamestown. Five years later the Company was dissolved and the colony was handed over to the Crown.

By this time another English colony had come into being in North America. Virginia was founded in order to make trading profits: this second settlement arose because its members wished to escape from an England where they were persecuted for their religion. The Reformation had released the Church in England from Rome, and Elizabeth's Church settlement of 1559 had created the Church of England. But the Reformation had not stopped there. Many people, the so-called Puritans, thought that the Church needed further reforms, and some, the extremists among them, had left the Church. Some of these Puritans, a group often known as Separatists, fled from Scrooby in Nottinghamshire to Holland and set up their own English congregational church at Leyden. Growing dissatisfied with their life there, many of them came back to England with the intention of sailing to the New World. The London merchants, scenting another trading venture, financed them, and in September, 1620, a party of 102 set sail from Plymouth in the *Mayflower* with the intention of reaching Virginia. These were the famous Pilgrim Fathers. They landed not in Virginia but near Cape Cod, in land now part of the state of Massachusetts, and they called their first settlement Plymouth. Like the early settlers at Jamestown, they too faced bitter hardships. Half of them died in the terrible cold of their first New England winter.[1] This settlement, too, survived; here it was the determination and organising ability of William Bradford, governor of the colony for nearly all of its first thirty years, that did much to prevent it dying. Unlike the Jamestown settlement, that at Plymouth did not become the nucleus of a larger colony. It remained independent, though never very large or influential, until 1691, when it was united with the Massachusetts Bay colony.

Large-scale colonisation began with the foundation in 1630 by a group of wealthy Puritans of a colony in Massachusetts Bay. This colony, efficiently organised on the basis of a charter granted in 1628, prospered from the start. It is said that in 1630 there were 2,000 settlers: by 1643 there were eight times that number, the great majority of them industrious Puritans who rapidly established themselves as farmers and merchants. The chief town, Boston, so called because many of the first settlers came from Boston in Lincolnshire, was founded in 1630. Right from its foundation Massachusetts was the chief colony of that north-eastern group of colonies to which the name New England is given. Two more colonies were founded in New England in the 17th century by settlers from Massachusetts. The Puritans of Massachusetts who had gone to the New World to escape persecution for their faith in the Old, were themselves persecutors. Dissent from the established Puritan beliefs was a crime in Massachusetts: a rigid censorship of speech and conduct was set up: and the right to vote in elections to the assembly of the colony for long belonged only to Church members. In 1635 Roger Williams, a Puritan who—quite contrary to the general practice of his age—believed in complete religious freedom for everybody, was expelled from Massachusetts, and next year he founded a small settlement called Providence, at the head of Narrangansett Bay. From this settlement Rhode Island, the smallest of the colonies, grew, and Charles II granted it a charter in 1663. Similarly, and at about the same time as Roger Williams departed, a number of settlers moved out of Massachusetts southwards into the land which lies to the west of Rhode Island: this new colony was called Connecticut. Puritan in outlook like Massachusetts, it was for long dominated by its northern neighbour. In 1643 the colonists of Massachusetts, New Plymouth, and Connecticut formed a defensive confederation against the Indians, the French, and the Dutch. It is the first confederation or league of colonies in American history.

South of New England there grew up a group of colonies which, from their position on the coast, were afterwards called the Middle Colonies. (In strict accuracy, the great mass of one of these colonies, New York, lies

---

[1] Those who survived were aided in planting crops by an English-speaking Indian, Squanto, who had crossed the Atlantic two or three times.

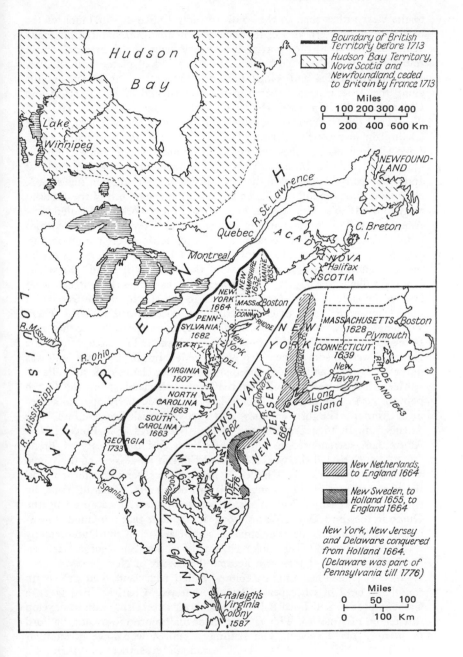

European Colonisation of eastern North America

to the west rather than to the south of New England. But much of the northern and western area of that colony remained uninhabited for many years: and the centre of gravity has always been in the extreme south, round the city of New York itself.) In the first half of the 17th century Dutchmen, Swedes and Finns built trading-stations at various points along the American coast between the eastern end of Long Island and Chesapeake Bay. In 1609 Henry Hudson, in the service of Holland, discovered the Hudson River, which runs south from the region of Lake Champlain to meet the Atlantic Ocean at New York—and which, with Lake Champlain, provides the only convenient through route from the northern U.S.A. to Montreal and the St. Lawrence. The Dutch West India Company, interested in the possibilities of fur-trading in this region, set up a trading-station on Manhattan Island at the mouth of the Hudson early in the 1620's. This was the beginning of New York, then called New Amsterdam. This settlement grew slowly, soon developing that cosmopolitan character which it has never lost: Dutch settlers were not numerous, and the fur trade attracted men of all lands. On the strength of the settlement Holland claimed as the colony of the New Netherlands the whole Hudson valley and a large area to the west of it, as well as the whole of what is now the state of New Jersey. Farther to the south, on the estuary of the Delaware River, a Swedish settlement was formed in 1638 where Wilmington now stands, and Swedish and Finnish traders penetrated farther inland into what is to-day Pennsylvania. The area round the Delaware was for some time called New Sweden, but the Swedish hold was never very strong, and in 1665 Sweden handed her claims over to Holland.

Meanwhile all was not well with the New Netherlands, from the Dutch point of view. The position of the colony laid it peculiarly open to settlement from the English colonies, and many English poured into New Amsterdam. In 1664 England and Holland went to war in Europe. New Amsterdam surrendered to an English fleet, and the Treaty of Breda (1667), which ended the war, recognised English possession of the whole of the New Netherlands. Charles II handed over New Amsterdam and the northern part of the colony to his brother James, Duke of York, by whom it was renamed New York. It was temporarily recaptured by the Dutch in the third Dutch War of 1672–4, but after that remained continuously in English hands. The smaller, southern part of the Dutch colony was given to two English noblemen, one of whom, Sir George Carteret, had been governor of Jersey: it became the colony of New Jersey.

Since 1633 another English colony, called Maryland, had grown up round the head of Chesapeake Bay. In that year Charles I had given a Catholic peer named Lord Baltimore a charter authorising him to develop this region of America. This charter made Baltimore the owner, or 'lord proprietor,' of Maryland. The Baltimore family, who have given their name to the chief town of Maryland, leased land to settlers in return for a rent. One purpose of the colony was to provide a refuge for Catholics,

THE PORTRAICTUER OF CAPTAYNE IOHN SMITH / ADMIRALL OF NEW ENGLAND.

Ætat 37
A.º 1616

These are the Lines that shew thy Face; but those
That shew thy Grace and Glory, brighter bee:
Thy Faire-Discoueries and Fowle-Overthrowes
Of Salvages, much Civilliz'd by thee
Best shew thy Spirit; and to it Glory Wyn;
So, thou art Braße without, but Golde within.

Captain John Smith, coloniser of Virginia, 1607

George Washington

although in fact the Catholics were never more than a small minority of the inhabitants of Maryland. In 1649 the Maryland assembly passed a Toleration Act, permitting any form of Christian worship in the colony. Toleration, and the splendid natural position of the colony at the head of Chesapeake Bay, attracted numerous settlers to Maryland.

North of Maryland and west of New Jersey lay land which was not settled by Europeans until late in the 17th century. Charles II owed Admiral Sir William Penn some £16,000. Penn died in 1670, and this debt was not finally cleared until 1681, when Charles paid the Admiral's son, another William Penn, by giving him a grant of land in America west of the river Delaware. The younger Penn was a Quaker, a member of a religious sect which was as bitterly hated and as vigorously persecuted as any in 17th-century England. He was anxious to find land which might serve as a refuge for those Quakers who wished to leave England. The first settlement in his new colony, called, after Penn's father, Pennsylvania, was made in 1682. The colony prospered rapidly in its early years under Penn's own leadership. It owed some of its success to the rich farmlands which the settlers cleared: some to the thrift and industry of the early settlers. Most were Quakers, but many were Germans, 'Deutsch', the so-called 'Pennsylvania Dutch.' The most remarkable achievement of the colony's first years was Penn's Treaty of 1683 with the Indians. Many of the settlers in the other colonies had soon found themselves in trouble with the Indians because of their use of fraud and force to obtain lands from them. Penn, a Quaker, refused to employ force in his dealings with the Indians, and insisted from the start on peaceful and fair dealing. As a result, Pennsylvania secured fifty years of freedom from Indian Wars. In 1682, in a dispute between Pennsylvania and Maryland, Charles II was persuaded to take the land which is now the state of Delaware from Maryland and hand it to Pennsylvania. It did not become a wholly separate colony until 1776.

The remaining three of the original thirteen English colonies in North America lay south of Virginia. In 1663 a group of prominent English noblemen obtained from Charles II a charter to settle the land which is now the states of North and South Carolina. The first large settlement was formed on the Ashley River in 1670, and in 1680 Charleston, the chief town of South Carolina, was founded. The colony was eventually divided into two, North and South Carolina. Georgia, the southernmost and youngest of the thirteen, was not founded until 1733. James Oglethorpe, an English general who was also a humanitarian, conceived the idea of founding in America a colony where Englishmen who had lost all they had and had been imprisoned for debt might start life anew. He obtained a grant of land south of the Savannah River, and settlement began at Savannah, at the river mouth, in 1733. The colony grew slowly, and remained backward throughout the 18th century.

By 1750 about 1,500,000 people lived in the English colonies, of whom perhaps 300,000 were black slaves. England and Wales at this time contained about 6,000,000 people. Most of the settlers were poor people, attracted by the chance of improving their lot in the New World, and hardly any were rich men or nobles. Some were criminals, some adventurers, some land speculators: a fair number were traders, in fur or tobacco, ships' stores or spirits. A great many had gone across the ocean as 'indentured servants' —they paid for their passage by promising to work for some landowner in the colony for a number of years: the captains of the ships which took them over acted as agents in the business and were paid in cash when they landed the servants. This system was very close to slavery. Among those who went in this way were many children and servant-girls, kidnapped by unscrupulous sea-captains, and convicts. The last were nearly all petty thieves, men and women guilty of trifling offences, and condemned under the harsh English penal code to transportation. Most of the settlers were British, though the Middle Colonies especially contained many Dutch, Germans and other Europeans. The great majority of the Negro slaves were in the southern states, and in South Carolina there were more Negroes than whites. The first boatload of Negroes had been imported to Jamestown in 1619.

Already by 1700 very different ways of life had developed in the different groups of colonies: the fact that the slaves were mostly in the southern states is one illustration of this. In 1700, as for long afterwards, the main occupation of most people in all the colonies was farming. In the south, where the climate was hotter, the summer longer and the land more fertile, tobacco, grown for export to England, was the chief crop. It was grown on fair-sized plantations, where most of the work was done by Negro slaves. Virginia was the chief centre of tobacco-growing. Other southern crops were wheat, barley, and rice. The southern 'planter' sent his crop to England, and bought from England the finer manufactured goods—his silverware, his linen, even some of his furniture and his clothes. Life in the southern colonies was already more aristocratic and more leisurely than in the north.

In New England, where winters were longer and harder, and the soil was stonier, farming was a more laborious process. Farms were smaller, and the settler grew Indian corn, hay, rye and fruit to meet his own needs. It was the sea rather than the land that was New England's road to wealth. New Englanders, thanks to their harbours and to the wood, pitch and tar in their forests, built ships: they caught fish from them—herrings and cod and mackerel, and above all whales: and they traded in them. They carried rum to Africa, and bought slaves with it: they took the slaves from Africa to the West Indies: there they picked up the molasses from which the rum was distilled, and brought it home. They carried timber, pitch, hemp, fish, tobacco, wheat or sugar from the various parts of America to England. New England seamen rapidly won a name for skill and courage. A great source of difference between the New England colonies and those of the south lay in religion. Whereas the Anglican Church was supreme in Virginia and the other southern colonies, New England was sternly puritanical.

The Middle Colonies—New York and Pennsylvania were the most important of these—had farms rather more fertile than those of New England, without the hot climate of the south. They grew barley, rye and wheat, and became known as the 'Bread Colonies.' As in New England there was a good deal of fur-trading in the forests. American traders bought, often for a few beads or a bottle of whisky, from Indian trappers the skins of beaver, fox, deer and other animals and sold them to European merchants. New York, a cosmopolitan port, and Philadelphia, a model of town-planning, both grew into thriving towns.

Life in all the colonies was hard, and men and women had to be strong, energetic and independent to survive. The immigrant, indeed, had to be pretty hardy to survive the voyage across the Atlantic. That might take anything from five weeks to six months, with passengers of every age and both sexes crowded together below decks in a tiny boat, where food was short and often mouldy, sanitation primitive and disease quite usual. The chief towns were on or near the coast, round the original 'tidewater' settlements; on the western edge of the colonies, in the mountain region, life was far less civilised. The pioneer on the frontier was thrown on his own resources, and rank and wealth mattered little with him: circumstances forced him to be independent and democratic. In Virginia and the southern colonies a sense of class, of a difference between rich and poor, arose fairly rapidly. The well-to-do planter of the tidewater region, already owning a number of slaves, felt himself superior to the struggling farmer of the frontier. Slavery made this social distinction worse, for it suggested that manual labour was something ignoble which no white man ought to do. Even by 1700 a class of 'poor whites' was growing up in the southern colonies. A poor white was a white man who owned either no land at all, or only a small piece which he worked himself, and who had no slaves: consequently the richer slave-owners despised him. In the northern states social distinctions were not so sharp, although they were beginning to grow as some men in the towns became wealthier than their neighbours.

All the colonies had elected assemblies which managed most of their affairs. The right to vote in elections to these assemblies belonged usually only to the more prosperous settlers: and for long in New England it belonged only to church members. In 1700 some colonies, like Pennsylvania, still had lords proprietors, members of the family to which the original grant of land had been made. Others were crown colonies, with governors appointed by the king in England—but paid by the colonists themselves. Two colonies, Rhode Island and Connecticut, elected their own governors. In them all, the amount of power which the English government could exercise was limited by the distance from England. But certainly in 1700 the colonies had no wish to be independent.

5. ANGLO-FRENCH RIVALRY IN THE 18TH CENTURY

The map on page 11 shows what American lands the three European powers claimed in 1700. During the next hundred years the two strongest of these powers, France and England, fought a series of wars. The battles in these wars were fought on the oceans and in three continents. Broadly the wars were about one great issue—which of the powers was to establish a world empire? In these wars the fate of North America was involved.

Between 1700 and 1763 there were three great Anglo-French wars. Each of them began, in part at any rate, over some European dispute (hence the names of the first two of the wars), and in each of them most European states fought; but here we are only interested in events in America, and in the effects of the wars on America. One point must be clearly remembered. A treaty between England and France and the end of official fighting in Europe did not mean the end of fighting in America. For one thing, the news of a treaty in Europe did not reach America until long after the treaty was signed. Again English and French frontiersmen and fur-traders in America pursued their quarrels without bothering about orders from Europe.

The first war was the War of the Spanish Succession (1701–13). In this war England was successful, and she won land in America, notably Acadia (Nova Scotia) and the Hudson Bay territory. This gave her a foothold in Canada. In reply to this the French began to develop their main plan in North America during this century (see map on page 21). This was to link up the mouths of the Mississippi and St. Lawrence by a line of French forts and settlements. If this plan had succeeded it would have shut the English colonies in behind the Appalachians, stopping their advance westwards. The French had one advantage over the English. They were explorers and soldiers, missionaries and traders, rather than farmers, and they did not usually seek to rob the Indians of their land. They pointed out to the Indians that they were only honest traders who paid the Indians for the furs they took: but that the English seized the Indians' lands, cut down the forests and set up farms, killing or driving away the Indians. Only one great Indian tribe, the Iroquois—those whom Champlain had defeated in 1609—sided with the English. But the English colonists greatly outnumbered the French; by 1750 there were only about 65,000 French settlers, against over twenty times that number in the Thirteen Colonies. The French would find it hard to pen the English behind the mountains, however many forts they built.

While Englishmen were pushing through the Appalachians and French traders were making their way down the Ohio, another war broke out in Europe—the War of the Austrian Succession (1740–8). Again there was war in Canada, and the quarrels on the Ohio grew fiercer. The Treaty of Aix-la-Chapelle which ended the war simply returned to each country the conquests it had made: so Louisburg, the great French fortress in

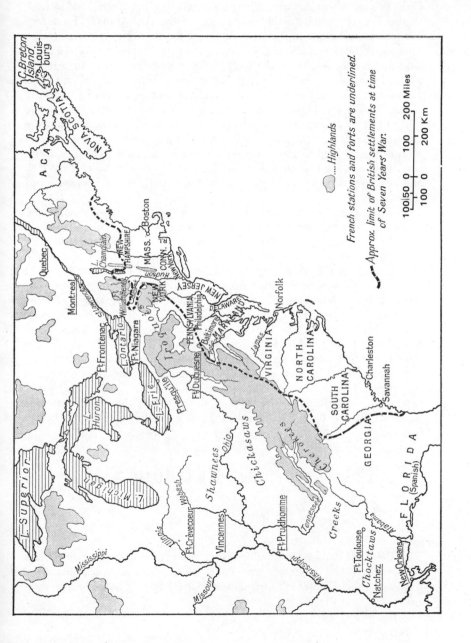

The French Design in the 18th Century

Cape Breton, which American forces had taken in 1745, was handed back to the French, much to the annoyance of the Americans. This treaty brought no real peace in America. In 1749, the year after it was signed, a group of Virginians formed the Ohio Company. Its object was to exploit land in the Ohio Valley, to the west of the mountains, and in 1752 it was granted a royal charter for this purpose. The French claimed the Ohio Valley as theirs, and such a grant merely encouraged war. In 1754 the French built Fort Duquesne, on the present site of Pittsburgh, and in the following year an expedition of British troops and American volunteers commanded by General Braddock set out to attack it. Among the volunteer officers was a young Virginian named George Washington. The expedition was disastrous, for French and Indian forces ambushed it, killed Braddock and destroyed most of his men. Washington's coolness and courage saved the rest.

In Europe the Seven Years' War, the third of the Anglo-French wars, broke out in 1756. The Americans saw it as a continuation of the struggle over the Ohio Valley, and called it the French and Indian War. Its effect on the balance of power in America was decisive. British forces under Wolfe took Louisburg in 1758, and Quebec fell in 1759: the capture of Montreal in 1760 set Canada in British hands. The French forts were taken after initial failures, including the massacre of the British garrison of Fort William Henry by the Indians in 1757. The Treaty of Paris of 1763 confirmed these victories. The French abandoned their claims to Canada and to all land east of the Mississippi, handing them over to Britain. In the same treaty they turned over to Spain all their claims to what was henceforward known as Louisiana, the huge territory across the Mississippi, and the region round New Orleans at its mouth. The French attempt to dominate North America had broken down, while the British attempt to do so seemed to be successful. 1763 is a turning-point in American history.

3   The American Revolution, 1763-83

The Treaty of Paris was signed in 1763. Twenty years later Great Britain acknowledged the independence of the thirteen American colonies. The purpose of this chapter is to explain why and how this happened.

1. THE BACKGROUND

Changes of this kind may happen very suddenly. But they are usually the result of causes extending over a long time. This is true of the American

Revolution. The series of events to which that name is given covered only the twenty years after 1763. Many causes of the revolution lay further back in the history of the colonies.

The settlers in the colonies went there to find a freer way of life. They found it, particularly in the frontier region, where the conditions forced men and women to show vigour and enterprise. Laws for the colonists were made chiefly by the colonial assemblies, and the government in London interfered little with their everyday life, except, as we shall see, in the one matter of trade. Most colonies had governors appointed by the King: these frequently quarrelled with the assemblies, who had one powerful weapon—control of the governors' salaries. Each colony had its own assembly, and the colonists soon developed the habit of free political discussion. In New England a very democratic institution called the Town Meeting arose: this was a regular meeting open to all the inhabitants of a settlement, at which all local problems and grievances were freely discussed. Newspapers developed—the first was published in Boston in 1704. The colonists were outspoken and critical, far more so than English people at this time. Further, they grew, during the 18th century, more conscious of their numbers and importance. By 1775 the population of the thirteen colonies had reached some 2,500,000. The colonies' jealousy of each other was great: for example, each colony hesitated to provide soldiers against the French and Indians until it was sure that its neighbours were giving theirs. In 1754 a Colonial Congress, a meeting of representatives of the colonies, took place at Albany. Here Benjamin Franklin put forward a plan for a federation or union of the colonies. The advantages of union were not yet evident, and the colonies turned it down.

It was certain that, if ever any grave cause of quarrel arose between the colonists and Great Britain, the colonists would speak freely and act vigorously. Such a cause of quarrel was growing steadily during the 18th century. It concerned the one issue on which Britain made laws that seriously interfered with the colonists—trade. In Britain during the 17th and 18th centuries it was generally believed by merchants and politicians that colonies and colonial trade existed simply for the benefit of Britain. The colonies were a market for British manufactures: colonial raw materials were to benefit Britain. Hence Parliament passed a series of laws regulating colonial trade. These may be summarised as follows:

1. By the Navigation Acts, directed originally against the Dutch (the first was passed in 1650), all goods to and from the colonies had to be carried in English or colonial ships: the majority of the hands on these ships had to be English or colonial born.

2. Certain kinds of produce, known as the 'enumerated articles,' could be sent to Europe only via England: these included furs, ships' masts, tar, pitch, turpentine, tobacco—in fact, most of the chief colonial exports.

3. Goods from Europe to the colonies had to go via England.

4. To prevent competition with English manufacturers, restrictions

were placed on some colonial industries: e.g. the Iron Act of 1750 attempted to limit the manufacture of hardware in America.

5. By the Molasses Act of 1733, a duty of sixpence a gallon was placed on molasses imported to the colonies from the French West Indies: the object of this duty, a very high one, was to make the colonists buy their molasses from the British West Indies.

The colonists got real benefits from this system. The Royal Navy protected their shipping, and they paid nothing towards its upkeep. The laws regulating trade prevented foreign competition and certainly helped the economic development of the colonists. Some of them, like the Virginia tobacco growers, had a monopoly of the British market. New England shipbuilders benefited greatly from the stimulus given by the Navigation Acts. The British government paid a bounty on the export of some colonial goods: the indigo growers of North Carolina, for example, were paid sixpence on every pound they sent overseas. Moreover, many of the more tiresome regulations were not seriously enforced; the Iron Act, for example, was largely ignored. Smuggling and contraband trading were easy, and the officials who administered the law were slack and open to bribery.

On the other hand the laws seriously damaged the colonists. They involved numerous inconveniences, such as the necessity of unloading and reloading in England colonial goods bound for Europe. Further, both European goods bound for the colonies and colonial goods bound for Europe had to pay customs duties in England. Many of these duties, however, were refunded when the cargo was re-exported from England. But the worst defect was not inconvenience or customs duties. The real trouble was that the whole system put the colonists at the mercy of English merchants, who controlled the prices of the goods they bought and of those they sold. Two examples will illustrate this. A colonist who bought goods from France had to bring them home by way of England, where they had to be transhipped before being sent on to America: the freight charges and commissions which had to be paid to English merchants raised the price of the goods, often to several times their real value. Again, a Virginian planter who wanted to sell his tobacco crop could do so only in England. He had no chance of trying to get a higher price for it elsewhere in Europe, and he had to accept what the English merchants offered. Virginian planters often ran heavily into debt. They had to leave the sale of their annual tobacco crop and the purchase of English manufactures to their agents in England, who frequently swindled them right and left. When the quarrel with England came, many Virginians, who might otherwise have supported Britain, were ready to break away and leave their debts unpaid.

The Molasses Act was a special grievance in New England. One of New England's major industries was distilling rum (remember the triangular trade between New England, Africa, and the West Indies mentioned in the previous chapter). The British West Indian islands could not provide anything like enough molasses to keep the New England distillers employed. Hence they bought it from the French West Indies. The sixpenny duty of 1733 was prohibitive—it made the price of French molasses so high that the New Englanders could not buy it. So they smuggled it instead. This was not difficult on the coast of New England with its numerous inlets, and smuggling became a large-scale business. It has been estimated, for example, that over 80 per cent. of the molasses imported into Rhode Island each year was smuggled. Some of the richest and most respectable colonial merchants made their fortunes by smuggling. The result of the Molasses Act, which was slackly enforced, was to encourage lawlessness—precisely what happened nearly 200 years later, when the Prohibition Amendment to the American Constitution became law (see Chap. 22). The colonists showed quite clearly that they had no intention of keeping laws—especially English-made laws—which it suited them to break.

These trading regulations did not produce a movement for independence before 1763. But they created irritation in the colonies, and encouraged the colonists to defy the laws made by a Parliament in England. This was the background against which events developed after 1763.

2. THE EVENTS LEADING TO WAR

In 1763 the Indian tribes west of Virginia made a sudden and violent attack upon that colony. It was led by the Indian chief Pontiac. British troops with a measure of American assistance—the colonies wrangled over the share each was to give—eventually defeated it. A Proclamation Act (1763) forbade American settlers to move into the lands taken from France across the Appalachians. The object of this was to prevent further disturbance of the Indians until some arrangement was made about the fur trade which the French had carried on. It was only intended as a temporary measure: to stop Americans from settling west of the mountains was about as possible as stopping the flow of the tides. But the act caused some irritation among western settlers.

There was worse to come. At the end of the war in 1763 Great Britain found herself with a national debt nearly double what it had been before the war. Much had been spent in America, in winning Canada from the French. Further, it was still thought necessary to maintain British troops in America, partly as a safeguard against a French rebellion in Canada, partly to protect the colonists from the Indians. The growth of the British Empire was proving costly. The colonists, on the other hand, had spent comparatively little money on the war. Great Britain had repaid most of the money each colony had spent on providing troops. Moreover, colonial merchants had made profits by supplying food and other goods to the British troops. (Some, incidentally, had done well out of supplying goods to the French in the West Indies, even while the war was going on.) The colonies in 1763 were flourishing.

George Grenville, who became Prime Minister in 1763, had these facts in mind. He began to tighten the control of American trade. He ordered stricter measures against smugglers and contraband; he set up Vice-admiralty courts to try those who broke the trade laws, and gravely offended the Americans by empowering royal officials to use 'writs of assistance,' which enabled them to search houses suspected of containing contraband. In 1764 the Sugar Act was passed; this replaced the useless Molasses Act of 1733, and put a duty of threepence a gallon on imported molasses. Grenville's object was simple. He wanted to obtain more money from the American colonists, in order to make them contribute towards the cost of keeping British troops in America. These first steps aroused hostility and protests. But the real storm of protest burst when Grenville introduced his next measure, the Stamp Act (1765). In England revenue stamps—stamps on legal documents, licences, wills, etc.—had been used for some time as a convenient form of taxation. Grenville proposed to extend the system to America. His proposals would not have raised a great sum, and there was little opposition to the bill in Parliament.

The results of the Stamp Act were astonishing. There was a general outcry of the colonists, rich and poor alike, against the tax. The newspapers attacked it violently: they were ordered to pay it, and some of them printed a death's head on the front page where the stamp was supposed to be. Mobs made bonfires and burned heaps of stamps: they also burned the effigies and houses of the tax-collectors. Workmen formed groups calling themselves 'Sons of Liberty'; radical leaders, like Samuel Adams of Boston, made inflammatory speeches against the stamps and the government. There were riots in New England and New York. The merchants formed a 'non-importation' agreement—they refused to import goods from England so long as the Stamp Act was law. The lawyers and the merchants, both of whom were hit by Grenville's policy, encouraged the mobs in opposing the stamps. A young Virginian lawyer named Patrick Henry made himself famous in American history by a speech in the Virginian assembly denying the right of the British Parliament to tax the people of Virginia. Finally, representatives of nine colonies met in the Stamp Act Congress at New York. This Congress passed a resolution saying that Parliament had no right to tax the colonies without their consent.

This furious agitation against the Stamp Act was ominous for the future of British rule in the thirteen colonies. The colonists found a battle-cry with which to challenge British rule—'No Taxation without Representation.' They argued that the British Parliament had no right to tax them unless they sent representatives to it. Distance prevented them sending representsative, and so only their own assemblies could tax them. This argument overlooked the fact that the colonies had long accepted laws made by

Parliament. But it showed that they were growing conscious of their own strength. At the Stamp Act Congress nine of the colonies united for the first time against Britain. Finally, the whole agitation showed up the weakness of British rule in America: the British authorities were powerless against the mobs.

In Britain itself opinion was divided. The King, George III, was—as throughout the quarrel—strongly against the Americans. Many politicians, and notably two of the ablest of the day, William Pitt, later Earl of Chatham, and Edmund Burke, argued that even if Britain had every right to tax the colonists, it was highly unwise to do so. In the end the Stamp Act was repealed in 1766, largely because of the influence of British merchants whose trade was killed by the 'non-importation' agreement. With the repeal went a Declaratory Act, declaring that Britain had every right to tax the colonists. To the Americans it seemed that they had successfully defied British authority. Such a feeling led them later to further defiance, and in the end to a demand for independence. Yet in 1765 few Americans wanted independence. The news of the repeal of the Stamp Act was received with wild enthusiasm in the colonies. The agitation ceased. The wound seemed to have closed.

It was reopened in 1767. The Commons in that year compelled the government to reduce the land tax, and Charles Townshend, the Chancellor of the Exchequer, decided to make up some of the deficit by taxing the Americans. So he introduced a new series of customs duties on paper, paints, glass, and tea. He argued that the colonists, although they might object to the stamp duty, could not reasonably oppose customs duties: indeed many colonists themselves had argued on these lines at the time of the Stamp Act. Having imposed the duties, Townshend died. Once again there were riots, furious speeches, pamphlets, violent newspaper-leaders: once again non-importation. The government made renewed efforts to stop smuggling, and the British garrison in Boston was strengthened. Most colonists were on the side of the smugglers, and informers, those who gave the smugglers away to revenue officers, were often tarred and feathered by crowds. In 1769 a mob in Rhode Island burned the British revenue ship *Liberty*.

1770 was a critical year. In January Lord North, an easy-going nobleman, whose weakness allowed George III himself to get control of policy, became Prime Minister. He repealed all Townshend's duties except that on tea. In America the so-called 'Boston Massacre' took place. The British soldiers in Boston were the victims of all manner of insults. Tempers soon frayed, and incidents were frequent. One of these, in March 1770, started with a brawl outside the custom-house. Soldiers fired on a crowd: three citizens of Boston were killed and five injured. The officers and soldiers responsible were acquitted, by an American jury, after a fair trial, in which they were defended by John Adams of Massachusetts, a leading opponent of Britain. But the event, a sign of a very awkward situation, was a splendid chance for revolutionary agitators, who soon spread exaggerated accounts throughout the colonies.

Yet from 1770 to 1773 the situation seemed to be growing less dangerous, although the burning by American patriots of the revenue ship *Gaspee* when she ran aground off Providence in 1772 showed that the Americans still supported the smugglers. It was North's Tea Act of 1773 that provoked the crisis which led directly to war. The East India Company, the chief importers of tea to Great Britain, found themselves with 17,000,000 pounds of tea on their hands in 1773. Most of the tea drunk in the colonies was smuggled tea. To enable the East India Company to sell their tea in America, North introduced a law permitting them to take it direct to the colonies in their own ships and sell it direct to American shopkeepers. This would reduce the price of the tea, and so, it was hoped, make it cheaper than smuggled tea. It would, in fact, have benefited the colonists. But the American merchants, who made profits out of smuggling, would have been hard hit. Once again they united with the radicals—those, like Samuel Adams, who opposed Britain on any issue—and stirred up popular feeling against the new act and the East India Company's tea. Late in 1773 the tea-ships arrived. In Charleston and elsewhere the tea was landed, but no one would buy it. Boston was the centre of opposition to Britain. Here the town meeting would not allow the tea to land: the governor of Massachusetts would not allow the ships to go out of harbour without unloading. The famous 'Boston Tea Party' solved the problem. A mob disguised as Indians forced their way on board the ships and threw the tea overboard.

For once the British government took firm action when the news of what had happened reached England. Some £25,000 worth of English property had been destroyed, in defiance of the law, and Parliament replied with the Boston Port Act (1774) and other measures to punish Massachusetts. The port of Boston was closed. The charter of Massachusetts was cancelled. Town meetings were forbidden without leave from the governor. Persons charged with capital offences could be tried in Britain instead of Massachusetts. General Gage was appointed governor, and more troops were sent to the colony. This was a challenge to Massachusetts. It was also a challenge to colonial freedom, and the other colonies backed Massachusetts. Relief was sent to Boston, where the closing of the port meant unemployment and starvation. Most important of all, the 'Committees of Correspondence,' which had grown up in order to keep all the colonies in touch over questions affecting their liberties, arranged a meeting of representatives from each colony.

This meeting took place in Philadelphia in 1774: it is called the First Continental Congress, and all the colonies except Georgia sent delegates. These were nearly all well-to-do citzens, coming not from the mobs which had taken part in the riots, but from the wealthier colonists. They included many distinguished men who were to be prominent in the struggle for independence and in the early history of the U.S.A.—George Washington of Virginia, John and Samuel Adams of Massachusetts, John Jay of New York. They were divided about what to do. Some advised caution, others wanted resistance. Few—yet—wanted independence. Eventually the radicals, those who wanted a vigorous resistance, triumphed. The Congress adopted the 'Continental Association,' an agreement against importing British goods: they also agreed not to export goods to Britain. They issued a Declaration of Rights, and agreed to meet again in 1775. This Congress showed that the colonists could unite with each other over big issues, however much they might squabble over small ones. The First Continental Congress took the thirteen colonies a long stride on the road to nationhood.

In Britain, George III and most members of Parliament were determined to quell this resistance. Early in 1775 several proposals for agreement were put forward: the most notable of these were North's Olive Branch Resolutions. They all broke down. The colonists, particularly in the northern colonies, were openly preparing rebellion, and more troops were sent to Boston. Yet Gage in Boston was not anxious to fire the first shot. But in April 1775 he sent out a body of troops from Boston to take possession of military stores at Concord, some twenty miles to the north-west. At Lexington his way was barred by a handful of colonists. Shots were fired and the colonists dispersed. The British troops went on to Concord, found the stores gone, and had to fight their way back through a countryside which had risen in rebellion. This episode—known for the story of Paul Revere's ride—cost over 250 British casualties. The American War of Independence had begun.

3. THE WAR OF INDEPENDENCE, 1775–83

The odds seemed to favour Britain. She had thrice defeated France in the 18th century. Her naval power was outstanding. She controlled Canada and the St. Lawrence. The colonies were thirteen separate units: many of their inhabitants were loyal[1] to Britain. They had always needed British troops to protect them from French and Indians. Yet they had on their side definite advantages, of which the most obvious was distance. The British government had to conduct its campaigns from 3000 miles away. It took at least three months for a message and its answer to cross the Atlantic. Further, the area of fighting was large and the number of British troops small; and they, unlike the colonists, had little experience of warfare in colonial conditions. These factors reduced Britain's advantage. Three others caused her ultimate defeat. First, Lord North's government was one of the most incompetent in British history. Secondly, France, anxious for revenge for the loss of Canada, was hostile to Britain, and eventually joined the colonists. Thirdly, the colonists discovered in George Washington one of the oustanding leaders of modern times.

Britain was faced with the problem of defeating rebellion. The rebels

[1] These loyalists were called Tories by the rebels.

had to be crushed wherever they could be found. This meant a series of piecemeal conquests, with attacks at the chief centres. Boston was in British hands in 1775: New York, Philadelphia and Virginia would have to be occupied and tamed. But there was never very much plan about British actions, and, moreover, the need to defend Canada distracted her generals: in 1775 American troops under Benedict Arnold took Ticonderoga and Crown Point, thus threatening an advance into Canada. One at least of those generals, Sir William Howe, who arrived at Boston with 10,000 reinforcements in 1775, had very little enthusiasm for his work.

In May 1775, a month after Lexington, the colonists set about organising for war. The Second Continental Congress met at Philadelphia. This body, which contained representatives of the colonies, created an army by taking over the militiamen which each colony had under arms. Most important, it appointed George Washington as Commander-in-Chief. This action was the first turning-point of the war. Washington, born in Virginia in 1732, had already distinguished himself in the disaster to Braddock's force in 1755. He was wealthy, a gentleman and a slave-owner. Finer qualities than generalship or wealth made him outstanding. His uprightness and honesty are proverbial: equally impressive were his unselfish devotion and his courage in adversity. These qualities of character have made him a supreme figure in American history.

While the Congress was debating, the first considerable battle of the war, Bunker Hill, took place. Howe captured a height dominating Boston and held by the enemy, but lost one-third of his army and over twice as many men as the Americans. The orderly retreat of the Americans showed the British that they were fighting something more than a collection of sharpshooters. The Americans held most of Massachusetts. To the south the people of Virginia drove out their governor; but to the north an attack on Canada, under Arnold and Richard Montgomery, failed.

1776 saw the second turning-point, the Declaration of Independence. The Americans for some time claimed that they were not fighting the King, but his ministers. But war widened the gulf between George III and the colonists. The King hired 20,000 troops from the German state of Hesse for service in America; and Tom Paine published his best-seller *Common Sense*, a vigorous statement of the case for complete independence. Both these events stimulated the demand for a complete break. So, even more strongly, did the wish to obtain French assistance. Therefore on the Fourth of July, 1776, Congress issued the Declaration of Independence. It was drawn up by Thomas Jefferson. After cataloguing the crimes of George III, it declared that 'these United Colonies are, and of Right ought to be Free and Independent States.' Its most famous clause comes at the beginning of the second paragraph—'We hold these truths to be self-evident, that all men are created equal, that they are endowed by their Creator with certain inalienable Rights, that among these are Life, Liberty, and the pursuit of Happiness.' This was strange language from a slave-owner, as Jefferson

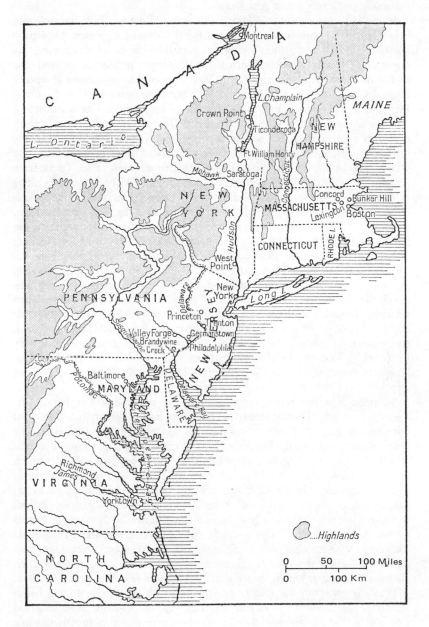

The War of Independence

was; but it does express the passion for freedom that was in the heart of Jefferson and many other Americans.

In this same year 1776 Howe evacuated Boston. But he defeated Washington at Long Island, and occupied New York, where he settled down for the winter, thus losing a splendid chance of destroying his opponent's much weakened army. Washington boldly re-crossed the Delaware River in a snowstorm on Christmas night, captured a thousand Hessians at Trenton, and a few days afterwards won another battle at Princeton, thus doing much to restore American morale. There was worse to come for the British cause in 1777. Lord George Germain, the Secretary for the Colonies, accepted a plan for cutting off New England from the other colonies. General Burgoyne took command of a force of some 8000 which was to work down the Hudson Valley to New York from Lake Champlain. Admirable on paper, the plan overlooked both the difficulties of the wild region through which the army would march, and the deficiencies of Burgoyne as a general. He over-burdened his men with baggage, and thirty waggons were needed for his own equipment, including silver plate and supplies of champagne; and he neglected the needs of scouting in the forested and trackless country. A supporting expedition from the west was driven back by the Americans. Worst of all, Howe, who had been expected—though not ordered, for Germain recognised the impossibility of tying generals down to detailed orders from home at so great a distance—to bring forces to meet Burgoyne, set off southwards instead. He defeated Washington at Brandywine Creek and Germantown, and installed himself in Philadelphia. Meanwhile Burgoyne moved slowly to disaster. Trapped by the Americans, abandoned by his Indian allies, he surrendered, with the 5000 men left of his army, at Saratoga in October 1777.

Saratoga was the third turning-point. It convinced Vergennes, the French Foreign Minister, that the colonists had a reasonable chance of winning. So in 1778 France came into the war on the American side. The French had supported the Americans from the start, seeing that the rebellion would weaken Britain; while the Americans had sought French favour because they wanted French money. The chief American agent in France, Benjamin Franklin, a shrewd and experienced citizen of Philadelphia, had obtained several loans from France. Moreover, before Saratoga, French noblemen had crossed the Atlantic to fight as volunteers in the American army. The most famous of these was the Marquis de Lafayette, who carried back to France with him revolutionary ideas and experience. After the alliance, signed in 1778, the most important French aid was sea-power, which, as we shall see, was at one vital point decisive.

Washington spent the winter of 1777–8 at Valley Forge. It was bitter and freezing; the army was hungry, ragged, and ill-paid; men deserted frequently. Yet Washington's determination kept an army together, while Howe helped by neglecting to attack. But no decisive fighting took place, either in 1778 or in 1779. In 1780 the British began to win a series of victories in the south, overrunning South Carolina. In the north the treachery of Benedict Arnold depressed the Americans. Arnold, who was genuinely dissatisfied with the way the war was being run, and was suffering from wounded pride, determined to betray to the British the important post of West Point, of which he was commander. But the British officer, Major André, who came through the American lines to arrange the details, was captured, and, after court-martial, hanged. Arnold escaped, and became a brigadier-general in the British army.

This was a severe blow. But next year, 1781, brought the Americans success. General Cornwallis, with the chief British army in the south, was trapped in the small peninsula of Yorktown, Virginia, by American and French armies under Washington and Rochambeau. He could still have been supplied by sea, or if necessary, embarked—so long as the British retained control of the sea. At that moment, September 1781, they lost that control. The French gained a naval victory and blockaded Yorktown. Cornwallis had to surrender, with 7000 men. It was the fourth, and decisive, turning-point. The war went on in name until 1783, but Britain was weary of it. Spain and Holland had joined the alliance against her, while Russia and other powers had formed the Armed Neutrality of the North, directed against Britain.

The peace treaty was signed at Paris in 1783. Britain recognised the independence of the thirteen colonies, and handed over to them all territory in America westwards to the Mississippi, except Canada, which she kept, and Florida, which she returned to Spain. The Americans agreed to recommend the separate states to allow loyalists to recover their property and British traders to recover the debts owing to them before the war. Thus the Americans won their independence. They owed their victory chiefly to British incompetence, to French help, and to George Washington. The treaty opened to them the vast area between the Appalachians and the Mississippi. But they were still thirteen separate states. The question of union lay ahead.

4   The Making of the Constitution 1783-9

The problem which the Americans faced between 1783 and 1789 is as easy to state as it was difficult to solve. It was that of combining union and freedom. Each of the thirteen states wanted to keep its freedom to manage its own affairs in its own way. Union was necessary for strength, to avoid disputes, and to deal with the new western lands won from Britain. The

Americans solved this problem by creating their Federal Constitution. This chapter tells the story of the making of that constitution, and gives an account of its main features.

I. THE ARTICLES OF CONFEDERATION

The thirteen colonies had, as we have seen, formed a kind of league in the war. The rules of the league were drawn up in 1777, though they were not finally accepted by all the states until 1781, and they were known as the Articles of Confederation. These provided for a Congress in which each state was represented, and which appointed various officers of state—for example, secretaries for foreign affairs and war. The Articles also said that citizens of each state were entitled to the full rights of citizens of any other state. But they went very little further. The Confederation was not a great deal more than an alliance of the thirteen states for the purpose of running the war. Congress was more like a meeting of ambassadors from separate countries than a meeting of a parliament. The states were extremely jealous of their separate rights and privileges. The Articles of Confederation were successful for the war period and for some time afterwards, but they were not satisfactory as a framework of lasting union. Very soon after the war was over they showed many signs of cracking.

2. POST-WAR DIFFICULTIES AND SQUABBLES

When the war was over the thirteen states found numerous difficulties in front of them. The end of the war brought its inevitable economic troubles. There was a certain amount of unemployment, notably in the northern states. The issue of paper currency during the war, notes which did not represent real wealth, made the situation worse. A peculiarly serious problem, one which crops up throughout American history, was that of debt. The farmers of the western regions of the states had borrowed heavily from the merchants of the eastern towns. After the war Britain closed the West Indian islands to American trade, and farmers could not sell their produce. Many of them were forced to sell their farms: others went to debtors' prisons. The position was worst in Massachusetts, and here in 1786 Shays' Rebellion broke out. Daniel Shays, an ex-officer, led mobs of farmers in attacks upon the courts, with the object of preventing judges from giving decisions in cases of debt. They refused to disperse when ordered to do so, and the movement turned into a rebellion which for a short time threatened Boston. Eventually the Massachusetts militia, armed with firearms, crushed the rebels, whose weapons were often pitchforks or clubs. This episode caused grave alarm among the richer inhabitants of the states, and made many men ready to welcome some stronger united government.

The jealousy which existed between the separate states showed itself very clearly after 1783 in a series of petty squabbles. In New England Connecticut quarrelled with most of her neighbours over minor matters of trade. New York and New Jersey quarrelled too, and New York taxed vegetables and chickens imported from New Jersey. Maryland and Virginia disputed the ownership of the Potomac River. Pennsylvania and Connecticut each claimed the Wyoming Valley (now in north-east Pennsylvania), and came to blows about it. Such disagreements threatened to destroy what little union existed among the states, and they were another argument for creating a firmer union than that which existed under the Articles of Confederation.

But the most serious post-war difficulty was that of relationships with foreign powers, particularly with those two that still held territory in North America, Britain and Spain. It was hardly possible for each of the thirteen states to send separate ministers to each of the major European states. And it was quite certain that no European state would regard with much respect a union whose members were perpetually squabbling with one another. A firmer union alone would entitle the states to respect in Europe. This was shown by the attitude of Britain towards the thirteen states after 1783. The Treaty of Paris left behind it various grounds for dispute. Both Britain and the states broke the Treaty, and there was plenty of futile but angry argument about which broke it first. Some of the bitterest disputes concerned the loyalists, those Americans who remained faithful to George III. Some 80,000 of them left the thirteen states, going to Britain, to Canada, where they formed the colony of Upper Canada or Ontario, or to the West Indies. The Americans in the Treaty had promised to recommend the separate states to give back to the loyalists the property which had been confiscated during the war. In fact many loyalists who returned in the hope of getting their property back were put in gaol or tarred and feathered and sent packing: others, more fortunate, remained and some became prominent American citizens. Moreover, in 1783, the British government issued an Order-in-Council forbidding American vessels to trade with Canada or the West Indies. This action deprived Americans of valuable trade which they had carried on in colonial days. It was unreasonable of the Americans to grumble at losing colonial privileges when they were no longer colonies. But this order strengthened the already strong anti-British feeling in the states. It also strengthened the movement towards a more effective union, for many Americans pointed out that the states could not retaliate until they were really united.

3. THE WESTERN LANDS

But it was the American possession of the western lands, the area across the Appalachians, that made strong union essential. Years before the war Daniel Boone and other pioneers had explored the rich lands of what are now the states of Kentucky and Tennessee. A steady stream of migrants crossed the mountains—outlaws and thieves, land-speculators, refugees, loyalists, men of all types: it has been estimated that by 1790 there were about 100,000 settlers in this region. Then the Treaty of 1783 gave the states possession of all English territory, north of Florida and south of the Great Lakes, as far west as the Mississippi. Some kind of government had to be provided for this vast region, some sort of law to govern its settlers, the backwoodsmen. Under the Articles of Confederation, the Congress had taken over control of all lands west of the mountains. In 1787 Congress passed the North-West Territorial Ordinance. This provided a system of government for all the lands north of the Ohio River which Britain had handed over under the Treaty. Its methods were extended later to all new lands which became part of the U.S.A. At first a newly settled Territory was governed by officials appointed by the President. When it contained 5000 people, it was allowed to send a delegate, who could not vote, to Congress, and to elect its own representative assembly. When its population reached 60,000 it was allowed to organise itself as a state, and was admitted to full membership of the union with the same rights as any of the original thirteen states. This principle of 'Territorial Government' secured the free development of the whole area of the United States, checking any rivalry among the original thirteen states to grab the western lands.

These western lands were the occasion of bitter disputes with Great Britain, and, as we shall see (Chap. 7), they were to contribute to causing the so-called 'Second War of Independence,' the War of 1812. The chief offence of Britain in connection with the Treaty of 1783 was her refusal to evacuate her military and fur-trading posts in the region south of the Great Lakes. As excuse for this she pleaded that the Americans had broken other clauses of the Treaty, but the real reason was that she did not wish to give up her fur-trading or her Indian allies. The fur-trading brought in £200,000 a year, and Canadian merchants protested to the government against handing this wealth to the Americans. Therefore Britain held on to the posts until 1796. The Montreal fur-traders encouraged the Indians against the Americans, who were encroaching on tribal lands, and for years among the backwoods there was continual warfare, marked by fiendish cruelty on both sides. The British government did not refrain from supplying the redskins with rifles and ammunition. For this reason the western settlers long hated Britain.

Farther down the Mississippi valley American settlers came into conflict with Spain. Spain had joined France on the American side in the war, and at the peace Britain handed over Florida to her: she already claimed vast territories to the west of the great river. Spain too encouraged the Indians against the Americans, and in the 'eighties there were terrible butcheries on the frontier of Georgia in fights between the settlers and the Creek and Cherokee Indians. But it was Spanish control of the mouth of the Mississippi that mattered most to Americans. The farmers of the west were already sending their corn and their salt pork on flat-boats down the Mississippi. Sometimes Spain granted 'right of deposit', i.e., free tran-shipment of goods at New Orleans, sometimes she refused it; she could open or close at her will the western farmers' door to their European markets. Here was a fruitful source of conflict.

The west was the gateway to the future for the thirteen states. The pion-eers of the 1780's were the leaders of a great host of Americans who followed in the next century. This western advance created new problems of government for the thirteen states; and it brought them into conflict with two great European powers. To meet these problems and this con-flict, a stronger union was essential.

4. THE PHILADELPHIA CONVENTION, 1787

These numerous difficulties and problems made the more thoughtful American statesmen aware that the existing Confederation was not strong enough. In February 1787 the Congress invited the states to send delegates to a convention to be held at Philadelphia for the purpose of revising the Articles of Confederation, in order to make the Union more fit to deal with the new problems of government, and to preserve the union. This Phila-delphia Convention met in May. Within four months it had drawn up the American Constitution, the document under which the U.S.A. has been governed ever since that time. Its members are known as 'The Founding Fathers.' They included most of the ablest American statesmen of the day, men who were the leaders of the U.S.A. in its early history. The list of names is impressive; besides George Washington, who was unanimously chosen President of the convention, and Benjamin Franklin, perhaps the two most notable were two of the youngest men present, Alexander Hamilton of New York and James Madison of Virginia. Hamilton was an alert politician who was determined to build a strong central govern-ment: Madison, later fourth President of the U.S.A., was profoundly learned in the constitutions of the past. The great majority of them represented the well-to-do: they stood for the richer landowners and the merchants rather than the small farmers.

5. THE AMERICAN CONSTITUTION

A constitution is a system of government. The main object of the 'Found-ing Fathers' was to build a constitution which would enable them to preserve and strengthen the union which the thirteen states had temporarily formed in order to fight the war. Here are some general comments upon the American Constitution, a short statement of its main details, and some special points to note about it.

A. *General Comments.* First, it is a written constitution. All its provisions are contained in one document. The British constitution is not a written constitution of this kind, but is a mixed collection of all manner of laws and customs, some of which are written down and some of which are simply traditional. But even written documents, however clear their writers try to make them, are at the mercy of lawyers, who interpret them in various ways. The American Constitution has been variously interpreted by lawyers, especially by judges of the Supreme Court.

Secondly, it is a federal type of constitution. The thirteen colonies (or, rather, the wiser statesmen in them) wanted in some way to preserve the union which they had formed: equally each colony wanted to sacrifice as little as possible of its own power. They solved the problem by creating a federal constitution. In this type of constitution each separate state which is joining the union retains its own government to deal with certain matters which concern itself alone: for other, more general problems—for example, foreign affairs, war, currency, inter-state commerce—the states create a central, federal, government in which they are all represented. It is this federal government which we mean when we talk of the government of the United States to-day. The Articles of Confederation were also a federal constitution, but one in which the central, federal government was very weak, while the separate states' governments were very strong. When the new constitution was being drawn up, some men considered that Americans should give most of their attention to making the federal government, the government of the whole nation, strong: others firmly believed that the rights of the separate states must come first. This division of opinion, between those who were nationalists and those who believed in states' rights, has continued right up to to-day. It was very important at certain crises in American history, especially, as we shall see, in the trouble between Andrew Jackson and South Carolina, and in the years before the Civil War.

B. *The Main Details.* Laws are to be made by Congress, which includes two houses.

The upper house is the Senate: this contains two members from each state large or small, and each senator sits for six years. The lower house is the House of Representatives (or, simply, the House). In this each state has members in proportion to the number of its inhabitants: they sit for two years. Among the powers given to Congress are the following:—it can collect taxes, and borrow money on the credit of the United States: coin money and establish post offices: declare war, raise and support an army: dispose of or govern all territory belonging to the United States: admit new states to the union.

Laws are carried out by the President. He is elected for four years, and is eligible for re-election. He is elected by electors themselves specially elected by this purpose by the people of every state. Each state elects as many electors as it has Congressmen (Representatives and Senators). His powers include that of vetoing laws (forbidding them) unless overruled by two-thirds of Congress. With the Senate he has the power of making

treaties and appointing ministers, ambassadors, and judges. He is Commander-in-Chief of the army and navy.

Courts of justice are to be set up, of which the chief is the Supreme
Court. Members of this court are appointed by the President and hold
their offices during good behaviour (in practice, for life). This court has
very wide powers. It may judge 'all cases, in law or equity, arising under the
Constitution: controversies to which the United States shall be a party: controversies between two or more states: between citizens of different states.'

Among other details the following must be noted. Each state is to
surrender criminals escaping from justice to the state from which they
came. Any person 'held to service or labour' under the laws of one state
who escapes to another is to be returned to his owner. The United States
guarantees a republican form of government to every state. Since slavery
existed in the southern states when the Constitution was made, it was
decided that in calculating the number of members which each state was
entitled to have in the House of Representatives every slave should count
as three-fifths of a free man: this was known as the 'Federal ratio.' (The
slaves of course had no right to vote.) It was made hard to alter or amend
the Constitution: amendments have to be supported by two-thirds of each
house of Congress or by the legislatures of two-thirds of the separate states,
and only become part of the Constitution when they have been ratified by
three-quarters of the states.

C. *Special Points to note.* The three branches of government—that is,
Congress, the President, and the Courts—are deliberately kept separate
from one another. Thus members of the President's Cabinet may not sit
in Congress, while judges hold office for life. Elections for the Presidency
are held every four years and for the House every two years. This leads to
difficulties, for it sometimes happens that a President of one party is in
office at a time when the majority in Congress belongs to another party.

The Senate is very strong. Each senator holds office for six years, whereas even the President is only elected for four. The fact that each state is
equally represented in it safeguards the small (for example, Rhode Island
or Delaware) or thinly-populated states (for example, nowadays the Rocky
Mountain states like Nevada and Wyoming) against the large or thickly-
populated states (for example, those of the industrial north and east, like
New York or Pennsylvania). It has made great use too of its power of
treaty-making: every treaty must gain a two-thirds majority in the Senate,
and in fact the Senate has rejected many treaties.

The Supreme Court occupies a position of great importance. Its judges,
notably John Marshall (Chief Justice 1801–35), have made full use of the
power left to them. The Supreme Court has made itself the interpreter of
the Constitution: it has taken upon itself to decide whether acts of Congress
themselves are lawful according to the Constitution. We shall see, for
example (Chap. 23), that it rejected some of Franklin D. Roosevelt's
'New Deal' laws as unconstitutional.

Up to date there have been only twenty-six Amendments. The first ten of these are known as 'The Bill of Rights' and were passed in 1791 (see below): while the twenty-first (1933) simply reverses the eighteenth, the famous Prohibition Amendment of 1918. Thus there have been few changes in the Constitution since it was first drafted.

The Constitution itself lays down nothing about the right to vote. It is left to the states themselves to decide who shall vote in elections, even of the President. This seems strange in the constitution of what has been from the start in many ways a most democratic country. In fact in 1787 many Americans, including such important ones as Alexander Hamilton, strongly distrusted the people. They had seen the power of the mob in the numerous riots of the 1770's and 1780's. In some states in 1787 the right to vote belonged only to a fairly small number of the people, though in others, such as Massachusetts, it extended quite widely. Only gradually during the next forty years was the franchise widened to include most male white Americans.

6. RATIFYING THE CONSTITUTION

The Fathers of the Constitution ended their labours in September 1787. It was one thing for a group of America's wisest statesmen to draw up an elaborate system of government; it was quite another to persuade the people of the several states to accept it. Indeed the hardest part of the struggle for a stronger union came after the Philadelphia Convention had broken up. The members of the Convention declared that the new Constitution would be in force when it had been ratified (that is, accepted) by nine of the thirteen states. Its publication aroused much hostility, for a variety of reasons. Some opponents pointed out that it gave far more power to the President and Congress than had ever belonged to King and Parliament in colonial days; others complained that it included no bill of rights stating the liberties of the individual; others said that it protected the property-owners and did nothing for the poor man. There was a spate of pamphlets and orations against it. Patrick Henry of Virginia, the most effective American orator of the time, attacked it: while Thomas Jefferson, the author of the Declaration of Independence and at that time American minister in France, suspected it because it contained no bill of rights.

Its supporters mustered all the arguments they could find. They could appeal to the need of a strong central government to maintain order: Shays' Rebellion had only been crushed at the beginning of 1787. They pointed out that the United States needed a strong and united government to overcome British obstinacy and Spanish intrigues in America. Washington's support was a powerful argument. Most important of all, Hamilton, Madison and John Jay wrote and published under the title of *The Federalist* a series of essays, which explained in clear and convincing language the merits of the Constitution. This propaganda certainly won over many waverers. But it is highly probable that if the outcome had depended solely on arguments in pamphlets and speeches the Constitution would have been lost. A good deal of shrewd manœuvring was necessary to get majorities in some states. The contest was very close: the majority in favour in the Massachusetts convention (special conventions were elected in each state to ratify the constitution) was 19, in Virginia 10, in New York only 3. Massachusetts tacked on to the Constitution a bill of rights, which was to be put before the other states and, if accepted, added as amendments. It was accepted, and it now forms the first ten amendments. These guarantee, among other things, freedom of speech and religion, freedom to assemble, freedom from general search-warrants, the right to trial by jury and security against cruel and unusual punishments. By the end of June, 1788 nine states had ratified, and so the Constitution became law. North Carolina was slow in ratifying, while Rhode Island stubbornly refused to do so until 1790. But before that time, on April 30, 1789, George Washington had been inaugurated as first President of the United States of America. The new republic had begun its course.

5   The New Republic

1. THE COUNTRY AND ITS POPULATION

George Washington had become President of a land great in size, but small in population. In 1789 the United States of America stretched along the Atlantic coast for some 1300 miles, and extended westwards from the coast to the long line of the Mississippi. Its total area was about 800,000 square miles. In this area there lived just under 4,000,000 people. The vast majority of them lived within 100 miles of the coast, and only about 100,000 were beyond the Appalachians. Only six American towns had more than 8,000 inhabitants each: Philadelphia, the capital and largest town, had about 45,000, and New York 33,000. The remaining 97 per cent. of the people lived on farms or plantations, in log-cabins or in hovels, in clearings in the great woods which covered most of the country. Thus most Americans lived scattered over the land. The difficulties of travel made distances greater. From Philadelphia to Charleston is some 600 miles; in 1776 it was over four weeks before the folk of Charleston heard that the Declaration of Independence had been signed. When Washington was first built, early in the 19th century, it took five days for a mail rider on horseback, and perhaps twice as long for the passenger in a stage-coach, to travel the 230 miles from New York.

2. AGRICULTURE AND INDUSTRY

The people of this area were still, as earlier in the century, nearly all farmers; and there had been little change in the kind of farming. In Virginia, indeed, where most great American leaders of the day came from,[1] the tobacco plantations of the tidewater region were less important, and the bigger plantations were now farther inland; on them the farming was much more mixed. Most of the people of Pennsylvania still grew corn and wheat, and most of the people of New England still struggled hard to grow anything at all on the stony soil of their land. In the towns, too, the occupations of the people were still the same. Philadelphia, New York, Boston, and Charleston were the homes of thriving merchants. Now that British rule had gone, these no longer made their fortunes by smuggling. None of them were wealthy, even by European standards of that time, but many of them were very comfortably off. New England was still dominated by its ship-builders and ship-owners, still noted for its seamen. On the whole, the U.S.A. was certainly not a wealthy land; the age of the millionaire had scarcely arrived—although merchants and financiers like Stephen Girard of Philadelphia were making handsome profits on trading voyages. On the other hand, it was not a desperately poor land. It did not suffer from the miserable poverty which was driving many of the peasants and workmen of France into wild and bloody revolution at this very time. And the age of slums also had not yet arrived in America.

There had not been much change in the ways in which Americans earned their living during the 18th century. But in 1790 they were on the edge of great changes. Already before 1790 a difference had grown up between the states to the North of Mason and Dixon's Line and those to the South of it. Both these sections of the U.S.A. depended mainly on farming. In the North farming was a small-scale affair: a farm was run by a man, his wife and his family, perhaps with two or three servants, more often without any. But in the South there had grown up plantations, on which black slaves did the manual work. Most of them were fairly small, but some contained many slaves. In 1790 there were about 700,000 slaves; some were in New York and other northern states, but the great majority were in the South. There they were employed in farming or in housework. Many southerners were already beginning to think seriously about freeing them. This was so even in Virginia, where 40 per cent. of the population were slaves.

But in 1793 an event occurred which fastened slavery upon the Negroes for another seventy years, and altered the whole history of the United States. Cotton had been grown in the South before 1790—for example, in South Carolina. There was a ready market waiting for it, for the British cotton industry was just getting into full stride, thanks to the use of power-

[1] Washington, Thomas Jefferson, James Madison, James Monroe, and John Marshall were all Virginians.

driven machinery. But it was a difficult crop to work. The great problem was that of getting the cotton off the seed; this was done by hand, and it took several hours to clean one pound of cotton. The land and climate of the South were ideal for cotton-growing, but there seemed no way round this problem, until 1793. In that year Eli Whitney, a young graduate of Yale University looking for a job as a teacher in Georgia, invented the cotton gin, a device containing a set of wire brushes on a roller. This simple machine got the cotton off the seed many times faster than any slave, and it revolutionised the life of the South. In 1792 the U.S.A. grew about 3 million pounds of cotton; in 1800 she grew over 36 million pounds. Hence the growing of cotton became by far the most important occupation of the South. And the idea of emancipating the slaves began to disappear from the minds of southerners, who now wanted all the labour they could get in the spreading cotton fields.

The North, too, began to undergo a change at about this time, although its effects were nothing like as dramatic or as sudden as those of Eli Whitney's cotton gin. In Britain the Industrial Revolution was well on its way by 1790, and many places in Lancashire were growing used to the sound of machinery in the cotton mills. Most of it was still driven by water-power, for James Watt had only produced his steam-engine in 1782, but it was machinery. Britain made every effort to keep the secrets of the new machines to herself, and passed a series of laws forbidding anyone to carry out of the country plans or models which might enable foreigners to set up the machinery, and thus compete with British trade. Secrets of this kind are impossible to keep, and in 1789 Samuel Slater, who had been a mill-hand in Lancashire, came to Rhode Island, carrying with him the design of the new cotton-spinning machinery—not on paper, but in his head—and set up a cotton-mill at Pawtucket. The development of machinery was slow in the U.S.A. at first. But when war came between France and Britain, and later between the U.S.A. and Britain, American industry began to grow. In this process, too, Eli Whitney played a part. He first used, in the manufacture of rifles, the principle of interchangeable parts, the principle on which modern mass production is founded. Thus the North became the manufacturing area of the U.S.A., while the South became the land where 'Cotton was King.' Between the two sections, in many ways so similar before 1790, a gulf gradually grew wider, until, seventy years after Eli Whitney had gone to Georgia and Samuel Slater had arrived in Rhode Island, the two sections fought each other in the American Civil War.

But in 1790 that was in the unknown future, and life in the new republic was still slow and simple. The farmers lived rather lonely and very primitive lives. There was indeed plenty to eat—fish in the streams and the sea, game in the woods, besides the crops which the farmers themselves grew. With a log cabin for his home, the farmer worked hard and long hours, especially if he lived in New England or on the western fringe of settlements in the Appalachians. In Virginia on the greater plantations life was in many ways similar to that in the England where some of their owners had been educated. The Virginian planter was not unlike the English country gentleman of the time; both gained their wealth from the land, both held the leading positions in the government of their countries; they worshipped at the same kind of church, often had the same outlook upon life, and wore the same kind of clothes. But the subjects of the one were English peasants; of the other, black slaves.

The rivals of the planters in importance were the prosperous merchants of the towns. These towns themselves were not unlike English country towns in appearance, with many pleasant houses and an air of connection with the countryside. On the other hand—also as in contemporary England—many of the houses in the lesser streets were dirty and dingy. There were no drains, and epidemics were frequent; there was, for example, a disastrous outbreak of yellow fever at Philadelphia in 1793. Philadelphia was the chief city, and the headquarters of the government until that moved to the half-built new city of Washington in 1800. Boston, the chief centre of the revolutionary disturbances in Stamp Act days, was very much a city of shipowners and seafaring men; New York, with its fine natural position at the mouth of the Hudson, already had its merchants and bankers like the Schuylers; Charleston, the chief town of South Carolina, was perhaps the country's gayest town.

3. THE U.S.A. AND THE WORLD

In the world of the 18th century the U.S.A. was not just a new independent state. It was a state of quite a different kind from any other that the 18th century knew. It was a republic in an age of monarchies. France, indeed, became a republic in 1792, but it was not long before she fell under the power of the despot Napoleon, who made himself an Emperor, and Europe's two other republics, Switzerland and Venice, also lost their independence through the rise of Napoleon. Further, the United States was the first great experiment in a federal type of government; the first large-scale attempt to combine a measure of independence for a number of separate states with a central government strong enough to unite them in their dealings with the rest of the world. No one knew whether it would succeed or fail. European statesmen at the time—notably those of Britain —regarded it with a faint amusement. Its problems were clearly great. The mere size of the land was one. The self-willed independence shown by the states was another. The presence of European powers as neighbours, Britain in Canada and Spain across the Mississippi as well as in Florida was a third. The redskins in the unoccupied area beyond the Appalachians were a fourth. The restless and vigorous pioneers thrusting into that area were a fifth. Taken all together, these problems provided a severe test for the new federal type of government.

In one other way, and that the most important, the United States stood for something new in the 18th century. Jefferson had stated it in the Declaration of Independence: 'We hold these truths to be self-evident, that all men are created equal, that they are endowed by their Creator with certain unalienable Rights, that among these are Life, Liberty, and the pursuit of Happiness.' The Founding Fathers had stated it in the introduction to that document: 'We, the people of the United States, in order to form a more perfect union, establish justice, insure domestic tranquillity, provide for the common defence, promote the general welfare, and secure the blessings of liberty to ourselves and our posterity, do ordain and establish this Constitution for the United States of America.' The new country stood for certain ideals—and above all for freedom and equality. It was to be a land where men might be free to live their lives as they wished, and where they would be on a level with other men. It proclaimed itself as a land of the free. There would be no tyrants, and no distinctions of rank. In setting these ideals before themselves, the Americans broke away from contemporary Europe. That was why those people in Europe who were discontented with Europe as it was hailed the American experiment with enthusiasm. That was why those French thinkers who at this time were criticising their own system of government praised the American experiment; that was why those few Englishmen who at this time were demanding Parliamentary reform took so great an interest in what the Americans were doing. Because it claimed to stand for freedom and equality, the United States was a challenge to Europe in 1789.

6   Early Years, 1789-1801

The U.S.A. was not born into an easy world. Within three months of Washington's first inauguration a Paris crowd had broken into the Bastille: a month before his second inauguration France had declared war on Great Britain. The French Revolution and the long Anglo-French war that it produced did not leave the U.S.A. untouched. She had broken with Britain, but she could not escape from Europe. The French Revolution provoked in the U.S.A., just as it did in England, wild enthusiasm among some people and shocked opposition among others: in this way it helped to create two distinct American political parties. The war between England and Revolutionary France set before the U.S.A. the problems which face a neutral trading country in time of war. American statesmen had to face all this at the very time when they were running in their new machinery of government and creating some kind of financial system. That they did so without serious disaster is a measure of their ability. The U.S.A. was fortunate in her early statesmen.

1. GEORGE WASHINGTON, 1789–97

She was most fortunate of all in her first President. George Washington was reluctant to become President: he wanted to retire to his estate at Mount Vernon, Virginia. But once he had accepted office he gave all his powers to its problems. Few leaders of successful revolutions in history have been more unlike the typical revolutionary than George Washington, the slave-owning patriarch of Mount Vernon. His quiet dignity of bearing was a national asset in the continuous disputes with European powers, and his firmness and honesty were generally respected, even by his political opponents. He had not the subtle brain of Hamilton, and he lacked Jefferson's enthusiasm for the idea of liberty; and he contributed little to the ideas of his government. But he showed a wise judgement which was frequently valuable to the nation in those early days. For most of his two terms of office he kept above party politics: but his natural sympathies were with the landowners who governed England rather than with the French revolutionaries. Thus he grew more ready to be friendly with England and more sympathetic to the Federalists, the pro-British party. This cost him a good deal of popularity, and in his last year of office he was heartily abused in the press. He was an aristocrat, not a democrat, and he tended to regard all opposition as treason. Yet, taken as a whole, his guidance was wise and his tenure of office successful. Washington has become almost an American legend. His patience and sureness of judgment helped the U.S.A. to establish itself in the world, in the middle of one of the great crises of world history. He showed the calm wisdom and sane judgment which marked the 18th century, and was unstained by its typical vice, corruption.

2. THE U.S.A. AND EUROPE, 1789–97

We have already seen that one of the reasons why the thirteen states adopted their new and stronger constitution was the policy of Spain and Britain in the lands which lay to the west of the U.S.A. Britain was refusing to withdraw from her trading stations and military posts in that region, while Spain was throttling the trade of the western settlers by forbidding them to send their goods down the Mississippi. Both countries maintained this attitude during most of Washington's terms of office. Both went on intriguing with the Indians: and both tried to detach lands from the Union by plotting with discontented settlers. It was fortunate for the U.S.A. that the two European powers did not combine against her. In 1789 they fell out with one another over the question of Nootka Sound. Nootka Sound, which lies on the Pacific coast of Vancouver Island, was at that time the centre of a fur trade between these regions and China. It was the market where furs were sold before being sent across the Pacific, and both Britain and Spain laid claim to it. The dispute obviously interested the U.S.A., which was ready to support Spain rather than Britain for fear of any further extension of British power in North America. The Nootka crisis at length passed, leaving Americans more suspicious than before about the motives of European powers.

Nootka was a small matter in comparison with the effects of the French Revolution. This was hailed in America with great enthusiasm. It was believed that the new age of liberty, of which American independence had been the first-fruits, was about to begin in Europe. But this early enthusiasm gradually turned into hostility, among many Americans—particularly among the rich and well-to-do. The growing violence and disorder which accompanied the Revolution alienated Americans as well as Englishmen. A reaction of feeling against the Revolution itself, and against the liberal principles which it proclaimed, set in. Yet there always remained a large number of Americans who believed in the Revolution, saying that its principles of 'Liberty, Equality and Fraternity' were those for which the thirteen states had fought against Britain, and that the mob-violence and Terror were only temporary phases which would soon disappear. Thus the Revolution split Americans into two political parties (see Section 4 below). This division became acute when, after 1793, the Revolution ceased to be a mere subject of argument for Americans, becoming instead a serious practical problem. In that year Britain and France went to war: the war lasted, first as the Revolutionary and then as the Napoleonic War, until 1815, with a short break from 1801 to 1803.

The war was a test for America's inexperienced diplomatists. The alliance of 1778 with France still stood, and under its terms the United States was bound to help France if Britain attacked the French West Indies; and Britain was certain to do this. France might have expected Americans to help her out of mere gratitude for her assistance in the winning of independence. Enthusiasm for France was still high, and anti-British feeling was strong. Yet an influential party, in which Hamilton was prominent, detested the Revolution. Washington himself was anxious to keep his country neutral, and in 1793 he issued the Neutrality Proclamation, stating America's intention to remain neutral and warning American citizens, on pain of prosecution in American courts, against taking any part in the war.

The French for their part erred seriously in an attempt to win the U.S.A. to their side. They sent as minister to the U.S.A. in 1793 a gay young man called Genet. Citizen Genet was a model of vanity and indiscretion, all that an ambassador should not be. He received a great welcome on landing at Charleston and on his way to Philadelphia, the capital, and this seems to have turned his head. He issued licences to privateers to attack British trade: founded Jacobin clubs: tried to raise American troops to fight under the French flag against Spain, which was an ally of Britain in 1793: and was extremely rude to American politicians. Even Jefferson, more sympathetic to France than the rest of the cabinet, found him impossible. This cabinet asked for his recall: his successor brought with him orders for Genet's arrest. Genet wisely stayed in America and became an American citizen. At the same time the republican government in France asked for the recall of Gouverneur Morris, the American minister to France, who had schemed to obtain the release of Louis XVI. Neither Genet's antics nor Morris' intrigue brought their two countries into more friendly relations.

In 1793 American relations with Britain were no better than those with France. The constant bickering over the western lands was at its worst in this year, largely on account of a plan produced by the British government, for erecting an Indian state between the Ohio and the Lakes. This plan, which the American government refused to consider, simply served to encourage Indian hostility to the Americans, and the hostility was fomented by the intrigues of the British lieutenant-governor of Upper Canada. Added to this there came the problems caused by the Anglo-French war. In 1793 the British government imposed a blockade on goods going into France or the French colonies. This meant a stoppage of much American trade: it meant also accepting the British claim to be free to search all ships suspected of carrying contraband either to France itself or to the French West Indies. The 'right of search' often meant the right to loot, for the crews of British naval vessels, many of whom had been collected from taverns and gutters by the press-gang, were frequently rascally and unscrupulous. In 1793 Britain was highly unpopular in the U.S.A.

Washington's judgment was of great worth to his country at this time, when war would have been disastrous to the young republic. On Hamilton's advice he sent the Chief Justice, John Jay, to Britain as a special envoy, with instructions to reach some settlement with Britain. Jay was well-known for his friendliness to Britain, and undoubtedly British diplomatists played on this fact and got the better of him. The Treaty, known as Jay's Treaty, which he signed in 1794 (it was ratified, after prolonged debate, by the Senate and accepted by Washington in 1795), was very favourable to Britain. When news of its terms spread there were riots during which Jay was burned in effigy, and it did much to promote party division in the United States. The chief American gain in the treaty was that Britain finally abandoned her claim to the frontier posts, which she evacuated in 1796. But this was only handing over to the Americans property which was really theirs according to the Treaty of 1783. In return for it, Jay accepted the British view about the rights of neutrals in wartime—he practically accepted the blockade: he also gave Britain several trading advantages in America: and he made no claim for compensation for the cost to the U.S.A. of Indian raids encouraged by British officials. Washington disliked Jay's Treaty, but felt that the only alternative to accepting it was war. He believed it to be more important that the United States should develop in peace. The settlement with Britain was costly, but it prevented a war which might have wrecked the young republic. Further, Washington

Alexander Hamilton, Secretary of the Treasury, 1789-95

Thomas Jefferson, author of the Declaration of Independence and President, 1801-9

also reached a settlement of frontier questions with Spain, by the Treaty of San Lorenzo (1795), which gave Americans the 'right of deposit' at New Orleans. This permitted the Western farmers, coming down the Mississippi, to unload their goods at New Orleans for shipment to Europe.

3. HAMILTON AND AMERICAN FINANCE

The chief domestic problem which confronted Washington's government was that of finance. The U.S.A. had to pay off the debts contracted during the war, and give European nations as well as American settlers confidence in her finances. Washington chose as his Secretary of the Treasury Alexander Hamilton. Hamilton, born in 1755, on the island of Nevis in the West Indies, of a Scottish father and a French mother, was perhaps the most brilliant of the American statesmen of these years. He led an attack at Yorktown: became after the war a lawyer at New York, and married into one of New York's wealthiest families: and wrote many articles in *The Federalist*. A clear thinker, writer and speaker, he had a peculiar genius for finance, and he used it to the full in laying the foundations of American national finance.

In 1789 Congress passed the first tariff, or list of customs duties, in American history. The duties were imposed on foreign manufactures, and they protected what little American manufacturing industry there was. Since that time the U.S.A. has always been a protectionist nation. Hamilton had nothing to do with this first tariff, although he was a protectionist. His achievement for American finance was embodied in his Report on Public Credit, which he delivered to Congress in 1790. In this document he first made clear the necessity of starting the U.S.A. on her course with an assured system of public finance, which would enable Americans and Europeans alike to trust the government of the new republic. He wanted in particular to win the support of well-to-do merchants and financiers in the northern states. To attain these ends Hamilton proposed four measures, all of which were adopted.

First, all the debts of the U.S.A., whether owed to Americans or to foreigners, were funded at par: that is, the government guaranteed to pay off all its debts at their face value. The total amount was about $54 million, including $42,500,000 owed to Americans and just under $12,000,000 owed to foreigners. A fair amount of the $42,500,000 domestic debt consisted of soldiers' pay certificates, paper promises to pay which had been given to soldiers in the war. These had depreciated and were worth much less than their face value. Hamilton paid the cost of this financial operation from the money brought in by import duties, and by excises—taxes levied on goods, such as whisky, manufactured within the U.S.A. Secondly, the government took over all the debts owed by the separate states. The total of these was about $21,500,000: but this was not evenly distributed, because some states had been extravagant and others cautious in their financial dealings. Therefore some states and especially Virginia, which had paid off most of her debts, opposed this 'assumption' of state debts. Others, such as Massachusetts, which owed more than any, welcomed it. Hamilton got this proposal through by a deal with Jefferson, Virginia's leading statesman. The Constitution provided that an area not more than ten miles square should be set aside as the site of the national capital. Jefferson agreed that Virginia would support the assumption if Hamilton would get the northern states to consent that this site should be carved out of Virginian territory. So it came about that the Federal government took over the state debts, and that the District of Columbia, containing the city of Washington, lies by the side of the Potomac.[1]

Hamilton's third measure was the creation of a Bank of the United States. This was in many ways similar to the Bank of England, notably in its close connection with the government. It was chartered for twenty years: its total capital was to be $10,000,000, of which the government was to contribute $2,000,000. Its powers included those of issuing notes, receiving deposits, and opening branches throughout the country. Fourthly, he established a Sinking Fund, a fund which would gradually be accumulated by the government in order to provide for paying off the principal of the national debt. This was the last of Hamilton's financial achievements of 1790. In 1791 he delivered to Congress a Report on Manufactures. This had no such immediate results as the Report on Public Credit, but it set out with lucid force the argument for protection as against free trade. In the following year he set up a national currency system, and a mint.

The success of these measures is enough to show Hamilton's skill as a finance minister. American stocks sold well in Europe: while all the debt, both domestic and foreign, was paid off by 1817. Hamilton turned an almost bankrupt group of states into a nation whose financial credit stood high. It was a brilliant feat. But he did not do it without provoking strong opposition. First there was the simple opposition of those who did not want to pay the taxes he imposed. This was illustrated in the Whisky Rebellion (1794) which took place in Western Pennsylvania; distilling was a considerable industry, and whisky was even used as currency in this region, and the farmers rose in protest against the excise duty. The rebellion was put down by state militia called out by the President. Much more important, on a long view, was the opposition created not just by taxation, but by the whole aim of Hamilton's finance. This kind of opposition did not produce rebellions: instead it led to the rise of political parties in the United States.

[1] In fact most of modern Washington is in Maryland. Laws for the District of Columbia are made, under the Constitution, by Congress; it is governed by a Board of Commissioners appointed by the President. Its inhabitants—753,000 in 1970—had no votes, until the Twenty-Third Amendment (1961) gave them the right to vote in presidential elections.

4. THE RISE OF POLITICAL PARTIES

The first two political parties in American history were the Federalists and the Republicans.[1] They arose during the 1790's, when Americans began to differ sharply from each other over major political issues; in particular, over financial policy and, more important, foreign affairs. In finance, it was Hamilton's policy that provoked the division.

Hamilton's political ideas reflect the opinions of the commercial upper class into which he had married. He did not believe that common folk were fit to take any share in government. He had, that is to say, no belief in democracy. 'The people,' he said, 'are turbulent and changing; they seldom judge right or determine right.' The rich, he argued, were more likely to be wise rulers than any other class, because they were better educated and had more to lose by misgovernment. So the rich must be won over to support the existing system of government. This was Hamilton's object in giving financial stability to the United States, in funding the debt and in creating the Bank. Rich men would support a government whose finances were secure.

Hamilton's opponents said that he had gone a great deal further than winning a rich class to support the new government. They maintained that he had put the country at the mercy of a rich class. They pointed to the privileged position of the Bank: they also pointed out that funding the debt had made fortunes for the speculators who had gone round buying up pay certificates from soldiers at cheap rates. They challenged the government's right to charter a Bank, saying that such action was unconstitutional. The leader of Hamilton's opponents was Thomas Jefferson of Virginia, Secretary of State in Washington's cabinet until 1794. Jefferson, a tall, carelessly-dressed man, was in personal appearance a contrast to Hamilton, who was small and neat: in ideas too they were completely opposite to each other. Jefferson lacked Hamilton's logical brain, but Hamilton had none of Jefferson's devotion to democracy. Jefferson believed —as the Declaration of Independence, whose author he was, shows—in the right of the common man to liberty: each man, he maintained, had a right to share in the government of the country in which he lived, and a right to be free from control by the rich. Whereas Hamilton was a realist, valuing men at their lowest, Jefferson was an idealist, seeing them at their highest. Hamilton regarded the Bank and his other financial measures as a necessary means of giving the U.S.A. sound government by winning the support of the wealthy: to Jefferson they were a device for putting the country in the hands of the rich class to which Hamilton's friends belonged.

The other great issue upon which parties arose, and on which Hamilton

[1] The Republicans called themselves this: their opponents called them Democrats, and the party later adopted that name: thus they are the ancestors of the modern Democrats. They have nothing whatever to do with the modern Republican party: this was founded just before the Civil War.

and Jefferson disagreed strongly, was the French Revolution and its outcome, the Anglo-French War which began in 1793. The Federalists under
Hamilton, whose sympathy for monarchy was well-known, opposed the
Revolution and supported Britain rather than France. Jefferson and the
Republicans welcomed the Revolution and preferred France to Britain.
This division of opinion was not just a matter of sentiment. It reflected
economic and sectional interest. The Federalist party included rich
merchants who had no liking for revolutionary mobs. It won most of its
support from New England and the northern states which carried on a
profitable trade with Britain. The Republican party attracted the farmers,
particularly the poor farmers of the western lands who loved liberty and
hated the merchants to whom they were in debt: it won much support,
too, in Virginia and the South, where the planters hated the British merchants who exploited them.

The rivalry of Jefferson and Hamilton grew more bitter, and party
feeling stronger as Washington's terms of office went on. In 1796 a
presidential election was held: it was a party contest. Washington, who had
grown steadily more Federalist in sympathy, had refused to stand for a
third term, and the Federalist candidates were John Adams of Massachusetts, who had been vice-president under Washington, and Thomas
Pinckney. The Republicans supported Jefferson and Aaron Burr. Adams
got 71 votes to Jefferson's 68, and the Federalists held power for the next
four years. Jefferson became Vice-President.[1] Washington retired in 1797,
having previously issued a farewell message, composed partly by Hamilton,
to his countrymen. Much of it was an attack on what he called 'the baneful
effects of the spirit of party.' But its most celebrated passage concerned
foreign policy, and advocated isolation from Europe. ''Tis our true policy
to steer clear of permanent alliances with any portion of the foreign world.'
The American parties of the day, energetically supporting either France
or Britain, seemed to take little notice of this, but it remained a constant
feature of American foreign policy until after the Second World War.

5. JOHN ADAMS, 1797–1801

John Adams was an unfortunate President. He was honest and blunt,
and had been a sturdy champion of independence. But he was also awkward and grumpy, lacking the dignity of Washington. He was unlucky
enough to cross Hamilton and so to split the Federalist party. Hamilton
was anxious for war with France, whose privateers, since the conclusion
of Jay's Treaty, had made severe attacks on American shipping. Moreover,
she was suspected of designs to rebuild a French Empire in the New

---

[1] This situation, whereby the President was of one party and the Vice-President
of the other, was awkward: the 12th Amendment (1804) provided that separate
elections should be held to each office, and now each party nominates a separate
candidate for each office.

World: even before Napoleon Bonaparte became First Consul in 1799, there seemed no limit to her ambitions. The episode of the XYZ Dispatches encouraged the war party. In 1797 Adams sent to France a mission to settle subjects under dispute between the two countries. Talleyrand sent three agents referred to in the dispatches as X, Y and Z, to try to persuade the Americans to buy an agreement with France by a cash payment, including a bribe for his own pocket. The Americans turned this scheme down, and described it in their dispatches, which were published, causing great fury against France. A series of naval fights followed, and Hamilton and his supporters confidently hoped for a general war. Hamilton had a wild vision of a war in which he would appear as the champion of a victorious America. Adams fought hard for peace, and saved it by sending a special minister to France in 1799: after long negotiations a settlement was reached with Bonaparte in 1800. Adams saved peace, but broke with Hamilton, and thereby made his own re-election to the presidency impossible.

At home he was equally unhappy. The fear of war with Revolutionary France brought repression in America, just as war itself did in Britain under Pitt. The Federalists in Congress passed three reactionary laws in 1798. The Aliens Act gave the President power to expel foreigners: the Naturalisation Act extended the period of residence required for natural- isation to fourteen years: the Sedition Act stated that all speeches or writings against the President or Congress, which seemed to be defamatory, were punishable. There was much clamour against foreign refugees, and a number of charges, under the Sedition Act, against Republicans. The acts brought protests from two states, Virginia and Kentucky. Both passed resolutions stating that the Aliens and Sedition Acts were unconstitutional. That of Kentucky was drawn up by Jefferson. These resolutions stated what is known as the 'states' rights' theory of the Constitution: they said that if any state considered an act of the Federal government to be un- constitutional, it would disregard that act. This theory became very prominent later in the dispute between North and South.

In the election of 1800 the two Republican candidates, Jefferson and Burr, tied with 73 votes each: John Adams got 65, with Hamilton per- suading some Federalists not to vote for him. The right to choose went to the House of Representatives. Here Jefferson was chosen. His victory brought Federalist rule to an end, and within twenty-five years the Federalist party was extinct.

7 Jefferson, Madison, and the War of 1812 (1801-14)

Relations with Europe still remained the greatest American problem for most of these thirteen years. James Madison, the second of the two Presidents of this period, allowed his country to slide into a war with Britain, the War of 1812. Yet the United States looked west to the new lands as well as east to Napoleon's Europe. Jefferson, by the purchase of the Louisiana Territory, made the greatest single territorial gain in the history of the Union.

1. THOMAS JEFFERSON, 1801–9

Jefferson, who was fifty-seven when he became President, had already been a leading figure in America for over twenty-five years. He was a man of very varied interests; besides being an amateur zoologist and an architect of some note (he had designed in the French style his own mansion of Monticello), he had studied Greek, Anglo-Saxon and American Indian languages and produced his own translation of the New Testament. Slovenly in dress, he once shocked the British Minister by receiving him attired in an old coat, red waistcoat, sloppy pantaloons and slippers. The rich were terrified of revolutionary changes when he was elected, and many honest Americans suspected him of being an atheist. In many ways he was a strange mixture. He was at once a shrewd politician and a dreamer. A slave-owner, he believed deeply in liberty. A supporter of states' rights and author of the Kentucky Resolutions, he did not hesitate to extend the power of the Federal government to acquire Louisiana. Lincoln alone among the Presidents has given to Americans a nobler vision of their land as the home of individual freedom.

His most spectacular achievement in office was the purchase of Louisiana. This wide region, which extended from the Mississippi to the Rockies, included the territories of thirteen of the present fifty states of the Union. It had been Spanish since 1762, but in the secret treaty of San Ildefonso (1800) Spain handed it over to Napoleon, who was planning conquests in the New World. Next year he launched an attack on the black republic of San Domingo. Jefferson heard of the secret treaty in 1801, and in the following year Spain, which was still in formal possession of Louisiana, withdrew from American citizens the 'right of deposit' at New Orleans. The U.S.A. faced a difficult situation—a Napoleonic design for domination of the New World, and the strangulation of the trade of her western lands.

In 1803 the American minister in Paris began to negotiate with Napoleon. Jefferson hoped to buy New Orleans, and kept the possibility of an alliance with Britain as a weapon in reserve. In the middle of the bargaining Napoleon offered the U.S.A. the whole of Louisiana. Yellow fever and the Negroes had beaten his San Domingo expedition: and he was on the edge of a new war with Britain. The Americans accepted, and clinched the deal for $15,000,000. To accept this new territory was, according to all Jefferson had ever previously said about the powers of the Federal government, decidedly unconstitutional. But the prize was too great, and Jefferson accepted the Treaty. So did the Senate, and at the end of 1803 the million square miles of Louisiana belonged to the United States.

At home the behaviour of Aaron Burr, the Vice-President (1801 to 1805), was a serious problem. Burr, a corrupt self-seeker, intrigued with members of the Federalist party to get himself elected as governor of New York in 1804. Hamilton, who for all his dislike of Jefferson had no sympathy with a man like Burr, used his influence against him, and he lost. Burr determined to revenge himself on the man who had frustrated his ambition, forced a duel on Hamilton, and killed him. In 1805 Burr, his reputation gone and his term of office as Vice-President ended, involved himself in a mysterious conspiracy, whose object may have been either the establishment of a new western republic or simply the enrichment of Aaron Burr. He was arrested in 1806, tried and acquitted: he went into exile in France.

Jefferson's first term, to 1805, was prosperous. Albert Gallatin, Secretary of the Treasury, practised sound economy: and American ships broke the power of the Tripoli pirates of the Barbary coast. The second term (1805–9) brought a multitude of troubles, the product of the Napoleonic War. Britain and France alike cared little for the rights of neutrals, but the superiority of British sea-power made her violence more obvious to the Americans. One constant, though much exaggerated, source of grievance was the British impressment of seamen from American ships. Sailors in the British navy, recruited by the press-gang, often deserted to American ships, as did men from British merchant ships, attracted by higher wages. British naval officers searched American vessels for British subjects: it was only too easy to impress an American by mistake. In 1806 Napoleon published the first of his Berlin Decrees, proclaiming a strict blockade of Britain: Britain retaliated in 1807 with Orders-in-Council, forbidding all trade with Europe. This meant British interference with all American trade to Europe.

In 1807 a British frigate, the *Leopard*, attacked an American naval vessel, the *Chesapeake*, and took off her three American citizens who had earlier been impressed into the British navy and had deserted. This incident caused a wave of war-feeling to sweep through the United States. But Jefferson had no wish for war: he believed that American trade was essential to Britain, and that he had only to stop it to bring Britain to heel.

He got Congress to pass, late in 1807, the Embargo Act, which forbade all export from the U.S.A. Jefferson's belief in this measure was misguided. It was futile, for American trade was not vital to Britain: British shipowners rather liked the Act, which caused much suffering and brought Jefferson much hatred in New England and New York. The shipowners of these regions opposed the embargo: some had accepted British inspection and licences and developed their trade under British protection, and American ships had captured much of the European carrying trade. This opposition grew most serious when New Englanders condemned the Force Act (1809), which allowed Federal officials to seize cargoes believed to be intended for export overseas. Jefferson got western support for his embargo, for the western farmers were ready to back any measure directed against Britain. But its failure was obvious: and just before Jefferson left office in 1809 he signed the bill for its repeal.

Thus Jefferson's presidency ended unhappily. Yet his position in American history is secure. He lived on until 1826. His gift to the U.S.A. may be summed up in the words which he himself chose for his epitaph— 'Here was buried Thomas Jefferson, Author of the Declaration of Independence, of the Statute of Virginia for Religious Freedom, and Father of the University of Virginia.'

2. THE ORIGINS OF THE WAR OF 1812

James Madison, elected to succeed Jefferson at this critical time, was an honest and high-minded man who had been very prominent in the making of the Constitution. A great reader and scholar, a far clearer thinker than Jefferson, he lacked the latter's force of character and flair for political problems. Under his government the United States drifted into war with Britain. Like Jefferson, he believed that the stoppage of American trade with Britain would force Britain to listen to American grievances. In 1809 Congress replaced the embargo by a Non-intercourse Act. This forbade trade with both belligerents: but it said that the U.S.A. would resume trade with either nation when it withdrew its regulations interfering with American trade. This device failed. Napoleon, in reply, published the Rambouillet Decree (1810), under which he seized $10,000,000 worth of American shipping in European harbours. Macon's Act (1810) turned the non-intercourse principle inside out: it allowed American trade with both countries, but added that if one of them withdrew its regulations striking at American trade the U.S.A. would stop trading with the other. American traders took advantage of this to begin trade again with Britain, and profited appreciably by it. When Napoleon, in an obvious attempt to turn the U.S.A. against Britain, offered to withdraw his decrees on condition Britain withdrew her Orders-in-Council, Madison accepted. Once more trade with Britain was suspended: this time, in the winter of 1811–12, it caused much distress in Britain. In the middle of June, 1812, after long delay, the British government announced the withdrawal of the Orders-in-Council.

It was too late. Two days after the withdrawal (long before the news had crossed the Atlantic) Congress declared war on Britain. Americans had tried for years, by embargo and suspension of trade, to put economic pressure on the British and thus compel them to stop searching American ships for contraband and impressing American seamen into the Royal Navy. Peaceful methods had failed: Britain believed that her actions were essential when she was fighting for survival against Napoleon. So the men who had voted for Jefferson's embargo now turned to vote for war. Only in this way, they believed, could American honour and recently-won independence be preserved.

There were other causes of quarrel. Canada was one. The pioneer farmers of the western lands, steadily breaking new ground, were moving into the region round the southern shores of the Great Lakes. In 1803 the state of Ohio was formed: north of it lay Lake Erie, on whose other side was the peninsula of Upper Canada, land which with its woods and springs was a frontiersman's dream. It was thinly inhabited. In 1810 all Canada contained about half a million people, most of whom were Frenchmen living in Lower Canada. It is not surprising that many westerners not only coveted it, but imagined they could easily seize it. Many American politicians argued that its capture would at least give the United States something to bargain with at the end of the war, to exchange for a firm British recognition of American rights on the high seas.

An attack on Canada might also have the further advantage of dealing with the Indian problem. Westerners believed that the British were supplying the tribesmen with guns and ammunition, which they needed if they were to have any chance of halting the merciless advance of the American frontiersmen. In 1809 a Shawnee Indian named Tecumseh and his brother, known as the Prophet, created a strong Indian confederacy. These two, the noblest champions of Redskin independence, were making a desperate attempt to halt the westward spread of the pale-faces. The Prophet awakened religious enthusiasm among the tribes around the Lakes, while Tecumseh tried to link tribes throughout the frontier-lands. British officials in Canada welcomed this movement as a check on American advance. This infuriated the westerners, who accused the British government of encouraging Indian savageries, and made them more than ever anxious to drive the British from Upper Canada. In 1811 William Henry Harrison, Governor of Indiana Territory, who had already tricked Tecumseh out of hunting-grounds, took advantage of the chief's absence to lead a military expedition into the Indian lands, where he destroyed Tecumseh's village near the mouth of the River Tippecanoe. This exploit made Harrison President of the United States thirty years later (see Chap. 11): at the time it was hailed as a triumph over the Indians and as a blow to British designs.

The Congress which met in 1811 contained a small group of vociferous representatives from western lands whose demand for an attack on Canada won them the nickname of 'the War-Hawks.' Two of them, Henry Clay of Kentucky, elected Speaker of the House in 1811, and John C. Calhoun of South Carolina, were to play notable parts in American history. This group clamoured for war, harping steadily upon a long list of grievances— impressment, the *Chesapeake*, neutral rights, the freedom of the seas, the supplies and encouragement given to the Indians. Many southerners supported them; Madison in 1810 had annexed part of West Florida, and now seemed the moment to snatch all Florida from Spain, who was the ally of Britain. But New Englanders, who represented the very shipping interests which the War-Hawks claimed to be avenging, opposed them; they foresaw that war would do far more harm than good to their trade. Madison wavered, and finally gave way to the demand for war, as the British delayed their withdrawal of the Orders-in-Council. Congress passed the declaration of war by 79 votes to 49.

3. THE WAR OF 1812

The American objective in 1812 was Canada, which the War-Hawks expected to overrun in a few weeks. It seemed likely to be easy prey: the population of the U.S.A. was some fourteen times as great as that of Canada. Britain was spending all her energies on the desperate struggle to defeat Napoleon: and twenty years of war had weakened her. She had been very anxious to avoid a war with the U.S.A., as the decision, made too late, to withdraw the Orders-in-Council, showed. When the war came, she treated it as a sideshow, until the first abdication of Napoleon in 1814 enabled her to send some of Wellington's veterans across the Atlantic. The problems of conducting a war at 3,000 miles distance were the same in 1812 as they had been in the War of Independence: and now the Americans had settled finances, a stronger Union, a stronger sense of nationality, and a population three times as great as in the earlier war. The naval pressure which Britain could exercise was limited by the fact that until 1814 her primary object at sea was a blockade of Napoleon's Europe. All these facts gave some substance to the War-Hawks' prophecies of a quick victory.

In fact, American troops at no time appeared likely to conquer Canada. This was in part the result of difficulties caused by geography. War in the region around the Great Lakes meant a series of complicated movements involving careful co-operation between land and sea forces, and such co-operation was not possible when Indian runners were the fastest means of communication. But two other causes stopped an effective attack on Canada. First, the American army in 1812 was small, badly-officered, and out of date in its ideas; while the state militias, who were called out to help, were useless, chiefly because they were unwilling to fight outside

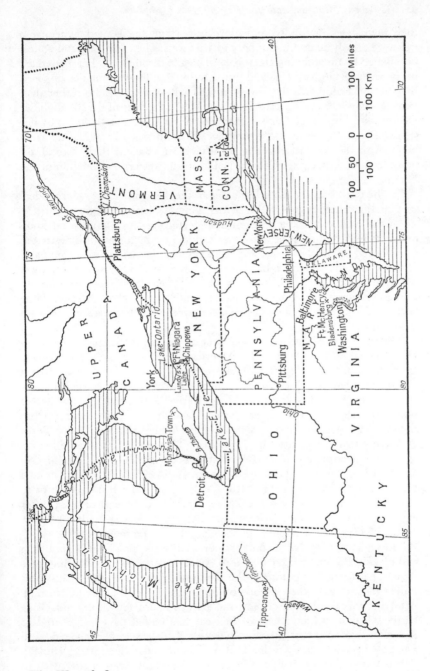

The War of 1812

their own states. Secondly, and more important, the United States were never genuinely united in support of this war. The New England states, dominated by the shipping classes, were hostile throughout. The Federalist party, strongest in New England but with much influence outside, opposed the war. In Hamilton's day the Federalists supported Britain rather than France; they had severely criticised Madison at the time of the Rambouillet Decree, and they argued that to declare war on Britain at the crisis of her struggle with Napoleon was wrong as well as unwise. They had no sympathy with the western clamour for attack on Canada: they were afraid that a conquest of Upper Canada would mean western domination of the Union.

On the open seas the Americans began the war with a navy a great deal smaller than that section of the British Navy which was stationed off the American coasts. It won a series of unexpected successes at first: but soon numbers told, and most of the American ships which were not destroyed were locked up in harbour for the remainder of the war. British command of the seas made possible a blockade, which grew stricter as the war went on, and it also enabled Britain, as we shall see, to send expeditions to various points on the American coast from Maine to New Orleans. Some successful coups by American privateers were poor consolation for these advantages.

The main area of land-fighting at first was the region immediately south of the Great Lakes. In 1812 the Americans attempted to invade Canada from each end of Lake Erie. The western attack ended in the British capture of Detroit, while the eastern one broke down because the New York militia refused to cross the Niagara River into Canada. This double failure was a poor start for the westerners' 'short war.' In 1813, after further failures on land, an American naval force under Captain Oliver Perry defeated a British squadron on Lake Erie. This victory forced the British to abandon Detroit, and it was followed by a considerable American success on the River Thames. Tecumseh, whose Indian confederacy had joined the British, was killed in this battle, which ended the Indian attempt to resist American advance in the Lakes region. At the end of 1813, after eighteen months of war, neither side had made any real advance. The events of 1814 were far more spectacular, though no more decisive.

Throughout 1813 Napoleon's power in Europe had been crumbling, and in 1814 Britain could dispatch to America veterans from Wellington's armies, hardened by fighting in the Peninsular War. The Americans forestalled the arrival of these troops by invading Canada by way of Niagara. After a victory at Chippewa, they took part in a hard-fought but indecisive battle at Lundy's Lane: before the year had ended they had retired to American soil. In the late summer the British veterans arrived, and attempted an invasion of the U.S.A. by the Lake Champlain–Hudson River route. This was halted by a second American naval victory, that of Commodore MacDonough off Plattsburg in Lake Champlain. Meanwhile, in the south, another British force, transported from Europe, had been landed in Chesapeake Bay, in order to attack Washington. It met a force of American militia at Bladensburg: after a very brief contest the militia ran away, thus giving the battle the title of 'Bladensburg Races.' The British advanced on the American capital, and Madison and the government left in a hurry. British officers arrived in time to eat the dinner intended for the President. The invaders then burned all the public buildings in Washington.[1] This was not the work of drunken soldiers out of control, but a deliberate retaliation for the Americans' action in burning the parliament house at York (now Toronto) in 1813. This British force next went on to attack Baltimore and to bombard Fort McHenry:[2] these activities failed.

Farther south still a British expedition advanced on New Orleans. One of the most astonishing men in American history, Andrew Jackson (see Chap. 10), a backwoods lawyer experienced in Indian warfare, was defending it against a British commander who had served under Wellington in Spain. Jackson threw up earthworks, upon which the British made a frontal attack. It was a terrible and costly failure. Over 2,000 British soldiers were killed, wounded, or missing; the American casualties were eight dead and thirteen wounded. Jackson became a national hero, and the victory restored national self-confidence by enabling Americans to forget earlier failures. It made no difference to the peace treaty. This had been signed at Ghent a fortnight before, on Christmas Eve, 1814, although news of it did not reach America until the battle was over.

At home, as we have seen, the country was not unanimous. New England, with Massachusetts at its head, grew less, not more ready to support the war, and a peace party was organised there from the start. Britain encouraged this opposition by omitting to blockade Massachusetts until 1814. In several ways New England did well out of the war. She sent out privateers who captured British ships; she began to develop industries of her own to supply the textiles formerly obtained from Britain: until she too was blockaded she was the gateway for all imports to the U.S.A., and her merchants made profits out of this: some of them, indeed, did not hesitate to trade with the enemy, either by sea or over the Canadian border. But all this did not make New Englanders want the war. They wanted it less when Britain blockaded their coasts and British landing parties raided their seaports.

Among the extremists in the Federalist party a movement arose for

[1] The President's house was burned: its walls remained, and, when it was reconstructed, were painted white to cover the smoke-marks: hence it has got the name 'The White House.'
[2] The fort was bombarded all night: at dawn the Stars and Stripes was still flying over it. This gave Francis Scott Key, a young American detained on one of the British ships, his inspiration for 'The Star-Spangled Banner.' Thus the United States gained a national anthem from the War of 1812.

seceding—that is, breaking away—from the Union, making a separate peace with Britain, and forming an independent republic in New England. These 'secessionists' hoped to get their own way at the Hartford Convention, a special meeting of representatives from the New England states summoned in 1814 to consider the situation. Their fear of the westerners was strong enough to make them ready to split the Union. They talked much of 'states' rights', saying that each state had the right to break from the Union if it could not agree with the policy of the Union. At Hartford, however, the wiser statesmen of New England prevailed, and the proposals of the extremists were turned down. Secession was an ominous word: it was to be heard again in the history of the United States.

Negotiations for peace went on intermittently throughout the war, and neither country was unwilling to stop it. In the U.S.A. western hopes of a triumphal march into Canada were dim: while British citizens who had paid for twenty years of war against France had no wish to pay for an indefinite period of war against the U.S.A. The final Treaty, signed at Ghent in 1814, said nothing whatever about the rights of neutrals, the ground on which Madison had declared war. As for Canada, the Treaty provided that four boundary commissions should be set up to decide exactly where the boundary between Canada and the U.S.A. ran.

If the results of wars are measured by comparing the treaties which end them with the objects for which men begin them, the War of 1812 was wholly indecisive. In fact, it was an important stage in American development. First, before 1812 the U.S.A. had been in many ways, and particularly in her foreign policy, at the mercy of Europe and European affairs. The Napoleonic War had governed American foreign policy. In 1814, the U.S.A. turned her back on Europe, only facing her again when it became necessary to warn European powers to keep off America. A hundred years of isolation began in 1814. Secondly, the war gave an impulse to a process that had started in the days of Jefferson's embargo—the growth of modern industry in the U.S.A. The stoppage of trade with Britain encouraged manufactures at home. The textile industries, and especially that of cotton, grew rapidly. There was widespread enthusiasm for wearing only American clothes, and the legislatures of at least six states passed resolutions asking their members to do so. The number of spindles in American cotton-mills increased from 8000 to 500,000 between 1807 and 1815. Two inventors of these years, Francis C. Lowell, who made a power loom, and Eli Whitney, who first developed the idea of standardised, interchangeable parts, have notably influenced the history of their country. Lowell set up at Waltham the first large-scale cotton factory in the U.S.A. Besides textile factories, foundries, rope-walks and other workshops grew up. The government took its first census of manufactures in 1810. Thus the War of 1812 set the U.S.A. on the course of her modern industrial development.

8   The Ever-moving Frontier

1. THE WESTWARD MOVEMENT, 1790–1829

Between 1790 and 1829 eleven new states were admitted to the Union. By 1830 there were over 4,000,000 people in these eleven states—one-third of the whole population of the Union, and more than there had been in the original thirteen states in 1790. Thus in forty years the population in the lands across the Appalachian Mountains had grown prodigiously. This growth was caused by the arrival of a host of settlers from the eastern states and from Europe. These western lands now stood for what the earliest colonists had sought—land in which to begin a new life, freedom in which to do so. Land and freedom were the chief reasons why so many millions moved west, ready to brave all the hardships of life on the frontier. In the South, in the rich lands of the lower Mississippi Basin, the planters from the states to the east broke new land for cotton-growing, and took their slaves with them. But the great majority of the settlers wanted the new land in order to set up small, independent farms. There was an un-limited amount of land available, and most of it was very fertile. It was sold by the Federal government at prices which grew lower as time went on. A succession of Land Acts were passed, fixing the prices to be paid for public land. That of 1820 was typical. It said that all land was to be paid for in cash: credit had been allowed previously, and the government had bad debts of millions of dollars. Further, the price was to be $1¼ an acre.

These pioneer settlers—of every age and both sexes—went by every means possible; by wagon and by coach, on foot, or by boat over such stretches of river as lay in their route. They moved sometimes in ones or twos, usually as families, or in fifties and in hundreds. Travel was difficult, and the steep slopes of the Appalachians did not make the journey easier going. This movement of vast numbers of human beings was a migration greater than that which brought the Angles and Saxons to Britain, and at first their means of transport were little better than those of the Angles and Saxons. But the movement itself stimulated improvements in com-munications: and settlers in states like Kentucky and Ohio wanted to be able to send their produce to market in the eastern cities. In the 1790's the Lancaster Turnpike road was built in Pennsylvania, and it served as a highway for countless travellers on their way westwards. In 1808 Congress voted money for the building of the 'National Road' or 'Cumberland Pike'; this began at Cumberland, Maryland, in 1808, and was then pushed on to Wheeling, Virginia (1817), Columbus, Ohio (1833), and ultimately to

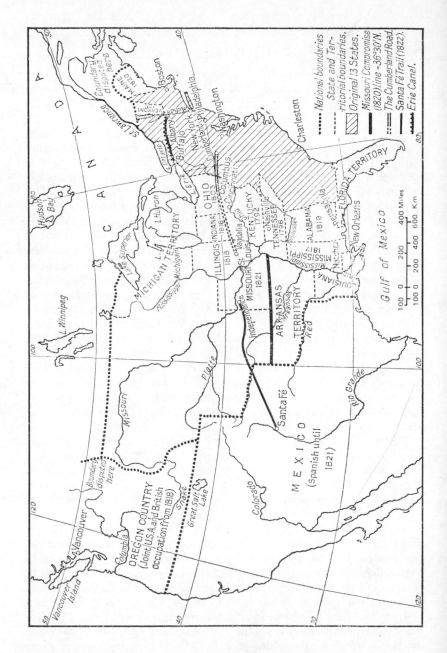

The Westward Expansion of the U.S.A. before 1829

Vandalia, Illinois (1852). This was the main highway for those journeying to land north of the Ohio until the middle of the century.

Canals were another way of crossing the Appalachians. It was the states, not Congress, which built most of the roads and canals, and the most important of the latter, the Erie Canal, was begun in 1817 by the state of New York. Its object was to connect Albany on the Hudson with Lake Erie. Completed in eight years, it was a vital link between east and west, enabling the farms of the Ohio Valley to send their produce down to New York, and the newly-developed factories of the east to send their manufactured goods to the farmers. It cut down the cost of carrying goods from Buffalo to Albany by about 90 per cent., and contributed greatly to the development of the wealth and importance of New York. Other eastern seaports produced plans to connect them with the west, but none could rival New York, with its site at the mouth of the Hudson. It was on that river that the first important experiment in steam navigation was made. In 1807 Robert Fulton sailed his paddlesteamer *Clermont* up the Hudson from New York to Albany. The steamboat gained importance gradually. It made much difference to life in the Mississippi Basin. Before its coming, western farmers floated their goods down the great river in flat boats, and when they reached the mouth they often sold the boats with the goods. To get a boat upstream on the Mississippi was a desperately slow business. The steamboat cut down the time over a long distance by many weeks; trade could now go both ways on the Mississippi and its wide tributaries, and during the 19th century great cities like Cincinnati, St. Louis, and Minneapolis grew up along their banks. All these improvements in communications in their turn stimulated the movement of people to the west.

Beyond the line of settlement went explorers and traders. In 1804–6 two explorers, Lewis and Clark, sent out by Jefferson, crossed the continent, reaching the mouth of the Columbia River, and brought back valuable information about the land through which they had passed. This far north-western region which they had reached, the Oregon Country, was rich in fur-bearing animals, and fur-trappers grew more numerous as the century went on. It was this region and the Missouri Valley which helped to found the Astor fortunes. John Jacob Astor, who came to the U.S.A. as a poor immigrant from Germany, made much money by questionable methods in fur-trading there. (He invested it in tenement property and land in New York, and died in 1848 worth $20,000,000.) To the south-west lay the great land which belonged first to Spain and then, after 1821, to Mexico. In 1822 there began the Santa Fé Trail. This was the 750-mile route from Independence, Missouri, to Santa Fé, over which caravans of American traders moved every year after 1822, carrying with them manufactured goods, to be exchanged at Santa Fé for skins and precious metals.

Yet these explorers and trappers and traders were only the heralds of the westward advance of the settlers. The real frontier line—the line where the white man's settlement ended and the spaces which still remained to the Indian began—was never fixed. It crept constantly westward, as more and yet more pioneers broke new ground, and new townships arose. This advance westward was never a movement planned and organised by the government. It was the work of millions of individual pioneers—emigrants from Europe wanting new land, Americans tired of life in the east, fugitives from justice, missionaries out to convert Indians, slave-owners seeking fresh soil for cotton-planting. The Federal government encouraged it by its Land Acts. When the pioneers had blazed the trail, and small townships had arisen, Congress went further by providing law and government. Under the North-West Territorial Ordinance of 1787 the system of 'Territorial Government' had been devised. This method of colonising new lands was first applied to the land north-west of the Ohio River, which became a Territory in 1798; it was later split up into smaller districts, and the first of these to be admitted as a state was Ohio, in 1803. Other western districts were also admitted as states in this way. But by the time the stage of admission as a state had been reached, fresh pioneers—or the same ones, tired of a settled life—had pushed the frontier many miles to the west of the new state.

2. THE FRONTIERSMAN

The typical frontiersman was hardy and enterprising because the conditions in which he lived made him so. There were many different kinds of frontiersman, from the daring pilot of the river-boats on the Mississippi to the lonely trapper of mountain areas. But the log-cabin farmer was the most typical of them all. He lived in a clearing—made by his own axe—in the woods. Timber was the centre of his existence. His house was made of it, his clearing was fenced with it; it provided him with fuel, furniture, mugs and platters. His staple crop was Indian corn, which grew well and gave him a sure supply of food. He was a hunter, of the wild animals which roamed in the woods, of game for his pot, and of the Indians with whom he was at perpetual enmity. His life—and that of the women and children who bore the hardships and the excitement with him—was rough and grim. The work of creating a settlement and of keeping back the wilderness never ended. Consequently the frontiersman was himself hard, like his work; he was rough and brutal, alert and ready to meet any danger. He was independent, believing strongly in equality and disliking all artificial differences between men, like those created by rank or riches. Self-confident and vigorous, he believed that the western lands had been made for him, and he swept away without scruple anything or anyone that stood in his path—the trees of the forest, the bears and other wild beasts, and the Red Indians.

3. THE FRONTIER IN AMERICAN HISTORY

It is scarcely possible to overestimate the effects of the westward movement in American history. Remembering that it went on after 1830, right
on indeed until the beginning of the 20th century, let us consider some
of the effects which were already visible before that date. The advance of
the pioneers brought the U.S.A. into contact—and into conflict—with
other peoples already settled in the North American continent. Foremost
among these peoples were the Indians. The pioneers engaged in a continuous struggle with them along the whole frontier line from the Lakes
to the Gulf of Mexico. It was a savage struggle, in which massacres and
scalpings were the methods of both sides. The redskins were fighting
desperately for the lands upon which their ancestors had roamed for
centuries. Consequently there was slaughter and bloodshed in thousands
of nameless encounters up and down the continent, and gradually the
redskins were pushed back, or exterminated. The Federal government,
on the whole, tried, on paper, to restrain the pioneers, and countless treaties
were made with Indian tribes, guaranteeing to them the remainder of their
tribal lands and safeguarding them against further advance. The treaties
were valueless, for no government could stay the advance of the pioneer,
and the advance of the pioneer meant the destruction of the Indians. It is
hardly possible to name definite stages in a movement of this kind. One
or two events were of outstanding importance. One was the battle of the
Fallen Timbers in 1794, in which 'Mad Anthony' Wayne defeated a force
of mixed Indian tribes near the western end of Lake Erie. This was
followed by the Treaty of Greenville (1795), by which Indian tribesmen
handed over more lands to the pale-faces. Another important event, as
we have seen, was the battle of Tippecanoe in 1811. Yet the destruction
of the redskins was a movement not of great battles, but of numerous
massacres, treaties made and broken, and seizures of land. In the years
before 1830 all the Indians of the lands east of the Mississippi, and some
to its west—including the Shawnee, Potawatomi, and Wyandot of the
north, the Cherokee, Creek, Chickasaw, and Choctaw of the south—
suffered alike from the relentless advance of the pioneers.

The frontier advance brought the U.S.A. into contact with other peoples
besides the Indians. To the south it brought them into contact with Spain,
the owner of Florida, and hence led to the purchase of Florida in 1819
(see Chap. 9). It led them also into contact with Mexico after that state
had shaken off Spanish power. In 1823 the Mexican government granted
Americans permission to occupy lands in Texas, then part of Mexico.
This in turn led to the American annexation of Texas in 1845, and contributed to the outbreak of a war with Mexico in 1846 (see Chap. 11). To
the north, the advance of the pioneers brought further contacts and
quarrels with Britain in the regions of Maine and Oregon (see Chap. 11).
Thus the westward advance created problems for the U.S.A. in her

relationships with other powers during the first half of the 19th century.

The frontier had equally important effects on the relationships of Americans with one another. First, it brought a new democratic element into American politics. The chief statesmen of the U.S.A. in its early years had been planters like Washington and Jefferson, or townsmen like Hamilton. With the growth of western states, whose people had been or still were pioneers, new politicians appeared on the scene. Henry Clay of Kentucky, the 'War-Hawk' of 1812, was one of these. More pushing and more ready to appeal to popular opinion than the older statesmen, they represented the vigorous and energetic pioneer farmers of the West. A new section had arisen, to rival the trading and manufacturing North and the cotton-growing South. The West, with its democratic farmers, was a new force in American politics. The westerners had not to wait long before they elected the first westerner to become President of the United States —Andrew Jackson of Tennessee, who became President in 1829 (see Chap. 10). Thirty-two years later another and a greater westerner became President. Abraham Lincoln was a son of the frontier. His family, like many western families, was restless, and fell into the habit of moving westwards. They had moved from Pennsylvania to Kentucky, where Abraham was born; from Kentucky to Indiana; and from Indiana to Illinois.

The western spirit of democracy was not the only effect which the frontier had upon American politics. Another and more serious one showed itself quite early in the history of the U.S.A. The opening-up of new western Territories soon aroused a thorny question—were they or were they not to be open to slavery? This question cropped up first in 1819–20, and was solved for the time by the Missouri Compromise of 1820 (see Chap. 9). But it was bound to recur, as each new group of pioneers broke new land and new Territories were created. In this way the steady advance of the frontier provoked a bitter quarrel between two sections of the U.S.A. over the question of slavery. In the 1850's this quarrel was the prelude to the Civil War (see Chap. 13).

Thus the advance of the frontier led directly or indirectly to most of the chief problems of American history in the 19th century—to the terrible strife with the Indians, to the wars with Britain and Mexico, to the quarrels with Britain in the 1840's, to the growth of a new and extremely democratic section, the West, and to the growth of the bitter quarrel between South and North over the extension of slavery. For this reason the 'ever-moving frontier' has been described as the most important influence upon American history in the 19th century.

9 Madison, Monroe, and John Quincy Adams, 1814-29

1. POST-WAR PROBLEMS, 1814-17

The War of 1812 began a new age in American history. Its immediate legacy was a measure of trouble. The U.S.A., indeed, did not suffer from the terrible distress which England was enduring in these same years. But there was severe unemployment in her newly-developed industries. At the end of the war English manufacturers dumped on the American market surplus quantities of goods accumulated during the war, offering them at low prices. This hit American manufacturers severely, many foundries and mills having to close down; and they clamoured for protection in the form of a tariff. In this cry the manufacturers of New York, New Jersey and Pennsylvania were supported by the farmers of Ohio, Kentucky and Tennessee, who reckoned that they would get better prices for their wool, hemp and flax in a protected home market than overseas, and by the sugar-planters of Louisiana, who wanted protection against Cuban and Jamaican competitors. Clay and Calhoun, the War-Hawks of 1812, led the demand for a tariff. Clay, a firm nationalist, who thought of the U.S.A. as a whole and not simply as a group of states or sections, had developed the idea of what he called the American System. According to this, all benefits which one section received by the increase of trade or industry ought to spread over the entire country. This would be achieved by a tariff on European manufactures. The North, protected by the tariff, would develop her industries: the growing population of the industrial towns would provide a market for the food grown by the farmers of the West and South: the farmers in their turn would buy the factory-made goods of the North.

This system was admirably thought out, and it does, on the whole, represent what has actually happened. Yet there were two flaws in it. First, New England was not, in the period after the Treaty of Ghent, unanimous about a tariff. The manufacturers welcomed it; the merchants and shipowners opposed it, because it interfered with their business. Secondly, and more serious, there was no real place for the South in Clay's system. While the sugar-planters wanted a tariff, the cotton-planters, far more numerous, for the South was becoming increasingly dependent on cotton, were not enthusiastic. They had no objection to English dumping, because they wanted to buy their manufactured goods as cheap as possible. And most of their cotton had, in any event, to go to England. The 'American System,' in fact, did not help the South. In 1816 Calhoun and the southern congressmen voted for the tariff bill that was introduced, and helped to pass it. They did so because there seemed then some chance of making the South an industrial area. But as the amount of southern wealth invested in cotton grew, southern opinion turned against tariffs which put money into the pockets of Yankee[1] manufacturers. Calhoun, who remained for many years the leading statesman of the South, became a determined opponent of the tariff.

One other notable act of Congress during what remained of Madison's second term must be mentioned. This, like the tariff, contributed to the growth of American industry. In 1811 the charter of the first Bank of the U.S.A. had expired and had not been renewed: in 1816 the second Bank of the U.S.A. was chartered for twenty years. One-fifth of its twenty-five directors were to be appointed by the President, and one-fifth of its capital of $35,000,000 was to be subscribed by the government.

2. JAMES MONROE AND THE ERA OF GOOD FEELINGS, 1817–25

Four of the first five American Presidents were from Virginia. The last of this 'Virginia dynasty' was James Monroe, who had been Madison's Secretary of State. He was elected in 1816 by 183 votes against his Federalist opponent's 34. The old Federalist party was dying, and the Republican party had itself adopted many Federalist ideas. For the only time in American history the spirit of party rivalry seemed dead, and for this reason the eight years of Monroe's presidency have been given the name of the 'Era of Good Feelings.' In 1820 he was re-elected unanimously except for the vote of a single elector.

Monroe's presidency saw rapid westward expansion. One sign of this was the fact that six new states were admitted to the Union. These were Indiana (1816); Mississippi (1817); Illinois (1818); Alabama (1819); Maine (1820); and Missouri (1821). Another sign was the speculation in land, which helped to create a serious commercial panic in the West in 1819. This speculation was encouraged by the Bank of the United States, to which many farmers fell heavily in debt. The position was somewhat eased by the Public Land Act of 1820, which both lowered the price of land bought from the Federal government and stopped purchases on credit. But the western farmers never loved the Bank, which they blamed for their troubles.

Southwards there was territorial expansion at the expense of Spain. The land now known as Florida was at this time owned by Spain: some of it was occupied by Creek and Seminole Indians who used it as a base for

---

[1] The word 'Yankee' was first used in America to mean any New Englander and, later, any inhabitant of the northern states: in England it came to mean anyone from the United States. English soldiers in the War of Independence talked of their opponents as 'Yankees': so did the soldiers of the South in the Civil War. How the word originally arose is uncertain.

plundering raids on the American settlers round the mouth of the Mississippi. In 1818 Andrew Jackson led an expedition against them and chased them into Florida: he then proceeded to take possession of Pensacola and other Spanish towns. Not content with this rash behaviour, he went on to put to death two British residents of Pensacola, named Ambrister and Arbuthnot, who had opposed his activities. Serious international complications might well have followed, and a majority of the cabinet opposed Jackson. Calhoun, Secretary of War, wanted him court-martialled. But John Quincy Adams, the Secretary of State, backed Jackson strongly and won the cabinet over to support him, while the British government withdrew its protests when it found that its two subjects had been in the wrong. Spain's power over her American possessions was fast declining, and she decided to take the chance of cutting her losses. She offered to hand Florida over to the U.S.A. provided that the American government would abandon claims which it had to Texas, and would take over the claims, amounting to $5,000,000, which American citizens had against Spain. The U.S.A. accepted the offer, and in 1819 Florida became American territory. It was admitted as a state of the Union in 1845.

It was in Monroe's day that there came the first serious outbreak of the bitter dispute over slavery which was later to split the nation. In 1818 the territory of Missouri applied for admission as a state of the Union. Slavery already existed in Missouri. John Tallmadge, a New York Congressman, proposed an amendment to the act of admission: this was to the effect that Missouri should only be admitted provided that there was no further extension of slavery in the state, and that slave children born after the state's admission to the Union should be freed at 25. This was virtually to demand the admission of Missouri as a free—that is, non-slave—state. Tallmadge was supported by New England and the North. His proposal raised two questions—slavery itself, and the whole political power of the South. The Northerners felt that if slavery spread through the lands of the Louisiana Purchase the Union would fall into the hands of men whose ideals and ways of life were those of the South, utterly different from those of the North. The South on the other hand knew that its political position was at stake. In 1820 the South had a population of 4,485,000, and 81 representatives in the House. The North had 5,152,000 people and 105 representatives in the House—and the population of the North was growing faster than that of the South. The South retained a balance of power by means of the Senate, where there were eleven free and eleven slave states. If the new states which were being carved out of the Louisiana Purchase were to be free, the political power of the South was gone.

Tallmadge's amendment aroused bitter debate all over the country. The House passed it, but the Senate rejected it. The problem was solved —temporarily—in the next session, when Maine, whose people wished to be separated from Massachusetts, petitioned for admission as a state.

There was a deadlock because the slave state senators prevented its admission as a free state as long as Missouri was excluded as a slave state. Finally a solution which partially satisfied each section was reached. This was the Missouri Compromise (1820). Both Maine and Missouri were to be admitted, Maine as free and Missouri as slave; it was added that there should be no slavery north of the 36° 30′ N. parallel of latitude (which is the southern boundary of Missouri) except in the state of Missouri itself.

One outcome of this episode was to strengthen the southern determination to defend slavery, for the South began to suspect that the North was aiming at the complete destruction of that institution. The South became more conscious of itself as a section, different in outlook and way of life from the North. It was quite clear that the question had in no way been solved. The more far-sighted statesmen saw the danger ahead. Ex-President Jefferson said, 'This momentous question, like a fire bell in the night, awakened and filled me with terror.' John Quincy Adams saw it as 'a title-page to a great, tragic volume.'

One of the questions that arose during the arguments over the admission of Missouri was the right of Congress under the Constitution to interfere with the institution of slavery inside a state. At this time the greatest of all Chief Justices of the Supreme Court was making history by his interpretations of the Constitution. He was John Marshall of Virginia, Chief Justice from 1801 to 1835. We have noticed that the American Constitution is inevitably open to the interpretations which lawyers put upon it, and that, in consequence, the Supreme Court, which has the right to try cases under the Constitution, has great power. Marshall, a vigorous thinker who was not afraid to set out his own interpretation of the Constitution in deciding the cases that came before him, made full use of this power. This in itself has been important, for later Supreme Court judges have followed Marshall's example and freely used their powers to decide whether acts of the states or of Congress are constitutional or not (see, for example, Chap. 23).

Two ideas in particular which Marshall held have been 'written into' the Constitution because he embodied them in the long series of decisions which he handed down while he was Chief Justice. He was a nationalist, standing firmly for the Federal government against any idea of 'States' rights.' Thus in the case of *McCulloch* v. *Maryland* (1819), a case which involved the position of the Bank of the United States, he ruled that the Federal government was the government of the people of the whole United States, and not just an agreement among the several states: the Federal government must therefore be able to make laws for the benefit of the people, and the separate states may not interfere with these laws except where the Constitution definitely permits them to do so. Again, he was a champion of the rights of property. In *Dartmouth College* v. *Woodward* he ruled that no state had the right to make laws which threatened the charters of private corporations (as distinct from public corporations like cities); these were protected by the clause in the Constitution which forbade any state to pass any 'law impairing the obligation of contracts.' The charter threatened in 1819 was that of a college, but Marshall's decision was important because it greatly encouraged the growth of private business corporations.

All these events of Monroe's presidency—the Florida Purchase, the Missouri Compromise, and John Marshall's decisions—are important in American history. Yet James Monroe will always be most clearly remembered because he gave his name to the most famous statement ever made about American foreign policy. This is somewhat unjust, for it was his Secretary of State, John Quincy Adams, who was entirely responsible for American foreign policy at this period. And this policy, from 1814 to 1824, was vigorous and successful, thanks to Adams. Florida, as we have seen, was acquired in 1819. A settlement of several boundary problems with Great Britain (but not in Maine and Oregon) was reached. The most notable part of this was the Rush-Bagot Agreement of 1817 which provided that there should be no naval units, but only police boats, on the Great Lakes.

But the most important moment of Adams' policy came in 1823. For some fifteen years before this date the several Spanish colonies in Central and South America had been breaking into rebellion, and the feeble power of the distant and decadent Spain proved quite unable to crush them. Several of them had proclaimed their independence. Spain, threatened with the utter ruin of her western Empire, had appealed to the other continental sovereigns of Europe—particularly to those of Russia, Austria, Prussia and France, the leading members of the Holy Alliance, whose main purpose was the quelling of all movements towards liberty—to help her to recover her lost colonies. They were anxious to help, for the germ of revolution might have crossed the Atlantic. But no help was possible without an assurance of assistance, or at least of neutrality, from Britain, the leading naval power. And Britain was quite unwilling to give such an assurance; for she had developed a flourishing and profitable trade with the new South American republics. In the U.S.A. most people emphatically supported the republics and opposed Spain and any threat of European intervention on behalf of Spain.

In 1821 the Tsar of Russia, one of the leading figures in the Holy Alliance, published an ukase, or imperial decree, in which he claimed as part of the territory of Alaska (which at this date was Russian) a considerable section of the western coast of North America. This claim was quite ineffective, but it alarmed American opinion, and in 1822 the U.S.A. replied by recognising the independence of the new republics of Argentina, Chile, Peru, Colombia and Mexico. In 1823 the intervention of France to put down a liberal revolution in Spain itself caused alarm in America lest the intervention should be extended across the Atlantic. Canning, the British Foreign Secretary, proposed in August, 1823, that the U.S.A. and

Britain should make a joint declaration that they would oppose any attempt by a European power to gain possession of the territory of the former Spanish colonies. Adams, who did not trust Canning, preferred that the U.S.A. should act alone. Hence President Monroe, in his message to Congress in December 1823, made the famous declaration that the American continents were not to be considered as 'future subjects for colonisation by any European powers,' and that any interference with the liberty of the Spanish colonies which had declared themselves independent would be regarded as 'the manifestation of an unfriendly disposition towards the United States.' Just as Europe was for the Europeans, so America was to be for the Americans. This was the Monroe Doctrine. Ever since that time the U.S.A. has adhered strictly to this statement of foreign policy laid down by Adams and stated by Monroe, opposing all European intervention in American affairs. In fact it was not seriously challenged during the 19th century; had it been, the British navy would have enforced it, for the United States was scarcely strong enough to do so. Americans did not even call it by its present name until 1854. Moreover, it must be noted that there is another side to the Monroe Doctrine. It implies, though it does not state, the supremacy of the U.S.A. over the whole American continent. While stopping European interference, the U.S.A. herself very frequently interfered in the affairs of Central and South America, especially in the early years of the 20th century.

3. JOHN QUINCY ADAMS AND THE ERA OF HARD FEELINGS, 1825–9

The lull in party strife which coincided with Monroe's presidency had clearly come to an end by 1824. The Federalists did not put up a candidate in the election of 1824: but the Republican party, which had split into groups, provided four. These were John Quincy Adams of Massachusetts, Andrew Jackson of Tennessee, Henry Clay of Kentucky, and William H. Crawford of Georgia. The election was noisy and bitter, quite different from the previous ones, which had been decorous and almost silent affairs. Jackson got 99 electoral votes, Adams 84, Crawford 41, and Clay 37. As no one had a clear majority, the decision had to be made by the House. Here Clay persuaded his followers to vote for Adams, who was elected. Adams later made Clay his Secretary of State. Jackson's supporters, nicknaming Clay 'The Judas of the West,' regarded the whole thing as a crooked political bargain, and their hostility towards the new President was very bitter. They were wrong; the honesty of Adams is above suspicion. But this was a bad beginning to a most unhappy term, which Adams' opponents devoted to trying to break him and to preparing for the election of 1828. Adams' personal qualities—he was often disagreeable and always awkward in manner, and contemptuous of public opinion—made a bad situation worse. Of the first seven Presidents of the United States five were re-elected at the end of their first term: the two who had only single terms were John Adams and his son, John Quincy Adams.

In foreign affairs, Adams' own special interest, his administration was unfortunate. Canning, until he died in 1827, was an awkward opponent. Poinsett, the American minister to the new republic of Mexico, had to be recalled because he helped to stir up civil war there. In 1826 Adams accepted an invitation to send representatives of the U.S.A. to a conference of American republics at Panama. Jackson's supporters, out to harass Adams on any pretext, opposed this in Congress. Many Americans were anxious that the U.S.A. should not become involved in South America's troubles. Some of the delegates at the conference would be men with negro blood in their veins, and some senators from the slave states said it would be degrading for the representatives of the U.S.A. to sit with them. Britain was also invited, and Canning sent a representative, who improved the occasion by suggesting that the U.S.A. had designs on Cuba and that the other American republics ought not to trust her. A United States delegation was eventually approved, but arrived after the conference was over.

At home Adams' opponents were preparing for the elections of 1828. The western farmers who had backed Jackson in 1824 intended to elect their hero this time. There were professional politicians about, too, men who wanted office and power for themselves and who reckoned they would get it by joining themselves to Jackson: outstanding among these was Martin Van Buren of New York, who became Jackson's chief party organiser. Office mattered more than the kind of laws that were passed. This was well illustrated by the tariff controversy of 1828. The eyes of every congressman were on the forthcoming election. A new tariff was proposed, raising the scale of duties higher than before. The northern states, especially the manufacturing areas of New York and Pennsylvania —which, by reason of their growing population, carried many electoral votes—wanted it: the cotton-growing states of the South did not. Jackson could rely on an overwhelming majority of votes in the West and South: New England would vote for the re-election of Adams, a Massachusetts man. Jackson wanted to secure New York and Pennsylvania, but could not come out strongly for the tariff, for that would have lost him southern votes: while if he opposed it, he would lose those two states and the election. Van Buren, the astute politician, produced the answer. He proposed alterations in the bill which put higher duties on raw materials like hemp and wool, which the northern manufacturers used in their factories, than on foreign manufactured goods. He anticipated that the New Englanders would vote against this and so reject the whole tariff, and that Adams would be blamed for their action. The plot miscarried, for they voted for the tariff and not against, and the bill was passed. The South was furious, and Calhoun gave the new bill the name by which it is known—'The Tariff of Abominations.'

10   Andrew Jackson, 1829-37

The election of 1828 began a new period in American history: it brought
into the White House the first true representative of the people. It replaced
the haughty and cultured John Quincy Adams by Andrew Jackson, a
backwoodsman turned general. Like that of 1824 it was hard-fought, and
so bitter had feeling grown that there was hardly any limit to the abuse
which each side showered on the other's candidate. This time the westerners succeeded, aided by the professional politicians. Jackson was elected
by a triumphant majority, with John C. Calhoun as his Vice-President.

I. THE CAREER AND PERSONALITY OF ANDREW JACKSON

The new President had a background entirely different from those of
his predecessors. He had been born somewhere on the boundary between
the Carolinas in 1767. His father, an immigrant from Northern Ireland,
died the same year. At fourteen Andrew Jackson ran away from home:
after being taken prisoner by British soldiers, he became a saddle-maker's
assistant, and then a school-teacher. In his spare time he studied law, and
at twenty-one he was appointed public prosecutor in the district court of
Nashville, Tennessee. Wit and eloquence were more valuable than much
learning in the rough trials of a frontier court, and he was a success. In
1796 he became a Representative for Tennessee, and in 1797 a Senator. He
was quite out of place in the Senate, and resigned after less than a year.
Early in the 19th century he became prominent in warfare against Creek
Indians. But it was his victory over the British at New Orleans in 1815
that first brought him national fame. When he followed this by his adventures in Florida in 1817–18, he became a presidential possibility.

'Old Hickory', as Jackson was nicknamed, was a remarkable man. Tall
and lean in appearance, he was in many ways a typical frontiersman—
simple and direct in speech, uneducated but shrewd, quick to take insult
and slow to forget. By the time of his election he was a well-to-do landowner and slave-owner in Tennessee. Throughout his terms of office he
showed himself dignified and courteous as well as honest and vigorous.
But he never spared financiers, as they were to find to their cost: in this,
above all, he stood for the democratic and debtor farmers of the West.
Yet he drew support from other parts of the country as well as the West—
from southern planters, from working men in the eastern towns, from
many small business men, even from bankers who disliked the power of
the Bank of the United States. The pattern of American life was beginning
to change: with the construction of roads and of the Erie Canal and the

beginnings of the steamboat, men were moving about more and seeking greater scope for business enterprise. More Americans were becoming interested in politics: the commercial panic of 1819 had brought demands for new laws to safeguard debtors, to improve the tariff, to provide more chance to acquire land. The new western states which had come into the Union gave votes to nearly all men, and some of the older ones widened their franchise. It is not surprising that these changes should be reflected in the election of 1828, and that Americans should turn to vote for a new type of leader, a national hero with simple and outspoken democratic views.

2. THE EVENTS OF HIS PRESIDENCY, 1829–37

His inauguration was surely the most astonishing ever seen in Washington. His speech accepting office was dignified and simple: but it was followed by a reception at the White House to which all his followers, rich and poor, were invited. Many came, and the White House was the scene of a great party. The crowd swarmed all over the place, spread mud over furniture and carpets, smashed glass and china, and drank a considerable quantity of punch: the President had to escape through a window. The respectable inhabitants of Washington were scandalised.

Politics, Jackson believed, should be open to all. In his message to Congress in 1829 he declared that 'The duties of all public offices are, or at least admit of being made, so plain and simple that men of intelligence may readily qualify themselves for their performance.' In practice, he is generally blamed for the introduction into American political life of what is called the 'Spoils System.' One of the charges made against Adams by Jackson's followers had been that of corruption in the civil service. This was untrue: but the civil service was certainly inefficient. The Jacksonians were interested in the chance of getting government posts for themselves. Washington early in 1829 was packed with them, all after jobs in the government service, ranging from cabinet offices to local postmasterships. They had won the election, and they felt entitled to the rewards; as one of them, Marcy of New York, put it, 'To the victor belongs the spoils.' This spoils system, whereby the victorious party in an election obtained for its members not merely the chief posts in the new government but also countless minor ones (which in Britain we regard as permanent civil service posts), already existed in state politics; and Jackson was unwise enough to introduce it into the Federal government. He dismissed many supporters or suspected supporters of Adams, and filled the vacancies with Jacksonians —ardent followers of himself, but often inexperienced, and even corrupt. In number the changes were not vast; only 252 out of 612 civil servants appointed by Adams, and 600 out of 8600 postmasters in the country, were dismissed. But it was a bad example which was followed later. Another much-criticised feature of his method of government was the so-called 'Kitchen Cabinet.' This was composed of various friends of Jackson who were not members of his official cabinet, but with whom Jackson certainly discussed the problems of government, behind the backs of his cabinet ministers. Linking the two cabinets together was Van Buren, Jackson's most intimate adviser, an acute and subtle politician who was to achieve his ambition by succeeding Jackson in the presidency. In fact, most of Jackson's chief advisers were well-to-do, many of them prospering in business.

In his remarkable rise to power Jackson owed much to southern support. But it was a southern state, South Carolina, that caused him the most serious troubles of his terms of office, and her leader was his own Vice-President, Calhoun. During the 1820's South Carolina steadily declined in prosperity. Her cotton lands were becoming exhausted, and the more energetic of her planters left for the richer soils of the Mississippi Basin. In the same period the rest of the country, and notably the northern manufacturing states, grew wealthier. This was partly the result of the tariffs which were imposed during these years. South Carolina developed no large-scale industries, and so the tariff did her harm and not good, making her people pay more for manufactured goods from abroad. As her wealth declined, so feeling grew in the state against the tariff and against the Federal government which imposed the tariff. They were blamed, quite wrongly, for all South Carolina's ills; the North, the manufacturing area, was accused of trying to dominate the South; and behind all this lay the haunting southern fear that the North would try to interfere with the South's 'peculiar institution,' slavery. Men in South Carolina began to claim that the Federal government was overstepping its powers, as laid down in the Constitution, by erecting a tariff which damaged the interests of any state.

Calhoun stated his views and those of his supporters in 1828 in a document known as the South Carolina Exposition. This document gives a clear account of what is known as the 'states' rights' theory of the Constitution. According to this theory the Constitution was simply an agreement between the different states; and each state had the right to decide for itself whether the Federal government was overstepping its powers in any particular matter. If a state did decide that the Federal government was overstepping its powers, then, according to Calhoun, it could 'annul' or 'nullify' the particular law with which it disagreed. This meant that it could say that that particular law was not to apply in its own state territory. And besides this right of 'Nullification,' Calhoun also said that any state had the right to withdraw from the Union, to secede; he claimed for each state the right of 'Secession.' These ideas of Calhoun, shared by many people in the South, threatened the very existence of the Union. In 1861 Civil War was to break out between North and South over the second of them, the question of Secession. In Jackson's day it was the first. the question of Nullification, that caused trouble.

In January 1830 there took place in the Senate the famous Webster-Hayne Debate, in which the whole question of states' rights was thrashed out. The debate began over a proposal that sales of public land in the west should be limited, but it soon passed to wider issues. Senator Robert Y. Hayne of South Carolina delivered a long address stating fully Calhoun's view of the Constitution as an agreement between the states which any state could break. To this Daniel Webster of Massachusetts made a reply that is one of the noblest pieces of American oratory. He maintained that the Union was made by the people, not by the separate states: and that no state had the right to secede. Secession would wreck the Union: the Union destroyed meant 'a land rent with civil feuds, or drenched it may be in fraternal blood.' His final words give the key to his speech—'Liberty *and* Union, now and forever, one and inseparable.' It was hoped by Calhoun and his supporters that at a banquet given to celebrate the anniversary of Jefferson's birthday Jackson would come out with a speech in favour of the states' rights theory. He did nothing of the kind. Instead, when it came to his turn to propose a toast, he rose, looked full at Calhoun, and proposed 'Our Federal Union—it must be preserved.' This marked a clear breach between President and Vice-President. Later Jackson found out that in 1818, when his own behaviour in Florida had been under discussion by the cabinet (see Chap. 9), Calhoun, then Secretary for War, had wanted to have him court-martialled. Bitter letters passed between the two; Jackson never forgave what he regarded as personal insults.

In 1832 the quarrel between Jackson and South Carolina came to a head. In that year Henry Clay introduced a new tariff bill into Congress. It got rid of some of the worst features of the Tariff of Abominations, but left high duties on imported manufactured articles. South Carolina took it as a challenge. A special convention was elected in the state, and this passed what was called an 'Ordinance of Nullification.' This said that the new tariff was not to be law, and the duties it imposed were not to be collected, in South Carolina; and it added that, if the Federal government were to attempt to collect them there, the state would leave the Union. This was defiance of the law. Jackson replied with a vigorous proclamation condemning the whole idea of nullification and warning the people of South Carolina of the dangers of such action. He was determined to send troops into the state. In return the people of South Carolina prepared to resist. Civil war seemed to be near. In reality no one wanted to press matters so far. Jackson did not want to use force, for once war had started there was no telling where it would stop; while the wiser heads in South Carolina were doubtful, for no other state in the South was anxious to support her. And Clay proposed that the tariff should be altered. It was, by the new tariff act of 1833, which provided for the gradual reduction of all rates of duties: South Carolina accepted this and repealed the Ordinance of Nullification, and all was well. Or, rather, it seemed to be. In fact this solution, like the Missouri Compromise of 1820, was only a temporary cure. Jackson believed that the tariff was only an excuse for nullification; that the real object of Calhoun and his followers was secession; and that the 'next pretext will be the negro, or slavery, question.' How right he was the coming of the Civil War was to show.

Next we come to one of the strangest episodes in Jackson's strange career, a good example of the way in which he let personal prejudice govern his public actions. In his early days Jackson had been the innocent victim of someone else's financial failure, and had been left heavily in debt to a bank. Ever since then he had disliked banks and the financial system of which they were the centre. History gave him an excellent chance of revenge. In 1816 the second Bank of the United States had been chartered for twenty years (see Chap. 9); so the government would have to decide before 1836 whether or not to renew that charter. His attitude towards banks was well known, and he had indicated his dislike of the Bank of the United States by saying, in his first message to Congress (1829), that he thought its charter was neither legal nor wise. In this attitude he was strongly supported by his western followers, impecunious farmers, who believed that the power of rich financiers was the greatest enemy of democracy—and encouraged by his own businessmen friends, who disliked the Bank's power.

His opponents decided to make the Bank the issue of the 1832 election; Nicholas Biddle, the President of the Bank, was an important member of the National Republican (or, as it was soon called, the Whig) party which opposed Jackson. This party nominated for President Henry Clay of Kentucky, and also brought before Congress a bill to recharter the Bank, which was passed in July 1832. Jackson promptly vetoed it, saying that the Bank was a monopoly and that its profits came out of the earnings of American citizens and went into the pockets of a few rich men. Jackson's supporters and the common people all over America liked this kind of straight talk, and Jackson, once more Democratic candidate, won the election easily. Having won this victory, he decided to kill off the Bank. He did this by using up all government funds in it. The Senate passed a vote of censure on him, but that did not worry Jackson. It is very doubtful whether his action was wise. The Bank no doubt brought far too much wealth into the hands of far too few people, and it encouraged political corruption; but these were arguments for reforming, not for destroying it. It helped the development of American industry, and its government backing made it safe. The smaller local banks, which had to do its work when it was gone, were thoroughly unsafe, and encouraged fantastic speculation; and the value of the notes they issued was quite uncertain. The government, which had to sell and be paid for public land, suffered from this, and in 1836 Jackson issued a Specie Circular, ordering that all payments for public land should be made in specie, that is, gold or silver. This tended to put up the price of land without doing much to stop speculation. This speculation, together with the absence of a strong

Andrew Jackson, hero of the battle of New Orleans, and President, 1829-37

John C. Calhoun (1782-1850), champion of the South

central bank, contributed to the disastrous panic of 1837 (see Chap. 11).

The election of 1832 is important for two other reasons besides the trouble over the Bank. Each political party chose its candidate by a national convention, a grand meeting of the local leaders of the party from all over the U.S.A., which decides which claimant for the presidential candidature is the most suitable: this is now the normal method. And at this election there was a third party, the Anti-Masons. At intervals throughout American history special political parties have arisen whose object has been to support some single idea, or to oppose some single institution. They have usually won some temporary support, but have never lasted very long. This one in 1832 did not like Masons. It came into being after the disappearance of a New York bricklayer named Morgan, who had revealed Masonic secrets. It put forward candidates at this election, who only succeeded in drawing numerous votes in New York and other northern states away from Clay. After this it fizzled out.

The typical westerner liked Indians as little as he liked the Bank of the United States. Jackson shifted as many Indian tribes as possible to the other side of the Mississippi. In the eight years of his presidency no less than ninety-four Indian treaties were made; through these many thousands of Indians lost their tribal lands and were either pushed or driven to the west. Most of them accepted calmly a process which they were unable to resist; some objected, and suffered in consequence. The Cherokee of Georgia were treated in a peculiarly scandalous manner. They were a civilised and well-behaved folk whose land had been guaranteed to them by a solemn treaty, made with the Federal government. Georgia wanted their land, more especially when gold was found on it, and tried to grab it. John Q. Adams, when President, sent Federal troops to protect the Cherokee, but Jackson withdrew them. The question came before the Supreme Court in the case of *Worcester* v. *Georgia*, and John Marshall gave a decision saying that Georgia had no right to interfere with the Indian territory. To this Jackson said 'John Marshall has made his decision; now let him enforce it.' Then part of the tribe was bribed to give up the lands of all the Cherokee in return for land across the Mississippi. The others objected, but were pushed out by 1838.

In foreign affairs Jackson was more successful than Adams, although he alarmed the country by nearly going to war with France. The U.S.A. had some old claims against that country for loss caused by Napoleon's blockade, and in 1831 the French agreed to settle them. The French assembly was slow in voting the money, and Jackson proceeded to order the Navy to prepare for war and advised Congress to seize the goods of French residents in the U.S.A. The French assembly retaliated by voting the money on condition Jackson apologised. He refused to do so, and so nothing was done about the debts until 1835. Then he said that he had had no intention of insulting France, though he still refused to apologise. Britain intervened to reconcile the U.S.A. and France, and the debt was paid. With Britain he kept on good terms, steering a clear course through the awkward boundary problem.

In 1837 Jackson retired to his home in Tennessee. The election of 1836 had decided that his successor was to be Martin Van Buren, the 'Little Magician' whose advice had been so valuable to him. He had proved a popular and on the whole a successful President; he had certainly been a democratic one. His natural good sense and his sincere devotion to freedom contributed to his success. 'Old Hickory' justified his western supporters without being the national disaster which his opponents had anticipated.

11   Manifest Destiny

1. THE WESTWARD MOVEMENT, 1829–61

Jackson was a westerner, and did all he could to encourage settlement in the West. The purpose of his large-scale removals of Indians from their tribal lands was to clear the way for new settlers. Thus the great migration to the West went on. In 1836 Arkansas was admitted to the Union as a state: by the end of 1861 ten more states had been admitted, all of them, except Florida, in the West. Some, like Arkansas itself, were admitted by the normal process, with Territorial government as a half-way stage; Texas and California, as we shall see later in this chapter, arrived in a different manner. The admission of each new state marked another step in the American people's conquest of their continent, and in some of them the population increased with astonishing rapidity on account of the ceaseless flow of settlers from the east. Between 1830 and 1860 the population of Michigan increased from 31,000 to nearly 750,000. Between 1840 and 1860 that of Wisconsin increased from 30,000 to 775,000. The frontier was pushed out beyond the Great Lakes and the source of the Mississippi, to include Minnesota and Iowa, as well as Michigan and Wisconsin; to the south it took in Texas. More remarkable, the Americans also penetrated to the Far West; California was admitted as a state in 1850, Oregon in 1859.

Beyond the Mississippi the land sloped gently to the Great Plains. American pioneers, used to the wooded lands of Kentucky, Tennessee, and Ohio, looked on this great grassland as a barrier. Explorers, like Lewis and Clark, had revealed all the difficulties which were obstacles to its settlement—the absence of timber: the sparse vegetation and the shortage of water in the western Great Plains: the alkali deposits of the same region: the extremes of climate, from fierce sunshine in summer to freezing cold in winter. And beyond the Plains lay the formidable obstacle of the Rockies. It is not surprising that the Plains were called 'The Great American Desert.' The pioneers, for a time, left them to the Indians, Sioux,

Shawnee, Crow and other tribes, huntsmen who shot down with bow and arrow the buffaloes which provided their food and clothing.

The pioneers themselves struck across the Plains, to south-west or north-west. To the south-west American settlers had already moved into Texas in the 1820's, and this advance went on in the thirties. It led, as we shall see, to conflict with Mexico. In the same direction the trade of the Santa Fé Trail increased. But the north-western route across the Plains was far more famous. This was the Oregon Trail, from Independence up the courses of the Missouri and Platte to the foothills of the Rocky Mountains, through the South Pass, across the dry Wyoming Basin, and then down the westward-flowing Snake and Columbia rivers to the Willamette Valley. In 1834 missionaries established themselves in the valley of this river Willamette, a tributary of the Columbia. Two years later Captain Bonneville led the first caravan of loaded wagons through the South Pass. The author, Washington Irving, gave Bonneville's adventures publicity in his *Adventures of Captain Bonneville*, and Americans grew interested in western Oregon. It was a most attractive land, wooded, well pastured, and possessing a temperate climate. So in 1842 there began the Oregon Trail. Many covered wagons, carrying pioneers, their families, goods, and supplies, set out on the 2000-mile journey from Independence to the Willamette. By 1843 there were about 1000 American settlers in Oregon, and many more followed them within the next two years. This north-western advance, as we shall see, brought the U.S.A. into contact with Britain.

In the 1840's, too, the most remarkable group migration in American history took place. This was the trek of the Mormons to the basin of the Great Salt Lake. In 1823 Joseph Smith, a seventeen-year-old farmhand in New York state, announced that he had been visited by an angel. The angel, he said, left him instructions to find certain buried plates with strange writings on them, together with magic stones which would enable him to read the writings. He found the plates (no one else ever saw them) and translated the strange writings, producing the *Book of Mormon* (first printed in 1830). This is an astonishing account of the early history of America and of certain lost tribes of Israel (the Red Indians), containing much inaccuracy and many quotations from the Authorised Version of the Bible. It brought Joseph Smith followers, and in the same year, 1830, he founded the Mormon Church, or, to give it its full title, 'The Church of Jesus Christ of the Latter-day Saints,' whose bible is the *Book of Mormon*. Its first home was in Ohio. The Mormons formed a self-contained and narrow community, industrious and financially astute. They moved from Ohio, first to Missouri, where they met with a good deal of hostility, and then to Nauvoo in Illinois, where they got a charter making their community practically independent. In Nauvoo in 1843, Joseph Smith had another revelation, permitting polygamy. This split the church and caused a local civil war in Illinois, in the course of which Smith was lynched

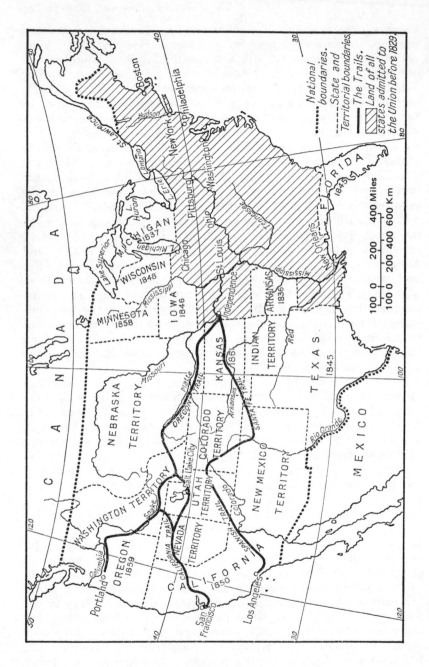

The Westward Expansion of the U.S.A., 1829–61

by a mob. A truly remarkable man, Brigham Young, followed him as leader of the Mormons. He was a born organiser, shrewd and unscrupulous, and a determined man of action. He realised that if the Mormons were to survive they must leave Illinois, where opposition was growing fast; and he determined to lead them into the West. In 1846 he led them out on the long trek to their promised land, just as Moses had led the Israelites long before. This promised land, unlike Canaan, was not flowing with milk and honey. It was the basin of the Great Salt Lake, high up in the Rockies, remote and barren. The Mormons had won many converts, notably in the Northern states and in the English industrial areas, and 12,000 people set out on the long and dangerous journey. The winter was harsh, and many died on the way. But by the end of 1848 there were 5000 settlers in the basin of the Great Salt Lake. In 1850 the area settled by the Mormons was organised as the Territory of Utah. For practical purposes it was independent, with Brigham Young as its ruler. President Fillmore appointed him its Territorial governor. He controlled every branch of life in Utah—religious, economic, political. Federal judges were driven out of Utah if they would not obey his wish. This dictator, who had twenty-three wives, organised the whole development of Utah, which grew in wealth and numbers, though not in liberty or culture.

Three years after the Mormons set out on their trek, a westward movement of a very different kind, inspired by utterly different motives, took place. This was the California Gold Rush. In 1848 gold was found in a mill-race in Sutter's Creek in the Sacramento Valley in California. The find was a good one, and by 1849 thousands of men, of all races, classes, tongues, and jobs, from every part of the U.S.A., were on their way to the valley, in a mad rush for quick wealth. They went by three main routes. The safest and slowest was by sea round Cape Horn; the quickest, and, by reason of the tropical fevers, the most deadly, was across the isthmus of Panama; the third was the vast distance overland across the Plains and over the Rockies. For most the rush was stark idiocy; fortunes were rare, and most men died on the way, or came home worn out and disillusioned. The rush destroyed the old Spanish civilisation in north California. The great haciendas broke up with the coming of the new mining camps with their ugly names, like Red Dog, Grub Gulch, and Poker Flat. The population of California shot up enormously, while San Francisco grew in a few months from a village into a fair-sized town. The miner—the 'forty-niner'—became a national figure.

No one knows how many perished on their way to the Far West. A large number of those who set out never reached their goal, whether it was the lovely valley of the Willamette, the sombre basin of the Great Salt Lake, or the diggings of California. The redskins killed many; many others, lost in the trackless wastes or the barren uplands of the eastern Rockies, died from hunger or thirst. But the risks did not check the pioneers, and an ever greater number of settlers moved into the Far West. By 1860 Utah contained 40,000 people, Oregon over 50,000, and California nearly 380,000. The principal westward advance of the 1850's, however, took place in the area between Missouri and the Canadian border. It was much stimulated by two new forces of this period—the rapid increase in immigration, and the coming of the railroad.

Between 1840 and 1860, 4,300,000 immigrants entered the U.S.A. Nearly 1,700,000 of them were Irish, and most of these went to New York and other eastern cities. Their willingness to accept lower wages than native-born Americans helped to encourage some of the latter to move out westwards. Another 1,3000,000 of the immigrants were Germans, many of them refugees after the failure of the German revolutionary movement of 1848. Most of these went out to the new western lands, and especially to those of Wisconsin, Iowa, and Missouri. They were hard-working and enterprising farmers who did much to open up the American prairies. These new settlers were quick to develop what was potentially one of the world's greatest cornlands. In this they were assisted by the second new force of the period—the railroad. The first American railroad, the Baltimore and Ohio, was begun in 1828, three years after the opening of the Stockton to Darlington Railway in England. Railroads developed comparatively slowly in the U.S.A. By 1850 there were only 9000 miles of them, but by 1860 there were 30,000; and lines ran into Wisconsin, Iowa, Missouri, Arkansas, and Louisiana. Chicago, which in 1830 had been a small settlement, was a city with many thousands of inhabitants by 1860, and already a great railroad centre, as well as the port through which the farmers of the thriving state of Illinois sent their produce on to the Great Lakes. By 1860 the railroads had begun to play an important part in opening up the prairies. They enabled the prairie farmer to send his corn and wheat to the cities of the east. They carried to him the manufactured goods of the east. They carried many thousands of immigrants on the first stage of their journey westwards. The railroads did all these things on a far greater scale after 1860; but already by that date they were helping to quicken the pace of the great movement to the West.

2. VAN BUREN, HARRISON, AND TYLER, 1837–45

Martin Van Buren, who succeeded Jackson as President in 1837, was unlucky. His term of office coincided with the worst commercial depression the U.S.A. had experienced up to that time. We have already noticed the speculation in land which went on during the 1830's. Such speculation encouraged unsound finance of every kind, particularly unsound banking, and created a thoroughly false appearance of great prosperity. In 1836 commercial depression began to strike England; banks failed, factories and mills closed down. England could no longer buy the cotton she had previously bought, and depression struck the cotton-planters in the South. Then American industry suffered; and banks failed and factories and mills closed down in the U.S.A. Farmers were hit because townsfolk could not buy when they were out of work. Merchants who had allowed the farmers to run up debts and banks who had lent them money were ruined. Many thousands were thrown out of work. All this happened within a few months of Van Buren's inauguration. The government did nothing to help, for such a gigantic and nation-wide depression had never been foreseen.

The direct political result was the defeat of Van Buren in the election of 1840. The government, which had very little more to do with causing the depression than the man in the moon, was blamed for it all, just as Herbert Hoover's government was blamed for the even more severe depression of the 1930's. The Whigs grew steadily stronger. The tactics they adopted in 1840 led to the most fantastic election in American history. Their candidate, as in 1836, was William Henry Harrison of Ohio, the victor of Tippecanoe. In order to win southern support, they chose as vice-presidential candidate John Tyler of Virginia. They offered no positive policy, but gave their energies to running down Van Buren, charging him with living in luxury while thousands of Americans were out of work. A Democratic newspaper unfortunately sneered at Harrison, saying 'Give him a barrel of hard cider and $2000 a year and he will sit the remainder of his days in a log cabin.' The Whigs seized upon a golden opportunity of drawing an excellent contrast between the champagne-drinking Van Buren and 'the gallant old soldier of Tippecanoe,' as one of their songs called Harrison. They ran their election campaign on log cabins and hard cider. They carried log cabins through the country on wagons, and provided barrels of hard cider for their audiences; what they said in their speeches mattered little, as long as they poked fun at Van Buren and made the crowds sing about log cabins. It was quite useless for the Democrats to point out that Van Buren did not spend all his time in eating and drinking, and that he did not scent his whiskers with eau-de-Cologne: that Harrison did not live in a log cabin or anything like one: that Tyler was a rich slave-owner: that the Whigs had no policy whatsoever. Reasonable arguments were drowned in a shout of 'Tippecanoe and Tyler Too.' Harrison won easily. He lived long enough to compose an inaugural address full of references to Roman history (Daniel Webster revised it for him, and after the revision reported that he had 'killed seventeen Roman proconsuls as dead as smelts'), and to deliver it. Then he died, one month after taking office, and Tyler succeeded him.

Harrison's death was unfortunate for the Whig party leaders like Clay and Webster, who had hoped to control him at their will. Tyler was a southerner, at heart more a Democrat than a Whig, and his term of office was one long fight between him and the party which had put him into the White House. After a few months all his cabinet ministers, except Webster, resigned, and Tyler replaced them by Democrats. Webster, after signing the Webster-Ashburton Treaty (see below, Section 3), went out in 1843, while Calhoun, the southern champion, joined the cabinet in 1844. Tyler used to good effect the President's power of vetoing laws. He vetoed a bill which proposed a new United States Bank, and vetoed it again when it was sent up to him in a revised form. The Whigs had intended to use the Federal government to carry out a programme of 'internal improvements' —the building of canals, railways, and highroads. Tyler believed that such activities were the business of the states, and vetoed the programme.

3. FOREIGN AFFAIRS, 1837–61

a. Great Britain and the Canadian Boundary. As we have seen, something had been done in the years immediately after 1814 to try to settle the disputed American-Canadian boundary. But the boundary commissions which the two governments had set up had been unable to agree about the exact position of the extreme eastern and extreme western sections of the line. This uncertainty was a continual source of friction: settlers of various kinds—trappers, farmers, fishermen, bandits, desperadoes—from each country were continually crossing into land which the other country claimed as its own, and local disputes and clashes were frequent. It was clearly a very hard task indeed to fix a definite boundary. The natural difficulties in some parts, for example in the Rockies, were vast; while the number of inhabitants, especially in the West, was very small, and many of these had no fixed abode. To make a bad situation worse, the men who made the Treaty of 1783, at the end of the War of Independence, from which any discussion of the boundary had to start, were exceedingly ignorant of American geography, misplacing mountains and assuming that rivers flowed in directions contrary to their actual courses. As a result, both countries made extensive and often wild claims to territory, and until the boundary was settled there would always be danger of war over some few square miles of wilderness.

In 1837 this danger came much nearer for causes unconnected with the charting of frontiers. In that year two rebellions broke out in Canada. Many Americans, who hoped that Canada would break away from Britain just as the thirteen colonies had done, sympathised strongly with the rebels, and gave them more or less open assistance, of guns, ammunition, money, and men, from those American states, Vermont and New York, that were nearest the centres of rebellion. One of the vessels that ran supplies across was the small steamer *Caroline*. One night in December 1837 a number of Canadians rowed, at great risk, across the Niagara River above the Falls, cut the *Caroline* loose from her moorings and set fire to her. The U.S.A. protested against this, and the two countries haggled about it for over two years. Then, in 1840, a Canadian named McLeod boasted in a New York bar that he had killed an American in the attack upon the *Caroline*; and he was arrested for it. Palmerston, British Foreign Secretary, had never admitted that the attack upon the ship had been at the orders of the Canadian government; now he turned completely round, claimed that it had been an official attack upon American pirates, and demanded that

McLeod should be set free at once. Van Buren and Tyler, both of whom wanted to keep the peace, found themselves facing a difficult situation.

This was all the worse because at this very time a long-standing dispute about the north-eastern section of the boundary between the U.S.A. and Canada grew more bitter. This Maine Boundary problem had persisted for some sixty years. Most of the north-east frontier country was a wilderness; in the Treaty of 1783 it had been agreed that the boundary should follow 'the Highlands which divide those rivers which empty themselves into the St. Lawrence from those which fall into the Atlantic,' but each country had produced a different meaning for this expression. In 1831 the King of Holland had been asked to arbitrate, but he had been unable to find the highlands, and had produced a solution which the U.S.A. had refused. In 1838 British settlers had seized a Maine official, and the local governors on each side of the (uncertain) boundary line had called out the militia. This so-called 'Aroostook War' had gone no further, but it was obvious that a second incident might not end without serious trouble. A change of government in Britain brought relief. Aberdeen replaced Palmerston as Foreign Secretary, and in 1842 he sent Lord Ashburton to Washington to settle the Maine dispute. He and Daniel Webster negotiated the Webster-Ashburton Treaty of 1842, which produced the present boundary. There was some difficulty in getting Senate and Parliament to ratify this Maine Treaty, and it was pushed through by what Webster called 'the battle of the maps'; each government discovered an early map which gave the other far more than the actual agreement had done. The McLeod affair, meanwhile, died a natural death.

Aberdeen was responsible for settling with the U.S.A. another and even more serious boundary dispute, by the Oregon Treaty of 1846. What was at this time known as Oregon included not only the present state of Oregon, but also those of Idaho and Washington and the present territory of British Columbia. Its ownership had long been disputed, and both countries claimed the whole of it. On three occasions John Quincy Adams had offered to divide it at 49° N., but Britain had refused, preferring the line of the Columbia River as the boundary. In 1818 a joint occupation was created until an agreement should be reached. In 1824 the Hudson's Bay Company built Fort Vancouver, as the centre of its trade in furs and fish, on the north bank of the Columbia. After the opening of the Oregon Trail in 1842 Americans settled in large numbers—6000 by 1845—in the Willamette Valley, south of the Columbia. Westerners began to clamour for American seizure of the entire Oregon territory, up to 54° 40' N., the border of Alaska. Calhoun in 1844 proposed Adams' old solution of the 49° N. line, but the British again refused. Next year James Knox Polk became President, and in his inaugural address he said 'Our title to the country of the Oregon is clear and unquestionable.' There arose in the U.S.A. the cry of 'Fifty-Four Forty or Fight.' But in reality neither government wanted to fight. Polk was plunging into war with Mexico (see below) and had no wish for a quarrel with Britain too; while the British attitude changed sharply when, in 1845, the Hudson's Bay Company, alarmed by the aggressive attitude of many American settlers south of the Columbia, moved its headquarters from the north bank of the river to Fort Victoria on Vancouver Island. This enabled Aberdeen, the British Foreign Secretary, in 1846 to propose the 49th parallel as the mainland boundary, provided that Vancouver Island was included in Canada. Polk accepted, and a treaty was signed on those lines.

In Central America too the U.S.A. met Great Britain. The U.S.A. was already interested in the idea of a canal across Central America. Polk obtained from Colombia a right of transit across the Panama Isthmus, and in 1850–5 a Panama railway was built with American money. Another possible canal route lay across Nicaragua. Here Britain had interests, for she owned part of Honduras and claimed a protectorate over the Mosquito Indians on the coast of Nicaragua. Possible dispute about the proposed canal was avoided by the Clayton-Bulwer Treaty (1850). By this each government agreed never to fortify or to obtain exclusive control over the canal, and to guarantee its neutrality. One clause in the Treaty was not clear, and further friction arose in the fifties. The activities of William Walker, an American filibuster who made himself President of Nicaragua in 1855 and wanted to add it to the Union as a new slave state, made the situation no easier. Finally, Britain withdrew by giving the Mosquito Coast to Nicaragua in 1860. Nicaragua had not heard the last of American diplomacy.

b. The War with Mexico. In 1823 the Mexican government, newly recognised by the U.S.A., gave to Stephen F. Austin, an American citizen, the right to settle two hundred families in Texas. Similar rights were given to others, and the Americans took advantage of them, and by the late 1830's there were probably five times as many Americans as Mexicans in Texas. That area was in many ways independent of Mexico, and naturally felt a stronger tie with the U.S.A. than with Mexico. The fact that by the Florida Treaty of 1819 the U.S.A. had renounced all claim to Texas made no difference. When in 1834 Antonio Lopez de Santa Anna became the leading figure in the turmoil of Mexican politics he determined to strengthen Mexican control over Texas; the Texans replied to his policy by declaring themselves independent. Santa Anna invaded Texas and massacred a number of settlers in the mission house of the Alamo in San Antonio. But in the same year (1836) Texan forces under Sam Houston defeated and captured Santa Anna at San Jacinto, and forced him to acknowledge Texan independence. In 1837 Andrew Jackson officially recognised the Lone Star Republic, as Texas was called from its flag. During the following years the Texans wanted admission to the Union, and they were supported in this by the slave states of the South. The election of 1844 was fought over this issue and over Oregon. James Knox Polk of Tennessee, the Democratic candidate, stood for the annexation of Texas, and he was successful,

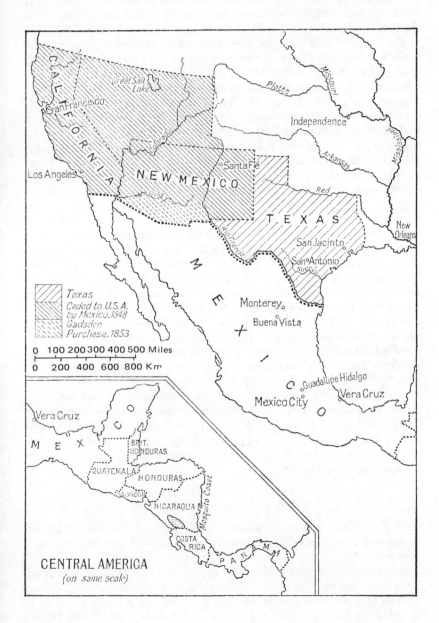

The Mexican War, 1846-48

defeating Henry Clay; and Tyler, right at the end of his term of office, annexed Texas. From the time of Polk's inauguration in March 1845 events moved steadily towards war between the U.S.A. and Mexico, and the war actually came in 1846.

The causes of this Mexican War were numerous. One of them was the desire to settle the Texan problem once and for all. This feeling was strong in the South, where it was hoped that Texas might be carved up into several new slave states, thus maintaining slavery and helping the South to keep its power in the Union. Yet Texas, it must be noted, was a state of the Union before the war began; Mexico had no real hope of getting it back, and this question might well have been settled by cash. The real causes of the war lay elsewhere. Chief among them was the desire of the U.S.A. to annex California. In this she was prompted by a fear of Great Britain, who was at this time extending her power in the Pacific. This desire was backed by the spread throughout the Union of an aggressive national feeling. Men began to talk of the 'Manifest Destiny' of the United States. The rapid expansion of the U.S.A. both in wealth and population encouraged the growth of the idea that her people were in some special way destined to bring civilisation to the so-called 'lesser' peoples of the American continent. Many Americans wanted to take over Mexico itself, as well as California and Texas; the same people who had clamoured for 'Tippecanoe and Tyler Too' in 1840 were now ready to shout 'Annex Texas' and 'Fifty-Four Forty or Fight.' Moreover, Polk, a dark horse as a presidential candidate, showed himself to be a man with a determined and vigorous foreign policy. Strongwilled and a very hard worker, he knew what he wanted and how to get it. California was the object of his ambition. Finally, the weakness and incompetence of Mexico encouraged both Polk's policy and the growth of 'Manifest Destiny.' Mexican methods of government were casual and erratic, and the land suffered from frequent revolutions. On the other hand, there was much opposition to the war in many parts of the U.S.A., notably in New England, where anti-slavery feeling was strong at this time. Many people regarded the war simply as a means of adding new slave territory to the U.S.A. As J. R. Lowell, the American writer put it—

> They just want this Californy
> So's to lug new slave-states in.

Others saw it as a war of aggression, in which a great state was taking advantage of a neighbour's weakness to grab some of her most valuable territory.

Polk's actions between his election and the outbreak of war were designed to create a situation in which he could declare war on Mexico with an appearance of justice. He sent an army under Zachary Taylor to the southern border of Texas, the Nueces River, to 'protect' the Texans against the Mexicans; and, after encouraging revolt in California, he sent an American naval squadron to its coast. To Mexico itself he sent an envoy, John Slidell, to discuss the Texan question and the heavy Mexican debts to American citizens. The Mexican government refused to receive Slidell. Polk then ordered Taylor's army to cross the Nueces and march to the Rio Grande; when the Mexicans attacked this force, Polk announced to Congress that Mexico had invaded the U.S.A. Congress thereupon voted $10,000,000 for war expenses, and authorised Polk to call for volunteers.

The war was brief. There were three regions of American attack— California, New Mexico, and Mexico itself. The main object of war, California, saw minor conflicts. An exploring expedition of Americans under John C. Frémont pushed into California and encouraged the inhabitants to rebel against the Mexicans and declare themselves a republic. Then Commodore Sloat of the United States Navy proclaimed California a part of the U.S.A., whereupon the Californians rebelled against the U.S.A. They were quelled and by 1847 the land was safely annexed. A handful of American troops took Santa Fé and New Mexico.

In Mexico itself American troops had to fight the country and the climate as well as the Mexicans, who resisted bravely but inefficiently. The U.S.A. found two successful generals—and future presidential candidates—in Zachary Taylor and Winfield Scott, while many of those who were later prominent in the Civil War fought in the Mexican campaign. Among these were Robert E. Lee, Ulysses S. Grant, and Jefferson Davis. There were two main lines of American advance into Mexico. Taylor crossed the Rio Grande and defeated the Mexicans first at Monterey and then, fighting against numerically superior forces under Santa Anna, at Buena Vista. Farther south Winfield Scott attacked and took Vera Cruz, the main seaport of Mexico, in March, 1847. He then advanced, through the heat of the summer, up the 7500 feet to Mexico City, which fell in September. The conquest of the capital meant the end of the war. Peace was made in 1848 at Guadalupe Hidalgo. The treaty gave the U.S.A. California and New Mexico (which included Arizona), and recognised the American annexation of Texas; in return the U.S.A. paid Mexico $15,000,000, and took over claims of American subjects against Mexico amounting to another $3,000,000. There was an appendix to this treaty in the Gadsden Purchase of 1853, when the U.S.A. paid $10,000,000 more to Mexico for some 45,000 square miles to the south of the Gila River; this addition completed the mainland territory of the United States.

The results of the Mexican War were considerable in American history. On the credit side it put the U.S.A. in possession of California just in time for the discovery of gold there in 1848. The debits were more important still. The war was an indication to the other republics of America what the Monroe Doctrine might mean to them. Mexico was the first victim, and henceforward the countries of Central and South America were apprehensive of the U.S.A. Secondly, the annexation of new lands aroused once more the bitter dispute over slavery, which had not been a major issue since the Missouri Compromise. In 1846 a Congressman named Wilmot introduced a resolution that there should be no slavery in any territory taken from Mexico. This Wilmot Proviso unleashed forces of sectional rivalry between North and South which grew in strength and hatred until they brought civil war in 1861.

c. Other Problems—Japan and Cuba. Both the boundary disputes with Britain and the war with Mexico were signs of the growing vigour of the U.S.A. in the middle of the 19th century. There were others. One of these, the Treaty of Kanagawa (1854), was very significant for the future. Japan had for centuries closed her ports to foreigners. It was the U.S.A., prompted by the desire for trade, which brought her isolation to an end. In 1853 an American naval squadron under Commodore Matthew Perry anchored in Yedo Bay, about thirty miles from the capital of Japan. He was forbidden to land, but the strength of his force so impressed the Mikado and his advisers that they were ready, when Perry came again in 1854, to sign the Treaty of Kanagawa. This gave the U.S.A. permission to establish a consulate, and allowed American vessels to trade with some Japanese ports. No one foresaw the consequences for the world, and particularly for the United States, of Japan's emergence from isolation.

The same year 1854 also saw one of the more unhappy episodes in American foreign policy. In 1848 President Polk had offered $100,000,000 for Cuba. The largest island of the West Indies, strategically important to the U.S.A., it had sugar plantations and a big Negro population; and Spanish rule was harsh and inefficient. The Madrid government rejected Polk's offer with contempt. But many Americans enjoyed adventure and profit in filibustering expeditions to Cuba, and there were disputes with the Spanish authorities, who started to interfere with honest American traders as well as with dishonest ones. Pierre Soulé, American minister to Spain between 1853 and 1855, was anxious to obtain Cuba for the U.S.A., and in 1854 he and the American ministers to France and Britain met at Ostend. There they issued a manifesto which stated that 'in the progress of human events the time has arrived when the vital interests of Spain are as seriously involved in the sale as those of the U.S.A. in the purchase of Cuba'; it added that if Spain did not sell Cuba to the U.S.A., the U.S.A. would be justified in taking it by force. Nobody took any notice of this document whose only effect was to make the U.S.A. look rather ridiculous. The ministers were reprimanded. Cuba remained a Spanish possession; as we shall see, it became in the 1890's the occasion of a war between Spain and the U.S.A.

12   The Sections and Slavery

After the end of the Mexican War one issue overshadowed everything else in American history. This issue was the growth of sectional rivalry between North and South, leading to the Civil War of 1861–5, the central crisis of the history of the United States. Before we look at the details of this story, let us correct one mistaken idea. Many people still think that the Civil War was begun in order to get rid of slavery; that the North was deliberately trying to free the millions of black slaves owned by the South, and that the latter was trying to stop them doing it; that this 'explains' the outbreak of the Civil War. This view is false. The truth is more complicated. The Civil War was a conflict between two parts of the U.S.A. in which very different ways of living had developed; most northerners followed one set of ideals, most southerners another, and the two sets were contrary to each other. The fact that the South had slaves and the North was free was only one example of the different ways of living. But it was much the most important example, and it was the one which led to the final dispute out of which the war came. Slavery was the central difference: without slavery there would, for example, have been no such bitter quarrelling over the development of western lands, as we shall see. The purpose of this chapter is, first, to describe the different ways of life in North and South and to show the contrasts between them; and then to explain the importance of slavery in the sectional rivalry.

1. THE NORTH

The area generally known as the North included in 1850 New England (the states of Maine, New Hampshire, Vermont, Massachusetts, Connecticut, Rhode Island), New York and New Jersey, Pennsylvania, Ohio, Indiana, and Illinois, Michigan, Iowa and Wisconsin. Its population then was over 13,000,000, and it was growing fast, largely by immigration. The period from 1840 to 1850 saw the first great leap in the number of immigrants from Europe. 1,700,000 people entered the U.S.A. in that time, and most of them went to the North. Many of them were swallowed up in the steadily-growing industry of the U.S.A. Although the northwestern states, like Iowa and Illinois, were almost wholly agricultural in 1850, and all the others were considerably so, the North was the industrial area of the U.S.A. By 1850 industry was firmly planted there, especially in Pennsylvania, New York and Massachusetts. The new industrial town, with its factory or mills, its crowded and ever-growing population, was part of the northern landscape. By 1840 there were 1200 cotton factories in the U.S.A., the overwhelming majority of them in the North.

The Industrial Revolution, the coming of machinery, brought with it to the U.S.A. much the same evils as it brought to Britain—overcrowding, overlong hours, child labour, and a fearful contrast between the few rich and the many poor. Southerners were quick to point out that the northern critics of slavery, in their enthusiasm for freeing other people's black slaves, quite often forgot all about their own overworked and ill-paid white employees in the factories. There were exceptions—for example, the factories of Waltham and Lowell, which were modelled on Robert Owen's New Lanark Mills in Britain. Moreover, there were at this time fewer slums in the U.S.A. than in Britain, and there was not the vast amount of dirt and smoke, for, until the sixties, most American textile mills were driven by waterpower. But the contrast between rich and poor was already great. By 1852 there were twenty-one millionaires ($) in New York City. In 1848 there had died John Jacob Astor, who left about twenty million dollars to found the Astor fortunes, money made partly by real estate speculation in New York at the expense of its citizens.

Wealth carried with it political power, and the Whig party—which, like the old Federalist party, drew most, though by no means all, of its support from the North—was largely controlled by rich men. But neither this nor the gulf between rich and poor affected the fact that the North was democratic in its ideals and in many of its ways of life. The northern workman regarded himself as a free individual, equal in political power to every other man. Although he was himself exploited by the rich factory-owner, he looked upon slavery as unjust, and thought of the whole southern way of life,—dominated by the ideas of the planter aristocracy, as a danger. This did not mean that he was ready to join in a crusade against slavery; until 1861 and for some time after it most northerners were ready to let the South keep its slaves. But it did mean that when sectional feeling ran high in the 1850's over the question of further extension of slavery, the northern workmen and the northern manufacturers would be united.

Perhaps the most striking fact about the North in the middle of the 19th century was its progress. It was developing fast, and it could look at the future with confidence. We have seen its growth in population. Its advance in industry and trade was just as impressive. America's chief deposits of coal and iron are in the northern states; American finance had early found its centre at New York; the protective tariff gave the northern manufacturers the chance of capturing the ever-growing home market; the railroads enabled them to send their goods throughout the states. It is not surprising that the Yankee business man was self-confident and enterprising. The North in 1850 was full of a vigorous and optimistic economic life, and foreign visitors noticed the energy and activity of its inhabitants.

Nor was it only in trade and industry that the North was forging ahead. It was progressing in other ways too. In education, for example, it was far ahead of the South. The Oxford and Cambridge of the U.S.A., Harvard and Yale Universities, were both in the North; both had been founded in colonial days, Harvard (at Cambridge, Massachusetts) in 1637 and Yale (at New Haven, Connecticut) in 1701. In the 19th century the separate northern states began to establish their own free universities, those of the north-west taking the lead. Admission to them did not depend on wealth or belief. Further, by 1850 free elementary education was firmly established in all the more thickly-populated northern states. In education the northern states were well in advance, for example, of contemporary England, where, until the 1850's, no one but an Anglican could receive a degree at Oxford or Cambridge, and where, until 1870, there was little elementary education except that provided by the Church schools. One noticeable consequence of this spread of elementary education was the rapid growth of newspapers. Two of America's outstanding papers, the *Baltimore Sun* and the *New York Tribune*, were born in the 1840's. The first great newspaperman of the U.S.A. was Horace Greeley, the editor of the *Tribune*, a power in the land in Civil War days.

In literature the North was supreme. Only one American writer of importance in the 19th century, Mark Twain the humorist, who came from Missouri, was born outside the northern states. The poets Walt Whitman, Henry Wadsworth Longfellow, and John Greenleaf Whittier—all of them in very different ways singers of freedom—were northerners. So were the novelists—Nathaniel Hawthorne, James Fenimore Cooper, Henry Thoreau, and Herman Melville. So too were the historians—John L. Motley and William Prescott. So too were the essayists Oliver Wendell Holmes, Edgar Allen Poe[1] and the man who expressed most clearly the American ideals of his day, Ralph Waldo Emerson. The great majority of these men came from New England, the literary centre of the United States.

In short, in 1850 the North was alert and prosperous, making progress in ideas as well as in wealth. It was making rapid industrial progress; its towns were becoming busier, its capitalists more wealthy, its population ever larger. The railroad had come to unite it as a section, and to link it with the democratic West. In politics its wealthy capitalists were its leaders and provided the driving force; but its common people were democratic in their outlook and hostile to all ideas alien to those of their section. Most important, the people of the North were conscious of the rapid growth of their section. The future belonged to the North, and its people knew it.

2. THE SOUTH

The easiest definition of the South would be 'all states where slavery was legal'; but it must be remembered that certain slave states (Maryland, Delaware, Kentucky, and parts of Virginia, Tennessee, and Missouri) were on the northern side in the Civil War. The most important southern

---

[1] Poe, however, did some of his writing while living in the South.

states were the cotton states of the lower South—South Carolina, Georgia, Florida, Alabama, Mississippi, Louisiana, Arkansas, and Texas. North of these was a group more or less firmly attached to slavery, but in which little cotton was grown, including North Carolina, Virginia, Kentucky, Tennessee, and Missouri; farther north still were Maryland and Delaware.

This area was almost wholly agricultural. In the more northerly parts of it agriculture was varied, with many tobacco and hemp plantations; in South Carolina and Georgia there were great rice fields; while at the mouth of the Mississippi, Louisiana, for example, grew a good deal of sugar cane. But in the lower South, one crop was supreme above all others. 'Cotton was King.' Nature had made the South one of the finest cotton-growing areas in the world, and since Eli Whitney's invention of the cotton gin cotton had grown to a position of overwhelming importance in southern agriculture. Some figures will illustrate this fact. In 1840 320,000,000 pounds of cotton were produced; in 1850, over 1,000,000,000 pounds; ten years later, on the eve of the Civil War, over 2,000,000,000 pounds. Such a vast increase was not achieved by any scientific methods of growth, but by a steady westward expansion of area. When cotton land was exhausted, the planters broke new ground, leaving the old plantations derelict behind them. Thus the great cotton area moved from South Carolina and Georgia to Alabama and Mississippi, filling the rich black soil of the river valley, then on to Louisiana and Texas. The new land was used at a prodigal rate, for the planter cared nothing for the permanent value of the soil and was simply out to get a good cotton crop from it. The labour used was ignorant slave labour. Southern cotton-growing was based on two facts— the continual breaking of new land, and the exploitation of slave labour.

The South was aristocratic. Of the white population of the South less than 6 per cent. were slave-owners; some 350,000 whites owned between 3,000,000 and 3,500,000 blacks. Among these 350,000 less than 8000 owned more than fifty Negroes apiece. It was these 8000 who were the real rulers of the South. The other slave-owners followed their lead, and so did most of the considerable number of non-slave-owning farmers. The humble poor whites, often despised by the slaves, who called them 'white trash', had little say in southern politics. The great planter's whole outlook on life, as well as the way in which he lived, was aristocratic. He saw himself as the ruler of a small kingdom, surrounded by his faithful subjects, the slaves, whom he cared for and to whom he dispensed justice. He was accustomed to giving orders and to having them promptly obeyed. Men of this type were unlikely to agree with the pushful Yankees. Proud of their way of life, they would certainly never yield to them on a matter so dear to southern hearts as slavery.

The dependence of the South upon cotton was in the long run disastrous. King Cotton brought ruin upon his subjects. His reign weakened the soil, and seemed to tie the southern planter to slave labour. In 1850 the South had practically no manufactures; its manufactured goods came either from

England or from the northern states. The southern economic system was one-sided and unbalanced. The profits of the cotton-planters depended on their ability to use fertile new soil every few years. This wasteful process had carried them westward until they had begun to draw near the natural limit of cotton production, the 100° W. line. Beyond this the land is arid and unfit for cotton-growing. Again, during the 19th century the price of slaves rose steadily, thus putting up the expenses of the planter —although it benefited the Virginians, who sold slaves to the Lower South. In 1857 a native of North Carolina, Hinton R. Helper, published a book with the grim title of *The Impending Crisis in the South*. Helper was very unpopular in the South because of what he wrote—he lived in the North and the North Carolinians threatened to tar and feather him if ever he showed his face again in his native state. He diagnosed the economic complaint from which the South was suffering, and proceeded to suggest a remedy. His diagnosis may well have been too harsh; later investigators have suggested that there was still abundant scope in the Lower South for profitable cotton-planting based upon slavery, and for developing a more balanced agriculture in the Upper South. Certainly most planters had no doubt that all was well with the South; as for Helper's remedy, that annoyed them more than the diagnosis, for he suggested the abandonment of slavery in favour of wage-labour.

The difference between North and South showed itself in many ways. In comparison with the North, the South was backward. Its railroads in 1860 were fewer, its roads far poorer. Its average standard of living was lower. Its people were mostly illiterate, and its contribution to American literature was very limited. Lack of education helped to make them disorderly and narrow-minded. One of the worst results of slavery was that it demoralised the whites. It made all whites despise manual labour, which they thought to be work fit only for blacks. It made the slave-owner haughty and unwilling to tolerate opposition. Consequently the southern gentleman sometimes had in him something of the bully, and bad temper often took the place of fine manners. Duelling was quite common.

The South, the land of the black slaves, the land where Cotton was King, was a backward country facing a crisis. Its planters, with their aristocratic outlook, could have no sympathy with the capitalists of the North. They dominated southern society, a society in which there were many more poor whites than slave-owners. Yet the whole section was united in defence of its 'peculiar institution,' slavery. Sectional feeling ran higher in the South than in the North. In both sections the events of the 1850's provoked hatred and distrust to the point where war broke out.

3. SLAVERY AND THE SECTIONAL CLASH

On several occasions before 1848 feeling flared up between North and South. The first of these was in 1820, over slavery itself, when the Missouri

Compromise had provided a temporary solution. Another had come in 1830, over States' Rights, when South Carolina had issued her Ordinance of Nullification; this had shown clearly the southern opposition to the tariff. A third, far less serious, had come during Tyler's Presidency, when the Northerners wanted to use the Federal Government to carry through a scheme of internal improvements, which Tyler, a southerner, had vetoed. But slavery was the greatest single issue over which sectional feeling arose. Slavery was the occasion of the fierce sectional hatred of the fifties. It will be well, before describing these events, to find out the facts and figures about it, and to look at some of the arguments put forward by each section.

In 1850 there were about 3,500,000 Negroes in the U.S.A. All but about 250,000 of these were slaves. Slavery existed only in the southern states, from Delaware and Maryland, Kentucky and Missouri southwards. This fact does not mean that northerners were better or more humane than southerners. It was simply the result of geography: the hotter climate of the South encouraged the use of Negro slave labour, the colder climate of the North discouraged it. The white population in the slave states was about 6,250,000, just under twice the black. But in certain areas the slaves formed over 50 per cent. of the whole population. These areas were in the cotton-growing states of the Lower South, and Virginia: Virginia no longer grew much cotton, but bred slaves instead, for export to other states. These slaves were the descendants of those who, from the days of John Hawkins until the early 19th century, had been shipped in boatloads, so many human cattle, from West Africa across the Atlantic.

Slavery was a basic feature of life in the southern states. The South called it her 'peculiar institution'—peculiar in the sense that it did not exist in the North. Most of the manual labour in the South was done by slaves. A man's wealth and his position in society were judged by the number of slaves he owned. A plantation with over 50 slaves was a large one; a 'middle-class' plantation of 400–1000 acres would have 10 to 50. Over half the 350,000 slave-owners were men with 5 or less slaves. Able-bodied slaves were chiefly employed as field-hands in the cotton plantations. This was the kind of work in which they could most profitably be used. Slave women did the housework on the larger plantations.

A movement for abolishing slavery had arisen early in American history. Quakers, following the lead of John Woolman (1720–72), were to the fore, and the first achievement came in 1808, when the legal import of slaves to the U.S.A. ceased. After this attempts were made to get individual slaves freed and sent back to West Africa, where, in Monroe's day, the state of Liberia was founded for this purpose. Such schemes were not highly successful, mainly because the Negroes considered themselves Americans, and did not want to be shipped back to an African wilderness, partly because Liberia itself did not develop happily; some of its black citizens made slaves of their fellows. The next landmark in the abolitionist movement came in 1831, when William Lloyd Garrison of Boston published the first edition of his anti-slavery newspaper *The Liberator*. Garrison was a single-minded idealist, who gave all his energies to the campaign for abolition. He would have no compromise, no gradual buying out of the slave-owners; slavery was to go, immediately and for ever. His object was to arouse the people of the United States to the sin of slavery in their midst, and he spared no violence in his language in his efforts to do this. If the South did not get rid of slavery, he maintained, then the North must quit the Union and have nothing to do with the slave-states. So the front page of his paper carried the words—'No Union with slaveholders. The United States Constitution is a covenant with death and an agreement with hell.' Other abolitionists, including Theodore D. Weld in Ohio and wealthy philanthropists like the Tappan brothers in New York, organised local anti-slavery societies.

In 1833, the year of the abolition of slavery in the British Empire, the American Anti-Slavery Society was founded. By 1840 there were over 150,000 members, in some 500 local organisations. It drew its support from humanitarians in the northern states; once again Quakers were prominent, and they gave to the abolitionist movement its poet, John G. Whittier. Propaganda of every possible kind was used to spread the message—speeches and public meetings, pamphlets and newspapers, sermons and pictures. But Garrison's fierce language brought upon him the wrath of the slave-owners, who used every possible means to silence the movement. Their fury was the greater because seven months after the foundation of *The Liberator* a rebellion, known as Nat Turner's Insurrection, broke out among the slaves of Virginia. Fifty whites were killed before it was put down with savage cruelty, and Garrison was denounced as responsible. The very violence of his language made the slave-owners less ready to listen to reason, and so helped to shut the door against a peaceful solution of the problem of slavery. This was one of the reasons why many northerners, including other abolitionists, were hostile to Garrison, whose campaign they considered dangerous to the Union. Moreover northerners as a whole, though disliking slavery, had no great enthusiasm for Negroes; free Negroes in the North were ill-paid and employed in the lowest-grade jobs. So it came about that northern mobs attacked abolitionists and burnt their property. The immediate political effect of the abolitionist campaign was small.[1] In 1840 an Anti-Slavery candidate, J. G. Birney, appeared in the presidential election; he won little support, but the Liberty Party, standing for opposition to slavery, put him forward again in 1844, once again with little success.

[1] One by-product was the 'gag' rule of 1836. So many abolitionist petitions poured into Congress that the southern members got a resolution passed saying that every future petition on the subject of slavery should lie on the table—that is, the House would take no notice of them. The ex-President, John Q. Adams, now a member of Congress, battled in session after session for the repeal of this interference with the right of the American citizen to petition Congress; he succeeded in his object in 1844.

There was violent disagreement about the way slaves were treated. Many writers said that the blacks were the innocent victims of every kind of injustice and cruelty. Among these was Mrs. Harriet Beecher Stowe, the author of *Uncle Tom's Cabin*. She had never been in the South and had no personal knowledge of slavery. She gave in her book (published in 1852) a most vivid and moving account of slavery as she imagined it to be, and the book had great influence in the North. The contrast which she drew between the simple and innocent slave and his wicked and cruel master made a great appeal. As a general picture of slavery the book was misleading. On the other hand, some of the southern writings about slavery, with their suggestion that the slave lived in a kind of earthly paradise, doing a limited amount of work and being excellently cared for, were even more fantastic. The truth lay in between the extremes. Slaves were worked for very long hours and punished by whipping or flogging. Their personal liberty was limited. Some of their songs, the beautiful 'spirituals,' express the terrible sorrow of a captive race. The southern planter said that the Negro was careless, somewhat lazy, and untruthful. Yet it is clear that slavery in itself certainly does not encourage a man to work carefully or hard, or to be honest. Slaves were cared for mainly because they were valuable pieces of property. The price of the most valuable type of Negro, the strong young male, was high and rising steadily through the 19th century, and on the eve of the Civil War it was as much as $1800, nine times the price of seventy years before. Twenty slaves represented a very large investment of capital, and each one of them was worth the utmost attention.

The subject aroused varied and passionate discussion in the U.S.A., and some of the arguments used give us an insight into the utterly different attitudes of the two sections. The central argument which the South used in defence of slavery was simple. They maintained that slavery was the essential basis of the whole of southern prosperity, which depended on cotton-growing; adding that the cotton crop was itself an essential of American national prosperity, because it provided two-thirds of the value of American exports. Further, they said that they could not afford to emancipate. All their capital—the money which the northerner put into his factory, his mill, and his tools—was invested in slaves. Slavery, too, they asserted, was the only means of getting the lazy black race to work, and the only way of civilising them. To emancipate them would be disastrous; and they drew gloomy pictures of a black revolution with numerous calamities in its train. Finally, countless more or less extravagant arguments appeared; among the least convincing of these were that slavery was clearly authorised by the Bible, that slavery was essential to true democracy, and that Negroes were not really human beings at all, but animals. The wisest southerners did not believe all these arguments. But most of them believed the first two, the economic arguments.

The noblest and ultimately the strongest of the northern arguments was that slavery was immoral and unjust; that it was wrong in the sight of God to make one man the property of another. But this particular argument found little support outside the comparatively small group of abolitionists like Garrison and John Brown. Many northerners opposed slavery on the ground that it was a contradiction of the free and democratic ideals for which the U.S.A. stood. The words of the Declaration of Independence, 'Life, Liberty, and the pursuit of Happiness' rang very hollow beside the accounts of slaves taken from their families and sold at auction like so many bits of furniture, flogged with hide, deprived by law of education, subject to a night curfew, hunted with bloodhounds and barbarously punished if they tried to escape. Such facts were accepted features of slavery in the Lower South. The South's most effective answer to this argument was to point to the mills and factories of the North and ask whether the white slaves in them had much chance of attaining Jefferson's ideal. Moreover, the North brought economic arguments against slavery. The slave was a very heavy capital investment who decreased in value as he grew older, until he finally became valueless. To keep a slave cost perhaps $35 a year on an average on a small plantation, $15 on a large one. The slave could not lose his job, and it was difficult for the planter to get a full day's work out of him. As Helper had said, cotton growing could have been more economically managed on free labour, for the planter would not have had to care for his workmen in infancy and old age, or to nurse them when sick. These economic arguments were by no means necessarily valid; indeed slave-owners generally were prosperous in the years before the Civil·War, and the fact that they were able to pay high prices for slaves was a sign of this.

13   The Coming of Civil War, 1846-60

I. THE WILMOT PROVISO

In 1846 a Pennsylvanian Congressman named David Wilmot proposed that slavery should be forbidden in any territory taken from Mexico. This Wilmot Proviso would not affect Texas, already a slave state within the Union, but it would apply to California and any other lands taken from Mexico. The southerners, led by Calhoun, were immediately indignant. According to the Missouri Compromise, the limit to which the South was ready to go, California would be part free and part slave, since the 36° 30' line passed through the middle of it. The Wilmot Proviso was carried in the House, but defeated in the Senate. It reawakened the old bitterness.

The solution of 1820 had failed to become permanent. Wilmot raised a vital question—was slavery to be permitted in those vast western lands of the U.S.A. which were not yet organised as states? There was no need of Wilmot's Proviso in California or New Mexico, for both were naturally unsuitable for slave labour. But the South felt his proposal as an insulting challenge. In the election of 1848 the Democrats, who were becoming an increasingly southern party, nominated Lewis Cass, because Polk, worn out by his work, refused to stand. The Whigs put forward 'Old Rough and Ready,' General Zachary Taylor.[1] A new party, the Free Soil Party, demanding 'Free soil, Free speech, Free labour, and Free men,' nominated ex-President Van Buren. It secured enough votes in New York and Pennsylvania to give those states to Taylor, and so to elect him. The Whigs were unlucky in their military Presidents, for Taylor died in 1850, and was succeeded by Millard Fillmore, his Vice-President, a man of few abilities whose influence on events was small.

2. THE COMPROMISE OF 1850

In 1849 the Gold Rush brought a sudden increase of population to California, and the inhabitants drew up a state constitution for themselves. This prohibited slavery throughout California, and thereby caused furious feeling in the South; although up to this time southerners, following Calhoun's states' rights theory, had always insisted upon the right of each state to decide for itself about slavery. The Californian constitution had to be ratified by Congress before the state could join the Union, and southern members opposed it strongly. Many southerners were already talking of secession from the Union, which would have meant civil war. The veteran, Henry Clay, saved the situation by bringing forward the series of proposals which is known as the Compromise of 1850. He suggested the admission of California to the Union as a free state; the creation of the Territories of Utah and New Mexico without reference to slavery; the prohibition of the slave trade in the District of Columbia; and a new and harsher Fugitive Slave Law, providing for the capture and return to their owners of escaped slaves. These were accepted after much debate, for there was something in them to please everybody. But the Fugitive Slave Law aroused bitter hostility in the North; the pursuit and recapture of runaway slaves in free states was a perpetual reminder to northerners of the existence of slavery. It stopped them from forgetting it, and there was little hope of peace unless they did forget it.

The Compromise was Clay's last achievement for his country. He died in 1852. Two great contemporaries, as devoted to the Union as Clay, Daniel Webster and John C. Calhoun, died about the same time, Calhoun in 1850 and Webster in 1852. With them there passed away some of the hopes of a sane solution to the sectional dispute; the way was open for less

[1] Taylor came from Louisiana and was a slave-owner.

experienced and more hasty politicians to take the lead. Rising passion
brought wild words in Congress and in the press. One episode of 1856
illustrated the rise of uncontrolled passion. In that year Senator Charles
Sumner, a Republican opponent of slavery, made a speech in the Senate
which contained offensive remarks about a Senator from South Carolina.
Shortly afterwards Congressman Preston Brooks, a relative of the insulted
Senator, strode up to Sumner's desk in the Senate and, while the latter
was writing, beat him into unconsciousness with his cane. Brooks bitterly
regretted his action afterwards; it was a sign of the rise of passions in the
'fifties. A worse sign was that many southerners admired his action, and
sent him more canes. Nor were the Presidents of the time men who were
strong enough to check the growth of hatred. In the election of 1852 the
Democrat Franklin Pierce of New Hampshire won an easy victory over
the Whig candidate, General Winfield Scott. Pierce's chief virtue in the
eyes of politicians was his lack of personality. James Buchanan of Pennsylvania, his successor, an abler man, was no more capable of giving the
nation a resolute lead towards a peaceful settlement.

3. 'BLEEDING KANSAS'

   Once again sectional feeling broke loose over the question of slavery in
the western lands. In the 1850's the U.S.A. needed a trans-continental
railroad to open up the prairies and the Pacific coast. Several routes were
possible. One was the Southern from New Orleans across Texas. It was
to make this one more likely that Jefferson Davis of Mississippi, Pierce's
Secretary of War, persuaded him to buy from Mexico in 1853 the land to
the south of the Gila Valley which formed the Gadsden Purchase, so named
from the business man who negotiated the deal. Another was the Central,
from St. Louis across the Rockies to the Great Salt Lake, and down the
California Trail to San Francisco. Senator Stephen A. Douglas of Illinois
was interested in this route, and in railroad and land speculation. He
wanted to attract settlers to the land of the Middle West through which
the new railroad would have to pass. More important, it seems probable
that Douglas, who was young and ambitious, wanted to raise some big
political issue which would reinvigorate the Democratic party and give
scope to his own talents. So in 1854 he proposed a bill to organise a
Territory in the Middle West; this would give law and government, and
so bring settlers. The area was that of the present states of Kansas and
Nebraska. The bill raised once again the slavery dispute. It was somewhat
altered by Congress and was finally passed as the Kansas-Nebraska Act
(1854). Its terms were simple. It created two new Territories, to be known
as Kansas and Nebraska; and it was left to the settlers of the new Territories to decide whether they would have slavery or not. The idea behind
this second clause was given the name of 'popular sovereignty.' This
apparently fair act was disastrous because of the vast number of Americans

who did not want any further extension of slavery in the west. Once again the Missouri Compromise had gone by the board.

Nebraska was unfit for slaves and the southerners made no attempt to gain it; but in Kansas the act provoked what was practically a civil war. Slave-owners came in from Missouri and other slave states; northern abolitionists formed companies to finance the settlement of northerners in Kansas. Both parties established Territorial governments and asked for the approval of Congress. 'Bleeding Kansas' was full of disorder and crime. Each side made armed raids on the other's property, and murders and even massacres were not infrequent. One of the worst of these was the Pottawatomie Massacre (1856). John Brown, a ferocious abolitionist, invaded with his followers the pro-slavery settlement of Pottawatomie. There they murdered five unarmed men at dead of night. The 'Kansas War,' which lasted for several years, was a preliminary to the Civil War. Gradually the northerners outnumbered the southerners. The latter got a constitution, the Lecompton Constitution, which the pro-slavery settlers had drawn up for Kansas, accepted by the Senate. But a majority of the people of the state rejected it; and in 1861 Kansas joined the Union as a free and not as a slave state.

4. ANTHONY BURNS AND DRED SCOTT

On the day after Congress passed the Kansas-Nebraska Act, a Boston mob tried to rescue from the local gaol a Negro prisoner. He was Anthony Burns, a slave who had escaped from Virginia and who had been caught in Massachusetts. According to the Fugitive Slave Law he was to be sent back to his owner. Abolitionists were numerous in Boston, where the law was bitterly resented. The attempt to rescue Burns failed. But he and his master had to be escorted to the quay, whence a ship was to take them back to Virginia, by over a thousand soldiers and the local sheriff's posse. It cost the Federal Government $40,000 to get Burns back to his owner. It was the last time the Fugitive Slave Law was enforced in Massachusetts.

Incidents of this kind led to the formation in 1854 of a new Republican party. This was a party from the North, led by northern men and concerned to defend northern interests. It opposed slavery in the Territories, and so its southern opponents called it the 'Black Republican' party. It put forward as candidate in the presidential election of 1856 John C. Frémont, chiefly notable for his somewhat dubious political adventures in California in 1848, and its slogan was 'Free Soil, Free Speech, and Frémont.' The Democrats chose more wisely; their man was James Buchanan, who had been Pierce's minister in London and had therefore not been involved in the Kansas business. Further, like Pierce, he was a northerner, and therefore more likely to capture northern votes than a southern Democrat would have been. A third party appeared—the 'Know-Nothings,' or the Native American Party. This had arisen because of many

Americans' dislike of the continuous stream of foreign immigrants. Between 1850 and 1860 over 2,500,000 arrived; over 900,000 of these were Irish, and in 1860 over 12 per cent. of the population of the U.S.A. had been born overseas. The forties and fifties were the great period of Irish immigration. The 'Know-Nothings' opposed the Irish, and therefore the Pope and Roman Catholics too; they opposed Germans as well, who were also arriving in large numbers. Their members got their name because, with the American love of mystery, they answered all questions about their party with the phrase 'I know nothing.' In the 1856 election they supported Millard Fillmore, who got 874,000 votes. Buchanan won, carrying every Southern state, plus Pennsylvania, Illinois, and Indiana. Frémont swept the rest of the North. Elections were becoming not party contests, but sectional contests.

Early in 1857 the Supreme Court published its decision in the Dred Scott Case. Dred Scott was a Negro from the slave state of Missouri whom his master had taken with him, first to the free state of Illinois and then to the territory north of 36° 30', where the Missouri Compromise had forbidden slavery. Scott claimed his freedom on the ground that he had twice been taken on to free soil. The Supreme Court under Chief Justice Roger B. Taney (Taney was from Maryland and four of the other eight judges were southerners) decided against him. They said that no Negro could be a citizen of the U.S.A.; that slaves were property, and that Congress had no right, when making laws for the Territories, to deprive citizens of their property. This judgment meant that the Missouri Compromise was null and void; and it suggested that all United States Territories (not states, which could decide for themselves) were open to slavery. It was felt as a severe blow in the North, and meetings of protest were held throughout the northern states.

5. THE LINCOLN–DOUGLAS DEBATES

It was in 1858 that Abraham Lincoln first became nationally famous, when he stood as Republican candidate against Stephen A. Douglas for election as Senator for Illinois. Born in Kentucky in 1809 of very humble parents, Abraham Lincoln had grown up in pioneer surroundings. As a boy his great physical strength had won him a reputation as a wrestler and runner. He had in all about twelve months' schooling, yet he read all the books he could get hold of. In 1830, after the Lincoln family moved to Illinois, he got a job as a storekeeper's assistant, and while in it helped to build a flat boat and float it down the river to New Orleans. Educating himself in his spare time, he showed an early enthusiasm for the law. In 1832 he was an unsuccessful candidate for the Illinois House of Representatives. He took a partnership in a store, and it went bankrupt; then he became a land surveyor, and began seriously to study law. In 1834 he was called to the bar, and elected to the Illinois House of Representatives. Here he showed his enthusiasm for democracy, as well as his opposition to any further extension of slavery. He did not come into national politics until 1846, when he was elected Congressman for Illinois. Here he opposed the government on the Mexican War, and voted for the Wilmot Proviso. He was a resolute opponent of the Kansas-Nebraska Act, and took a leading part in Illinois in the movement which led to the formation of the Republican party.

Yet the nation did not hear of him until his contest with Douglas in 1858. The two rivals held a series of joint debates throughout Illinois during the summer and autumn of that year. The contrast between the two men, in person as well as in ideas, was great. Douglas, nicknamed the 'Little Giant.' was short, well-dressed, dynamic, combative; Lincoln tall and shambling, untidy, droll and casual. The high level of their eloquence, the adroitness of their replies to one another, and the tense political situation, gave the debates a nation-wide audience. Douglas stood by his idea of popular sovereignty—that the settlers in the Territories should have the right to decide for themselves about slavery. Lincoln maintained the Republican party's view—that slavery must be outlawed in the Territories to prevent its further spread. Lincoln's strongest argument in the debates was that slavery was morally wrong. Douglas in defending popular sovereignty was championing the right of the majority to choose their own way of organising society. No doubt he recognised that for geographical reasons slavery could not be extended into western territories like Kansas and Nebraska where neither the climate nor the soil suited the plantation system, and therefore he did not concern himself with the moral issue. Douglas was re-elected as Senator; but the future was with Lincoln.

6. JOHN BROWN AT HARPER'S FERRY

The year 1859 saw an event which seemed to justify the belief of southerners that the North was engaged in a gigantic conspiracy to free all the slaves in the U.S.A. It was a terrible warning of the coming of what the northern politician William H. Seward had in 1858 called the 'irrepressible conflict' between North and South. John Brown was an abolitionist,[1] and an incredible mixture of cruelty and saintliness; deeply religious, he was ready to to to any length of brutality against slave-owners. This astonishing character devised a crack-brained scheme for stirring up a slave revolt in the South—an invasion of Virginia and the seizure of the United States arsenal at Harper's Ferry, followed by a summons to the slaves to

[1] He was one of the numerous abolitionists who helped to run what was known as the Underground Railroad, a means by which some slaves escaped. A slave who got away made his way as best he could to free soil: here abolitionists took charge of him and, hiding him and disguising him, passed him on from one farmhouse to another until he was clear of danger. Canada was the ultimate goal, for the Fugitive Slave Act did not apply there. Some 75,000 Negroes are believed to have escaped by this means over the years.

rise in revolt. The scheme was wildly impracticable. On October 16 John Brown with about twenty followers seized the fire engine house at Harper's Ferry. Here they were besieged; not one slave rose in support. His two sons were killed at his side. When he was eventually captured,[1] on the morning of October 18, all but four of his men had been wounded or killed. He was tried for treason, murder and criminal conspiracy. His guilt was obvious, and he was executed on December 2, 1859. The effect of this terrible episode was to inflame hatred in North and South almost beyond power of control, to drive reason out of American minds. The South was plunged into an orgy of fear—fear of Yankee barbarism, of black revolution with the arson and massacre which it would bring, of the complete destruction of all it knew as civilisation. The North had gained a martyr. Emerson was only expressing the sincere belief of thousands of northerners when he described John Brown as 'that new saint, than whom nothing finer or more brave was ever led by love of men into conflict and death,' and said that he 'will make the gallows glorious like the Cross.' The North also had a marching song.

7. THE ELECTION OF 1860

1860 was the fateful year. It saw the election to the Presidency of one who was known to be an unyielding opponent of any further extension of slavery, and whom the South—quite wrongly—believed to be determined to stamp out slavery in the South itself. Lincoln was the Republican candidate, chosen mainly because the party did not want Seward, a far more prominent figure. The party was clear about slavery. There was to be no more slavery in the Territories; there was to be no interference with slavery in the states. The South was frantically suspicious. The cotton states wanted slavery permitted in all the Territories. Before the election, they threatened to secede from the Union if any 'Black Republican'—one, like Lincoln, known as an opponent of any further extension of slavery— were elected. The election was vital for the South. Since the election of Pierce in 1852 it had controlled Congress by means of its domination of the Democratic party; if the Democrats lost this election, the Southern hopes of slavery in the Territories were gone. The extremists in the South were not content with Douglas' view that the settlers in each Territory should choose for themselves; they took their stand on the Dred Scott decision, that all the Territories should be open to slavery. The Democratic party convention of 1860 split over this question. The moderates supported Douglas as candidate for the election; but the extremists from the Lower South would not have him. The latter walked out, formed a new convention of their own, and nominated John C. Breckinridge of Kentucky. The former nominated Douglas. A fourth candidate, from the Constitutional

---

[1] The commander of the Federal forces which compelled him to surrender was Robert E. Lee.

Union Party, a moderate party who saw the dangers ahead and hoped to overcome them by pretending not to see them, was John Bell of Tennessee; his platform did not even mention slavery. The result of the election, the most important in American history, was a victory for Lincoln. The figures illustrate the complicated American system of electing a President; they also show that Lincoln was chosen by a minority of the American people. They were as follows:

Lincoln	.	.	1,866,452 popular votes,	180 electoral votes		
Douglas	.	.	1,376,957 ,,	,,	12	,, ,,
Breckinridge	.	849,781 ,,	,,	72	,, ,,
Bell	.	.	588,879 ,,	,,	39	,, ,,

8. ABRAHAM LINCOLN

The Republicans had their President, a northern President—he had carried all the free states in the election. You can see a photograph of Lincoln opposite page 113 and you will note his lean and angular face, with its shrewd and melancholy gaze. In 1860 many Americans knew little of him. He was by no means the leading figure of the Republican party: William H. Seward of New York, who became his Secretary of State, had a greater claim to that position. The nation had seen few signs of those qualities of greatness by which we know him to-day. In 1860 a great section of the nation regarded him as the embodiment of all they suspected and hated most. Lincoln was a villain, not a hero, to the South. In the North, too, many politicians regarded him with some alarm, not unmixed with scorn for his western ways. Quite certainly, also, the national crisis which coincided with his presidency brought out in Lincoln qualities that were half-hidden before.

Patient and unselfish and utterly honest, Lincoln was no simpleton. His mind was wise, and acute, penetrating at once to the heart of a subject. His alarming habit of telling odd, whimsical stories concealed a clear and quick-thinking brain. His noblest qualities were his devotion to freedom and his deep tolerance of the views of others; and it is by these that he expressed all that is finest in American tradition. Democracy, to Abraham Lincoln, was a living thing, not just a word to which politicians pay lip-service: and when he talked, as he did in the famous speech at Gettysburg in 1863, of 'government of the people, by the people, for the people,' he was not coining a clever phrase. He was stating a belief that was a part of himself, the belief in the right and ability of men to be free to govern themselves. He believed profoundly in self-government, and hated injustice, whether it affected white men or black. That was why he hated slavery, with its abominable traffic in human life, its exploitation of the Negro and its denial of all real freedom to its victims. Slavery was in Lincoln's eyes a moral wrong. He was not an abolitionist; he did not believe that in his day social equality between the two races in the United States was practicable, and he advocated the foundation of Negro settlements overseas as the best solution of the problem. But he did believe, as he said in the first debate with Douglas, that 'in the right to eat the bread, without the leave of anyone else, which his own hand earns, he [the Negro] is my equal, and the equal of Judge Douglas, and the equal of every living man.' Until the middle of the Civil War, Lincoln was willing to recognise the right of the southern states to choose for themselves on the question of slavery. He would have no slavery in the Territories; yet he would have no interference with it in the states that wanted to keep it. His view changed during the war, when his main concern was to save the Union. The time came when he felt that the Union could best be preserved by freeing the slaves, and so in 1862 he issued an Emancipation Proclamation.

Lincoln's way of speech was direct and unaffected, both in conversation and on the public platform. He spoke and wrote in clear, bold English, and his political beliefs can best be understood from his speeches and letters. His phrases were sometimes peculiarly pointed: he once described wealth as 'a superfluity of the things one does not want.' More often his words expressed a burning sincerity in a simple, balanced style. At times he was inconsistent in what he said, but few can doubt either his sincerity or his belief in freedom. Two of his best known statements on slavery are outwardly inconsistent. In 1858, in the debates with Douglas he uttered a prophecy about slavery. 'A house divided against itself cannot stand. I believe that this government cannot endure permanently half slave and half free.' Four years later, in a letter written to Horace Greeley of the *New York Tribune*, who had written complaining that Lincoln was not acting quickly enough about slavery, and published in that paper, he said 'If I could save the Union without freeing any slave, I would do it; if I could save it by freeing all the slaves, I would do it; and if I could do it by freeing some and leaving others alone, I would also do that.' Throughout his career he tried to act in the spirit of the noble phrase of his second inaugural (1865)—'With malice toward none, with charity for all.'

14   The Civil War

1. SECESSION, NOVEMBER 1860–APRIL 1861

Lincoln was elected President in November 1860. By the Constitution, as it then was, the President-elect did not take office until March of the following year.[1] This left an awkward gap even in normal times. Buchanan's situation in the intense crisis of 1860–1 was impossible. The southern states had already threatened secession if Lincoln were elected. South Carolina

[1] By the 20th Amendment (1933) this interval has been cut down to two months: the new President now takes office on January 20 in the year following his election.

was the first to go, and the others followed. In February, 1861, represent-atives from the seven chief cotton states (South Carolina, Alabama, Florida, Georgia, Mississippi, Texas and Louisiana) formed the 'Confederate States of America,' and elected as their President Jefferson Davis of Mississippi. This action was the decisive step on the road to war. There was much dispute whether, under the Constitution, a state had the legal right to secede. But it was not really a question of law at all. To permit states to secede would mean the collapse of the Union; it would make the 'United States of America' a mere name. Lincoln was firm in his intention to preserve the Union, whatever the cost. On this point most northerners, before long, agreed with him. They feared that to divide the Union into two would lead North America into a state similar to that of Europe—a mass of nations all striving to maintain a balance of power and periodically going to war with one another. To permit secession was to acknowledge the failure of the whole American federal experiment. Lincoln summed up this view by saying 'Physically speaking, we cannot separate.'

Buchanan, a well-meaning man who loved peace, and others made attempts to solve the problem peacefully. The most notable of these was the Crittenden Compromise, which suggested that slavery should be permitted in the Territories south of the old Missouri Compromise line, 36° 30′ N. They all failed. Meanwhile, in the South, forts, government offices, and other buildings fell peacefully into Confederate hands—except Forts Sumter and Pickens. The first of these, Fort Sumter, at the very mouth of Charleston Harbour, became a test issue. Would the garrison surrender it and so admit the South's right to secede? Or would the Federal government resist, and so start the war which men even yet hoped to avoid? The South was busy arming. Jefferson Davis called for 100,000 volunteers, and got them; yet many men on each side did not anticipate war. Lincoln was inaugurated in March, 1861. His inaugural speech was clear about secession: he said, 'I hold that, in contemplation of universal law and of the Constitution, the Union of these states is perpetual.' Yet he hesitated to take action about Sumter, and thus to cast his country into the hazards of civil war. But he refused to evacuate it; and in April he sent ships to reprovision it. On April 12 southern troops attacked Fort Sumter. Before the attack on Sumter many northerners, unlike Lincoln, felt ready to let the South go in peace. The action of the South, in firing on the Stars and Stripes, altered that. It produced a great outburst of northern enthusiasm for chastising the rebels, an outburst which carried the North into war. The fort's commander, Major Anderson, surrendered after two days. The Civil War had begun.

2. THE TWO SIDES, UNION AND CONFEDERACY

The American Civil War was in some ways a war greater than any which the world had seen, the first of the fiendishly destructive wars of the last

Brigham Young (1801-77), Mormon leader

James Knox Polk, President during the Mexican War (1846-48)

Abraham Lincoln

hundred years. It was fought over a vast area, considerable parts of which were laid waste in the course of the four years for which the war went on. It cost the lives of some 600,000 American citizens. Inevitably, the great majority of these were young men. Nearly three-quarters of those who enlisted in the Union army were under twenty-one. It saved the Union but it left behind it problems, notably that of the Negro, which the U.S.A. has not yet solved. When it ended, there followed twenty years of the most corrupt and disgraceful politics in American history. Few foresaw any of this in 1861.

Seven states had formed the original Confederacy. These were the cotton states of the Lower South. There were other slave states whose attitude was not so clear, those farther north like Virginia and Kentucky, and they hesitated to join the others; instead they took the lead in putting forward proposals for a compromise settlement. They were not so sure that the southern cause was a good one, and they knew that if war came their lands and not those of the Lower South would be the chief battlefields. Indeed, one reason why war did not come for five months after Lincoln's election was that the extremists on both sides were waiting to see which way these important border states would jump. Eventually, after the attack on Fort Sumter had made war certain, Virginia—faithful to her old southern traditions—Arkansas, Tennessee, and North Carolina joined the Confederacy, bringing the total of rebel states to eleven. Part of Virginia, the western mountain area, declared its loyalty to the Union, and was admitted as a separate state to the Union in 1863. Tennessee contained a loyalist enclave in the east. Delaware and Maryland remained loyal. Missouri was split throughout the war. Kentucky tried for about six months to be neutral, but at length was compelled to join the Union. There was no doubt about any free state, and in all twenty-three states fought for the Union in the Civil War.

To us nowadays it must seem that all the factors which give victory in war lay with the North. There were over 20,000,000 people in the North. The South contained only 9,000,000, and of these 3,500,000 were black slaves whom the South dared not arm. The North was bound together by a railway system useful for strategic as well as for industrial reasons. The North also contained all the chief industrial areas of the U.S.A.; in pre-war days the South had depended for manufactured goods on the factories and workshops of the North, and this meant that the North had an overwhelming advantage in the power to produce munitions. This southern disadvantage might have been rectified by imports from Europe—but the North possessed the great bulk of the navy, and early established command of the sea. Finally, the North possessed in Lincoln a leader far beyond Jeff Davis in shrewdness as well as in moral strength. Davis, for all his devotion to his cause and his great abilities, lacked both the political judgment and the nobility of Lincoln. This northern asset was not clear in 1861, when Davis was known as a politician with a high reputation,

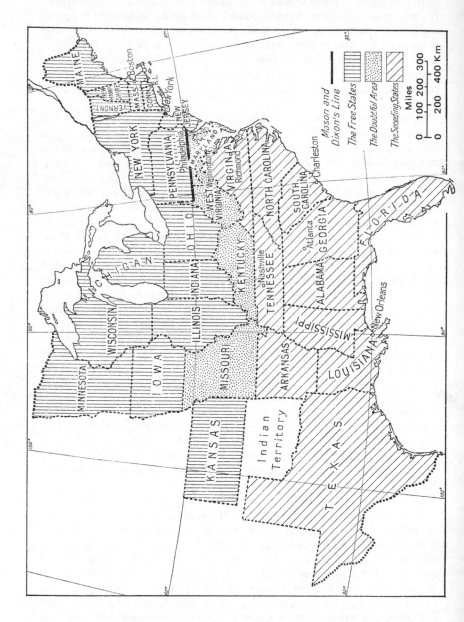

The Civil War—Union and Confederacy

while Lincoln was, to many folk, an inexperienced westerner; but it became increasingly evident as the war went on.

All these facts, taken cumulatively, indicated that all the probability of victory was with the North; and they did in the long run bring a northern victory. But there were other factors to be considered. On the purely military side, southern men had the advantage of being more used to outdoor life and conditions, and to habits of command. The conscript armies on which both sides were ultimately forced to rely brought into the northern armies men weakened by life in the industrial towns; almost every southerner was in some way connected with farming. Again, the South produced quite as many able generals as the North, and two outstanding ones in Robert E. Lee and 'Stonewall' Jackson, both of them Virginians. What is more, the South found its generals straight away: the North suffered several chief commanders before Ulysses S. Grant took command. Many southerners, of whom Lee was the chief example, left the Federal army at the outbreak of war to go and fight for their section, and this weakened the northern forces in the early days of the war.

Beyond these military advantages there were others, more important. The whole situation out of which the war had arisen set the North a gigantic task. The South had withdrawn from the Union; the North had to force it back again. Not until then would it have won. Any peace settlement which acknowledged the independence of the southern states or permitted the South to extend slavery to parts of the new western lands would be the equivalent of a northern defeat. The Confederacy had not to defeat the North. It had merely to avoid being defeated. If it could fight on long enough to make the North tired of the war and ready to come to some compromise, it would have won. The North could only win by defeating the South and conquering it—for no one doubted the southern readiness to resist to the last. And conquering the South was a prodigious problem; in area the South contained over half a million square miles.

Further, the objects for which the two sides were fighting gave the South a great advantage. Southerners could easily maintain that they were fighting to defend their homes and their states against northern invaders—this was the more true because nearly all the fighting was actually done on southern soil—as well as for the right to secede and to organise their lives in their own way. The North was fighting for something more remote and intangible, the ideal of Union. Such considerations as these were responsible for the belief, held by most statesmen in Europe in 1861, that the North would be forced to acknowledge the independence of the South.

3. THE BEGINNING OF THE WAR

The ground on which the two sections were to fight for four weary years was vast. It extended from Pennsylvania to New Orleans, and from the Atlantic Ocean to Kansas. In this area there were two main theatres of war. The first and more important was in the east, where fighting centred round Virginia. The second was in the west, in Tennessee and along the line of the Mississippi. The preliminary objects of the war in northern eyes were to secure Washington itself against enemy attack, and to place in northern hands the border states of Maryland, Missouri and Kentucky. The next task was to conquer the South. To overrun every square yard of southern soil was clearly impossible, and the North set about the problem in several ways. The most important of these were the naval blockade; the breaking of the South's slender rail communications and the capture of key transport centres like Richmond, Atlanta, and Vicksburg; and the penetration of Union armies so deeply into the South that they cut the east of the Confederacy off from the West.

The South began full of enthusiasm for the war, and of confidence in the easy victory which it expected. One southerner, it was said, could lick five Yankees. The first battle of the war seemed to give point to this boast. It took place near Washington, which, from its position near the Virginian border, was immediately threatened by Confederate forces. The two armies met near the little river Bull Run; the Union forces seemed to be winning, when suddenly panic seized them, and dropping their arms they ran as fast as they could go into Washington. Luckily for the North, the Confederates were themselves too disorganised to pursue. Some celebrated too heartily, others thought the war was over and went home. After this encounter men on both sides realised the serious struggle that lay ahead. Both sides gave their energies in the latter half of 1861 to occupying strong positions and to building up their armies. The most important event of the remainder of that year was not a land battle; it concerned not the clash of the two armies, but relations between the North and Europe, and was the outcome of northern control of the sea.

4. THE BLOCKADE AND EUROPE

Throughout the war the northern Navy held command of the sea. The South never really had a navy. The Confederate government gave much attention to the problem of sea power. The armoured gunboat *Merrimac*, captured by the South as she lay in the naval yard at Norfolk, Virginia, was a cause of grave alarm to Lincoln's government: and on one day of 1862 she did great damage to the wooden battleships of the Union. On the following day she was confronted by a Union ironclad, the *Monitor*, and the indecisive fight which followed was the first battle between ironclad vessels. The South, however, lacked the industrial resources which alone made possible the building of a fleet of modern warships. The first submarine also made its appearance in this war, built for the Confederates. It was highly dangerous to those on board, and sank six times, with great loss of life. The real strength of the South on the sea lay in her privateers, which preyed upon northern shipping. The most notorious of these was

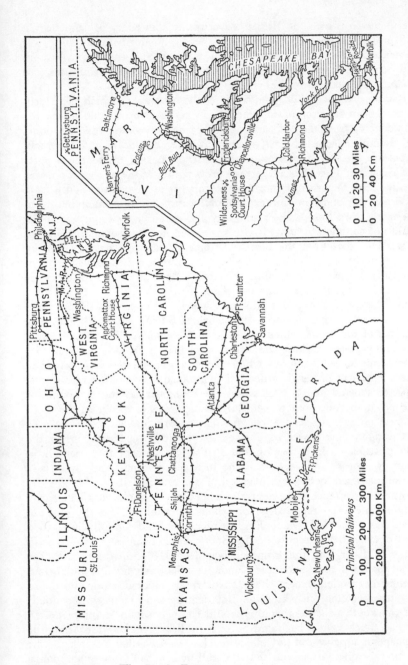

The Civil War—The Battle Zones

the *Alabama*, which the British government allowed to be launched in 1862 from Birkenhead; the damage she did to northern shipping was immense, and led to a later demand for compensation from Britain, and hence to an awkward disagreement between the two countries (see Chap. 15).

But no privateer could greatly affect the advantages which the North derived from superior naval strength. First, the North could attack the Confederacy from the sea, landing troops on her coasts; this was done, for example, against New Orleans in 1862. Secondly, and far more important, the North was able to impose a blockade on southern ports and harbours. This blockade, which grew tighter as the war went on, was an important factor in the northern victory. It prevented the South from exporting her most important product, cotton. It prevented her from importing from Europe the machinery and munitions without which she could not continue to fight; it also prevented her from obtaining, except at fabulous cost from the blockade-runners who were daring or lucky enough to get cargoes through, any of the countless minor conveniences of life which she had formerly bought from Europe. In the end the blockade practically strangled the economic life of the South.

But the blockade was not all advantage. It led to serious friction with foreign powers, especially with the strongest trading nation, Britain. The incident of the *Trent*, which occurred in November, 1861, was the outstanding example of this. The *Trent* was a British mail steamer; she was proceeding to Southampton when she was stopped by a Union naval vessel. American officers boarded her, and took off two Confederate agents, J. M. Mason and John Slidell, who were among her passengers, bound for Europe in an endeavour to get European powers to recognise the Confederate government. There was an outcry in Britain, who was technically in the right. The advice of Prince Albert, aided by the failure of the Atlantic cable, helped to stop the British government from sending a violently worded message to Lincoln's government. And eventually Lincoln, advised by Seward, released Mason and Slidell.

Britain and France stood neutral during the war, neither of them giving to the Confederacy the recognition which she wanted. Neutrality did not mean lack of interest. Many English aristocrats and some business men were outspoken in support of the South. Both Palmerston, the British Prime Minister, and the Emperor Napoleon III sympathised with her rather than with the democratic North. The South confidently anticipated foreign intervention on her behalf. The northern blockade stopped supplies of southern cotton, on which the Lancashire cotton industry depended; and the South believed that this would compel Britain to intervene. In fact, so much cotton had accumulated in Britain before 1861 that the stoppage of supplies did not affect the Lancashire mills until 1863. The position then became serious. But the mill-owners had made much money by that time; while the mill-hands, though thrown out of work by the shortage of cotton, were strongly democratic and, led by John Bright, opposed to slavery. So 'King Cotton' once more deceived his subjects; he could not bring Britain into the American Civil War on the Confederate side. Napoleon III, beginning to pursue his unhappy dream of a French Empire in Mexico, was very sympathetic to the South. He conspired vigorously but erratically with Confederate agents, of whom Slidell of the *Trent* was one. But he was not anxious to act without British co-operation. Consequently he never acted.

5. THE WAR, 1862–3

In 1862 the particular aim of the North was to take Richmond, the chief city of Virginia and the seat of Jefferson Davis' government. George B. McClellan, the Union commander-in-chief, was a thorough and painstaking soldier who prepared his attack with such deliberation that he was severely criticised for his delay; and the earliest important events of that year came in the west. Here the two chief Confederate centres were Vicksburg on the Mississippi and Nashville, the chief town of Tennessee, and the Union aim was to drive in between these two and cut the Mississippi Basin off from the remainder of the Confederacy. In this process the North discovered the general who eventually won the war, Ulysses S. Grant. Grant had distinguished himself in the Mexican War, but had later been cashiered for drunkenness; and he had become a rather unsuccessful assistant in his father's store at Galena, Illinois. On the outbreak of the Civil War he had come back into the army and had obtained a commission as a brigadier. In February 1862 he won a victory at Fort Donelson which led to the surrender of Nashville: it was followed by another, extremely costly, at Shiloh. In April Union naval and land forces took New Orleans, and the way was open for an advance on Vicksburg, whose capture would mean the capture of the whole line of the Mississippi for the Union.

In the east the costly Seven Days' Battle of June, fought in front of Richmond, failed to achieve the Union's object of taking the city. In September Lee invaded Maryland. This serious threat was halted by McClellan in the battle of the Antietam. On the strength of this victory Lincoln issued his Emancipation Proclamation, which set free, from January 1, 1863, all slaves in the rebel states. This move accorded with Lincoln's own deepest feelings and helped to win the support of British public opinion for the Union. It gave the North something clearer to fight for, something for which many people in Europe already believed them to be fighting, the freedom of the black race. So it would help to achieve Lincoln's supreme object, the saving of the Union. Thus he felt his proclamation justified. But in December came the disaster of Fredericksburg, when 12,000 Union soldiers were killed in a wild attempt to take a position strongly held by Lee.

The next year, 1863, brought decisive events, in the east as well as in the west. In May Union troops were crushed at Chancellorsville. But the Confederates suffered a severe loss in this battle by the death of their general, Stonewall Jackson, shot by mistake by his own men in the gathering dusk. Lee, realising the need of an early victory if the South were to win at all, carried the war into the North by invading Pennsylvania. Union troops met him at Gettysburg, and, after three days of severe fighting, he was forced to retire to Virginia. One day after Gettysburg, a thousand miles away to the west, Vicksburg, the western stronghold of the Confederacy, surrendered to Grant after a prolonged siege in which Grant displayed to the full the obstinate perseverance which was his most notable characteristic as a soldier. Gettysburg and Vicksburg were decisive. Gettysburg broke Lee's offensive, Vicksburg shattered the Confederacy in the west; henceforward Union armies would strike relentlessly and steadily southwards. A further victory, won by Grant at Chattanooga in November, 1863, threw open the road to the heart of the Confederacy. The South fought on for two years more, two years of grim and desperate resistance, conscious of what the cost of defeat would be.

Gettysburg is known in history not only for the decisive battle fought there: it is equally famous for Lincoln's greatest speech, delivered in November, 1863, at the dedication of a national war-memorial on the battlefield. It was a short speech, and at the time attracted far less attention than the two-hour address which another speaker had delivered. Now that other speech is wholly forgotten, while Lincoln's words are part of the heritage of all who speak English. From its first fine sentence—'Four score and seven years ago our fathers brought forth on this continent a new nation, conceived in liberty, and dedicated to the proposition that all men are created equal'—to the famous final phrase—'that government of the people, by the people, for the people, shall not perish from the earth'— it is a masterpiece of clear and moving prose.[1]

6. BEHIND THE LINES

It may be well to pause at this point in the narrative of the war, to consider what life was like behind the lines. Certain features of wartime life were common to both North and South, as indeed they have been common phenomena of every large-scale war of modern times. Among these were higher taxes and higher prices; the introduction of paper-money to meet war expenditure; the growth of profiteering; conscription; and a reduction of individual liberty. The North introduced an income-tax, and printed great quantities of 'greenback' notes, thus causing a measure of inflation. The South introduced conscription nearly twelve months before the North, and on the whole it was probably less unpopular there. In neither area was it popular, and there were many deserters from each army; while

[1] It is very short and easily accessible: perhaps it may be most conveniently found in the *Oxford Book of English Prose*.

the Northern conscription acts produced serious riots, including the famous Draft[1] Riots. These took place in 1863 in New York, and were only quelled after great loss of life. They reflected opposition by Irish immigrants to the Emancipation Proclamation, which they feared would lower their standard of living; and opposition to the fact that the rich could buy themselves out of the draft. In the South the phrase 'a rich man's war, but a poor man's fight' arose. There the owners of the larger plantations were exempt from service; but there the overwhelming mass of the population joined readily in the struggle, whether they were rich planters or just poor whites, and only gradually tired of it. Profiteering gave added point to the phrase. The profiteers in the North were the manufacturers whose industrial production was swollen by the war; in the South they were the blockade-runners. Northern profiteers made more profits, though the activities of those in the South were more spectacular. Fundamental opposition to the war, as distinct from the mere desire to get out of taking part in it, was considerable. Quakers, for example, who had been to the fore in the movement for the abolition of slavery, felt unable to fight even when Lincoln's proclamation had made the war one for the abolition of slavery. Those who opposed the war were the victims of laws which interfered with personal liberty. Such laws were passed both in North and in South; the most famous instance of their operation occurred in connection with the northern copperhead[2] Vallandigham. He was tried by a military court and sentenced to imprisonment for the duration: Lincoln banished him instead. On the whole there was probably less interference with freedom than during the First World War.

The South suffered from the war infinitely more than the North—and this was so not merely because she was defeated. Her sufferings during its course were far greater. The first and most obvious cause of this was the fact the the war was fought almost wholly on her soil. Virginia, where most of the battles took place, Georgia, the scene of Sherman's March, and the Carolinas, where Sherman carried out another and if possible more destructive march, suffered most severely; in these states huge areas of land were devastated, cities were burned, houses, farms and crops wrecked and ruined. The North, apart from brief inroads, suffered nothing of this. Moreover, the South in proportion gave more freely of her manhood. 250,000 men died on the Confederate side, out of a white population of about 5,500,000; 360,000 on the Union side, out of a population of over 20,000,000.

Further, the Confederacy suffered great hardship from the blockade,

---

[1] 'Draft' is the word which Americans use in connection with compulsory military service, much as we use 'conscription.' Strictly it means a selection or chosen group of men. A certain proportion of those conscripted in the U.S.A. is called up: that proportion is called the draft; it is now chosen or drawn by lot.

[2] Copperhead, so called from the copperhead snake, was the northern nickname for those who opposed the war.

whereas the North had no blockade to endure. While the war stimulated northern industry, the South and its businesses were bankrupted. Confederate paper-money became practically worthless; the transport system of the South was thrown into chaos. The people of the South suffered very severe privations, of everything that they had in pre-war days bought from the North—clothes, shoes, furniture, railroad rolling stock and engines, machinery, paper, ink, matches. In the North, life went on practically normally. Perhaps the strongest indication of this lies in the immigration figures of these years. 800,000 immigrants came in from Europe during the war. The great westward trek of population still went on; railroads grew, industry developed, financiers prospered; pioneers broke new farmland, sank oil-wells in Pennsylvania, struck silver in Nevada and gold in Colorado. The Civil War hardly interrupted the vast process by which man conquered the North American continent and seized its riches for himself. While the South was suffering desperate hardship in a struggle for life, the North was piling up the profits—and reinvesting them in the great business of opening up the continent.

Finally, beyond this extraordinary contrast, there was a special problem which Lincoln's Emancipation Proclamation brought upon the South— the problem of the freed Negro. This grew more severe as the war went from defeat to defeat for the South, and the Yankee armies advanced into the South as the champions of black freedom. Over 100,000 Negroes fought in the Union army. Many—possibly most—of the slaves followed their masters to the end, either from loyalty or from habit. But there were many gangs of darkies about, men who had nothing to live on but what they could steal, who had no idea whatever of what to do with their freedom, and who were only too ready to pay off old scores. This problem, coming on top of all the other hardships which the southerners endured for their cause, added the atmosphere of racial bitterness and sometimes of frantic terror to all the strain of a hopeless and unequal struggle.

7. THE COMING OF THE END

1864 was a grim year, of desperate resistance by the South, of determined effort by the North not to lose the fruits of the victories of 1863. Grant was appointed Commander-in-Chief of the Union armies, and took charge in the east. The kind of fighting which took place is indicated by a phrase from one of his dispatches—'I propose to fight it out on this line if it takes all summer.' It did, and longer. He drove doggedly southwards on the eastern front at ghastly cost in human life, winning victories at the Wilderness and Spotsylvania, and being repulsed at Cold Harbor. Meanwhile, General William Tecumseh Sherman, perhaps the most brilliant of the Union generals, carried out his notorious 'March through Georgia.' Having taken Atlanta, he led his Union troops through to Savannah on the sea coast, destroying all he could find in a belt of rich land sixty miles wide. This was not just the plundering of uncontrolled soldiers; it was a deliberate act, ordered by Sherman and rigidly organised. The words of the song describe the easy pleasures of the march for the soldier who took part in it—plenty to destroy, plenty to eat, hardly anyone to fight. In the North 1864 was election year, an election in which only the loyal states took part. The Democrats put up General McClellan as Lincoln's opponent; but they were discredited through their pre-war connection with the South, and Lincoln was re-elected. So he led the United States into the fourth and final year of the war.

1865 brought the end that had, humanly speaking, been inevitable since Gettysburg. Broken by the blockade, their territory cut into slices by invading armies, their losses in manpower irreplaceable, the Confederates had no hope. In February Lincoln met southern representatives in a peace conference at Hampton Roads, Virginia. It failed, so the war went on. It was no longer so much a war as a last series of attempts by hunted armies to escape the nets closing in upon them. Lee, with the main Confederate army, tried in vain to elude the persistent Grant. On April 9 he surrendered at Appomattox Court House. It was an odd scene. Lee, the defeated, was in splendid uniform with a jewelled sword; Grant, the victor, in a dirty private's uniform. They talked for a while of pre-war days in the American army, and then Grant wrote out the terms of surrender. A month later Jefferson Davis was taken prisoner, and on May 26 the last Confederate army surrendered. The war was over.

The war was over. The Union had been saved, but the cost of saving it had been vast. High among that cost must be set the immeasurable problems which the war left behind it. The United States had a hard course to run after 1865. And the one man who might have guided her, the President who had grown in the course of the war from an almost unknown politician to a figure of dominating national importance and international fame, was dead. On the night of April 14, five days after Lee's surrender, Lincoln was attending a performance at Ford's Theatre in Washington. A mad actor named John Wilkes Booth crept into the box in which Lincoln was sitting, and shot him from behind, through the head. Booth leaped down on to the stage and escaped, but was found and shot a fortnight later. Lincoln never regained consciousness, and died early next day. His assassination deprived the United States of his honesty and shrewdness at that time when she most needed them. The events of the years after the Civil War are the best measure of the loss which Lincoln's death meant to his country.

15   Reconstruction, 1865-77

1. THE SOUTH AFTER THE WAR

The end of the Civil War found the South utterly shattered. The Confederate government had collapsed and its chief was a prisoner. Law and order had crumbled, and in some regions of the South gangs of armed desperadoes—freed Negroes, deserters from the two armies, criminals and looters of the worst type—terrorised the inhabitants. The northern army had laid waste whole districts, some of them the fairest lands of the South. Parts of many southern towns, like Richmond and Charleston, were in ruins, through siege or fire. Neglect had added to the desolation, and throughout the South crops had rotted in the fields and grass grown in the streets. The pick of southern youth were gone, and those who remained, whatever the class from which they had come, were desperately poor. The economic life of the whole South had cracked under the war. Trade was at a standstill, factories were closed, banks had shut their doors; railroads were scarcely able to work, with their rails often torn up, and engines and rolling stock too dilapidated to run. 'King Cotton' was now a penniless beggar in rags; the huge cotton fields were in many places choked with weeds, and it was ten years before the southern crop reached pre-war level. The power of the rich planters had gone. The war had paralysed schools and churches. As a hurricane wrecks and shatters a town, so the long agony of the Civil War had in the end wrecked and shattered the whole life of the South.

On the whole the South accepted its defeat; there was bitterness and hatred for long after the war, but there was no attempt to raise again the Confederate flag. Some southerners went into exile; most stayed on to try and rebuild southern life. Lee was an example to his fellows; he bore with the abuse which the northern press hurled at all who had been prominent on the Confederate side, and spent the remainder of his life as head of Washington College, Virginia. Others, like the colonel who had to hawk his wife's home-made pies or the general who became a railway worker, had a harder trial to endure. There was one result of the war which southerners would not easily or willingly accept—the emancipation of the slaves. From this fact, and from the use to which northern politicians put the emancipation, sprang most of the bitterness and hatred which the South felt after the war. Slavery, we have seen, was an essential feature of the southern way of life. Emancipation upset the whole labour system of the South.

The emancipation of 3,000,000 black slaves would have been a formidable task even if it had been done gradually and by a process of law. The

Negro was the victim of generations of slavery; uneducated, and frequently lazy, he had little idea of how to fend for himself. The manner in which emancipation actually came—suddenly, and as a direct result of a war between two sections of the U.S.A.—did much harm to the Negro. Some Negroes believed that life was now to be one long holiday: others used freedom to rob and plunder: many rushed straight from the plantations to the towns in a vain hope of finding work: very few had any real idea of how best to use their freedom. One immediate result of emancipation in the South was an outburst of lawlessness. Coupled with it went an increase in the Negro death-rate. This was only partly the result of crime: it was mainly the result of disease and poverty. Slavery had given the Negro the certainty of food and shelter. Freedom guaranteed neither. And everywhere he went in the South he came up against race-prejudice. Lincoln's proclamation could not wipe out two hundred and fifty years of slavery. The white man could not step suddenly out of his habit of looking upon the black as an inferior being: he could not bring himself to see the ex-slave as his equal. The best southern whites, men like Lee who had sold their slaves before the war, tried to make the Negro's change to his new status as smooth as possible. But most southerners were incapable of treating their former slaves as free men. The poor whites were worse than the planters in this respect. The war had broken the planters, and the poor whites had no wish to see the blacks seize power instead.

Out of this indestructible prejudice came the 'Black Codes' of 1865. These were a series of laws passed by the southern states in 1865. Their general aim was to keep the Negro in what southern whites regarded as his place. These laws acknowledged his freedom, and guaranteed certain rights to him; but in other ways they discriminated against him. Negroes were not to marry whites; they were not to bear arms; they were to have some steady job—but in some states all jobs except those of farmhands or domestic servants were closed to them. Some of the laws were sensible in that they recognised the need for special treatment of the freed slaves. But they were obviously designed to keep the Negroes permanently under white control, and they aroused a fierce outcry in the North. They served as a splendid pretext for the activities of the Republican politicians of the North in the following years.

Meanwhile the North had put forward, as a temporary measure for the emergency, its own solution of the problem of the freed slave. In March 1865 the Freedmen's Bureau was set up, as an office of the American War Department. Its purpose was relief work in general, and looking after the freed slaves in particular. It lasted until 1872, and did much useful work. It saved many thousands, black and white, from starvation: it found work for many Negroes: and it set up many schools and hospitals for them. Yet it was bitterly detested in the South. The reason for this was that it fell into the hands of the Republican Party, who used it as a means of encouraging black hatred for southern whites, and thus of maintaining Republican power in the South. Many of its officers were dishonest and corrupt: even Grant, a Republican, called them 'a useless and dangerous set.' The Freedmen's Bureau made southerners less sympathetic than ever towards the Negroes.

2. THE RADICALS AND ANDREW JOHNSON

Lincoln had had a great vision of an American nation genuinely re-untied after the war. In his second inaugural speech (1865) he had called upon the American people 'to bind up the nation's wounds.' Had he lived, he would certainly have tried to make his vision a reality by pursuing a reasonable and generous policy towards the South. His death left the way clear for lesser men and meaner policies. The extreme, or Radical, wing of the Republican party was determined to have revenge upon the South, and to use the North's victory as a means of securing the Republican party in power. This group won support from other Americans whose motives were higher: from those who honestly believed that the South ought, in justice, to make some retribution for all the loss and suffering which her act of secession had caused, and from those who wished to give the Negro immediately all the rights of an American citizen. The Radical view of reconstruction, of rebuilding the South, was utterly different from that of Lincoln. And in nothing did it differ more than over the freed slave. Lincoln wished sincerely to educate and fit the freedmen to take their place alongside other American citizens. The Radicals wanted to give the freedmen the vote in order that they might vote Republican in elections. To Lincoln the Negro was a human being: to most of the Radicals he was just a possible Republican voter.

Lincoln was dead. His successor in office was the Vice-President, Andrew Johnson of Tennessee. Johnson was born a poor white, and had made his way in the world purely by his own intelligence and strength of will: he had at one time been a village tailor, and his wife had taught him to write. He had been put forward as candidate for the Vice-Presidency because he came from a southern state and had been a Democrat, and was therefore likely to win support among those who opposed the Republican Party. To him the Civil War was a war for the defeat of the southern planter aristocracy which had always kept the poor whites down. At its end he was very bitter against Davis and other Confederate leaders. But he had no particular enthusiasm for the Negro: he had owned slaves, and did not wish to see blacks and whites as equals. When the murder of Lincoln brought him to power, he tried to carry on Lincoln's moderate policy towards the South. In doing so, he came into violent collison with the Radicals. He lacked Lincoln's skill in overcoming opposition, and he was a rash speaker. Moreover, as a Republican who had once been a Democrat, he could not win full support from either party.

The Republican party had a clear majority in Congress and in 1866 the Radical wing quickly got control. The Radicals used Congress as a means of thwarting Johnson's policy, and of carrying through their own plan of reconstruction. Their leaders in Congress were remarkable men. The two most notable of them were Thaddeus Stevens and Charles Sumner. Stevens, aged seventy-four, sarcastic, sincere in his belief in Negro suffrage yet vitriolic in his hatred of the South, was a subtle politician. Sumner was a fanatical enthusiast for the equality of blacks and whites, an eloquent speaker whose words often seemed deliberately chosen to wound.[1] Stevens hated the southern whites, Sumner was determined to make Negroes and whites equal. Between them they got Congress to reject Johnson's plans for reconstruction, and to accept Stevens's plan. This plan finally destroyed the power of the southern planters: put the South under military rule: and gave the vote to the Negroes.

Lincoln had begun to reconstruct in the middle of the war. In 1863 he issued a plan for those areas which had already been recaptured: it was to apply to other areas recovered later. When one-tenth of the number of those who voted in 1860 in any given area had taken an oath of allegiance to the Union, that area was allowed to set up a civil government. Stevens and other Congressional leaders were violently hostile to this '10 per cent.' plan. Parts of Arkansas and Tennessee accepted; but Congress refused to admit their representatives. In May, 1865—while Congress was not in session—Johnson began his scheme of reconstruction. He issued a general amnesty, pardoning all who had taken part in the rebellion except its chief leaders and any former Congressmen and officers in the U.S. armed forces. Then all the other citizens of the southern states, provided they were loyal to the Union, were allowed to elect their own governments and their own representatives in Congress. All the southern states did this. And all except Mississippi ratified the Thirteenth Amendment to the Constitution, abolishing slavery. Thus by the end of 1865 every southern state had its own government, and reconstruction had begun.

But the real struggle had not begun. Congress met in December, and Stevens took command. Congress refused to admit the members from the southern states, and set up a Joint Committee on Reconstruction which was to draw up Congress' own plan of reconstruction. The real battle with Johnson began in the next year (1866). Congress passed a Civil Rights Act, giving equal rights to all citizens whatever their colour: Johnson vetoed it, but Congress passed it over his veto. In April the Committee on Reconstruction brought in the Fourteenth Amendment. This amendment was the heart of the Radical plan to dominate the South. It struck at the

---

[1] Sumner once called Johnson 'an insolent, drunken brute in comparison with whom Caligula's horse was respectable.' Caligula was a mad Roman Emperor who had his horse admitted as a member of the Senate. Johnson was never able to live down the unfair charge that he had been drunk when he was inaugurated as Vice-President; in fact he had just recovered from typhoid fever, and the single drink he took to steady his nerves was too much for him.

'Black Codes' by saying that any state, which for any reason denied the right to vote to any of its citizens, would, in proportion, lose a number of representatives in Congress: and it shut out from Congress and civil and military office all leaders in the rebellion. But its most important clause was the first, which said that all persons born or naturalised in the U.S.A. were citizens and that no state should make laws limiting the 'privileges or immunities' of citizens. It went on 'nor shall any state deprive any person of life, liberty, or property, without due process of law; nor deny to any person within its jurisdiction the equal protection of the laws.' The immediate aims of this Amendment were to shut out the southern leaders from power and to protect the Negro. It was rejected by all the southern states, who regarded it as humiliating. Savage anti-Negro riots that summer in Memphis and New Orleans convinced many northerners of the need for drastic action in the South. In the autumn of 1866 the biennial Congressional elections were fought over a straight issue—Johnson's plan of reconstruction versus Congressional reconstruction. Johnson helped his opponents to victory by going on tour of the country and making a series of irresponsible and undignified speeches, shouting to crowds 'Hang Thad Stevens!' Thus the Radicals won the election, and Congress met with two objectives before it—to destroy the governments of the southern states, and to break Johnson.

It attained its first objective by passing a law (the First Reconstruction Act) replacing the existing governments of the southern states by military governors, backed by an army of occupation of 20,000 men. The military governors set about forming new lists of electors, which included Negroes: the new governments elected by these were allowed to continue if they would ratify the Fourteenth Amendment. By 1868 all but three of the former Confederate states had done so: by 1870 the remaining three, Mississippi, Texas, and Virginia, had ratified. Thus military rule, which had lasted three years at the most, disappeared by 1870.

Meanwhile Stevens and the Radicals were trying to get rid of Johnson. They planned to do so by impeachment:[1] if this had succeeded, Ben Wade, the Radical who was President of the Senate, would automatically have become President, and the whole power of the U.S.A. would have been in their hands. They began by passing a Tenure of Office Act, which stopped the President from dismissing his own ministers without the Senate's permission. It was doubtful whether Congress had any right under the Constitution to pass such an act. Johnson proceeded to defy it by ordering the dismissal of Stanton, his Secretary of War, who revealed Cabinet secrets to the Radicals. Stanton refused to go, and the Radicals impeached

[1] The Constitution provides a process of impeachment: by it, high officers of state who are charged with serious offences against the state may be accused before the Senate. It says: 'The Senate shall have the sole power to try all impeachments . . . and no person shall be convicted without the concurrence of two-thirds of the members present.'

Johnson. The impeachment was very nearly successful. In May 1868, thirty-five members of the Senate voted for impeachment and nineteen against. Seven of the latter were Republicans who had not lost their sense of honesty and fairness. This was one short of the necessary two-thirds majority. Thaddeus Stevens died in August, a disappointed man.

In the election of 1868 General Ulysses S. Grant, the Republican candidate, was victorious, thanks probably to Negro votes. Johnson had been a most unfortunate President; only in foreign affairs, where Seward remained as Secretary of State, was he successful. Here the outstanding achievement of the administration was the purchase in 1867 of Alaska from Russia. Alaska cost the U.S.A. $7,200,000. Seward too was responsible for annexing the Midway Islands, which lie to the west of Hawaii— the first step towards the overseas empire of the U.S.A.; for concluding a treaty of friendship with China; and for intimating to Napoleon III of France that he should give up his designs on Mexico.

3. BLACK RECONSTRUCTION, 1868–77

'Black Reconstruction' is the name given to the brief period when Radical Republican governments were in power in the former Confederate states. It lasted, with considerable variations in the several states, from 1868 to 1877. The name is somewhat misleading. In no state did the Negroes control the government; only in one, South Carolina, did they have a majority in the elected legislature, and there only for a short time; relatively few Negroes held important posts. The new governments rested upon the support of those ex-slaves, most of them illiterate, who had been given the vote, and upon two groups of whites whom hostile white southerners nicknamed 'carpet-baggers' and 'scalawags.' The carpet-baggers were from the North, allegedly doubtful characters who descended upon the South to get what pickings they could from its carcase; in fact, they were men who had come for various reasons—ex-soldiers from the Union army who had liked the South they had seen in the war, teachers with a mission to educate the coloured people, Federal officials, business men both honest and dishonest, as well as mere adventurers. Scalawags were condemned as disloyal; yet they too were a mixed bag—independent farmers who had never liked planters or the Confederacy, poor whites, business men and merchants who wanted to co-operate with the North to restore law and order, as well as self-seekers. From the start there was much opposition from former Confederates, who wanted to get rid of the new governments as soon as possible. These were expensive, for the South had to be rebuilt in a period of inflation, when prices were rising. As well as high taxation, there was a good deal of graft and corruption. In South Carolina, the extreme example, the members of the legislature dined and wined at state expense in a special restaurant, voted themselves costly furnishings and delicate foods, and compensated the Speaker for

$1000 he had lost on a horse race, while a governor of Louisiana collected $500,000 during four years in office. Corruption was encouraged in nearly all the reconstructed states by the fierce competition between rival railroad companies for grants of land and money. But this was an age of graft in the U.S.A.; whites as well as blacks, ex-Confederates as well as Republicans, took part; and things were even worse at this time in the North under Grant's presidency.[1] On the other side of the picture, the new governments did notable constructive work, not merely in re-equipping their states with roads and bridges, railroads and public buildings, but also in providing the South for the first time with a system of free public schools. Moreover, it was to the credit of Black Reconstruction that its governments passed no vindictive laws against the former slave-owners.

But they did not last long. The opposition, standing for white supremacy and organised once more in the Democratic party, regained control in eight states by 1875; only Florida, South Carolina, and Louisiana remained in Republican hands after that date. There were various reasons for this. On one side the better carpet-baggers returned North, disgusted with the electoral frauds perpetrated by the Republicans, who used illiterate Negroes as pawns to maintain their party supremacy; on the other, many Democrats dismissed from their jobs Negroes who took part in politics. Violence, with the intimidation of Negroes, Republican politicians, and Federal officials, played an important part. The most celebrated manifestation of violence was the Ku Klux Klan, originally the outcome of a frolic in 1865 by a circle (kuklos) of young men in Tennessee who dressed in white sheets and hoods for a party, and enjoyed themselves in scaring Negroes. Organised over several states under the command of a Grand Wizard in 1867, with prominent white southerners among its leaders, the Klan rode by night through Negro camps, beat up scalawags and carpet-baggers, whipped and hanged Negroes, and frightened coloured voters away from the polls. Its influence has been exaggerated; Congress passed a series of laws against it, and Federal troops and courts virtually extinguished it by 1871. But its members turned to other devices of the same kind, like the bands of red-shirted rifle companies who effectively took over Mississippi in 1875 and secured a Democratic victory at the elections.

Yet the main reason for the collapse of Black Reconstruction was a change of feeling in the North. Here wartime bitterness was dying away by the 1870's; most of the old Radical leaders had disappeared from the political scene; many Republicans disliked what was being done in their name in the South; the Democratic party was recovering fast; the Supreme Court was showing itself critical of Reconstruction laws; above all, business men wanted reconciliation so that they could the more securely invest their capital in the South and exploit its re-development. The post-war

[1] See below, pp. 131–2.

military occupation of the South did not last long; in the 1870's, once the new governments had been organised, there were relatively few Federal troops left. By the middle of the 1870's there were many signs, in the North as well as in the South, that the days of Reconstruction were almost over.

4. THE GRANT ADMINISTRATION, 1869–77

Ulysses S. Grant had been a successful General in the Civil War, but he proved a highly unsuccessful President. He had taken little interest in politics before his election, and it was said that he had only voted in one presidential election. He had little understanding of the political problems of the day: he was a hopeless judge of men: and, if not corrupt, he was blind to a great deal of what went on around him. He was the nominee of the Republican party 'bosses,' who meant to do well out of Grant's presidency. The Republicans who wanted to keep power for themselves were hand in glove with the financiers and capitalists who were determined to make all they could out of the vast expansion of trade, transport and industry that was taking place in these years (see Chap. 16). The result of this unholy alliance was an orgy of fortune-hunting and corruption, and much of the political history of Grant's terms of office is the story of unsavoury scandals.

Grant himself was not dishonest. But he was only too easily influenced by gifts which he was simple enough to regard as mere marks of esteem for himself. And his great virtue, that of loyalty to those whom he regarded as his friends, led him into very difficult corners, because he was quite unable to judge men's honesty. He was remotely involved in the notorious Gold Corner of 1869, when the financiers Jay Gould and Jim Fisk juggled with the market in gold in order to make a prodigious fortune for themselves. Perhaps worse for the reputation of his administration was the Crédit Mobilier affair. The Crédit Mobilier was a company formed (before Grant took office) by the directors of the Union Pacific Railroad, to construct their permanent way. They then gave themselves huge contracts, paying themselves out of money borrowed from the government. Thus the Union Pacific Railroad Company itself was nearly bankrupt; but the Crédit Mobilier is said to have netted a profit of about $23,000,000. This scheme meant a good deal of bribery of Congressmen and others connected with the government. When it was investigated in 1872, Colfax, the Vice-President, was found to be deeply implicated.

Such scandals as these shook Grant's administration, but did not shake him out of office. An opposition group calling itself the Liberal Republican Party, led by Republicans disgusted with the corruption, put forward Horace Greeley as candidate in 1872. Grant, strongly backed by financiers and big business, won the election: men still thought of him as the symbol of Union victory in the Civil War. So the bribery and scandals went on.

The most bare-faced action of the whole period came in 1873, when Congress, led by a Republican majority, voted to its own members and the President an increase in salary, and made the increase date from two years earlier. This 'Salary Grab' or 'Back Pay Grab,' as it was called, was too much: and public opinion compelled Congress to repeal it later in 1873. But all manner of financial scandals went on, and in many of them Congressmen or government officials were involved. Democrats as well as Republicans dabbled in these crooked deals. 'Boss' Tweed, the head of the notorious Tweed Ring in New York, and his associates stole nearly $100,000,000 from the city before he fled to Europe. The South, already suffering Black Reconstruction, had also to bear the exploits of northern financiers and company promoters, who bribed Republican politicians to get contracts and special privileges. She suffered less than the North, because she offered less prospect of profit. It is a sordid story, and it shows the lowering of standards of honesty that came in the years after the Civil War. There were honest politicians about, and these were mainly responsible for forcing enquiries. They often lost office through their honesty: this happened to Benjamin Bristow, Secretary of the Treasury, who exposed the Whisky Ring. This notorious episode of 1874 was the affair which came closest to Grant. The Whisky Ring was a group of distillers who had robbed the revenue of many millions of dollars by non-payment of taxes on whisky. A Congressional investigation, started in 1874 after the Democrats had gained a majority in the Congressional elections of that year, found a trail leading to Grant's private secretary, Babcock. Grant publicly declared Babcock to be innocent, and the investigation was dropped: but it was noticeable that Grant dismissed Babcock from his post. In 1876 Belknap, the Secretary of War, was found to be selling trading privileges on the Indian reservations. This catalogue of crooked deals was not Grant's fault. But his weakness and his utter inability to grasp the responsibilities of his office contributed gravely to the mess.

In foreign affairs alone was his administration successful. His Secretary of State was Hamilton Fish, a tactful and level-headed statesman who steered the U.S.A. through several difficulties. He adroitly prevented American intervention in Cuba when the people of that island broke into rebellion against Spain in 1868. In his dealings with Britain he smoothed over the difficulties which arose because the Irish Nationalist societies, the Fenians (there were two of them, each claiming to be the only true Irish Republic), had launched attacks upon Canada from United States soil. Grant himself intervened in foreign affairs by sending Babcock to Santo Domingo, where he made an agreement with the man who happened to be dictator at the time by which its territory was handed over to the U.S.A. The Senate rejected the treaty. Foreign affairs were better left to Fish, whose greatest achievement came in 1871. The Union and Britain had been haggling for some years over American claims for the losses caused during the Civil War by the *Alabama* and other Confederate privateers launched from Britain. In 1871 Fish made with Britain the Treaty of Washington, whereby both nations agreed to submit the whole case to an impartial tribunal at Geneva for arbitration. The tribunal's decision, published in 1872, awarded the U.S.A. $15,000,000, a handsome recompense for the damage to property caused by the Confederate privateers. Gladstone, the British Prime Minister, accepted the decision without hesitation. The *Alabama* settlement was a great triumph for the principle of settling international disputes by impartial agreement rather than by war. Unfortunately it has been almost the only great practical triumph of the principle.

5. THE ELECTION OF 1876 AND THE END OF RECONSTRUCTION

The presidential election of 1876 was perhaps the most remarkable, and certainly one of the most important, in American history. The Democrats, whose strength had grown steadily during the 1870's, nominated Samuel J. Tilden of New York; the Republicans chose Rutherford B. Hayes of Ohio. When the votes were counted an extraordinary situation appeared. Tilden got about 250,000 more popular votes than Hayes. In the electoral vote by states, it was necessary to score 185 in order to win. Tilden got 184, Hayes 165; 20 electoral votes were disputed, 1 of them in Oregon and the other 19 in the southern states of Florida, South Carolina, and Louisiana—the three southern states where there were still Republican 'Reconstruction' governments. There was no clear method prescribed in the Constitution for solving such a problem and nearly three months' wrangle among the politicians followed, while men began to fear the possible recurrence of civil war. Eventually, late in January, 1877, a special electoral commission was established to settle the question. This commission awarded all the disputed votes to Hayes, who was peacefully inaugurated as president in March. Behind this decision lay a series of informal bargains between Republicans and Democrats, the so-called 'Compromise of 1877.' Northern business men, strongly represented in the Republican party, wanted peace; southern Democrats wanted northern investments in the South; and they joined together to overrule the northern Democrats, who wanted the presidency for their party. So Hayes became President; and the remaining Federal troops were withdrawn from the South. Reconstruction was over. The nation was at peace. The Democrats, the party of white supremacy, became masters of the south; the Negro, abandoned by the Republicans, was left to their mercies. In effect, the North accepted the southern view of the inferiority of the coloured man.

16   The Rise of Big Business

1. THE END OF THE FRONTIER

During most of the period 1877–97 the history of the United States was being made in places very different from the White House and the Capitol at Washington. It was being made on the quay-sides where the immigrants landed; in the valleys of the Rockies where the railwaymen were linking Atlantic and Pacific; on the cattle-ranches and wheatlands of the Great Plains, in the silver mines of Nevada and the copper mines of Montana; in the stockyards of Chicago and the steel foundries of Pittsburgh; in the bankers' headquarters in Wall Street, and the offices of the great business men like Andrew Carnegie. These years were the greatest age of American expansion, when the people of the U.S.A. made their land the greatest agricultural and the greatest industrial nation on earth. No country had ever seen such material progress on so great a scale in so short a time, as the U.S.A. made then.

The population, 31,000,000 in 1860, had soared to nearly 76,000,000 by 1900. In those forty years 14,000,000 immigrants had arrived, over 5,000,000 of them between 1880 and 1890. Within the United States the ceaseless move to the West had continued. Between 1861 and 1900 eleven new western states were admitted. Those admitted in the 'sixties and 'seventies included the farming states of Kansas and Nebraska, and the mining states of Nevada (admitted in 1864 in order to provide extra votes for Lincoln in the election of that year) and Colorado. Then Montana, North and South Dakota, and Washington were admitted by the Omnibus Act of 1889; Idaho and Wyoming in 1890; and Utah, which had only in 1890 agreed to forbid polygamy, in 1896. Historians have called this process of filling up the remaining large empty spaces 'the end of the frontier.' In the sense that there was no longer any great part of the U.S.A. in which men had not settled, this phrase is true. But it does not mean that there was no longer any free land available. For many years after 1890 there was room for settlers in the West.

The call of the West was as strong as ever. It was at bottom still the call of unbroken land, the urge to move west, to conquer both nature and the Indians, and to find a new way of life. The Homestead Act of 1862 encouraged the westward flood. It gave 160 acres of land to anyone willing to cultivate them; at first the offer was only open to northern citizens, but the damage which the Civil War caused in the South encouraged many southerners, after 1865, to try their luck in the new lands. Many demobilised men from both armies were among the post-war frontiersmen.[1]

[1] But only about one-eighth of the available public land before 1900 went to genuine homesteaders; speculators and the railroads between them got most of it.

These men faced a new kind of frontier, and they conquered it by new methods. Timber had been a mainstay of the earlier pioneers. They had hewn down forests, and converted the felled trees into logs to build their cabins and into stakes to fence their clearings. The pioneers of the 'sixties and 'seventies had to conquer one of the world's great treeless areas— the vast Great Plains, extending from the Mississippi Basin to the Rockies, thousands of square miles of open grassland. It would have been far too costly to transport across the Plains timber for fencing. American inventors, aided by the great development of American industry, overcame the difficulty. Barbed wire was the answer. It first appeared in 1874. One more stage was passed in the American conquest of the West. Other inventions enabled these pioneers to convert the northern part of the Great Plains into one of the great grain-producing regions of the world. In 1831 the first McCormick mechanical reaper appeared. Since then American factories had turned out an ever-increasing quantity of farm machinery—reapers, threshing machines, binders, rotary ploughs, combine harvesters. These machines made possible wheat and maize farming on a colossal scale over the broad level lands of the prairies. So it came about that in 1895 the U.S.A. grew three times as much of these two crops as in 1860. The area of wheat and maize growing gradually shifted west as ever more people came pressing in from the east. By the turn of the century the chief wheat lands were in the Dakotas; the main maize area included Illinois, Missouri and Iowa, Nebraska and Kansas.

Wheat and maize were by no means the only magnet pulling Americans west. These same years saw the golden age of the cowboy. The rolling grasslands of the Plains, where for centuries the Indians had hunted buffalo, were found to be ideal grazing ground for cattle. The area which became the state of Wyoming was the centre of the cattle lands. The animals were driven in great herds to winter on the higher western Plains; the railroads took them to the slaughterhouses of Chicago. The famous 'long drive,' northwards from Texas and the southern Plains, made the cowboy, with his sombrero, his lasso and his mustang, a great figure of American story and legend. The picture of the cowboy performing wonderful feats of horsemanship in controlling the mad rushes of thousands of horned cattle and facing the innumerable hardships of the 'long drive,' is true, not fanciful. But, like the Indian, the cowboy became a picturesque survival. The barbed wire which saved the other frontiersmen helped to destroy him by penning the cattle within ranches. The winters of 1885 and 1886 brought a terrible drought killing many thousand head of cattle. Since that day cattle ranching has come to stay, and the real cowboy has vanished.

There was a third and very different type of pioneer in these years— the miner. He, too, illustrates the unbelievably rapid opening-up of the vast natural resources of the U.S.A. The California Gold Rush of 1849 was the herald of later rushes. Ten years after it silver was found at the huge Comstock Lode in Nevada, and gold at Pike's Peak, Colorado. Later finds included more gold in Idaho, Montana, and Wyoming; more silver in Arizona, Idaho, Utah, and Colorado; copper in Arizona, Montana and Wyoming. Thus the Americans uncovered the mineral wealth of the whole length of the Rockies. The scenes of '49 were repeated, on a smaller and less fantastic scale, and against different backgrounds. These Rocky Mountain mining areas, high and containing much barren ground, have remained, despite later developments of farming and ranching, the least thickly populated parts of the United States. But their mines were one more summons to the West, and the response to it was one more sign of the vigour and vitality of American advance in these years.

The early pioneers of the West had gone to the frontier on wagon, horseback, or foot. The later ones went as far as they could by railroad. It would be too much to say that without the railroad none of this advance would have been possible; but it is certainly true to say that the railroad made possible so rapid and so vast an advance. The railroad linked Atlantic and Pacific (the first transcontinental line, the Union Pacific, was completed in 1869, and there were three more by 1884); brought the farmer his machinery and took his grain to markets in the cities of the East; took live cattle to the new city of Chicago and frozen meat (the first refrigerator car was on the rails in 1875) to the older cities of New York and Philadelphia; brought the miner the new engineering machinery without which he could not work, and bore away the precious metals eastwards. And above all the railroads took immigrants westward. The transcontinental lines advertised in Europe for immigrants, to develop the country through which they ran. The railroads themselves developed prodigiously, in size of engines, variety of rolling stock, number of safety devices,[1] and above all in length of track. The railroad mileage of the U.S.A. was 30,000 in 1860; in 1900 it was 192,000. In 1890 Great Britain had about 20,000 miles of railway.

No one can measure the effect of the railroads in American history. Unquestionably the size of the U.S.A. made them in some ways more important than they have been in British history. In these years they brought the frontier to an end, carrying hundreds of thousand of passengers to the western states. They created cities like Omaha and Seattle where a generation before there were empty spaces or tiny villages. But they were not an unmixed blessing. Their very importance made them a danger. Control of the railroads fell into the hands of a very small number of men —men who saw the railroads not as an essential public service, but as a source of private profit. Typical of such men was the unscrupulous 'Commodore' Vanderbilt, the ruler of the New York Central Railroad. When someone told him that the state of New York had passed a law which his railroad was required to obey, he exclaimed 'Can't I do what I like with my own? What do I care about the law? Hain't I got the power?' It

---

[1] The famous Westinghouse Brake was invented in 1869.

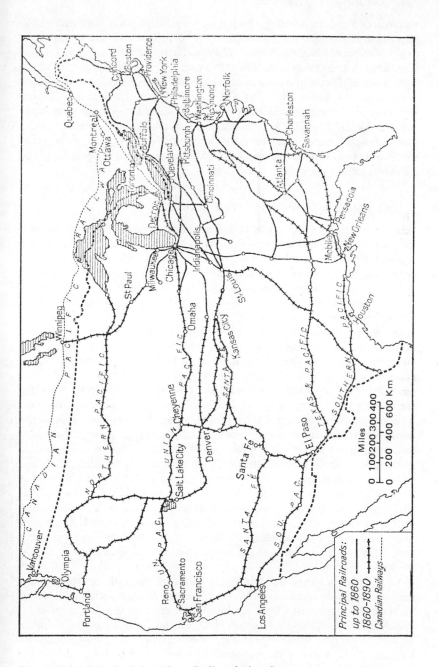

Some of the Principal American Railroads in 1890

was men of Vanderbilt's kind who put up freight charges so high that whole farming communities were ruined, and who bribed politicians wholesale to get laws passed in their favour. They had little cause to complain of the way the U.S.A. treated them, for in the years 1851–71 the western railroads were given extensive grants of lands alongside their tracks, as well as huge loans from the states. By 1871 the railroads were the nation's largest landowners. The return which they made was sometimes sheer swindling, like the Crédit Mobilier scheme; almost invariably they tried to make every cent they could, no matter who suffered. This was part of the price the U.S.A. paid for the opening of the West, and the development of her immense natural resources.

2. THE FARMERS AND THEIR TROUBLES

In the last thirty years of the 19th century more new land was put under cultivation in the United States than in the entire history of the American people from the first settlement at Jamestown up to 1870. During the same period the output of all the main staple crops, such as wheat, cotton and maize, increased two- or threefold. Millions of settlers poured westward into Kansas and Nebraska, the Dakotas, Wyoming and Montana. Agriculture still remained the principal occupation of the United States, in number of people employed, until after the end of the 19th century; even if the proportion of Americans engaged in farming was falling steadily, the total numbers of the farm population increased. And there were many notable improvements, of various kinds, affecting agriculture, as well as the two which have already been mentioned, the development of farm machinery and the advance of the railroad. These included the beginnings of large-scale irrigation, in Mormon Utah and the Gadsden Purchase area of the South-West; the invention of canning and packing processes; the introduction of grain elevators; improvements in the technique of large-scale flour-milling; the establishment of a Federal Department of Agriculture; and the advancement of scientific agriculture. The last was made possible by two acts of Congress: the Morrill Land-Grant College Act (1862) which provided for the allocation of public land in each state for the setting-up of agricultural and industrial colleges, and the Hatch Act (1887), under which agricultural research stations could be established in every state of the Union. The long-term importance of these two laws was immense.

Yet, despite all this, the last thirty years of the 19th century were a period of chronic discontent among American farmers, with widespread movements of protest. Behind the discontent lay the harsh physical conditions of the farmer's life, especially on the Great Plains—the frozen cold of winter and the savage droughts of summer, the plagues of grasshoppers, the erosion of treeless soil, the dust-storms, above all perhaps the terrible loneliness, in days without automobile, radio and telephone, a loneliness felt most by the farmer's womenfolk and at times of illness or childbirth. But the basic cause of the discontent was economic. For most of these years the price the farmer got for his produce was falling, and the more he grew the worse things seemed to get. Wheat prices, which averaged 106.7 cents a bushel over the years 1870–3 were down to 74.8 in 1886–9 and 63.3 in 1894–7; maize and cotton fell in the same way. The trouble was that American farmers were producing more than American cities could consume, and therefore were competing in a world market with Russian, Canadian, Argentine and Australian farmers. They got the low prices the world was prepared to pay, and no more—and these prices were not enough to meet their costs. Though conditions improved temporarily in the early twentieth century, this 'farm problem,' of rising production and low and falling prices, became a lasting one, as the farmers of the 1920's were to realise; no effective attempt was made to solve it until Franklin Roosevelt's New Deal of the 1930's.[1]

There were other sources of trouble, nearer at hand, which the farmer could understand and blame more easily. The railroads—whose advertising had tempted many an American to 'go west'—were in his eyes the principal villains of the piece. They charged excessive rates for carrying his produce east, and often also controlled the warehouse charges he had to pay for storing it. The railroads were particularly hated because they charged very low rates to favoured industrial companies in the East, and compensated themselves by asking rates several times as high from western farmers. Grain elevator owners demanded exorbitant fees. Moreover, big industrial firms set the prices the farmer paid for his machinery, his fertilisers, his barbed wire, even his wretched furniture. Bankers and loan companies charged extortionate interest rates—up to 15 or 20 per cent.— on the loans they had made him to enable him to buy and set up his farm. The West became a land of mortgages, on farms, cattle, and crops. One authority has calculated that by the late 1880's, in the five farming states of Kansas, Nebraska, North and South Dakota and Minnesota, there was at least one mortgage for every family. Twenty-seven per cent. of all American farms worked by their owners were mortgaged in 1890, and the proportion was rising; behind this figure there lay over the years countless forced sales and bankruptcies. In view of such economic conditions it was not surprising that wheat and maize growers sometimes found it paid better to burn their crops to keep their houses warm.

But they responded in other ways also to their desperate economic plight. From the late 1860's onwards a series of farmers' movements, aiming at getting states and, later, the nation, to pass laws dealing with their grievances, spread through the farm belt from the Dakotas and Minnesota to the South. These included the Patrons of Husbandry, better known as the Grange, strongest in Illinois, Iowa, Wisconsin and Minnesota in the years after the serious commercial panic of 1873, which got these states

[1] See below, pp. 182 and 204–5.

to pass laws regulating railroad rates, and also attempted unsuccessfully to create co-operative organisations in order to reduce the farmer's costs; the Greenback Party of the 1870's, an eastern movement which wanted the Federal government to continue 'greenbacks' (the paper currency issued during the Civil War) in circulation and which appealed to debtor farmers; and the Farmers' Alliances of the South-West and North-West in the 1880's, whose demands included currency reform and government ownership of railroads. These movements had abundant sincerity and won short-lived victories, getting control of some state legislatures and electing a few members to Congress. But they failed ultimately for a variety of reasons. They won no lasting backing from the major national political parties, they met very tough opposition from the railroads, the several farming areas had different economic interests, and they allowed themselves to get sidetracked into reliance upon currency reform, with its demands first for paper money and then for the free and unlimited coinage of silver. Out of them, as we shall see,[1] arose in 1892 a new and short-lived national political party, the Populists.

3. THE GROWTH OF INDUSTRY

The rapid and extensive growth of railroads could only come about through a parallel growth of the heavy industries—coal-mining, steelworks, engineering. In these industries in particular, and in industry in general, the U.S.A. made gigantic progress in these years. Two sets of figures will tell the tale shortly. Between 1859 and 1899 the total value of American manufactured goods increased sevenfold. In 1860 Great Britain was making one and a half times as many manufactured goods as the U.S.A.; by the end of the century the U.S.A. was making over twice as many as Great Britain. Thus, in the last forty years of the 19th century there was an enormous expansion of industry in the U.S.A., which became the world's leading industrial nation.

Many factors combined to make this advance possible. The U.S.A. had great supplies of raw materials. The swift rise of her population created a huge and ever-expanding market. This market, offering the possibility of great profits, encouraged the discovery of coal, iron, and oil, the building of factories, and the invention of mechanical devices. In these years vast new resources were exploited. They included the iron-fields round Lake Superior; coal-fields in Illinois and Ohio, and in Alabama; and oil-wells in California. Industry was no longer confined to the old cities of the East. It was beginning to move to the Middle West, to the five great states of Ohio, Indiana, Illinois, Michigan, and Wisconsin. There great new industrial cities arose—Cincinnati and Indianapolis, Cleveland and Milwaukee, and above all Chicago. Yet the East still remained supreme. Pennsylvania, where oil was first struck in 1859, developed especially

[1] See below, p. 148.

rapidly; Pittsburgh, with its huge steelworks, was the central city of her growth. New York remained the financial metropolis of the country: the wealth some of her citizens controlled rose to astronomical figures.

In these years there were thousands of new inventions, ranging from the typewriter to the telephone and from the refrigerated rail car to the cash register. Thomas A. Edison (1847–1931) has some claim to be considered the greatest single benefactor of mankind whom the U.S.A. has produced. Among everyday features of modern life which he invented or helped to develop are the dynamo, the incandescent lamp, the moving picture and the electric train. Along with inventions came advance in the technique of mass production and the use of standardised parts, both of them best illustrated by the motor-car industry which grew up right at the end of this period. Mass production meant specialised labour: it meant that each man was to work at the same comparatively simple job all day and every day, instead of doing a variety of different jobs. The labour which was organised in this way consisted partly of immigrants, newcomers from Europe who were satisfied with lower wages than native Americans.

No single factor was as important in the growth of American industry as the development of the 'trusts.' A number of steelworks or textile factories competing against one another to sell their goods had to reduce their prices in the effort to defeat one another. Manufacturers soon realised that if they combined with one another they would not only save money in various ways, but they would also be able to sell their goods to the public at higher prices, often at whatever prices they chose. Thus were born the great corporations, or trusts, as they are called. They were huge alliances of firms in the same industry or trade. Good examples of them were the railroad combines, controlling 15,000 or more miles each. Other prominent trusts were the Standard Oil Company and the United States Steel Corporation, which towered far above all rivals in these industries. Such trusts gradually came to dominate American industry towards the end of the 19th century.

Through them a handful of men gained vast power and wealth. These men—the best-known names include those of John Pierpoint Morgan the banker, John D. Rockefeller of Standard Oil, P. D. Armour the meat king, and E. H. Harriman of Union and Southern Pacific Railroads—were the real rulers of the U.S.A. in these years. A giant, even among them, was Andrew Carnegie, a poor lad from Dunfermline in Scotland who emigrated to America in 1848. He made himself the steel 'king' of the U.S.A., creating a vast steelworks at Pittsburgh. He bought up other steel-works; he bought coal-mines, iron-mines, and a fleet of ships to carry his iron ore through the Lakes; he imported immigrants in order to avoid paying high wages. When he retired in 1901, having sold out his works, he was said to have a fortune of $350,000,000. Vigorous, enterprising, unscrupulous, wholly self-made, Carnegie exercised great control over the life of the American people. Between 1901 and his death in 1919 he gave huge sums to various educational and philanthropic endowments in the United States, England and Scotland.

Trusts did much to develop the industrial resources of the U.S.A. But they also did great harm to American life. Their methods in pursuit of money were utterly ruthless. They struck at all competitors and smashed small firms with every weapon at their command. They deliberately cut their prices so as to undersell their rivals and force them out of the market; bribed railroads to give them preferential freight rates; used police armed with tear-gas bombs and troops armed with rifles to break strikes; and bribed politicians, congressmen, senators, and government officials to attain their ends. It soon became clear to Americans that the land of the free was in fact in the hands of a small group of wealthy men, and gradually public opinion began to turn against the trusts. Laws were passed against them, in some of the states and in Congress. The most notable of the acts of Congress was the Sherman Anti-Trust Act of 1890, which forbade the formation of 'combinations or conspiracies in restraint of trade.' Its aim was to stop the growth of trusts and to break down those already formed.

It was one thing to pass laws; it was quite another to get them to work. The opponents of trusts came up against two strong forces. The first was the old American belief in private enterprise, the belief that a man ought to make his own way in the world and that the less government regulation there was the better for everyone. The second was the Supreme Court and its interpretation of the Constitution. In this connection the 14th Amendment, introduced during the Reconstruction period, was highly important. That Amendment had said that no state was to 'deprive any person of life, liberty, or property without due process of law; nor deny to any person born within its jurisdiction the equal protection of the laws.' Now legally a company or trust is a person. It can buy and sell goods, sue people in court for fraud, inherit fortunes, and in other important ways behave as though it were a living person; and it is in one important way better off than ordinary persons—it never dies. Thus it was argued that the 14th Amendment protected the trusts against state laws, and the Supreme Court agreed with this view. Consequently any laws passed by states against the trusts were nullified by decisions of the Supreme Court. And in 1895 the Supreme Court showed even more strongly its support for the trusts. In that year a case was brought under the Sherman Act against the great Sugar Trust which controlled about 98 per cent. of the American sugar-refining industry. The Supreme Court ruled that manufacturing or refining sugar was not commerce and that therefore the act did not apply. With the Supreme Court taking this line, there was little hope of achieving any real control of the trusts, and they continued on their way unhindered. No real attack was made again until the presidency of Theodore Roosevelt (see Chap. 18).

In general the government, instead of stopping the growth of the trusts, helped them on their way. The most notable of the methods by which they did so was that of tariffs. American manufacturers demanded tariffs to protect their infant industries against the long-established British ones. They feared that if British manufacturers were allowed to enter the U.S.A. they would undersell American products. This attitude, which had much to support it in earlier days, had less to recommend it when the U.S.A. had become the world's greatest industrial nation, and when American manufacturers could put on the market goods quite as cheap as those made in Britain. The tariff was scarcely needed as a barrier any longer. It simply served to keep up the prices of goods in America and to put a wholly unjustified profit into the pockets of the American manufacturers. Yet the tariff remained. There were a number of variations, at certain times and in certain goods, but there was no real reduction in the tariff. In 1888 Cleveland came out strongly in favour of lowering it: he was defeated in the presidential election of that year. In 1890 the Republicans brought in the McKinley Tariff, putting on imports a number of higher duties: and in 1897 the Dingley Tariff was higher still. In this way the great business magnates protected themselves against foreign competition, and used the laws to benefit themselves at the expense of the citizens of the U.S.A.

4. TRADE UNIONS

This period, which saw the astonishing growth of American industry, saw also the first effective development of American trade unionism. The rise of great towns brought many thousands of workmen together; while the manufacturers in their lust for profits reduced wages and increased hours of work, thus compelling the workmen to act together in self-defence. Before these years trade unions had led a very uneasy existence in the U.S.A., and had not been a very important influence in American life. In many ways the U.S.A. was unfavourable soil for them. The size of the country made any attempt at a nation-wide organisation difficult. The steady inflow of immigrants from Europe hindered the efforts of unions to raise wages, because the newcomers were ready to accept low wages, and thus helped to keep the wages of Americans down. But the most important reason why it did not grow was what may be called the mental climate of the U.S.A. Americans from the start of their history were individualists; they believed in the right of every man to make his own way in the world without interference. The Pilgrim Fathers had acted on that principle, and so had every pioneer who had shaken off the east and made for the frontier. The self-made man was an American hero. Consequently most Americans did not look with any enthusiasm on bodies like trade unions which drew up lists of rules and interfered with the right of the ordinary workman to bargain on his own with an employer. Still less were most Americans ready to support any movement for government interference with industry, or any proposals that the Federal or state governments should regulate wages or hours of labour. Thus trade unions in the U.S.A. had a hard struggle against public opinion as well as against the employers, and they had great difficulty in getting any laws made in their favour. Therefore they grew very slowly and suffered many setbacks.

The years 1870 to 1900 were a period of almost continuous conflict between masters and men in the U.S.A. It was clear that the workmen were not getting their fair share of the great increase in the national wealth. Again, every time a new labour-saving machine was introduced, it threw men out of work temporarily; and on the other hand, the new machines frequently produced far more goods than could be sold, and so workmen were lying idle until this over-production had been remedied. This last fact was one of the reasons for the terrible commercial panics of 1873 and 1893, with their long queues of unemployed men. The fierceness of the struggle is ample evidence of the bitterness felt by both sides. The great corporations fought the unions with the utmost violence. Their weapons included gangs of private police and detectives, lockouts, injunctions (orders obtained from the law-courts against the workmen), and, in the last resort, Federal or state troops. Their great wealth and their control of the government gave them the victory, in these years. But it was only gained after a long series of strikes, of which the first was the desperate railway strike of 1877, centred in Pennsylvania and nearby states. Some of them were almost local wars in their extent and in the damage which they did.

Two large American trade unions were formed between the end of the Civil War and 1900. The first of them began as a secret society of the tailors of Philadelphia, and called itself the Noble Order of the Knights of Labor. This organisation's aims were as lofty as its title sounded. Its object was to attract workmen of every kind (sellers of intoxicants, lawyers and bankers, however, were left out) and unite them in the pursuit of social reforms like the provision of education for the poor, the abolition of child labour, and the eight-hour day. In 1879 Terence V. Powderly became the Grand Master of the Knights. He was a conceited man but an admirable propagandist, who made endless speeches throughout the U.S.A., and gained more influence for the Knights. But the real increase in their strength came after a victory in another railroad strike in 1884, in which they forced Jay Gould, ruler of 16,000 miles of railroad, to come to terms. Their triumph was short. In 1886 there took place a widespread strike for the eight-hour day. In its course bombs were hurled into a crowd in the Haymarket, Chicago; public opinion turned against the Knights, even though they were not involved in the bomb-throwing, and they steadily lost influence from that time.

The second and greater union was formed in this same year 1886. This was the American Federation of Labour. Just as the U.S.A. itself is a federation of separate states, so the A.F. of L. was a federation of different craft unions. Its organiser was a young Jewish cigar-maker of New York named Samuel Gompers. Gompers believed that trade unions should

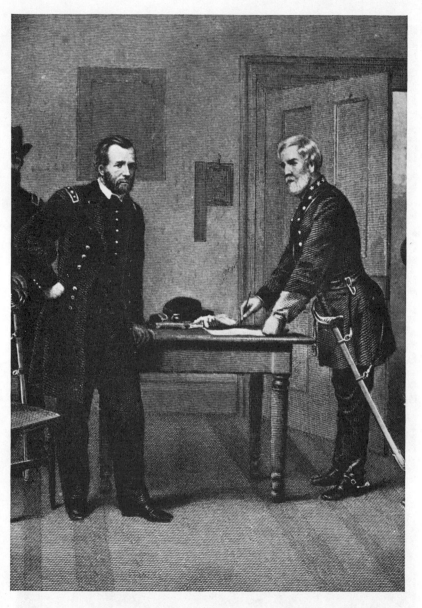

Lee surrenders to Grant at Appomattox Court House, April 9, 1865

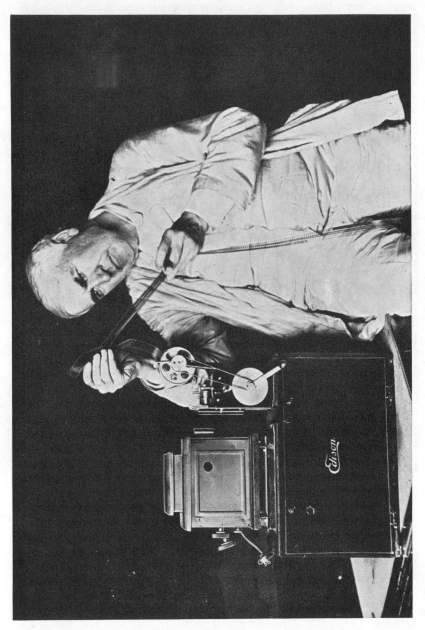

Thomas Alva Edison (1847-1931), the greatest of American inventors

concentrate solely on getting employers to grant shorter hours and higher wages. His unions were unions of skilled men; he believed in the strike as a weapon, but opposed any extremists who wanted to overturn the whole capitalist system. The A.F. of L. grew steadily, and by 1900 its membership was over half a million.

Two great strikes occurred in the 'nineties. In 1892 Henry C. Frick, the manager of Carnegie's works at Homestead, Pennsylvania, cut wages in order to destroy the Iron and Steel Workers' Union. The result was a strike, leading to a pitched battle between the workmen and Pinkerton detectives employed by Frick. Eventually Frick and Carnegie got 8000 state troops brought in, and broke the strike and the union. The Homestead affair did much to check the spread of trade unionism in the steel industry. Next year the crisis of 1893 broke upon America, and one of its results was the Pullman Strike of 1894. George Pullman, the manufacturer of Pullman cars, dismissed a number of his employees and cut the wages of the others by about twenty per cent. The Pullman workers went out on strike, and when Pullman refused to negotiate, the American Railway Union, a much larger body led by Eugene V. Debs, came out in support. Railroads in many parts of the country were idle. The railroad managers backed Pullman. They asked the government for troops, and Cleveland sent them into Chicago, even though the Governor of Illinois, John Altgeld, told him that there was no need to do so. The Federal government had come out on the side of the employers. The managers also got an injunction from the courts directed against Debs and the strikers, on the ground that they were a 'combination . . . or conspiracy, in restraint of trade,' and were therefore breaking the Sherman Anti-Trust Act. This was turning the Act inside out. After the coming of the troops there were riots and disturbances in Chicago; a good deal of property was burned and a number of people killed. Debs was arrested for defying the injunction, and sentenced to six months' imprisonment; and the strike broke down. It was a severe defeat for trade unions, and the weapon which achieved it, the Sherman Act, was used again later on for a similar purpose.

5. THE COMING OF 'JIM CROW'

The end of Reconstruction in 1877 left the Negro problem, in effect, to the rulers of the South, for there were still relatively few Negroes in the North; and nearly all southern whites had no doubt at all that, as one of them put it, 'the supremacy of the white race of the South must be maintained forever.' In economic matters this supremacy remained clear, uninterrupted by Civil War and Reconstruction. Most southern land stayed in white ownership; no serious attempt was made to divide it up amongst the former slaves. Most Negroes continued to work on the land, and it was largely their labour which brought about the recovery of the cotton fields, so that by 1900 the cotton crop of the South was twice what it had been in 1860. Instead of owning the land, they often worked it as sharecroppers, with the landlord providing land and implements and receiving half the crop in return; a system which prevented effective agricultural progress and kept the tenant chronically poor. Some coloured people went to work in the small textile mills which were arising in Georgia and the Carolinas; others got jobs in the tobacco industry of Virginia and North Carolina, already a giant enterprise within twenty-five years of the end of the Civil War; and others went to the coal and iron industry which grew up around Birmingham, Alabama, after about 1880. For intelligent younger Negroes the schools which began to be established during Reconstruction provided a road to professional and 'middle-class' employment; but only a very few were persistent and lucky enough to be able to take it.

Some politicians, southerners as well as northerners, for various reasons tried genuinely even after Reconstruction to treat the coloured man as politically the equal of the white, and in most parts of the South large numbers of Negroes voted in elections until about 1900. But by that time southern whites were successfully adopting several devices—compelling all voters to pay a poll-tax which most Negroes could not afford, or requiring them to own property, or imposing literacy tests on Negroes who could not read—to get round the Fifteenth Amendment (1870) which says that no citizen shall be denied the vote 'on account of race, color, or previous condition of servitude.' Moreover around 1900 southern states and cities passed many 'Jim Crow' laws which segregated—i.e. separated—the two races in an extraordinary range of public services. Blacks were forbidden to share with whites the use of street-cars, trains, lavatories, schools, deaf and dumb institutions, telephone booths, hospitals, cemeteries, waiting-rooms, exits from public buildings, parks, and many other facilities. Proprietors of hotels, circuses, soda-fountains and the like imposed similar restrictions; many white doctors attended only white patients. Segregated housing areas grew up in every southern city and town; and in them, as in all the public services, the provision for coloured people was far worse than that for whites. A series of decisions by the U.S. Supreme Court backed the laws against coloured people. In the case of *Plessy* v. *Ferguson* (1896) a majority of the judges maintained that it was legal to provide 'separate but equal' railway accommodation for white and coloured people. This opened the way to segregation in education and condemned generations of Negroes to inferior schools. And behind all this there lay the terrible shadow of lynching, the sudden outburst of mob savagery ending in the hanging of a Negro.

The Negro was thus firmly stamped as a lesser creature; so firmly that some of his own leaders at the end of the 19th century took the view that only after a long period of evolution, in which he won economic independence, would he be wise to challenge white supremacy. The most distinguished coloured man of the time, Booker T. Washington—who had been born in slavery and had in 1881 opened a Negro college at Tuskegee in Alabama—in a famous speech at Atlanta, Georgia (1895) accepted segregation and the inferior position of his people, saying 'The wisest among my race understand that the agitation of questions of social equality is the extremest folly.' But other coloured leaders, especially in the North, including W. E. B. DuBois, a gifted Massachusetts Negro, educated at Harvard and influenced by Marxism, sharply disagreed with this. In 1909, they and a group of white reformers formed the National Association for the Advancement of Colored People (N.A.A.C.P.) to agitate for political and civil rights for the Negro.

6. POLITICS, 1877–97

The story of American politics in this period is dull and sordid. Unquestionably the chief concern of most politicians was office-holding. There was no important election issue until 1896. Business interests dominated politics, and particularly the Republican party: Congressmen were looked upon not as the representatives of states, but as the representatives of great groups of business men. They spoke and voted for the oil or railroad or some other great business interest. Such groups of business men wielded immense power in their control of land, mines, oil-wells, railroads, factories, and newspapers; and they dominated the political parties. Consequently nearly all the Presidents of the time were colourless figures, men whom the 'machine politicians'[1] could control and who were unlikely to strike out on any independent course. Four of them—Rutherford B. Hayes (1877–81), James A. Garfield (1881), Chester A. Arthur (1881–5), and Benjamin Harrison (1889–93)—were Republicans. They were competent and experienced, but wholly undistinguished. The fifth, the only Democrat, was Grover Cleveland (1885–9, and 1893–7). Cleveland was a resolute man, abler than the other four, and courageous in following his own line; he was, too, rather more awake to the new problems set by the industrial expansion of the U.S.A.

The goal of the politicians was to hold office. The goal of the financiers and business magnates was to put into office men who would vote the right way. The combination of these facts led to bribery and corruption. Yet the nauseating scandals of Grant's time did not recur. Both Hayes and Arthur tackled a number of serious frauds and made an attempt to reform the civil service. Arthur's achievement was the more remarkable because he had been a notorious New York 'spoilsman'[2] himself. He came into

[1] The 'machine politicians' were those party leaders or 'bosses', who managed the party organisations—worked the party 'machines' at election times. Typical of them was Mark Hanna, a wealthy business man of Ohio, who got 'Bill' McKinley elected in 1896.

[2] 'Spoilsman' is the American term for the man who hunts an office or place for himself or for his friends in the Federal or state governments, as spoils of victory in an election.

office as President when in 1881 an unsuccessful office-hunter shot Garfield. Dishonest officials and others had been swindling the Federal Post Office out of money allotted to the main postal routes, the Star Routes, and Arthur's first success was to track them down. In 1883 the important Pendleton Civil Service Act was passed, throwing open to competitive examination about 12 per cent. of civil service appointments. It did something to save the President's time as well as to improve the civil service, and some, but not all, later Presidents used it in order to throw open more posts to competition. In 1884 the Republican party split over the question of corruption. In that year James G. Blaine was nominated as Republican candidate for the election. He was a great orator and a highly popular politician, but he was also thoroughly corrupt; he had once been Speaker of the House of Representatives and had used the office as a means of filling his own pocket. The reformers in the party, disgusted with corruption and unable to tolerate Blaine, joined the Democrats. Blaine's supporters called them 'Mugwumps,' but the Democratic candidate, Cleveland, won the election.

Silver became a major political issue in these years. This was in part the result of the rapid growth of silver production in Nevada and other western states. In 1860 only $156,800 worth of silver had been mined in the U.S.A.; the figure had risen to over $57,000,000 by 1890. The 1890's saw a great controversy, argued vehemently by citizens who knew nothing about the money question as well as by economists who thought they knew everything about it, over the standard on which American coinage should be based. The orthodox economists said that gold alone should be the standard; they were supported by most of the Republican party and by the business men of the east. The bimetallists maintained that both gold and silver should be standards; they were supported by the mining communities of the west, and by an increasing proportion of the Democratic party. This second group went on to demand that there should be free and unlimited coinage of silver. Silver-mine owners grew more emphatic about this as more and more silver came out of the mines, and as, in consequence, the price of silver fell. They won two victories in Congress. The first, the Bland-Allison Act (1878), made the government buy each month at least $2,000,000 worth of silver. The second, the Sherman Silver Purchase Act (1890), made the government buy each month 4,500,000 ounces of silver at the market price. Neither act achieved much in the long run.

But the silver question became far more than a monetary question. Silver, in the 'nineties, became the symbol of all those who opposed big business and the Republicans on any issue. A new party appeared at the presidential election of 1892—the People's Party, or Populists. It grew up out of the Farmers' Alliances, and for a short time swept parts of the West and South like a crusade, with its vigorous evangelists like Mary Elizabeth Lease who told farmers to 'raise less corn and more Hell,' the Kansas farmer 'Sockless Jerry' Simpson, and 'Pitchfork Ben' Tillman, leader of the poor whites of South Carolina. Its platform, or programme, suggested numerous reforms, including an eight-hour day, public ownership of railroads, the creation of post office savings banks and an income tax, as well as the free and unlimited coinage of silver. This platform was looked upon as revolutionary, and made little appeal to the East, but the Populist candidate polled over a million votes. The Democrat Cleveland won the election, defeating the Republican Harrison. Big business had dominated American politics since the end of the Civil War, and the Populists uttered the first challenge to that domination.

That challenge was repeated, more loudly and more dramatically, in 1896—this time by the Democratic party. Once more 'free silver' was a major issue; once more it was the emblem of the opposition to wealth. Cleveland grew unpopular for various reasons. The chief of these were the severe financial and industrial depression of 1893, and the remedies which he applied. The depression, the worst yet seen, broke over five hundred banks and sent millions into unemployment. Cleveland, making bold efforts to relieve the depression, took two steps which free silver men thought sheer treachery. In an attempt to safeguard the United States Treasury against a drain of money, he got Congress to repeal the Sherman Silver Purchase Act; and he sold government securities to Wall Street bankers—notably John P. Morgan—for gold. In 1894 his attitude towards the Pullman Strike convinced thousands of workers that he had gone over to the side of the financiers and the employers. The accumulated opposition to Cleveland split the Democratic party, and gave a chance to those advocates of free silver in the party who wanted to strike a blow for the poor against the rich. In 1895 the Supreme Court ruled that a federal income tax was unconstitutional; this increased the general discontent in the country, and strengthened those who wanted radical change. In the Democratic convention of 1896 the free silver men carried the nomination of William Jennings Bryan of Nebraska as Presidential candidate. Bryan was a brilliant orator of thirty-six, shallow in mind and narrow in outlook, yet sincerely devoted to the well-being of the poor and boundlessly energetic in campaigning for his cause. His final speech before the party convention was a tremendous challenge to the rich, culminating in his final words— 'You shall not press down upon the brow of labor this crown of thorns, you shall not crucify mankind upon a cross of gold!'

The election of 1896 is a landmark in American history. The Populists joined the Democrats in nominating Bryan. The Republicans put up William McKinley of Ohio. Big business spent about $3,000,000 on his campaign; it was an investment, for Bryan represented a threat to everything that big business stood for. The latter got his support from the free silver men, from those who had voted for the Populists in 1892, from the workmen who had lost their jobs in 1893, from the western farmers who still, as in Jackson's day, hated the financiers of the east. Bryan, without the vast wealth of the business men to back him, carried out an astonishing personal campaign, touring the country and making speech after speech in crowded halls. The Republicans were not scrupulous in their choice of weapons. They slandered him in the press; manufacturers threatened to sack their men if Bryan were elected. The Republican slogan was 'a full dinner-pail,' which they promised McKinley's election would bring. The American people chose McKinley, and the business men felt great relief. Free silver was an unfortunate issue, confusing the real question—the question whether the rich men's control of the United States was to continue. The Populists faded away. But the memory of Bryan's campaign lived on, and later Presidents—notably Wilson and the two Roosevelts—led the country towards the cause for which Bryan's supporters voted in 1896.

17   McKinley and Spain, 1897-1901

The year 1897, in which William McKinley became President, brought an abrupt change of scene. The central interest of American history moved from the steel-works of Pittsburgh and the railroads of Chicago to the sugar plantations of Cuba. Neither strikes nor the rights of corporations were the chief problem of McKinley's term of office, 1897–1901. Overseas expansion had taken their place. Americans argued no longer about free silver. Instead, they argued about the right of the United States to annex the Philippine Islands.

I. THE GROWTH OF IMPERIALISM

In the 1890's the U.S.A. became an imperialist power, anxious to develop an overseas empire. This desire to expand resembled that of the 1840's, the period of 'Manifest Destiny.' There were many reasons for it. The chief one was precisely that industrial development from which the overseas expansion seems at first to be so distant. The U.S.A. had become a great industrial nation with a surplus of goods for export, and she had already developed a considerable overseas trade, notably in the lands round the Caribbean Sea, and across the Pacific to the Far East. Such trade needed secure bases, and so tempted the U.S.A. to acquire islands in those areas. Further, Americans had invested much capital in commercial enterprises. The sugar-plantations of Cuba and Hawaii were run by American money and their profits went into American pockets. The expansion of American trade, the need to hold secure markets for the sale of manufactured goods, the investment of money—all these facts made the U.S.A. an imperialist nation in the 1890's.

Others helped. The 'end of the frontier,' the fact that there were no more great undeveloped areas in her own continental territory, was one. The American people had filled up the great mass of their first empire, the United States itself. Now they turned overseas to find other lands to exploit. They were not alone in such a policy at this time. All the powers of Europe were doing the same; these were the years of the 'Grab for Africa,' the very descriptive name given to the process whereby European countries carved up most of a continent for themselves. American imperialism was part of a general world movement, undertaken by those nations which had developed their industrial resources and needed both markets and sources of raw materials. It was to be expected that the U.S.A., now the world's greatest industrial nation, would take part in such a process. There was a great variety of interests in the United States ready to support overseas expansion—Americans who wanted to sell iron and steel goods overseas; Americans who wanted to be sure of their rubber supplies from the East Indies; Americans who had money invested in sugar plantations in Cuba or in banana groves in Central America; and, not least important, American newspaper-owners who could put up their sales by boosting the idea of an American empire.

2. THE SPANISH-AMERICAN WAR, 1898

The most dramatic illustration of the new American imperialism occurred in 1898, when the U.S.A. went to war with Spain over Cuba. Many Americans during the 19th century had cast their eyes on Cuba. In the days of slavery Polk, Pierce, and Buchanan, all three Democratic Presidents, had wanted to get hold of it for its great store of unemployed Negroes. Later, sugar had become a greater attraction than slaves, and many thousands of American dollars had gone to develop Cuban sugar plantations. This had given Americans an interest in the island, and in the way it was governed. Spain, weak, backward, and poor, misgoverned the island scandalously, and the inhabitants, most of whom were of mixed Spanish, Negro, and Indian blood, were always ready to rebel. There had been ten years of desperate rebellion (the so-called Ten Years' War) between 1868 and 1878. American citizens had helped Cuban revolutionaries; but the government had remained neutral, in spite of the incident of the *Virginius*. This ship, flying the Stars and Stripes, was carrying munitions and men to Cuba in 1873, when she was seized by a Spanish gunboat and towed to Santiago. Here fifty-three of her crew were shot. In 1895 another and fiercer revolution had broken out, and all the efforts of the Spaniards had failed to put it down. They had met terror with terror, setting up concentration camps and building lines of barbed wire, with blockhouses at intervals, in a futile endeavour to crush the Cubans. The cheap press made sure that Americans did not forget Cuba, by printing atrocity stories; these increased the circulation of the newspapers, and stimulated a noisy popular demand for American intervention.

Cleveland refused to intervene. McKinley, a weaker man and a nominee of the Republican party, with its great financial interests, began with the intention of keeping out. But two events made the popular cry for war with Spain stronger than ever. After American pressure had made the Spanish government ready to grant reforms and abolish the concentration camps in Cuba, the *New York Journal* got hold of and published a letter by the Spanish ambassador in Washington which described McKinley as 'weak and a bidder for the admiration of the crowd.' Then, on the night of February 15, 1898, the United States battleship *Maine*, which had been sent to Cuba to protect American interests, blew up in Havana harbour, with a loss of 260 lives. Instantaneously the country was raging for war, especially when an American commission of enquiry reported, probably erroneously, that the explosion had been caused from outside, not from inside the ship. The press and most of the politicians wanted it; some of the latter were quite unblushing in their enthusiasm, like the Senator who said the 'war would increase the output of every American factory.' Prominent among them was the assistant Secretary of the Navy, Theodore Roosevelt. McKinley wavered, and then gave way to the clamour; he admitted a year later that the U.S.A. could have achieved what she was asking at this time—the withdrawal of Spanish troops from Cuba—without going to war to get it. So the United States declared war on Spain in April 1898.

The Spanish-American War of 1898 was an easy triumph for the Americans. The United States Navy, which had been kept strong during the previous years, won two of the most astonishing victories in history. In May 1898 the Pacific squadron under Commodore Dewey destroyed the Spanish fleet in the bay of Manila, in the Philippines, without losing a single seaman. In July a second Spanish fleet, which had sailed out of its harbours in the Cape Verde Islands and created a mild panic along the Atlantic coast because no one knew where it was, and had then got into Santiago Harbour in Cuba, was totally destroyed. This time the Americans had one casualty. The American army was not so fortunate; but nearly all its misfortunes were the work of the American commissariat department and of disease, not of the Spaniards. It had to eat what the soldiers called 'embalmed beef,' and some of the troops were sent to fight a summer campaign in Cuba dressed in thick winter uniform. But it won three quick victories in Cuba. The Spaniards had about 200,000 troops in the island, but never raised a single force in battle of more than 2000; and the fall of Santiago, thirteen days after the destruction of the Spanish fleet in its harbour, meant the end of Spanish rule in Cuba. A week later American troops overran Puerto Rico with the greatest of ease. The long story of the Spanish Indies, which had begun with Columbus, was over. On the other side of the earth American troops had not found it so easy to take Manila, the chief town of the Philippines. This was finally achieved in August 1898.

The American nation as a whole thoroughly enjoyed this war. The enthusiasm which the press had whipped up found plenty of outlet. There was no conscription. Only 298 soldiers were killed in the war.[1] It was fought in a popular cause, against Spanish oppression; Americans contrived to forget that the Cubans had shown themselves to be quite as bloodthirsty terrorists as the Spaniards. Its extremely decisive victories brought prestige to the Stars and Stripes. One of the politicians summed it up by calling it 'a splendid little war.' The problems came afterwards. The peace treaty itself set some of them. At the start of the war, by the Teller Amendment, the U.S.A. had stated that it had no intention of permanently annexing Cuba. But Puerto Rico and the Philippines were a different matter. By the Treaty of Paris, 1898, Spain acknowledged the independence of Cuba, and handed over to the U.S.A. Puerto Rico, Guam in the Ladrones, and the Philippines. For the last the U.S.A. paid over $20,000,000. This treaty left three questions behind it. How real was Cuban independence to be? Would the United States Senate ratify the treaty? And what would the Filipinos think about it all?

3. THE AMERICAN EMPIRE

In their expansion across their own continent the American people had looked westwards. In their foreign policy in the later 19th century, they looked in the same direction. American traders, whalers, missionaries, manufacturers, all found their goal in or across the Pacific Ocean. The policy which brought the United States an empire was a Pacific policy. That empire stretched across the Pacific from Alaska to the Philippines by way of Samoa. The Panama Canal is a vital link in American imperial communications: and the American possessions in the Caribbean Sea are part of the defences of the Canal.

The U.S.A. acquired overseas possessions before the 1890's. Seward, Lincoln's Secretary of State, had obtained Alaska and the Midway Islands in the north Pacific. He also proposed to buy the small islands which formed the Danish West Indies, but the Senate would not agree. Hawaii (or the Sandwich Islands) engaged the attention of American whalemen, missionaries, and sugar-planters early in the 19th century. In the 1890's the Americans on the island engineered a revolution which removed the royal family; and in 1898 the government of the U.S.A. annexed Hawaii. Spain handed over the Philippines, Puerto Rico, and Guam in 1898. The last formed part of a slender belt of American islands linking the U.S.A. and the Philippines. Others in the belt are Wake and French Frigate Island. Tutuila in Samoa was acquired in 1899. The last American annexation, the Danish West Indies, came in 1917, purchased for $25,000,000. These small islands, of which St. Thomas is the chief, became the American Virgin Islands.

[1] Thirteen times as many died from disease.

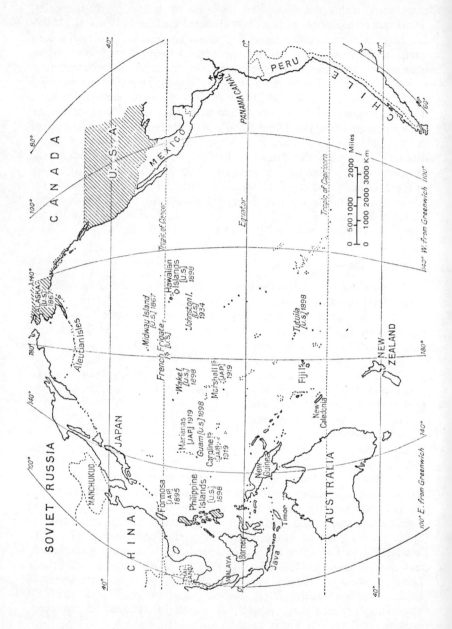

The U.S.A. and the Pacific in the Early 20th Century

Most of these possessions are small islands. They were used as naval bases and as stations on the Trans-Pacific air route. Of the larger ones, Alaska, the largest and the most difficult to develop, was the scene of several exciting but short-lived gold rushes in its Klondyke region. It became a Territory of the United States in 1913 and a State in 1959. Hawaii became a Territory in 1900 and a State in 1959; the memorable date in its history was 1941, when its naval station of Pearl Harbor, the base of the U.S. Fleet, was bombed by the Japanese, the event that marked the entrance of the United States into the Second World War. Puerto Rico has benefited from American control in many ways—in education, roads and drains. But it is heavily overpopulated, and most of its population of 2,700,000 are desperately poor.

The remaining possession, the Philippines, has been the most important in American history. By the Treaty of Paris in 1898 Spain sold the Philippines to the United States. The latter found that she had bought a revolution as well as a group of islands. The Filipinos, who had been fighting the Spaniards when the Spanish-American War began, wanted their new masters no more than their old ones. It took four years of war, marked by atrocities on both sides, to subdue them. Meanwhile, there was much argument in the U.S.A. over the question of annexing the islands. The Treaty had to be ratified by two-thirds of the Senate, and at one time there seemed every likelihood that it would be rejected. The opponents of the Treaty, of whom Bryan was the most notable, pointed out how contradictory it was to enter a war to free Cuba, and to finish it by forcing seven million Filipinos, against their consent, to become subjects of the U.S.A. They said that taking new territories by force was clean contrary to everything for which the Americans had fought in the War of Independence; and that the Constitution did not permit the annexation of a large subject population. But the enthusiasm for imperialism was still strong, and many Americans were nervous about the activities of European powers in China at this time (see Section 5, below). So the treaty was ratified, and the Philippines passed under American rule. William Howard Taft was the first American governor of the islands, and he began the process of giving the islanders all the benefits of American civilisation, from education to drains, and from hospitals to baseball. It was Taft who coined the phrase 'our little brown brothers' for the islanders. The Jones Act of 1916 gave them self-government, and promised eventual independence. Wilson proposed to give it them in 1920, but the grant was postponed. Under another scheme drawn up in 1934, the Philippines were due to become independent in 1946. The little brown brothers always were anxious for independence, and American sugar-growers, whose pockets suffered from the competition of Philippine sugar, encouraged this desire. But the outbreak of the Second World War brought the Filipinos into world history, and temporarily changed their fate—though it did not alter the date at which they achieved independence.

4. THE U.S.A. AND LATIN AMERICA

There are more ways of making conquests than by going to war, and the U.S.A. has found dollars almost as effective as guns in the Caribbean area. The method has been extended to South America too. It forms one side of the relationships between the the U.S.A. and the countries of Latin America. Another side is the movement for the strengthening of the ties between all the republics of the American continents—the movement called 'Pan-Americanism.' Somtimes these two methods have worked hand-in-hand. More often they have contradicted one another.

The first conference of American republics met at Washington in 1889. It was not particularly effective. Much more important was President Cleveland's behaviour over Venezuela in 1895. Great Britain and Venezuela had long had a dispute over the boundary between Venezuela and British Guiana, and both countries made very extensive claims indeed. In 1895 Cleveland, on the strength of the Monroe Doctrine, determined to take a hand, and his Secretary of State, Richard Olney, informed the British government that 'To-day the United States is practically sovereign on this continent, and . . . its infinite resources combined with its isolated position render it master of the situation and practically invulnerable as against any or all other powers.' Such strong language created an awkward situation. But Cleveland never wanted a breach with Britain, while British statesmen, realising the isolation of their country in Europe, did not want to quarrel with the U.S.A. Joseph Chamberlain (who had married as his second wife an American) took the lead in moving for a settlement, and the boundary question was referred to arbitration. The decision, given in 1899, was favourable to Britain.

Towards the end of the 19th century Americans began to invest money in the small republics of the Caribbean Sea area. There were plenty of opportunities for investment; as for example in Cuba, the 'the sugar-bowl of the world,' or in Costa Rica and the other Central American states, where, in 1899, the Boston United Fruit Company began operations. Hence this area became a United States sphere of influence. In these tiny republics revolutions were frequent, governments rose and fell with incredible rapidity, and debts were difficult to collect. The American owners of property looked to the American government to help, American marines were landed, and enforced order; sometimes they withdrew, sometimes they remained while American officials put the republics' finances in order and collected the debts. This process, whereby the American government intervened to safeguard American investments, and thereby obtained political control, was criticised as 'Dollar diplomacy.' It was not merely a matter of dollars. There were strong strategic arguments, especially after the opening of the Panama Canal in 1914, for American interest in the Caribbean republics. Americans knew that what

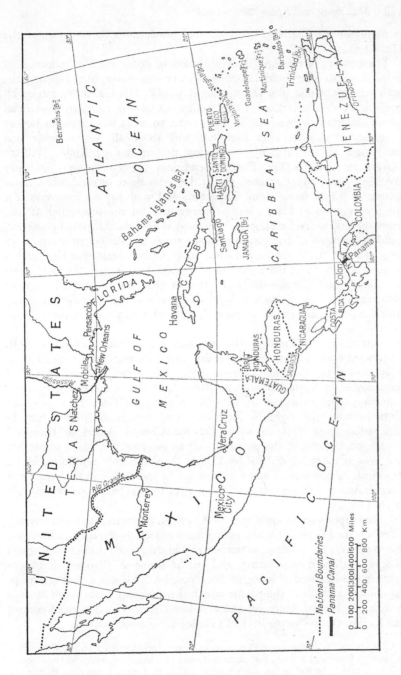

Central America and the Caribbean Sea in 1918

went on in the Caribbean was of vital concern to the security of the United States.

The landing of marines, the restoration of order and the collection of debts have been repeated—with local variations—many times during the 20th century. Cuba, the Dominican Republic, Haiti, and Nicaragua all provide ample illustration of this policy. Cuba was ruled by American governors from its conquest in 1898 until 1902. It was given an honest government; schools were founded: and above all, yellow fever was conquered by the hygienic revolution undertaken by Major William Gorgas in Havana. The Platt Amendment (signed in 1903 and not abolished until 1934) granted the U.S.A. the right to establish a naval station in Cuba, and—more important—allowed her to intervene 'for the preservation of Cuban independence and for the protection of life, property, and individual liberty.' Leonard Wood, the American governor, handed over to a Cuban government in 1902. But American troops were back again in 1906[1] and stayed until 1909. United States marines landed in 1912 and in 1917; from 1917 they remained until 1922. In fact Cuba, nominally independent—she held a seat on the Council of the League of Nations in 1927–8—became a dependency of the U.S.A., largely because American citizens owned so great a part of Cuba's sugar-plantations, railroads and mines.

Haiti and Santo Domingo—the two states on the island of Haiti—both underwent a similar process. In Haiti American marines remained from 1915 until 1934, and when they went the U.S.A. still retained control of the finances. In Santo Domingo an American financial agent took over the collection of the customs in 1904: a treaty three years later gave the United States the right to intervene: and American troops were in occupation from 1916 to 1924. On the Central American mainland Nicaragua, because of the possibility of an inter-oceanic canal across her soil, was of more interest to the U.S.A. than the other republics. Much American money was invested there early in the 20th century. American intervention was found necessary from 1912 to 1925, and again from 1927 to 1933.

Dollar diplomacy brought gain to American investors. It also in obvious ways benefited the small states, giving them orderly government, education, improvements in medicine, sanitation and health, roads, technical progress in agriculture and engineering, and on the whole an all-round improvement in the standard of living of their peoples. This was a clear service to mankind. But most of the profits which this progress made possible went into the pockets of American shareholders. Moreover, American control was foreign control in the eyes of peoples of Central America.

---

[1] The occasion of this intervention was the revolution caused by the re-election in 1905 of President Palma; his supporters were so eager to ensure his re-election that they faked the voting too successfully, giving him more votes than there were electors.

5. THE OPEN DOOR IN CHINA

One more episode of American foreign policy at the end of the 19th century must be recorded here. American trade with the Far East had grown steadily during the 19th century, and therefore the U.S.A. grew more interested in what happened in China. In 1894 Japan attacked China, and won a series of easy victories. Russia, Germany, and France, concerned about a possible danger to their Chinese trade, stopped Japan from retaining any of her conquests except Formosa. Four years later they, with Great Britain and Italy, proceeded to take various Chinese bases for themselves. Russia took Port Arthur, Germany Kiao-Chow, and Britain Wei-hai-wei. The result of this was the Boxer Rising of 1900, when infuriated Chinese nationalists massacred Europeans in Peking, and besieged the Legations of the European powers. The U.S.A. sent troops in the international expedition which relieved the Legations. The Chinese government was forced to pay an indemnity to those powers whose citizens had been killed and property damaged. The U.S.A. returned half her share in this; the Chinese government applied it to founding scholarships to enable Chinese students to study in America.

For the U.S.A. the most important outcome of this series of events appeared in a statement by John Hay, the American Secretary of State, which put forward what is known as the policy of the 'Open Door' in China. In a note to the great European powers in 1899 Hay demanded equal opportunities for all nations to trade in China; and in a second note in 1900 after the Boxer Rising he called on all countries to respect Chinese territorial integrity. In a vague general way the other powers accepted these aims; in practice the American government was not able or ready to take active steps to enforce them. 'The Open Door' fitted in with the genuine concern of American missionaries for China, and probably won some support for the United States in that country. It was certainly not a statement of an effective policy.

18 Theodore Roosevelt and Taft, 1901-13

In 1900 McKinley was re-elected as President, defeating Bryan, who was again Democratic candidate. In September 1901 he was shot by a mad anarchist. His Vice-President, Theodore Roosevelt, succeeded him.

1. THEODORE ROOSEVELT

That anarchist's bullet changed the history of the United States. The new President was the ablest since Lincoln, and in every way a contrast to his predecessors. He was only forty-two when he entered the White House but he had already had a remarkable career. He came of a wealthy New York family and had been educated at Harvard: had gone ranching in Dakota: been Police Commissioner of New York, and Assistant Secretary of the Navy: and had thrown up the latter post to lead a company of 'Rough Riders' in the Spanish-American War, and had won a reputation at the battle of San Juan.[1] In 1898 he was elected Governor of New York and he showed himself so keen a reformer that the Republicans there had him nominated for the vice-presidency in 1900 in order to get him out of the way. His versatility was amazing, and he was well-known to the American public as writer, soldier, politician and naturalist. Equally amazing was his ability to get on with people of every class. He revelled in publicity; never minced words about those with whom he disagreed (he once wrote that McKinley had 'no more backbone than a chocolate éclair'); and gloried in physical strength, taking a cold bath before break-fast, riding bareback, and playing energetic tennis. Enthusiastic, impetuous, full of vitality, Roosevelt came into American politics like a blast of fresh air.

McKinley and other Republican Presidents since 1869 had been dim figures, often controlled by the party managers. 'T.R.' came into office determined to lead, and to put his own policies into force. The possibility of a clash with the party chiefs did not bother him; it encouraged him, for he loved a fight, and he knew he could use his own personal magnetism to win over public opinion. His tireless energy enabled him to tour the country making frequent speeches. In foreign affairs he was intensely nationalist, bursting with patriotism and prepared to promote American interests regardless of principle. At home he showed himself full of sympathy for the poor, and anxious to tackle the many social problems which confronted the United States at the beginning of the 20th century. A special feature of his character was his love of the West. When President he liked to escape from his work to his ranch where he lived the life of a cowboy, and he was always deeply interested in western affairs.

2. ROOSEVELT ABROAD

Roosevelt took the United States into world affairs. He did not break traditional American isolation by involving her in alliances, although he

---

[1] This made him a popular hero. He wrote an account of his experiences in Cuba; a contemporary American satirist said he ought to have called it 'Alone in Cuba'.

kept on good terms with Britain. Yet he took a leading part in settling disputes between the powers. He ended one war by helping Russia and Japan to come to terms in the Treaty of Portsmouth (New Hampshire) in 1905, and he postponed the outbreak of another one when he persuaded France and Germany to refer their dispute over Morocco to an international conference held at Algeciras in 1906. Thus his activities as an arbitrator were a real contribution towards peace.

But the sphere in which Roosevelt's activities were most dramatic and most characteristic was the Caribbean Sea. Venezuela, Santo Domingo, Cuba, and, above all, Panama, felt the force of his personality. In 1902 Britain, Germany, and Italy combined to try to compel General Castro, the sinister tyrant who was President of Venezuela, to pay debts owing to them. Roosevelt restrained them from armed intervention, and the matter was settled by arbitration. He followed up this defence of the Monroe Doctrine when, in 1905, he forced Santo Domingo to accept American control of her finances. Here he used the Doctrine as an excuse for inter-ference by the U.S.A. with the affairs of her neighbours. He argued that the finances of Santo Domingo were so chaotic and that she was so much in debt that European powers were likely to intervene in order to collect their debts. The U.S.A. could not permit this: equally the European powers could not be deprived of money to which they were entitled. Therefore, said Roosevelt, the U.S.A. herself must intervene, take charge of the finances, see that the revenues are properly collected, and allot to each European power her fair share. This argument, which came to be known as the 'Roosevelt corollary' to the Monroe Doctrine, gave the U.S.A. a claim to interfere in the affairs of the Caribbean Republics. In 1906 there was another intervention, this time in Cuba, under the terms of the Platt Amendment.

But Panama provided the most notable illustration of Roosevelt's methods. 'I took Panama,' he said. The statement is true; it is not just an example of his complete lack of modesty. In a speech he once quoted an old saying—'Speak softly, and carry a big stick, and you will go far.' The supreme example of Roosevelt's use of the 'big stick' was his seizure of the Panama Canal zone. The U.S.A. had long been interested in the Panama region,[1] and the interest increased with the growth of an American empire across the Pacific. Before 1903 Panama was part of the republic of Colombia. The narrow isthmus was an obvious site for an inter-oceanic canal, and in 1878 a French company got a concession from Colombia, permitting them to dig a canal. They began work in 1881, with Ferdinand de Lesseps, builder of the Suez Canal, as engineer. After eight costly and terrible years, they stopped, beaten by landslides and fever. In 1898 the war with Spain and the annexation of the Philippines focused American

---

[1] Between 1855, when an American company completed a railroad across Panama, and 1903, there were thirteen landings of American, and three of British, marines on the isthmus.

attention on the question of a canal. A Panama Canal Company had bought from the bankrupt French company the right to build the canal and was very anxious to sell it to the United States. In 1902 Congress passed the Spooner Act, permitting the government to buy if it could obtain from Colombia the lease of the strip of land across the isthmus. In 1903 the government made a treaty with Colombia gaining the lease. But the Colombian senate was slow in ratifying the treaty—largely, it seems, because Colombia wanted a share of the cash which was to go to the Panama Company. Roosevelt became extremely impatient: in his private correspondence he was highly abusive about Colombian politicians. In 1903 various Americans and citizens of Panama hatched a plot to set up a separate state of Panama. Roosevelt knew about it, and, without giving official sanction, made it clear that he would welcome this solution. In November 1903 a revolution took place in Panama, which proclaimed itself independent of Colombia. The United States Navy helped by stopping Colombian troops from landing to put it down. Within a fortnight the new Republic of Panama had signed a treaty with the U.S.A. giving that country the lease, for ever, of a strip ten miles wide across the isthmus (except the towns of Colon and Panama): the U.S.A. was to have the right to fortify this strip, and if necessary, to police Colon and Panama. The whole affair was a severe shock to Latin America in particular, and to the world in general. It was a further revelation to the other American republics of what the reverse side of the Monroe Doctrine could mean, while it showed Europe that the U.S.A. had nothing to learn about imperialist methods. Roosevelt wanted his administration to go down in history as having created the Panama Canal, and cared little how he did it.

The Canal itself was a wonderful achievement. Work began in 1904; Colonel Goethals was appointed chief engineer in 1907, and within seven years ships were passing through. It is an essential link in the communications of the United States' empire, and also a great highway of the world's traffic, saving shipping a 6000-mile journey round Cape Horn. It has been described as 'the greatest liberty man has taken with nature,' and this is true not only of the conquest of forests and mountains made in its fifty-mile course, but also of the triumph over yellow fever and malaria, achieved by the same Colonel Gorgas who had cleansed Cuba. In 1921 the U.S.A. signed an agreement with Colombia, paying her $25,000,000 compensation.

3. ROOSEVELT AT HOME

In home affairs Roosevelt was a reformer; it was this fact, not his pugnacious foreign policy, that caused consternation among his fellow-Republicans. He came to power at an appropriate moment in American history, for many reforms were needed. Public opinion in the U.S.A. was just awakening to this fact, and Roosevelt's presidency coincided with the development of what American writers have called the 'Progressive Movement.' The rapid growth of the Industrial Revolution in the United States had brought with it a great mass of problems, and the need for social reform on a gigantic scale. In many ways the country was backward. The sudden rise of new industrial cities created countless problems—a spread of slums, the need for great sewerage schemes, the development of diseases like tuberculosis, great fires like that at Chicago in 1871, utter poverty, crime and disorder, the control of essential services like light and gas by private monopolies, and, a central problem, the existence of corruption and incompetence in the government of almost every great city in the land. The factories around which the new towns had arisen had their problems too—ventilation and light, an appalling rate of accidents, hours of work, child labour. The huge advance of American industry had been achieved at the expense of outrageous inroads upon the natural resources of the country, and it was urgently necessary that the waste in land, timber, natural gas and oil should be stopped. Beyond these problems were other wider ones—the position of the Indian, the exploitation of the Negro; the growth of drinking; the agitation for the emancipation of women. The phenomenal growth of immigration at this time made most of these problems more urgent. Between 1900 and 1910 over 8,790,000 immigrants entered the U.S.A.: Italy and Austria-Hungary sent over 2,000,000 apiece, and most of them went into the great cities, not to the open farmlands. Towering over the whole scene were the trusts, those prodigiously wealthy combines whose wealth was steadily growing.

Such questions as these had been brought before the American public not by the politicians, but by men and women with a burning hatred of injustice, and with an itch to set human conditions to rights. Among them were many journalists and novelists, the 'muckrakers' as Roosevelt called them, whose investigations of scandals and publications of the results aroused the conscience of many Americans. These revelations—whether they were about the corruption of San Francisco politics, the effects of drink, the appalling conditions of life in tenement houses in New York or the methods by which the Standard Oil Company made its vast profits —made it clear that all was not well with the United States. The Populist Movement a few years earlier had appealed mainly to farmers in the rural areas of the West and South. Now the Progressive Movement won its support from middle-class men in the cities, deeply perturbed by the developments which were taking place around them—from professors, clergymen, lawyers and other professional men, from many small business men who feared the trusts, even from a few very wealthy men. The remedies they propounded were numerous. Among the most famous of them was that contained in a book published in 1879 by Henry George, called *Progress and Poverty*. George proposed as a remedy for the great difference between rich and poor that there should be one tax and one only, that on land, from which, he argued, all wealth ultimately came. This book has been widely read ever since, making its author famous as 'Single-Tax George.'

Out of the great series of writings and arguments over these countless questions, one thing soon became clear—that nearly all the reformers demanded some extension of government control, whether it was by the Federal government or by those of the separate states. Most social questions, under the American Constitution, are the responsibility of the states. The first really effective law regulating hours of labour in the U.S.A. was the Massachusetts Ten-Hour Act of 1884. In Roosevelt's day the states of the Middle West, like Wisconsin and Illinois, with their factory laws, state control of public services, prison and numerous other reforms, set the pace for the rest of the country. Two state governors, Robert LaFollette of Wisconsin and Woodrow Wilson of New Jersey, were among the leaders of reform. Yet it was evident that there were major problems which the Federal government alone could tackle. Roosevelt was ready to tackle them. He talked of 'trust-busting' and of giving a 'square deal' to labour. He was genuinely humanitarian, very willing to do battle with the trusts, and ready to make more extensive use of the powers of the government than any of his immediate predecessors. He said that it was 'not only his right but his duty to do anything that the needs of the nation demanded, unless such action was forbidden by the Constitution or by the laws.'

He did a great deal. In 1902 he settled, in favour of the miners, a strike in the anthracite coal-fields of Pennsylvania. In 1903 he set up a Department of Commerce and Labour as a new department of state. In 1906 he got Congress to accept a Pure Food Act, safeguarding food against adulteration. This was the direct result of the public indignation caused by the revelations in a novel called *The Jungle*, written by Upton Sinclair, which described the shocking conditions existing in the meat factories of Chicago. Some of Roosevelt's finest actions concerned the open spaces which he himself loved so deeply. He destroyed a network of fraud through which the forests of the country were being plundered; created a national forests reserve of 150,000,000 acres; established national game preserves, and wild bird sanctuaries; got Congress in 1902 to pass a Reclamation Act to develop irrigation; and in 1907 called a national conservation conference.

But his major battle was with the trusts. They had grown yet stronger under McKinley's benign influence. In 1901, the year when Roosevelt became President, the United States Steel Corporation was formed by J. P. Morgan and others. Its capital was $1,321,000,000, and it controlled about 60 per cent. of the steel production of the U.S.A. Roosevelt determined to attack those 'malefactors of great wealth,' as he called the rich men who controlled the fate of millions and exploited the natural resources of the American people for their own personal gain. Among the largest and most pernicious trusts were the railroads, and he struck two blows at them. The Elkins Act of 1903 prevented them from giving rebates (special reductions of rates) to certain companies at the expense of others; this practice had enabled the bigger companies, like John D. Rockefeller's Standard Oil Company, to ruin their competitors. He followed this up by bringing and winning in 1904 a case under the Sherman Act against the Northern Securities Company, which controlled thousands of miles of railroad north-west of Chicago. In 1906 Congress passed the Hepburn Act, whose aim was to enable the Inter-State Commerce Commission, a body set up in 1887, to control the charges made by the railroads. It was not highly successful, but it was a beginning. Further, Roosevelt brought more cases under the Sherman Act, and succeeded in breaking some of the trusts.

Yet, taken as a whole, his campaign against the rich was not as successful as might have been expected. In spite of Roosevelt's 'sound and fury,' his actual achievement was limited. This was partly because Congress would not pass the bills he wanted. Big business was too strongly entrenched there. But it was also because Roosevelt himself was at heart only a moderate reformer. He was prepared to hit the trusts hard, but he had no sympathy with extreme ideas like socialism; and in practice he was ready to compromise. His great achievement was to open the door of national politics to the reformers, and thus to give the Progressive Movement its chance. In home affairs, his presidency was a tonic.

4. TAFT AND THE REPUBLICAN SPLIT

Roosevelt's personal popularity was immense. He was re-elected in 1904, and could have run for a third term in 1908 if he had wished. He declined to stand, but his party nominated William Howard Taft, his personal friend, and his own choice as successor. Taft won the election; Bryan, Democratic candidate once more, failed for the third time. Roosevelt, his term of office over in 1909, went off to Africa to shoot big game. The U.S.A. had not heard the last of him.

'Big Bill' Taft was a very different man from Roosevelt. He had been one of the latter's most loyal followers, and had been a successful ruler both of the Philippines and of the Panama Canal Zone. But he was much more ready than Roosevelt had been to yield to the party leaders. The best example of this came with the Payne-Aldrich Tariff of 1909. Taft had said that he expected the level of the tariff to be reduced. When Congress met, a revised tariff was introduced, lowering many duties; by the time the Republican leaders in the Senate had done with it, the general level of duties was higher than before. Taft accepted the changes with very little protest. Besides showing himself weak, Taft was unlucky. His proposal for a Reciprocity Treaty with Canada broke down through no fault of his own. The treaty offered Canada a reduction of American duties on imported farm produce, provided the Canadians reduced their duties on imported manufactured goods; it would thus have helped both Canadian farmers and American manufacturers. But a Congressman named Champ Clark of Missouri let fall in a speech the unfortunate remark that he favoured the treaty because he hoped 'to see the day when the American flag will float over every square foot of the British North American possessions clear to the North Pole.' This aroused great indignation in Canada, the Canadian government fell, and Taft's treaty failed. Yet his worst stroke of luck, as we shall see, was Theodore Roosevelt.

Nevertheless under Taft's administration several important changes, beneficial to the American people, took place. During his term of office two Amendments to the Constitution were proposed—the Sixteenth, giving Congress the power to impose an income tax, and the Seventeenth, providing that Senators should be elected directly by the people of each state and not, as previously, by the state legislature. Both these were ratified in 1913. Two new states were admitted to the Union in 1912, Arizona and New Mexico, bringing the total up to 48.[1] A parcel post and postal savings bank were created, further offices in the civil service were thrown open to competitive examination, and the government brought more cases against the trusts under the Sherman Act. In some ways Taft's administration did more for the people than Roosevelt's had done.

But Taft did not please the progressive group inside the Republican party, and this attacked him vigorously in Congress for going too slowly. Its members, led by Robert LaFollette of Wisconsin, formed in 1911 the Progressive Republican League to try to lead the party towards reform. And in 1910 a more formidable figure than LaFollette had reappeared. Roosevelt returned to America in 1910 after shooting lions in Africa, making speeches in many European countries, and attending the funeral of Edward VII in London. He could not keep out of politics; his thirst for power and action was too great, and he believed that Taft had failed him by not carrying out his policies. He began to make speeches, putting forward a series of ideas called the 'New Nationalism,' whose central point was the need of more government interference to secure the well-being of the people. He quarrelled with Taft. In spite of an earlier statement that he would not run for a third term, he began to put himself forward as a possible candidate for the election of 1912. The Republican party convention rejected him, choosing Taft instead; there was some suspicion of trickery in the way the votes were counted. Soon a new Progressive Party was formed, and this, with tremendous enthusiasm, nominated Roosevelt. It was known as the 'Bull Moose' party, because of Roosevelt's remark 'I am feeling like a bull moose.' This behaviour of Roosevelt split the Republican party, and was a golden opportunity for the Democrats. They nominated the Governor of New Jersey, Woodrow Wilson. He, like Roosevelt, offered a programme of reforms, and the contest was an exciting one. The real competitors were Roosevelt and Wilson; Taft had

[1] Oklahoma had been admitted in 1907.

little chance. Wilson won, although only a minority of the American people voted for him. He got nearly 6,286,000 popular votes, and 435 electoral votes; Roosevelt's totals were 4,126,000 and 88. The way lay open for reform by the Democrats.

19 Woodrow Wilson, 1913-21

The new President, Woodrow Wilson, was known to be a supporter of reform. But in 1913 few Americans suspected that he was an unusual man, with ideals as noble as those of the greatest of his predecessors. None knew that Wilson, after making desperate efforts to keep the U.S.A. out of the greatest war the world had seen, would take her in to play a decisive part. None knew that he would cross the Atlantic to try to give the world a lasting peace, and that his efforts would be wrecked upon the selfishness of European politicians and the narrow-mindedness of his opponents at home as well as by his own obstinacy. No American President has suffered so cruelly in seeing his ideals and plans rejected by his own people.

1. WOODROW WILSON

Woodrow Wilson was born in Virginia in 1856. Much of his life had been spent at Princeton University, where he had been successively student, professor, and president of the university. In the last post he had tried, with only limited success, to break down the barriers which gave advantages to wealthier students. He had entered politics in 1910, as Governor of New Jersey, and had done much to clean up the government of that state, which had suffered from corrupt politicians. This was a quietly distinguished record, but it gave little indication of what was to come. Like Lincoln, Wilson 'grew to his task.' His high qualities, scarcely known when he became President, gradually revealed themselves while he held office. Wilson was a great liberal, devoted to the idea of the United States as the land of the free. In this he was in the line of the great Presidents—Jefferson, Jackson, and Lincoln himself. His belief in freedom was well-known before he came to power. What men did not expect was the ability which he showed to capture the imagination of the people and to lead men. His faults were obvious. His life as a university professor had helped to make him remote and unapproachable, while he was very often too confident in the solution which he himself gave to a problem, and was unwilling to accept advice. These faults helped to bring the failure of his policy, and to make the end of his career more bitter. Yet he was a tremendous figure. His greatness is only thrown into higher relief by the terrible failure of his peace aims, both in Europe and in America.

His first inaugural speech, delivered in 1913, gave the key to his ideals

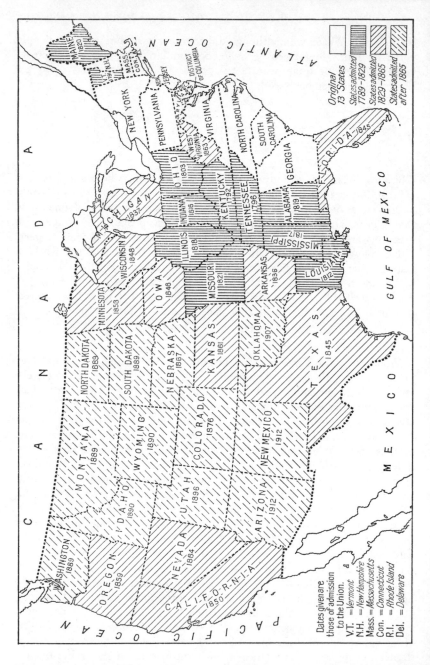

The States of the U.S.A. (To these must be added Alaska and Hawaii, admitted in 1959)

and to his policy. He pointed out the evils which the industrial development of the United States had brought—'the human cost of lives snuffed out, of energies over-taxed and broken, the fearful physical and spiritual cost to the men and women and children upon whom the dead weight and burden of it all has fallen pitilessly the years through.' He denounced the wealthy men who had controlled American politics. 'The great government we loved has too often been made use of for private and selfish interests, and those who used it had forgotten the people.' Finally he outlined the reforms which the government should make. They included reduction of the tariff; reform of the banks; attention to the natural resources of the country, to public health, and to the conditions of labour. He ended, as Lincoln might have ended, by calling on 'all honest, all patriotic, all forward-looking men' to help him set the American people free.

2. THE NEW FREEDOM

The name given to this programme was 'The New Freedom.' In the four years from 1913 to 1917 he carried through a great part of it. He struck vigorous blows at the three main pillars of wealth—Trusts, Tariffs, and the Banks. To combat the trusts, he got Congress to pass in 1914 the Clayton Anti-Trust Act. This law set out to break the big corporations by encouraging competition. It forbade corporations to acquire shares in other companies which were competing with them; it stopped any deliberate variations in price which were intended to lessen competition; and it forbade among the big firms what were known as 'interlocking directorates' —that is, it prevented the directors of one great trust from being also the directors of another. This law was complicated. Its effect depended on the way in which the judges interpreted it; and the judges in the Supreme Court did not permit it to be used against the wealthy as Wilson had intended. The Federal Trade Commission, set up at the same time to investigate unfair methods of trade (for example, dishonest advertisements or adulterated goods), was much more successful.

The second pillar, the tariff, was undermined by the Underwood Tariff of 1913. This cut down the general level of duties from 37 per cent. to 27 per cent.: and allowed many important goods, such as wool, iron ore, and sugar, to come in duty free. To make up for the loss of revenue this caused, an income-tax—on incomes of $3000 and over—was tacked on to the Underwood Act. The third great reform was the Federal Reserve Act of 1913. This created a new federal banking system. A Federal Reserve Board, appointed by the government, was created, and a Federal Reserve Bank was set up in each of twelve districts of the U.S.A. These banks controlled the banking system of the country. They helped to make money circulate more easily, and made the financial system of the country less liable to sudden collapse. Three years later the Federal Farm Loan Act created Farm Loan Banks, to make loans to farmers.

Beyond these major achievements there were others. Among them were the LaFollette Seamen's Act (1915), improving conditions in the merchant marine; the Federal Aid Road Act (1917), providing money from Federal funds for road-making; a civil service Workmen's Compensation Act (1916); and the Adamson Act (1916), which created an eight-hour day on inter-state railroads. Wilson and his party could be proud of their reforms. Yet these were only a start. The coming of the Great War wrecked the Democratic party's programme.

3. WILSON AND LATIN AMERICA

In its dealings with Latin America Wilson's government did not cut so liberal a figure. It acted on the lines of the 'Roosevelt Corollary.' Bryan, Roosevelt's old opponent, was Secretary of State; but he continued the policy of 'dollar diplomacy.' Thus under Wilson American marines were maintaining order—and looking after American investments—in Nicaragua, Haiti, and Santo Domingo. Mexico was the worst problem of Latin America. Its dictator Porfirio Diaz, who had ruled by savage repression, fell in 1911, and years of anarchy followed. In 1913 Victoriano Huerta seized power. He was backed by Britain and by the American business men who controlled the majority of Mexican mines, oil-wells, and plantations. Wilson refused to recognize his government, and in 1914 sent marines who captured Vera Cruz to obtain satisfaction for an insult to the American flag. When Huerta was turned out later in that year the disorder grew worse. Bandits roamed the country, and many American citizens lost their lives and property. One bandit, Pancho Villa, led raids into New Mexico. In 1916 an American army under General Pershing invaded Mexico to catch Villa. It retired nine months later without having caught him. Wilson managed to maintain peace with such governments as Mexico had. This in itself was a considerable feat, in view of the provocation offered by Mexican bandits, and the desire of many Americans to go to war with Mexico.

4. THE U.S.A. AND THE FIRST WORLD WAR, 1914–17

Before Pancho Villa began to pester the U.S.A., a far more ominous shadow had fallen across the land. The First World War broke out in August, 1914. It immediately created great problems for the American people and for Wilson. Wilson proclaimed American neutrality at the outset, and nearly everyone in the country supported him. The U.S.A. was a 'melting-pot' of Europe's peoples, and could hardly take sides in a war between two groups of those peoples. 11,700,000 of America's citizens in 1910 had been born in Europe. By tradition she was neutral, and she had kept clear of Europe's affairs since 1814. Washington had advised her to keep out of other people's quarrels; Monroe's famous Doctrine had stated that the U.S.A. would not interfere in Europe. Moreover, American trade might reasonably expect to benefit from a policy of neutrality, and did in fact do so. For these reasons American public opinion was over-whelmingly neutral in 1914. Wilson stood firmly for this neutrality. He used his position as head of the greatest neutral state to attempt, several times, to mediate between the Allies and the Central Powers, to see whether peace could be made. He was unsuccessful in this, but he remained no less firm in his neutrality.

But Americans—Wilson included—were much more sympathetic to-wards the Allies than towards the Central Powers. There were many reasons for this. The most obvious of these were language and tradition. British and Americans shared a common language, even if there were many different peoples in the U.S.A., and they shared, too, a common political tradition, that of self-government. This link was effective in innumerable ways, notably through the press and in the persons of American statesmen. Wilson himself, a student of English literature and history, was from the start much more sympathetic towards the Allies, however hard he tried to convince himself that he was strictly neutral; he could not help being so. A more glaring example was Walter H. Page, the American ambassador in London, a convinced supporter of the Allies; he used all his powers to get the utmost American support for them, and was often hand in glove with the British government in their attempts to do so. A second factor which made the U.S.A. more sympathetic towards Britain was propaganda. From the start of the war both sides set out to capture American opinion by any means possible—lectures, press articles, rumours, and atrocity stories. British propaganda was thorough and imaginative. German propaganda was equally thorough, but it was clumsy. And its effect was often marred by stupid political actions, like the sinking of American merchant ships or attempts to blow up railroads, or by revelations like that of the secret papers of Dr. Albert, the German propaganda chief in the U.S.A. Moreover, Britain had one great advantage on her side; she controlled all the news that went into the U.S.A., except by wireless (then little developed) or by diplomatic mail-bags.

The third and most important link between the Allies and the U.S.A. was trade. Wilson might declare his country neutral, and say she was ready to trade with either side. In reality, the British blockade soon made German trade with America dwindle to nothing. Trade between the Allies and America rose steadily. Its most important commodity was munitions. In 1914 the U.S.A. exported $40,000,000 worth of munitions; in 1916 she exported $1,290,000,000 worth. This trade went steadily on, despite British interference with American ships carrying cargoes to the neutral countries of Europe. British Orders-in-Council, issued in 1914, established a blockade of Germany. Mines were laid in the North Sea, and the block-ade grew far more rigid than any previous one. The list of contraband articles gradually grew longer, and eventually included food. Many

American firms were 'black-listed'—that is, British traders were forbidden to trade with them because they were suspected of trading with Germany; the goods of American citizens were kept waiting for weeks in British ports; letters to American subjects were tapped. Wilson protested against these practices, but in vain. Such British activities made the phrase 'the freedom of the seas,' on which Americans set great store, meaningless. Yet at least they did not cost the lives of American subjects as German torpedoes did. And the profitable American trade with Britain went on. It drew the U.S.A. out of commercial depression in 1915. Most important, it made American firms financially interested in keeping the Allies going. If they collapsed, the profits of the Du Ponts, the great armament manufacturers, and other big firms collapsed too.

Yet none of these things by themselves were sufficient to make the U.S.A. enter the war on the Allied side. They prevented her from joining the Central Powers and made her sympathetic towards Britain—that was all. It was the submarine that ultimately brought her into the war. Germany began submarine warfare in February 1915, and in the following month the first American lost his life as a result of submarine action. May brought the sinking of an American tanker, followed by an event which aroused very bitter feeling in the U.S.A.—the sinking without warning of the British liner *Lusitania*. Over 1100 people were drowned; 128 of them were Americans. Wilson addressed strong notes to Germany. There was a lull in the sinkings; then more sinkings, and more protests from Wilson. In May 1916 the German government promised to sink no more merchant ships without warning. 1916 was election year in the U.S.A., and Wilson fought on the slogan 'He kept us out of war.' There was strong opposition from the Republicans; Roosevelt, who hated Wilson, had gone back to his old party, and attacked him violently on the ground that he was not taking a firm enough stand against Germany. Wilson's victory was a narrow one.

1917 was the year of decision for the U.S.A. In January Wilson made a speech in which he proclaimed to the world the idea of a 'peace without victory'—a peace based on justice, in which neither side would be called on to make humiliating concessions and there would be no grabbing of territory from a defeated enemy. That same month the German government announced its intention of beginning unrestricted submarine warfare again. This step was taken with the full knowledge that it would almost certainly bring the U.S.A. into the war on the Allied side. The German government calculated that the submarines would bring starvation to Britain, and therefore victory to Germany, before American help could be effective. Two further events precipitated the American decision. In February Britain passed on to the American government the Zimmermann Note, an offer from Germany to Mexico that in the event of German victory in a war with the U.S.A. she should have Texas; in March came the first Russian Revolution and the dethronement of the Tsar, which meant that if the U.S.A. joined the Allies she would not do so as an ally of the corrupt and autocratic Tsardom. In April Wilson sent a message to Congress, demanding war against Germany. Wilson knew well what the war would cost America—the collapse of his plans for reform, the loss of lives, the reduction of liberty at home. He believed that, in view of the declared German intention to sink all merchant ships around the shores of Britain, he could not take any other action. Congress passed the declaration of war by a large majority.

5. THE UNITED STATES AT WAR, 1917–18

The United States played a considerable and decisive part in the First World War. Her direct contribution was twofold. First, she loaned to the Allies vast sums of money. The total Allied debt at the end of the war was estimated at over $10,000,000,000. The Allies spent most of it in America. Secondly, she contributed man-power. Her navy joined the British in the campaign against submarines. In April 1917 Britain, according to Page, the American ambassador, was within six weeks of starvation. American destroyers, together with a steadily growing American merchant fleet (on Independence Day, 1918, 95 vessels were launched in the U.S.A.), relieved the pressure. On land the U.S.A. raised a vast army within eighteen months, by a series of conscription acts, under which 24,000,000 men were registered. Of these 2,180,000 were taken, under the draft, for the army, which with regulars and volunteers totalled 4,000,000. 2,000,000 of them went overseas, and 1,390,000 fought in France. The first American troops arrived in France in June 1917. Under General Pershing, they took part in the Allied resistance to the German spring offensive in 1918; in the decisive Second Battle of the Marne in July; and in the successful advance of the autumn. According to the German generals, who had anticipated that the war would be over before the Americans got to Europe, their arrival was a vital factor in the German defeat. They were fresh, fitter and less war-weary than both Allied and German troops. Their losses, considering the short period during which they were in the front line, were not small; 50,000 men were killed, and 206,000 wounded.

At home the remarkable fact of the war was the extension of government control. The government's powers covered every sphere of American life. The conscription of men was only the most striking example. The government took over the railroads, and William McAdoo, Secretary of the Treasury, became their Director-General. McAdoo was also responsible for financing the war, which cost the U.S.A. over $20,000,000,000. He raised one-third by taxes; the rest came from gigantic 'Liberty Loans,' issues of war-bonds, which McAdoo sold by nation-wide campaigns of lectures, canvassing, and street-corner sales. The government controlled American industry under a War Industries Board which fixed a limit to the production of all essential goods, eliminated waste by reducing the types of articles, and shut down non-essential industries. Herbert Hoover was appointed to take charge of a Food Administration which controlled food supplies, and the country had 'meatless' and 'wheatless' days. The government controlled Americans' minds as well as their bodies, by setting up a Committee on Public Information. Its director, George Creel, used every device of propaganda—speeches, films, press articles, lectures, posters, rumours—to persuade Americans to hate Germans and support the war. Those suspected of opposition to the war were harshly handled. Severe laws were passed against sedition and espionage; among the victims of these was Eugene V. Debs, the Socialist leader, who was sent to gaol for ten years. Sentences of this kind were wholly contrary not only to the liberty for which Wilson claimed to be fighting, but also the 1st Amendment to the Constitution, which guarantees freedom of speech.

6. THE PEACE

The Allies attained their immediate object when in October 1918 the new German Chancellor, Prince Max of Baden, asked for peace terms. Now, Wilson believed, was his opportunity. The United States had not entered the war to gain territory. Wilson had believed, and millions of ordinary Americans had believed with him, that she had entered it in order to 'make the world safe for democracy.' In his war message he spoke of fighting 'for democracy, for the right of those who submit to authority to have a voice in their own government, for the rights and liberties of small nations.' The Kaiser's Germany threatened the rights of small nations, and the right of each man to have a share in his own government. Thus Wilson's aim was to make a new world in which both democracy and small nations would be safe.

In January 1918 Wilson stated Fourteen Points upon which he believed it would be possible to make peace. These Fourteen Points may be summarised as follows:

1. An open treaty, not a secret one decided by diplomatists among themselves.
2. Freedom of the seas for all shipping.
3. Equality of trade between nations.
4. Reduction of armaments.
5. A settlement of colonial problems, paying attention to the peoples of the colonies.
6. The evacuation of Russian, French, and Belgian territory by Germans.
7. Self-determination (that is, the right to choose their own form of government for themselves) for the peoples of Austria-Hungary and Turkey.
8. The independence of Poland with free access to the sea.
9. The establishment of a 'general association' of nations, in order to safeguard the independence of each nation.

This statement was highly important, especially in its emphasis on self-determination and upon the association of nations. It offered, in Wilson's view, the hope of a new world, free from the threat of war. The ideas it contained were an important part of Allied propaganda. Millions of pamphlets in German carried them to the German people, and so undermined their support of the war. When the Germans asked for peace terms, they did so on the basis of the Fourteen Points.

Wilson decided to go to Europe himself to negotiate the peace settlement, which was to be made at Versailles. Before he left, he had a warning of one of the difficulties that lay ahead. The biennial elections to Congress, held in November 1918, gave his opponents, the Republicans, a majority in both Houses; and this was in spite of a personal appeal by Wilson to the people, asking them to show their support for his policy. It was a sign of the steady growth of American feeling against Wilson, caused partly by a belief that he was likely to treat the Germans too leniently. But in Europe he received an amazing welcome. Millions of Europeans, utterly weary after four years of war, hailed him as the saviour who had come to give them a lasting peace. The crowds in London gave him a welcome such as no other foreign statesman has ever received there.

The peace conference began in January 1919. Wilson headed the American delegation. He found himself facing an uphill task. He wanted a peace based on the Fourteen Points; many European politicians wanted one based on revenge. They wanted heavy reparations for the damage caused by the war; and they wanted territorial gains at Germany's expense. In the course of the war they had made secret treaties, each country allotting to itself a share of the spoils of victory. Wilson knew of these treaties, but evidently believed he would be able to get round them in the settlement. He was mistaken. The Peace Treaty was made by the 'Big Four,' the representatives of France, Britain, Italy, and the United States. Two of these men, Clemenceau of France, who had no time for Wilson's idealism and the Fourteen Points, and Lloyd George of Britain, were astute politicians whose aims differed from those of Wilson, and who were frequently able to out-manœuvre him. Thus Wilson was forced to compromise.

The Treaty of Versailles of 1919 was, from Wilson's standpoint, a mixture of good and bad. It provided for some of the Fourteen Points. Germany had to restore all the land she had occupied. The idea of self-determination was recognised, and new national states like Czechoslovakia and Yugoslavia replaced the old Habsburg Empire. Germany was stripped of her colonies, but they were handed over, in name at least, to a newly-created League of Nations. This last, an attempt to guarantee international law and order, was Wilson's own peculiar contribution to the Treaty, and the part which he valued most highly. On the other hand, the treaty also contained clauses quite contrary to Wilson's aims. Among these was the clause insisting that Germany should pay a vast sum as reparations for war-damage; and the other one whereby Germany was compelled to admit herself guilty of causing the war. Moreover, the manner in which the Treaty had been made hardly agreed with the first of the Fourteen Points, stipulating open treaties, while there was no 'equality of trade' so far as Germany was concerned.

Wilson sailed home in June 1919. The Treaty had, under the American Constitution, to be ratified by the Senate before it became law. The majority of the Senate was Republican; and Wilson, unwisely, had failed to appoint any Senator as a member of the American delegation to Versailles. During his absence the Republicans had carried on a campaign against the suggestion that the U.S.A. should join the League of Nations. They said that to do so would be to break with the American tradition of isolation from Europe. Many Americans, already repenting their country's entry into the war, supported them. There were others who opposed Wilson on different grounds; among these were the Irish-Americans, angry because of Britain's repression of the Irish rebellion at this time, and some Democrats who believed that Wilson had betrayed his ideals by accepting any compromise at Versailles.

Wilson, already overtired by his work in Europe, came back to confront this opposition. The Republican leader in the Senate was Henry Cabot Lodge. He was an able and persuasive politician who won support from many quarters for his policy of isolation. To Wilson's call that the United States should show the way towards the new age of peace and democracy which he hoped the League of Nations would bring, Lodge replied that the League would enable other powers to summon American troops and ships to serve in any part of the world. Wilson, obstinately declining any compromise over details, determined to make a desperate bid for success. He would tour the West and win over the people. He was almost exhausted by the immense labour of the days since 1917. Yet he faced the prospect of the utter failure of all he had given his strength for, if America rejected the Treaty and the League. So he set out on a long speaking tour, delivering nearly forty speeches in less than a month.

It was more than he could bear. On September 25, 1919, he collapsed. For the next seventeen months the U.S.A. had virtually no President. Wilson was an invalid, hardly able to move out of the White House. The story of the Treaty was soon ended. The Senate rejected it; they passed instead a resolution for a separate peace with Germany, which Wilson vetoed. The final blow was the election of 1920, in which the Republican candidate Warren Harding overwhelmed the Democrat and pro-League James Cox. Wilson had failed.

7. THREE WARTIME CHANGES

The war altered American life in many ways, quite apart from the direct changes, like government control of food, railroads, industry, and public

Andrew Carnegie (1835-1919), the steel 'king'

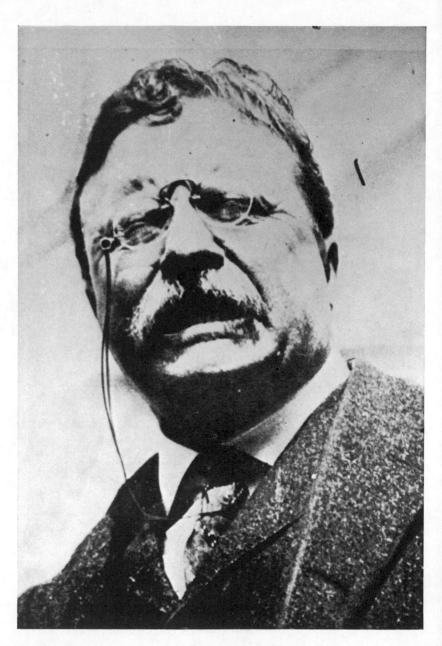

The first Roosevelt—Theodore, President from 1901-9

opinion, which were introduced to mobilise American resources. It hastened the arrival of changes which had been on their way before 1917. Three of these may be noted here.

In 1917 an Immigration Act was passed, whose object was to restrict the entry of immigrants. It forbade the entry of all aliens over sixteen who were unable to read. There had been earlier laws about immigration. Congress had at various times forbidden the entry of persons considered undesirable—for example, idiots, paupers, drunkards, anarchists, and Chinese labourers (the last were unpopular in the western states). Some states had made their own laws about immigration. The most notable among these were California and other western states, which stopped Japanese immigrants from owning land after their numbers rose from 26,000 in 1890–1900 to 130,000 in 1900–10. But the act of 1917, which was caused mainly by the great inflow of illiterate labourers from Central and Eastern Europe, marked a great change in American policy.

In 1919 the 18th Amendment to the Constitution was ratified. This forbade, after one year from ratification, 'the manufacture, sale, or transportation of intoxicating liquors within . . . the United States.' By the Volstead Act of 1919 it was decided that an 'intoxicating' liquor was one containing one-half of 1 per cent. of alcohol. Thus the U.S.A. went 'dry.' The country did so with very little reluctance; only two states (Connecticut and Rhode Island) refused to ratify the Amendment. Opposition to alcohol and its evil effects had long been powerful in the U.S.A. The Anti-Saloon League, founded in 1893, was a very strong force in politics because it was supported by so many voters in rural areas in the U.S.A. Five states had passed 'dry' laws before 1900; over two-thirds of all the states had done so before 1918. But such laws could not be effective so long as liquor could still be made in 'wet' states and taken across the borders into 'dry' ones. Only a national law could stop that. Such a law was passed by Congress during the war, on the ground that alcohol hindered the war effort; and it was now, in 1919, made part of the Constitution. Its effects were soon to appear (see Chap. 22).

Another Amendment came in 1920. This, the 19th, gave the vote to women by saying that 'the right of citizens of the United States to vote shall not be abridged by the United States or by any state on account of sex.' This was the most important stage in the road by which American women were gaining equal rights with men. Wilson himself was a strong advocate of it, and spoke before the Senate in its favour. Like the two changes previously mentioned, it had been on its way before the war, which accelerated its arrival. All three changes had important effects on American life, and those caused by Prohibition immediately became clear.

20 'Back to Normalcy'

1. THE POST-WAR REACTION

The ending of the war brought to all peoples a feeling of relief and reaction. This was obvious in Europe, which had suffered the full horrors of the war. America had suffered comparatively little; yet her people, too, felt relief and reaction, but in a different way. President Harding described their feelings when he talked of getting 'back to normalcy.' Americans saw the war as something that had taken them out of the normal path of their national development, and they wanted to forget it as quickly as they could, and get back to their own affairs. They were tired of Europe and tired of Wilson's idealism which had made them intervene in a European quarrel; while many of them disliked the peace settlement, and soon after the war was over began to wish that the U.S.A. had kept out of it. They wanted to be rid of the government control which had interfered with their lives during the war, and to get on with their own private affairs. This led the majority of them to give their votes at elections to that party which had generally opposed government interference with business or with the other occupations of the private citizen, the Republicans.

Moreover, events in Europe encouraged this feeling of 'one hundred per cent Americanism.' The success of the Bolshevik Revolution in Russia, with its attack upon individual liberties and particularly upon the liberties of capitalists and property-owners, and the brief success of Communist movements in other European countries, caused great alarm in America. Events in America itself heightened this alarm. The great profits which the war had brought to the manufacturers had not been shared by the workmen, and the years immediately after the war saw a succession of bitter strikes in nearly every important American industry. Some of the workmen were turning towards socialism as a way out of their difficulties, and employers readily encouraged the belief that these strikes were the work of 'Red' agitators. A series of bomb and dynamite outrages frightened Americans even more than the strikes. The worst of these came in 1920, when a bomb exploded outside the headquarters of the firm of J. P. Morgan and Company, the financiers, in Wall Street, New York. Such events caused a panic in the U.S.A., and there was a mild 'reign of terror.' Some six thousand Communists and suspected Communists were arrested, and the five Socialist members of the New York legislature were expelled. This 'Big Red Scare' made the American people very unwilling to bother about the League of Nations. It was a scare and nothing more, but it helped to make Americans even more suspicious of Europe, and anxious to forget all about the war and to return to normal life.

2. HARDING AND THE SCANDALS, 1921-3

The Republican President in 1921 was Warren G. Harding of Ohio. No man could have been a greater contrast to Wilson. Formerly a newspaper-proprietor in the small town of Marion, Ohio, he had sat in the Senate since 1915. He was handsome and good-natured; he looked a President, while his warm handshake and genial smile were great assets to him. It was typical of the change from Wilson to Harding that the latter immediately opened the grounds of the White House to the public; in Wilson's last days it had been a fastness, with its gates shut and barred. Unfortunately Harding was no more than a good fellow. He was weak, easily led, and always willing to oblige his friends; and he was quite unable to understand the economic problems of the day. In these as in other ways he was very like Grant; each was President after a great war, and the presidency of each brought shocking revelations of corruption in politics. Under Harding the 'Ohio Gang,' as the group of cronies with whom Harding used to play poker and drink illicit whisky was called, got their hands on the rewards of politics.

In 1921 these things were not known, and Harding began well. It soon became clear that the Republicans were going to remove all wartime government controls and allow the business men free play. One sign of this was the appointment of Andrew Mellon, one of America's richest men, as Secretary of the Treasury. The two ablest members of the Cabinet were Charles Evans Hughes as Secretary of State, and Herbert Hoover as Secretary of Commerce. Both showed initiative, Hughes by his activities at the Washington Conference (see below, Section 4), and Hoover by using the Department of Commerce to encourage the growth of even bigger industrial corporations. On the other hand, Harding made two very unwise appointments, those of Albert B. Fall as Secretary of the Interior, and Harry M. Daugherty as Attorney-General. The activities of these two were to make Harding's administration notorious. Yet for some time all went well. Harding was popular with the people, while business men found him the most satisfactory President since McKinley. The Immigration Act of 1921 was popular because it almost closed the doors on foreign workmen. In 1921 the U.S.A. made peace with Germany. The Washington Conference brought prestige to Harding. The Fordney-McCumber Tariff of 1922 sent up the tariff rates higher than ever before.

Then ugly stories began to spread. Colonel Forbes, whom Harding had appointed Director of the Veterans' Bureau, the organisation looking after disabled ex-soldiers, left his post in a hurry. Investigation showed that he had swindled the Treasury of millions of dollars. There were unpleasant rumours about the sales of the naval oil reserves at Elk Hills, California, and Teapot Dome, Wyoming. Harding visited Alaska in the summer of 1923; he was taken ill on the way home, and, after making an apparent recovery, he died suddenly of what was said to be a fit of apoplexy. It was later revealed that on this trip he kept asking Hoover and others what a man should do 'whose friends had betrayed him.'

The truth came out later, through the investigations of Committees appointed by the Senate. The worst scandal concerned the oil reserves. These originally belonged to the U.S. Navy, but Fall had persuaded the Secretary of the Navy to transfer them to the Department of the Interior; he had then leased those at Teapot Dome to an oil magnate called Sinclair, and those at Elk Hills to another called Doheny. Sinclair paid him over $200,000, and Doheny $100,000. Fall was later tried and sentenced to a fine of $100,000 and one year's imprisonment. Attorney-General Daugherty also was tried for conspiracy to defraud the government; investigations showed that he had been involved in selling, for his own gain, permits to buy intoxicants and permits to let convicts out of gaol, and in other illegal activities. There was no suggestion that Harding himself had been dishonest. But he had been criminally weak in letting his Ohio friends play their crooked games. His friends had let him down. It seems probable that he had realised what was happening, and that the knowledge killed him.

3. COOLIDGE AND PROSPERITY, 1923-9

His Vice-President and successor was Calvin Coolidge, a silent and sour-faced man from Vermont. He had become Vice-President largely on the strength of a famous telegram. There was a police strike in Boston in 1919, and Coolidge, who was at that time Governor of Massachusetts, had been asked by Samuel Gompers to intervene on behalf of the strikers; he had replied with a telegram saying that there was 'no right to strike against the public safety by anybody, anywhere, any time.' This phrase showed him to be a safe man, and in 1920 the Republicans nominated him for Vice-President. Coolidge never went out of his way to gain popularity, and he certainly was not a man of outstanding ability. Yet he was one of the most popular Presidents the United States has ever had. He was easily re-elected in 1924, in spite of the scandals which Harding's administration had brought upon the Republican party; and had he wished he could have been renominated by the party in 1928.

The reason for his popularity was not his personality. It was the great material prosperity which the U.S.A. enjoyed under 'Silent Cal.' The years from 1923 to 1929 were a period of soaring trade returns, high profits, rising wages, and great speculation. Coolidge, who once said 'the business of the United States is business,' was fortunate in his presidency. There were several reasons for this prosperity. Countries overseas, reconstructing after the war, bought large quantities of American goods; and American financiers loaned them cash to enable them to do so. Further, American industrial methods were developing fast; it was estimated that the average production per man in American industry increased 53 per cent. between 1919 and 1929. The signs of the prosperity were numerous, and visitors from Europe talked of 'America the Golden.' The most obvious signs were the prodigious growth of speculation in stocks and shares, and the rapid increase in the number of cars on the roads.

During the war the government had, as we have seen, extended its control over industry. When the war was over it began to abandon that control, and to leave industry to private enterprise. The Republicans and their three Presidents, Harding, Coolidge and Hoover, pursued this policy. Thus the Shipping Board, which had taken control of the American merchant marine during the war, sold numerous ships—at bargain prices—to private owners. Thus also Coolidge in 1928 vetoed a bill which would have enabled the government to supply the public with power from the dams built during the war at Muscle Shoals on the Tennessee River. Indeed, the government actively encouraged private enterprise in several ways. Three of these were particularly important. First, high tariffs continued. The Fordney-McCumber Act of 1922 had created a Tariff Commission which could vary the tariff levels on separate articles of trade. Under Harding and Coolidge there were 37 variations; all but 5 of these were increases, and the 5 reductions were on articles of trifling importance. Second, taxes were reduced; prosperity brought a great increase in the revenue, and Mellon, the business man at the Treasury, saw that tax-reduction would help business. Thirdly, Hoover, at the Department of Commerce, encouraged the great business corporations to join together in even greater combines. The Sherman and Clayton Anti-Trust laws were practically ignored. There was no pretence at the limitation of trusts now; the government was encouraging them. This policy was so successful that, by 1933, 594 vast corporations owned 53 per cent. of the corporate wealth of the entire country. This process no doubt made for efficiency. It also increased both the profits and the power of a small group of business men.

There was opposition to this policy, from many people. It was expressed in the election of 1924 when a new Progressive party was formed, with Robert LaFollette as candidate. This party's programme asked for public ownership of railways and water-power, public control of the banks, a lowering of the tariff, farm relief, and an amendment to the Constitution prohibiting child labour. But the Republicans fought their campaign on the slogan 'Keeping Cool with Coolidge,' and won easily against both Democrats and Progressives.

Yet Coolidge's presidency was not entirely free from difficulty. Prohibition, as we shall see, brought bootlegging, graft, and crimes of violence in its train. The Veterans of the Great War were a source of embarrassment. They were a well-organised group, and they pressed vigorously for increased pension rates, not merely for disabled men or their widows, but for anyone who had been in the army during the war. Many Congressmen who privately thought the Veterans' demands excessive were afraid to speak or vote against them because of their influence in the country. Harding vetoed one pension scheme in 1922. But in 1924 an Adjusted Compensation Act was passed over Coolidge's veto. This gave every war Veteran an endowment and insurance policy payable in 1945, or at death if the Veteran died before 1945. This Act cost the nation $3,500,000,000. The Veterans had made a successful raid on the Treasury.

The most serious of Coolidge's difficulties concerned the farmers. American farmers did not share in the prosperity. They had done well in the war, but then came a slump. Competition from Canada, Russia and the Argentine grew; European countries developed their own farmlands and tried to make themselves more nearly self-supporting in food; the American tariffs stopped foreign countries from sending to America goods for which they might have exchanged American wheat, cotton, and other farm products. So the farmer's prices came tumbling down. Wheat sold at $1.82 a bushel in 1920; it was 38 cents in 1932. Maize dropped from 61 cents to 32 cents a bushel, and cotton from 16 cents to 6 cents a pound over the same period. The Middle West and the South suffered alike. The value of the farmer's land fell, too, during this period; over the country as a whole, farmlands lost about 36 per cent. of their value. In face of this situation—which led to much distress among farmers and much agitation by Middle Western and Southern Congressmen in Washington—the Republicans were not idle. Their simplest, most used, and most ineffective remedy was a tariff on foreign farm products. There were five of these between 1920 and 1930; they were of little use since the farmers already grew more than they could sell in the U.S.A. itself. Another remedy was contained in the McNary-Haugen Bill passed by Congress in 1927 and 1928. The government was to buy all crops the farmer could not sell in the U.S.A., and sell them, even at a loss, overseas. The amount it lost would be spread out evenly over all sales of farm-produce, and each farmer would pay his share by what was called an 'equalisation fee.' He would, it was hoped, be able to do this because the whole scheme would enable him to charge more for the produce he sold in America. The scheme was never proved, because Coolidge disliked it and vetoed the bill twice. On the whole, the Republicans' most useful help to farmers under Harding and Coolidge was to continue activities begun by Wilson's government—loans to farmers, encouragement of co-operative schemes, and research into the causes of pests and drought. These did a little to lighten the farmer's burden; but he still carried most of it himself.

4. FOREIGN POLICY UNDER HARDING AND COOLIDGE

Just as Americans wanted to get 'back to normalcy' in their own lives at the end of the war, so they wanted to do so in their relations with other countries. 'Normalcy' in foreign affairs meant freedom from entanglements with other countries. It meant that America would do what she had done before 1914—isolate herself, as far as possible, from all dangerous connections with other powers. The most striking example of this isolationism was the Senate's refusal in 1919 to ratify the Treaty of Versailles with its clause committing the U.S.A. to membership of the League of Nations. Instead, the U.S.A. made a separate peace with Germany in 1921.

But in fact many forces were pulling the U.S.A. into world affairs. The re-building of world trade after the war was the greatest; the U.S.A., like other manufacturing countries, was hunting for new markets and new supplies of raw materials and this brought her into contact with other powers. One method of increasing her trade was by overseas investment. Americans in this period of prosperity had plenty of money available for investing. By 1930 over $3,000,000,000 of American money was invested in South America, and over $3,900,000,000 in Canada; the figure for Europe was higher still. This meant that Americans owned industries, mines, shops, forests, and land in South America, in Canada, in Europe, and elsewhere all over the world. Ford opened motor-car factories and Woolworth's opened sixpenny stores in Great Britain and other European countries. The American Standard Oil Company forced its way into the oil-fields of the Middle East and the Dutch East Indies. Such facts meant that the United States could not ignore what went on in the rest of the world.

Moreover, the war itself had left behind a link tying America to Europe. The Allies owed $10,000,000,000 to the United States. The problem of these War Debts was a persistent source of irritation throughout the post-war years. It soon became clear that the Allies were not very anxious to pay their debts. They argued that the American loans were really part of the American war effort; that the money had been spent in America, and that the Americans had done very well out of it. The American point of view was stated simply, if crudely, by Coolidge when he said 'They hired the money, didn't they?' Americans wanted repayment. Three facts made the position awkward. First, the total debt was a huge sum, difficult to pay in normal times, and almost impossible at the end of a great war. Secondly, the Allies hoped to get the money to pay the Americans out of the reparations which the Germans had been ordered to pay to the Allies. If the Germans did not pay reparations, then, the Allies maintained, they could not pay War Debts. Americans did not accept this argument that the payment of War Debts depended on the payment of reparations. Nevertheless, the Germans were, in fact, unable to pay reparations, which had been fixed at a high figure; and so the Allies argued that they were unable to pay War Debts. Thirdly, the American tariff was a hindrance to payment. In the long run the debts could only be paid by sending goods from the Allied countries to America. But the American tariff prevented this. Thus it was not difficult for the Allies to point out that America's own action in raising so high a tariff prevented the payment of War Debts.

Various attempts were made to solve the problem. In 1922 Congress created a Debt Funding Commission which was to make individual agreements with the countries owing money to America. These agreements were made, and from the American point of view they were very generous. They gave the various countries a long time—until 1985—to pay; and they cut down the rate of interest from the original 5 per cent. to very low levels, varying from country to country—for example 1·6 per cent. for France and 0·4 per cent. for Italy. Further, Americans took the lead in devising plans by which Germany might be enabled to pay reparations; these plans were the Dawes Plan of 1924 and the Young Plan of 1929. But the Allies paid very little, and paid it grudgingly.

War Debts were a rather uncomfortable link between the U.S.A. and Europe. A happier one was the willing co-operation of the U.S.A. in some parts of the work of the League of Nations. American representatives took part in League Conferences on the opium traffic and the trade in armaments. The U.S.A. still kept out of the League itself. But in 1928 the Secretary of State, Frank B. Kellogg, took the lead in proposing the Pact of Paris (sometimes known as the Kellogg Pact) by which sixty-two nations solemnly renounced war as an instrument of national policy. Even the Senate raised no objection to this treaty, which proved quite meaningless in practice. The Senate gave a truer indication of its attitude towards Europe and world affairs when it rejected in 1923 a proposal from Harding that the U.S.A. should join the Permanent Court of International Justice at the Hague. This Court—usually known as the World Court—had been established in 1922 to settle disputes between nations. Most Americans supported it, but the Senate was extremely cautious. In 1926 the proposal came up again. The Senate accepted, but added a reservation which meant that disputes which in any way concerned the U.S.A. should not be considered by the Court at all. This time the nations on the Court would not accept the U.S.A.

The areas in which the U.S.A. was most directly interested were still Central America and the Pacific. 'Dollar diplomacy' in Central America became less obvious. American troops left Santo Domingo in 1924. They left Nicaragua in 1925; but their departure was the signal for an outbreak of civil war, so they went back again. Mexico seriously alarmed the American owners of its oil-fields and mines by its new constitution, which contained a clause stating that the Mexican government owned all minerals and oil in the country. American investments in Mexico ran into hundreds of millions of dollars. Kellogg—the author of the peace pact—tried to bully the Mexican government into submission. But Coolidge eventually sent Dwight Morrow as ambassador to Mexico. Morrow contrived to persuade the Mexican government to refrain from any large-scale attack on American holdings in that country, and the trouble between the two countries subsided. The background to all these activities was the steady growth of American investments in Central America. The total of these had reached over $1,000,000,000 by 1930. Such a vast investment in a comparatively small area necessarily meant an extension of American control.

United States interests in the Pacific were the occasion of the Washington Conference of 1921–2. This was the most important single event in American foreign policy in these years. It was a meeting of representatives of all the powers with interests in the Pacific. Harding and Hughes summoned it in order to deal with Japanese expansion and to check the race among the naval powers to build bigger fleets. Ever since Hay's declaration of the 'Open Door' in China in 1900 Japanese power had grown steadily. Strengthened by her alliance with Britain she had used the opportunity of the Great War to annex Shantung and to obtain mandates of German Pacific Islands; and she had extended her power into Manchuria and Mongolia, and claimed 'special interests' in China. The 'Open Door' had become less of a reality than ever. In 1917 the U.S.A. had signed a treaty with Japan recognising the latter's 'special interests' in China. During the Bolshevik Revolution in Russia Japanese troops had occupied Eastern Siberia. All this growth of Japanese power was very alarming to the U.S.A.; but few Americans wanted to go to war against Japan to stop it, and many were anxious to withdraw from the Far East.

The Washington Conference produced two treaties dealing with the Far East. The Four-Power Treaty (1921) was signed by the U.S.A., Japan, Britain and France; each of these four powers agreed to recognise the rights of the others in their island possessions in the Pacific Ocean. All the Pacific powers signed the Nine-Power Treaty (1922). This guaranteed the independence of China, and recognised the 'Open Door.' Further, Japan agreed to evacuate both Shantung and Eastern Siberia. A third treaty, the Five-Power Treaty, was signed by the U.S.A., Japan, Britain, France and Italy, the five greatest naval powers. They agreed to a plan outlined by Hughes, the American Secretary of State. No battleships were to be built for ten years; while the total tonnage of Japanese naval ships was to be three-fifths of that of the U.S.A., which was in turn to be equal to that of Britain. This treaty slowed down the naval armaments race for a short time; it did not, however, limit the building of smaller ships, such as cruisers, destroyers and submarines. The Washington Conference was hailed at the time as a great success, and the Senate ratified the treaties. It limited armaments and re-stated the principle of the 'Open Door,' making nine powers responsible for maintaining China's independence. Events were to show that its success was only temporary. It gave Japan the opportunity to dominate the western Pacific.

21   Hoover and the Depression, 1929-33

1. HERBERT HOOVER

Coolidge could have been nominated again by the Republicans in 1928, if he had wished. He did not 'choose to run,' and the party nominated the Secretary of Commerce, Herbert C. Hoover. The Democrats chose Al Smith, four times Governor of New York. Smith was a man of great ability who was very popular in New York. But he was also a Roman Catholic and a 'wet,' and both these facts lost him votes. Hoover won forty states, and split the South, which normally voted 'solid' for the Democrats. This smashing victory, like Coolidge's popularity, was the result not of personal ability but simply of prosperity. Americans saw no reason to turn out the Republicans while business was so good. Hoover, a sincere humanitarian, looked forward to the abolition of poverty in the near future. In his speech accepting nomination he said, 'We in America to-day are nearer to the final triumph over poverty than ever before in the history of any land.' In March, 1929, most Americans shared this optimism.

Herbert Hoover had been a successful mining engineer and business director. He had displayed great efficiency in all he had undertaken—in organising Belgian Relief and in controlling America's food during the war, in organising Russian Relief and as head of the Department of Commerce after it. He believed firmly that the best way to run business was by private enterprise, and spoke about the merits of 'rugged individualism'; he was himself a millionaire. The government was not to take control of business, but it was to encourage and guide individual enterprise. Hoover had little experience of politics, and the presidency was the first elective office which he held. He was an unlucky President, for it was his misfortune to encounter the worst economic depression in the history of the U.S.A. The 'Great Engineer' had no plan ready to meet disaster when it came.

2. THE STOCK MARKET

The prosperity of Coolidge's day benefited the majority of Americans. Some—for example, most wage-earners in industry—gained only a little. Others gained much. The people who gained most of all were those who owned shares in the great industrial combines. The profits which the combines made went to them in the form of dividends. They were a comparatively small number of people. In 1929, 78 per cent. of the dividends from the great industries, railroads, oil companies and other combines went to 0·3 per cent. of the population—to about 366,000 people out of 122,000,000; at the head of this group was a handful of multi-millionaires.

But there is another way of making money from shares than by receiving dividends. In a time of prosperity when industry is doing well more people want to become shareholders, and so the price of shares goes up. Thus the market for the sale of shares becomes busier, buying grows keener, and—most important of all—speculation in shares is encouraged. Because the price of shares is rising and seems likely to go on rising, people buy them, not in order to get regular dividends, but simply in order to sell them again in a short time and so make a profit. As ever more buyers do this, so their prices rise higher, and so the temptation to speculate in the 'stock market' grows stronger. A gigantic whirl of speculation arises; and it goes on spinning of its own accord without much regard to the actual conditions of industry—provided that a certain measure of prosperity is maintained. This, in brief outline, is what was happening in the U.S.A. in the late 1920's. America in those years was a land of crazes, and the stock market craze was the greatest of them all.

This craze offered the possibility of an easy fortune and wealth for life. And so people of every type and occupation in America—cowmen from the Middle West and professors from New England, clerks, poets, plumbers, storekeepers, old ladies with plenty of dollars and workmen with a few savings—bought shares. Sometimes they knew what they were buying, more often they did not, leaving it to the brokers; it mattered little, as long as they could sell again at a profit. The stock market became a kind of national mania, or a gigantic gambling game, with hundreds of thousands playing. Perhaps it appealed to those whose lives were normally dull and secure; perhaps it satisfied some pioneering urge in the souls of Americans; certainly it offered the prospects of quick reward to anyone who had saved or could borrow a few dollars. Whatever its causes, it conquered America.

The results of all this were phenomenal. The prices of shares rose—not steadily, but on the whole—to fantastic heights, growing higher than ever during 1928 and 1929. In March 1928 General Electric Company's stocks were at 128¾: eighteen months later they had risen to 396¼. This rise was typical of dozens of others. The daily volume of business done on the New York exchange rose to over $5,000,000. No stockbrokers on earth had ever done such business before. Sometimes, indeed, the business was rapid selling. The rise in prices was erratic, and there were days of wild panic when prices came tumbling down, and shareholders were ruined in a few minutes. Yet the movement was in the main upward. This fact encouraged the Americans to believe in endless prosperity. The stock market has long served the Americans as a kind of barometer by which business prosperity may be measured; and thus, so long as the prices on the stock market were soaring upward, they believed that all was well with American business.

3. THE CRASH AND THE DEPRESSION

Herbert Hoover was inaugurated in March 1929. Six months later the stock market reached its highest price-levels. Then came the crash. Prices began to fall. They had fallen before, and recovered. For some time everyone anticipated recovery. But this time there was no recovery—particularly after one terrible day, October 24, when nearly 13,000,000 shares were sold. The bottom had fallen out of the stock market. Many thousands were ruined. Deep pessimism followed the wild optimism of the days when prices were soaring; and this in itself, by destroying confidence, made a bad situation worse.

The immediate cause of this collapse was the fact that so many people were speculating with borrowed money on a very small margin of safety. Just as a rise of a few points in the price of shares might bring fortunes to their owners, so a drop of a few points might bring ruin. Once prices began to fall, these speculators had to sell out quickly to avoid being saddled with a debt which would ruin them. And once selling on a large scale began, people's confidence fell, and so selling went on at an ever-increasing rate. This was what happened in that terrible autumn of 1929. The lowest point of prices came in June 1932.

But this stock market collapse was not the product of such selling and speculation alone. It had far deeper causes. It was the most spectacular piece of evidence that the U.S.A. was entering a disastrous commercial and industrial depression, the worst in its history, which would bring unemployment to about 14,000,000 of its people. The reasons for this depression were numerous and complicated, and it is only possible to suggest the chief of them here. Most of them were signs that something was fundamentally wrong with the private control of industry under which American business was managed.

First, it was a depression which hit not America alone, but Britain, Europe, and the world as well. In a way, it was a kind of delayed-action result of the dislocation which the Great War brought to world trade.

Secondly—and perhaps chief among the causes which primarily concerned America—came the fact that American manufacturers, encouraged by the high profits of the years of prosperity, had made too many goods. This overproduction led them eventually to start cutting down the number of goods they made; and this meant dismissing workmen. Unemployed men had less to spend; this meant fewer goods sold, and this in turn meant further lowering of the number of goods made—and more workmen unemployed—and so the process continued. Thus the depression gathered momentum as it went on.

Thirdly, we have seen earlier that most (78 per cent.) of the profits made by industry went to a very small proportion (0·3 per cent.) of the people. There was a limit to the amount of goods this 0·3 per cent. could buy; whereas, if the profits had been more evenly distributed among the whole population, the manufacturers could have sold many more goods. So the fact that the profits of industry went to a very small proportion of the people meant, in the long run, less profits. By 1929 American industry was feeling the effects of this. The 'domestic market'—that is, the American people—was not able to absorb the huge quantity of goods which was pouring from the factories. Moreover, many of the farmers, who formed a considerable part of that domestic market, were very poor throughout the prosperity period.

Fourthly, American foreign trade had fallen off. This was partly a result of the American tariff. Since the U.S.A. erected a tariff barrier against goods coming from foreign countries, these countries retaliated by erecting tariff barriers against American goods. In 1930 Congress passed the Hawley-Smoot Tariff Act which raised the level of duties on a great many imported goods. This provoked further retaliation, and the quantity of American goods sold overseas fell still lower after 1930.

Fifthly, the growth of speculation on the stock market was only one example of a general readiness to gamble on the future. Two other examples were the vast growth of debts, among huge industrial combines as well as among private individuals; and the habit of buying goods on the instalment system. Americans were banking heavily on prosperity in the future. When the prosperity began to fail, the whole of this great structure of debt collapsed. Companies went bankrupt, and their stock holders were ruined; innumerable Americans found themselves with houses, motor-cars, carpet-sweepers, wireless sets, furniture on which they could not pay the remaining instalments.

Finally, there were a number of deeper factors outside industry which helped either to cause the depression or to make it worse once it had come. The population was still increasing, but it was increasing much more slowly; the disappearance of the frontier meant that Americans could no longer move westwards in bad times; the crash, notably on the stock markets, came so suddenly, and its effects were such a contrast to the rosy pictures of the future which many Americans had painted for themselves, that many people lost heart and let it overwhelm them.

The depression, beginning in 1929, grew deeper as Hoover's term of office went on. Unemployment was its most obvious sign, and its most terrible result. There had, even in prosperity years, been much unemployment, averaging about 1,500,000; but the country had never dreamed of the shocking figures which the depression brought. By 1930 there were 3,000,000 unemployed; by 1933, about 14,000,000—a figure far worse, even in proportion, than anything reached in Britain, also suffering at this time from the worst depression in her history. American factories in 1933 were producing about half the amount of goods they were producing in 1929. American trade with overseas countries in 1932 was less than one-third of what it was in 1929. These figures are just the bare record of a severe industrial crisis. Behind them lies the story of America's great depression—the story of factories, mills and mines lying idle, of banks with closed doors, of families plunged from comfort into poverty, of bread queues in the cities, of people starving. All this happened in the world's greatest industrial nation, the land whose material civilisation had reached a higher standard than any other in man's history, the land where prosperity was expected to go on for ever.

4. THE GOVERNMENT AND THE DEPRESSION

Hoover was faced with a terrible problem. Inevitably the government was blamed for the depression. For some time Hoover, in common with many Americans, refused to believe that it would last. Recovery, it was maintained, was just round the corner. At the beginning of 1930, Mellon, still Secretary of the Treasury, said that there would be 'a revival of activity' in business 'in the spring.' In May Hoover said he believed the worst was over. It soon became clear that the worst was very far from being over. Moreover, Hoover throughout refused to depart from his firm belief in 'rugged individualism.' He believed that the American people would find their way through the depression by resolution and determination. He did not believe that the government ought to beat the depression by introducing a far-reaching and radical scheme for relief and recovery. He opposed government control of industry, and in 1931 vetoed a bill which would have enabled the government to sell electric power generated at dams on the Tennessee River. Government activity of this kind, in Hoover's opinion, weakened the self-reliance and energy of individuals; and the United States had been built up by the self-reliance and energy of its citizens. He maintained this attitude consistently, and a great many Americans agreed with him.

This did not mean that Hoover and his government did nothing while the country sank lower into depression. Hoover believed that the Federal government ought to do all it could to encourage individuals and the separate states to tackle the problems set by the depression. In this direction the government did a great deal. It was uphill work, for public opinion soon turned strongly against him when it became clear that he had no grand plan to overcome depression. The Congressional elections of 1930 gave the Democrats a majority, which blocked many of his proposals. And his own qualities were a hindrance; he disliked publicity and could not arouse enthusiasm; while his lack of experience of politics handicapped him in dealing with politicians. Yet his government made some attempt to deal with the problems created by the depression. Hoover called to the White House conferences of employers, whom he encouraged to keep wages high and to refrain from dismissing workmen. Extensive loans were made to farmers; more important, the Reconstruction Finance Corporation (1932) was set up to lend money to banks, railroads, and industries, and it saved many from bankruptcy. The Federal government encouraged private charities, and city and state schemes for relieving distress. It accelerated its own public works programme, and encouraged states and cities to do the same, in order to absorb some of the unemployment. In 1931 Hoover attempted to ease the world's financial position, and thus, indirectly, that of America, by declaring a 'moratorium' on war debts—that is, by saying that foreign countries need not pay any interest on war debts to the U.S.A. for twelve months.

All these were genuine attempts to relieve the plight of the country. They achieved little; and they certainly did not form a revolutionary plan to conquer depression. This was to come from Hoover's successor.

22   The United States between the World Wars

In the years between the two World Wars the ways in which Americans lived changed rapidly. The object of this chapter is to describe in some detail the chief changes and causes of change, paying special regard to those features of American life which attracted the attention of the rest of the world. Among these last were such different things as prohibition and the rise of gangsterism, the talking picture, the growth of the new American trade union called the C.I.O., and the revived Ku Klux Klan. When people in the rest of the world thought about the U.S.A., these were the things that came into their minds first. It may not be quite true to say that more human beings heard of the gangster Al Capone than heard of President Coolidge: but it is certainly true that Charlie Chaplin was far more famous than Coolidge. The U.S.A. was known to mankind not so much through its politicians as through its film-stars and crooners, its gangsters and city bosses, its airmen and athletes. The world was far more interested in Henry Ford's latest model or in Charles A. Lindbergh's solo flight across the Atlantic in a 220-horsepower monoplane, or in the Negro Jesse Owens' Olympic victories in 1936, than in the debates in Congress. This was not surprising. But it gave the world a rather one-sided impression of the U.S.A., and the capacity of the Americans for advertising themselves, especially through the films, helped to stamp this impression very deeply.

1. PROHIBITION AND THE GANGSTERS

When the U.S.A. went 'dry,' by the passage of the 18th (Prohibition)

Amendment in 1919, many Americans thought that a new age of sobriety and temperance had dawned. Few realised the difficulties that the attempt to enforce the Amendment would bring: and no one foresaw that the most important consequence of this noble experiment would be a great increase in crime. The Amendment was introduced during the First World War, when the country was in a mood of idealism, and self-sacrifice. To forbid beer, whisky, and other alcoholic liquors would, it was believed, greatly increase the efficiency of the American people and so further the war effort. When the war ended, that mood passed away, and the Americans gradually began to realise the difficulties of prohibition.

In practice, a law against drinking or importing drink was very hard to enforce. The U.S.A. had over 18,000 miles of coastline and land boundary, and it was easy enough to run cargoes of illicit liquor ashore or to get them across some lonely part of the Canadian or Mexican border. It was even easier for the citizen to set up his own secret still in his cellar, while large-scale illegal distilleries proved hard to eliminate. Moreover, alcohol was used in industry for numerous purposes, and, although the government ordered various substances to be put into industrial alcohol in order to prevent its use as a drink, it was not difficult to get round these regulations. The number of men employed by the Federal government to investigate the different methods of evading the law was never sufficient; these Federal agents were poorly paid, and many were very willing to be bribed to turn a blind eye to illegality. Finally, there was always a large number of Americans ready to break the law in order to get a drink. A large minority had opposed prohibition throughout; many more, while quite anxious to stop others from drinking, had no intention of stopping themselves. The Americans, with the tradition of the pioneers still strong in them, had never been a particularly law-abiding people, and the Prohibition Amendment simply encouraged lawlessness.

Its direct results were disastrous, and they illustrate the difficulty of enforcing any law which a large minority is prepared to break. Bootlegging, the making or importing of illegal liquor, developed on a gigantic scale, becoming one of America's major industries. Rum-runners lay off the coasts and swift launches landed their cargoes in lonely coves: lorries carried cargoes of beer through city streets in defiance of the law. Illicit distilleries turned out millions of gallons annually, while several million gallons of industrial alcohol were 'diverted' from their lawful use each year. Home brewing and distilling spread. Thousands of 'speak-easies,' bars where it was possible to obtain alcoholic liquors, sprang up in the large towns. In cities like New York, where the population was strongly 'wet,' the law was scarcely enforced. Drinking, largely because it was forbidden, became fashionable. The government spent $10,000,000 a year and arrested about 50,000 people annually in its attempt to enforce the law, but failed completely to check drinking or bootlegging.

This failure was serious enough. But prohibition had even worse results.

It was the chief cause of a great increase in crimes of every kind, and especially in crimes of violence. In bootlegging, as in every great industry, rivalry grew and disputes became more bitter, just because the profits at stake were so great. Other big industries could settle their disputes in court: bootlegging, being illegal, could not. Therefore the bootleggers devised other means of protecting their own interests and ruining their rivals. The ordinary citizen began to realise what prohibition involved when he heard of miniature battles between rum-runners and Federal agents, or when he saw lorry-loads of liquor protected by toughs armed with machine-guns proceeding through the streets of his own town. Bootlegging, being an illegal business, inevitably attracted criminals: and the bootleggers protected their business or smashed their rivals by means of hired gangs of criminals. So the gangster became an important figure in American life. Prohibition was not the only cause of the outbreak of crime which followed. The war had left behind it a spirit of unrest. The gulf between rich and poor had widened. There was no longer any frontier to which the adventurous could go. Modern inventions, especially the automobile and the machine-gun, were admirably suited to the gangster's work. All these factors encouraged crime. But prohibition and the resultant growth of bootlegging were undoubtedly its chief causes.

What the coming of the gangster meant may be illustrated from the story of Al Capone and of the city which was the centre of gangsterism, Chicago. Alphonse Capone, or 'Scarface Al,' was a gangster of Sicilian ancestry. He was for several years the most powerful man in Chicago, the second largest city in the U.S.A. He made a fortune of many millions of dollars, partly by bootlegging, partly by 'racketeering'[1] of various kinds. His activities were well known, but for years he defied the law—or bought its representatives. The city government of Chicago, from its notorious mayor, 'Big Bill' Thompson, down to the lowest ranks of the police, was riddled with corruption. Capone's victims were sprayed with bullets as they stepped from their own front doors, or carried away in cars and shot in some lonely part of the city. On one occasion, in broad daylight, a rival gang drew up in cars outside Capone's headquarters in Chicago, and raked it with machine-gun fire. On another, seven members of a rival gang were 'arrested' by three of Capone's men dressed as policemen, and then lined up against a garage wall and shot by two more of Capone's men, while the 'policemen' watched. The most effective law in Chicago was gang law. Other cities suffered from gangsters, though to a smaller extent: and New York's mayor, 'Jimmy' Walker, was at least as corrupt as 'Big Bill' Thompson. Other bootleggers made fortunes, though none was so

---

[1] A 'racket' was a crude form of blackmail. Gangsters forced owners of businesses or shops to pay them money by threatening to destroy their stock or premises, or even to shoot them; in name, the unfortunate victims paid for 'protection'! Racketeering even extended to laundries, window-cleaning, and the sale of artichokes.

eminent as Capone, with his armoured cars and private bodyguard, his estate at Miami, and his vast control of speak-easies, distilleries, gambling-dens, and liquor-importing.

As crime grew, so did the opposition to prohibition. In 1929 Hoover appointed the Wickersham Commission to investigate the working of the prohibition law. This body issued in 1931 an extremely muddled report, saying that prohibition did not work, but ought to be maintained. By that time the depression had greatly strengthened the 'wets.' States short of money saw that taxes on spirits would increase their revenue, while the unemployed were tempted to find a refuge from their troubles in beer. In the 1932 election the Democrats came out firmly against prohibition. In 1933 the 21st Amendment was passed, repealing the 18th and thus abolishing Federal prohibition. Several states still remained 'dry' by their own laws. But the 21st Amendment was an admission that the whole experiment had failed.

The ending of prohibition, by making bootlegging unnecessary, did something to stop crime. Now that gangsters and racketeers no longer served any purpose in helping the citizen to get his drink, public opinion became firmer against them. The Federal government took stronger action, through its Criminal Investigation Bureau under J. Edgar Hoover, and its agents, the 'G Men.' Even Al Capone was sent to gaol—for income-tax evasion. Yet prohibition left an unhappy legacy of crime, which could not be cured either by the repeal of the 18th Amendment, or by the work of the 'G Men.' One peculiarly American crime, which reflected the lawlessness of the time, was kidnapping; the kidnapping of the baby child of Colonel Lindbergh was a notorious example. Worst of all its effects was its influence on thousands of adventurous young men. These, who in earlier days would have gone out to the frontier and become valuable citizens, had instead become criminals, attracted by the excitement as well as by the profits of the gangster's life. Herbert Hoover called prohibition 'a great social and economic experiment, noble in motive.' The results of the experiment were a national disaster.

2. FILMS, RADIO, AND AUTOMOBILES

It was the films that brought gangsterism most effectively before the eyes of the American people—and of the people of the rest of the world. The moving picture industry, with its centre at Hollywood, a suburb of Los Angeles, was one of the great industrial developments of the post-war years. The 1920's were the golden age of the silent pictures: the domination of the talkies began about 1930. The cinema became a feature of American life. Moreover, American film-producers spread their wares all over the globe. In 1940, nearly two-thirds of the world's films were produced in the U.S.A., despite the elaborate attempts of other lands to stimulate their own film industries. Through the films the world gained its idea of how ordinary Americans lived; it also gained a very extensive knowledge of the more lurid or romantic features of American life, of gangsters and night clubs, of cowboys and lumber-camps. Through the films, 'stars' like Charlie Chaplin and Rudolf Valentino in silent days, and Greta Garbo, Will Rogers and Shirley Temple in the early days of the talkies became world-renowned. The profits of this new industry were huge, and the film magnate of the 1930's was almost as prominent a figure as the railway king of the 1890's. The effects of the films upon American life were much disputed. Some said they were thoroughly unwholesome, encouraging crime and loose living, and creating an undesirable atmosphere of artificial excitement. Others said that they were the one genuine form of art which the American people had produced. Whatever the merits of the argument, whatever the weaknesses of the films, the box-office returns demonstrated the popularity of the cinema. By the end of the 1930's over 80,000,000 Americans were going to the films every week.

Another great new industry whose products became a normal feature of American life in the post-war years was the radio. The first American broadcasting station was KDKA, opened at Pittsburgh in November, 1920. Broadcasting was slow in developing, and then suddenly became a craze in 1922. From the start American broadcasting stations were privately owned, making their incomes from advertising patent medicines and other products. The Federal government did little more than exercise a general supervision, settling disputes and arranging wavelengths and similar problems: it did not set up its own stations. By 1940 there were over 700 stations in existence in the U.S.A. No one can assess the general effects of radio on American life in these years. But three special effects, of different kinds, may be noted. First, the radio did more than anything else to popularise the dance band. Secondly, radio became one of the chief American industries with hundreds of millions of dollars invested in it. Thirdly, it proved highly important in politics. Political questions of every kind were thoroughly discussed over the air. Great political events, like the Conventions of the major parties, were relayed. The use of the radio was a great asset to an accomplished speaker like Franklin D. Roosevelt. His radio addresses, including, after he became President, the 'fireside chats,' did much to help him to win and keep power. It was an advantage that none of his great predecessors, Jefferson, Jackson, or Lincoln, had enjoyed.

A third great industry of the post-war years was the automobile, or motor-car, industry. It was not a new industry, for it developed in the U.S.A. before the war: but it improved vastly after the war. In 1919 there were nearly 7,000,000 automobiles in the U.S.A. Ten years later there were nearly 24,000,000. The progress continued, though not at the same rate, and the U.S.A. had far more cars in proportion to her population than any other land in the world. Among the manufacturers Henry Ford was the outstanding personality leading the way in the use of mass-production methods. The results of this vast expansion of the number of automobiles were very great. The automobile satisfied the desire for speed which many Americans showed; greatly increased the number of fatal accidents; caused great improvement in the construction of American roads; helped bootleggers and gangsters to ply their trades; opened up extensive areas of lovely country to Americans on holiday; enormously increased the use of petrol and the profits of the oil companies; and enabled thousands of Americans to make their living not only out of selling petrol, tyres, and spare parts, but also out of selling ice-cream, cool drinks, hot dogs, and similar commodities to the millions of people who travelled daily on the roads. In short, the automobile produced far-reaching changes in American life.

3. BUSINESS AND TRADE UNIONISM

During the years of prosperity, when American industry and trade were flourishing, the business man was much admired in the U.S.A. He was regarded as a model of efficiency. This produced many somewhat strange results. Universities began to advertise their courses by the methods of business salesmanship. They offered degrees in business management and in similar studies. Clergymen preached sermons praising the means which brought success in business. Great numbers of books pointed out to their readers that the way to success in life lay in cultivating the methods of the business man—in being efficient, in practising the arts of salesmanship. Clubs of business men prospered, the most notable among them being the Rotary Club. When the depression came, and neither the businessmen nor President Hoover, himself a highly successful business man, could stop it, the general enthusiasm for business methods waned. Yet it never perished, and business efficiency remained an American ideal.

Trade unionism followed a different course in post-war America. The coming of the First World War had done little to improve relations between employers and workmen in the U.S.A., and once it was over the strikes and industrial conflicts which had been common before 1917 broke out again with all the old violence. Between 1916 and 1935 there were on an average well over a thousand strikes a year: even during the prosperity years they went on. The strongest American trade union movement before 1935 was the American Federation of Labor, whose membership reached a high peak of over 4,000,000 in 1920. After that it fell away, until by 1926 it was down to 2,800,000. A slight rise before 1930 was negligible compared with the further drop caused by the depression. The A.F. of L. declined for various reasons. Prosperity itself was one of them, tempting workmen to forget the need of trade unionism. The failure of a railroad strike in 1921 brought unions into disrepute. The death of Samuel Gompers removed the A.F. of L.'s wisest leader. But the two most important reasons of all were its unsatisfactory organisation and its cautious policy. The A.F. of L. was mainly an organisation of craft unions—that is, of skilled men. It did not satisfactorily organise the unskilled workers. This was a serious weakness, for the rapid development of mass production meant that an increasing number of Americans were unskilled workmen. This was especially true in the newer industries, like the automobile industry. Henry Ford himself had pointed out that 43 per cent. of all the jobs in his works could be done by men with only one day's training, while only 1 per cent. needed a year or more of training. Again, the A.F. of L., under the leadership of William Green, was very cautious, anxious to avoid any extreme policy.

One union, the Industrial Workers of the World, founded in 1905, had attempted both to organise the unskilled workers and to provide an energetic policy. But it had never obtained many members, because its policy was too bold. It preached militant socialism and the destruction of capitalism, and its marching song was entitled *Paint 'Er Red*. The government locked up many of the leaders of the I.W.W. during the First World War, and it petered out soon afterwards. Not until the great depression of the 1930's was there a powerful demand for a new union.

4. DEMOCRACY?

At the entrance to New York Harbour the Statue of Liberty—a gift from the French people—had since its dedication in 1886 welcomed millions of immigrants who had fled from poverty or persecution to what they believed to be the land of the free. But, as we have seen,[1] American policy towards immigrants had begun to change with the First World War. An Act of 1921 set up the 'quota' system. The annual entry of persons from any country into the U.S.A. was limited to a small percentage (3 per cent. in this act, smaller still later) of the number of people born in that country who were living in the U.S.A. in 1910. The effect of the 1921 act was that only 357,803 immigrants could enter in any one year. The process of limiting the numbers went on in the post-war years; thus the National Origins Act of 1924, which came into force in 1929, reduced the figure to 150,000. The object of these acts was not simply to limit immigration, but also to favour certain kinds of immigrants and keep out others. More immigrants were permitted from western Europe than from eastern and central Europe. The act of 1924 did not apply to Canada or Latin America, but it totally excluded Japanese. In sum, the American doors, once and for so long wide open to all strangers, had been almost closed. The famous lines inscribed on the base of the Statue of Liberty—

> Give me your tired, your poor,
> Your huddled masses yearning to breath free

—were the welcome of an older America that was no more.

In Lincoln's phrase, the United States stands for 'government of the

[1] Above, p. 177.

people, by the people, for the people.' The noblest of Americans—poets like Whitman, statesmen like Jefferson and Wilson—had always seen their country as the land of democracy. Millions of the common people held the same faith; thousands had, as they believed, died for this faith in the Civil War and in the First World War. Yet throughout American history there had in fact been serious limitations upon American democracy. Government of the people had frequently been neither by the people nor for the people. In Washington's day, for example, government had been by the wealthier landowners. After the Civil War itself, in Grant's day, government had been in the hands of the business men. In the years between the World Wars, too, there were limits to the reality of American democracy. We have already come across one of the factors that limited it. The strength of Wall Street—that is, of the big business men and the financiers—was still great, and even the depression did not break them. Through their great wealth and their domination of industry and transport they remained very powerful and able to influence in many ways the lives of millions of Americans, and, what is more to the point here, able to exert a good deal of pressure on the government.

And there were also brutal forms of oppression to be found in the United States at this time. The example which caught the public eye in the 1930's was that of Huey 'Kingfish' Long, effective dictator of Louisiana for some years before he was assassinated in 1935. Able, unscrupulous, a brilliant orator whose speeches were an extraordinary mixture of pathos, buffoonery, and coarse abuse, unlimited in his arrogance, Huey Long secured virtually complete control of his state by his appeal to its many illiterate poor whites and by corrupting and bullying its politicians. He silenced almost all hostile newspapers, kidnapped his opponents, and surrounded himself with an armed bodyguard. Nor was he without national ambitions. After serving as Governor of Louisiana, he entered the U.S. Senate in 1932, where his eccentricities—he once created a diplomatic incident by wearing green pyjamas when he received a German admiral—his vulgar clothes and his flair for nicknames did not endear him to his colleagues. In 1934 he founded a 'Share Our Wealth' organisation whose slogan was 'Everyman a king but where no man wears a crown'; its programme was to confiscate all fortunes over $3,000,000, give every family enough money to buy a home, an automobile and a radio, provide a national minimum wage for a shorter working week, supply everybody over 60 with a pension, and send all deserving boys to college. The movement won millions of sympathisers. Huey Long wanted to be President, and might indeed have been a serious candidate by 1940. Many Americans in these depression years saw him as a possible saviour; others thought him an American version of the contemporary European fascist dictators, Hitler and Mussolini.

Yet perhaps the most serious weakness of American democracy in these years was the treatment of minorities. Any country contains minorities of some kind—groups of people who differ from the majority of the inhabitants in colour, race, nationality, politics, or religion. How the majority treats these groups provides a fair test of the reality of democracy —for a majority can be quite as tyrannical in its behaviour as a dictator. The U.S.A., because of its size and because it has been the 'melting-pot' of so many different peoples, contains many minorities. It contains, for example, a great number of national minorities—groups of Germans, Italians, Poles, Scandinavians and others, who, although American citizens, yet perhaps speak their own language rather than English. But the most important minority groups in the 20th century have been the Negroes, the Jews, and the Roman Catholics. They are all very large minorities. But the fact that they are large is no safeguard; rather, it is a danger to them, for it renders them more likely to be regarded with suspicion and with fear by the majority of the people.

In 1930 there were nearly 12,000,000 Negroes in the United States: almost one American in every ten was coloured. Broadly, the pattern set up around 1900 still remained in the South: great numbers of Negroes were deprived of the vote, and 'Jim Crow' laws of segregation were almost universal there. Certain features of it, for example, segregation in housing, had grown up in the North also. In the North Negroes were treated more fairly by the white majority; yet in practice they were generally employed in poorly-paid, low-grade jobs, for example as bootblacks, waiters, and railroad attendants, and they lived in the slums of the great cities. Harlem, the big Negro quarter of New York City, was in many ways desperately backward and squalid. As a result of the First World War, during which 360,000 Negroes served in the armed forces, and many moved from the South to better-paid jobs in the North, there seemed to be signs of improvement. But this in itself caused fear among the poorer whites, and in 1919 there was a series of savage race riots, in cities both South and North; that year, too, seventy Negroes were lynched, some of them soldiers in uniform. During the 1920's there was much racial tension. 'Jim Crow' laws were further extended in parts of the South; to taxis and buses, as transport developed, and also to boxing, race-tracks, and other sporting activities; in Birmingham, Alabama, white and coloured people were even forbidden to play dominoes together. In the North there was hostility from many trade unions to Negroes, and many were driven out of the better jobs they had managed to secure during the war period. The years of depression and the New Deal brought some modest signs of improvement, but not until the Second World War and its aftermath did real change begin.

The other great minority groups, the Jews and the Roman Catholics, were penalised very little by the law. No attempt was made, for example, to stop Roman Catholics from practising their own faith. But prejudice against them showed itself in other ways. In 1928, as we have seen, Al Smith lost votes in the presidential election because he was a Roman

Catholic. The most remarkable sign of this prejudice was the rise in the years immediately after the Great War of a new Ku Klux Klan. This body, like the earlier Klan, was first organised in the southern states. It stood for 'pure Americanism.' It attracted attention and support by an elaborate ritual; Klansmen wore white hoods and robes and were summoned to meet by a fiery cross. Its members opposed everything they considered un-American—Negroes, Roman Catholics, Jews, immigrants, and Communists. Their opposition was not merely vocal. Klansmen flogged Negroes and boycotted Jewish and Catholic merchants: forced Negroes to sell them land, and refused to lease land to Roman Catholics. This Ku Klux Klan of the 1920's gained a very large membership in the south, yet it was strongest in the rural northern states of Oregon and Indiana. It appealed strongly to the prejudices of rural Americans who disliked cities because foreigners congregated there. It was very influential in the affairs of the Democratic party, and in 1924 that party's Convention, which had met to choose a presidential candidate, became a bitter squabble over the merits of the Klan. It was never widely popular in the North, and its influence fell away greatly in the 1930's. But the mere existence of such a body showed how easy it was to arouse prejudice against any group which differed in any important way from the mass of Americans.

All these things were in different ways limitations upon, and dangers to, the working of a democratic system of government. During these years many Americans criticised them and fought against them. Huey Long by no means silenced all his opponents in Louisiana. There were constant white champions of the Negro. And the dangers must be kept in proportion. The Klan was in no way comparable in scale or in method, for example, with such a movement as Nazism in contemporary Germany. Huey Long was a peculiar and dangerous figure; but he had very little political influence outside Louisiana, and 'Share Our Wealth' faded out very quickly. Above all, the American people met the great crisis of the 1930's, the depression, not by turning to a dictator—as happened over so much of continental Europe at this time—but by accepting the reforms introduced by a democratically-chosen government under Franklin Roosevelt.

23   Franklin D. Roosevelt and the New Deal

I. FRANKLIN D. ROOSEVELT

It was practically certain that the Republicans would lose the presidential election of 1932. Prosperity had given them success in 1924 and 1928; depression would defeat them in 1932. They had already lost the

Congressional elections of 1930. They chose Hoover as their candidate once again, while the Democrats nominated Franklin D. Roosevelt of New York, a distant relative of Theodore Roosevelt. The election was an exciting one, even if its result was hardly doubtful. Roosevelt toured the country, travelling 20,000 miles in four months and delivering speeches promising the people a 'new deal' of reforms. His programme included unemployment relief, lower tariffs, the removal of prohibition, government operation of the dams on the Tennessee River, and a revival of industry and agriculture. Hoover attacked this programme, saying that the extension of government control which it would involve would destroy the energy and self-reliance of Americans. Roosevelt won a great victory. Nearly 23,000,000 Americans, over 57 per cent. of those who voted, voted for him; and he won 472 electoral votes against Hoover's 59.

Franklin Delano Roosevelt was born in 1882, of a wealthy Hudson Valley family. He was educated at Groton and Harvard, the Eton and Oxford of the U.S.A. In 1910, after a short career as a lawyer, he was elected to the New York State Senate, and was a supporter of Wilson, who appointed him Assistant Secretary to the Navy in 1913. He held this office throughout the First World War, and in 1920 was the Democrat candidate for the vice-presidency. In 1921 he suffered a blow which seemed certain to end his career; he was struck down by infantile paralysis. Saying 'I'll beat this thing,' he determined not to become an invalid, and succeeded, although the illness left him unable to walk without assistance; and in 1924 he came back to politics to organise Al Smith's unsuccessful presidential campaign. He was elected Governor of New York in 1928 and again in 1930, and in this office he gave the people of New York reforms which were a foretaste of the New Deal. In 1932 he was the outstanding leader of the Democratic party, and the obvious candidate for the presidency.

His personal qualities made him a particularly suitable candidate in the middle of a depression. Ambitious, energetic, resourceful, and full of common sense, he possessed a remarkable charm of manner. He thoroughly enjoyed popularity, and no president has ever known so well how to win it. The cheerful smile and handshake, the joking replies to the journalists, the broadcasts in which he took the American people into his confidence—all these were weapons in Roosevelt's armoury. Already before 1932 he had shown himself to be a vigorous reformer. Once determined on an end, he let no obstacle hinder him from reaching it. His wealth and his conquest of infantile paralysis were both important factors in his career. The former had given him a good education and the power to travel and to get to know people in every part of the U.S.A. The latter had developed his will-power; his triumph over his disability had strengthened his lively optimism and unbounded confidence in himself. He was ready to make full use of the power which he had obtained by his election, and he came into office with a far-reaching programme of reforms. His ideas were very like those of Woodrow Wilson; his flair for popularity was like that of Theodore Roosevelt. Few American Presidents have entered office with such a combination of personal qualities and popularity.

He needed all his cheerfulness, energy, and common sense. On the day of his inauguration in 1933 about 14,000,000 Americans were out of work, and every bank in the country was shut. This was just the kind of situation that brought out Roosevelt's qualities. His inaugural address attacked the system that had brought the U.S.A. to such a plight, and pointed the way to recovery. 'This nation asks for action, and action now!' And action he took, immediately.

2. THE NEW DEAL

The 'New Deal' is the name given to the great series of actions undertaken by Roosevelt's administration to lift the American people out of depression, and to lead them to a new future.These actions do not form one carefully-planned scheme. In 1933 time was short and the need urgent, so that many of Roosevelt's measures were steps taken in a hurry to deal with immediate problems. But at the back of them all were three main aims. Relief was the first; those millions of Americans who were in desperate need of food and cash had to be helped. Recovery was the second; the government had to lead the country out of depression. Reform was the third; glaring wrongs had to be set right in order that the U.S.A. might go forward to a new future. Relief, Recovery, Reform—these were the three great aims of the New Deal. In practice they included a wide variety of purposes. Roosevelt wanted to help the poor—not only poor people throughout the country, but also poverty-stricken industries, like the bituminous coal industry, and poverty-stricken regions, like the farmlands of the South and West. He wanted to attack the rich employers and financiers, and to help the workmen to organise themselves into trade unions in order to be able to bargain fairly with their employers. He wanted to safeguard democracy, 'government of the people, by the people, for the people,' against the power of the rich. He wanted to help industry to recover, not, as Hoover had done, by making loans to bankrupt business firms, but by enabling the ordinary American to buy more from the business firms. And he wanted to stop the waste of America's natural resources—her oil, her land—in order to keep them for Americans of the future.

The methods which Roosevelt used to put the New Deal into action were bold and skilful. First, he made it clear that it was his own personal policy. The New Deal was not the policy of the Democratic party; it was the policy of Franklin D. Roosevelt. Secondly, he used to the utmost the full powers which the Constitution allowed him. No previous American President ever wielded such great power in peace-time. Thirdly, he made full use of expert advisers. He collected round him a group of comparatively young men, college professors,[1] experts in finance, economics, and similar subjects. This group, known as the 'Brains Trust,' planned many of the details of the New Deal. Fourthly, Roosevelt cleverly used his own genius for winning popularity in order to gain popular support for his policy. Examples of this were the 'fireside chats,' and the White House press conferences. In the 'fireside chats' Roosevelt spoke over the radio to his fellow-countrymen as an American sitting by his own fireside and talking over their common problems with them. At the press conferences, held twice a week at the White House, he let the journalists crowd into his study and fire off at him whatever questions they liked. His quick answers, his great friendliness, and his willingness to crack jokes won him popularity among the pressmen.

Many able people of very varied opinions—like Harold Ickes (Secretary of the Interior), Frances Perkins (Secretary of Labor, the first woman to be appointed to cabinet office in the United States), Harry Hopkins (Federal Relief Administrator), and Henry Wallace (Secretary of Agriculture, and Vice-President during Roosevelt's third term)—contributed much to carrying out the New Deal. But Roosevelt's team changed substantially over the years, and so did the New Deal itself, so much so that it has become customary to talk of two 'New Deals', not one. What has become known as the 'First New Deal' lasted from 1933 to 1935 and concentrated mainly on the immediate problems—of restoring the banking system, providing jobs for the unemployed, raising agricultural prices to help the farmers, setting industries on their feet again. Then, in political language, Roosevelt moved to the left. The 'Second New Deal,' from 1935 to 1938, brought more measures of lasting reform; involved heavy expenditure and an unbalanced budget, as well as higher taxation of the rich; and showed far less sympathy to business and more to such groups as trade unions. The change was neither so clear-cut nor so sudden as this simplified division may suggest, for the actions of government were numerous and complicated and took time to come into effect. The reasons for it were various. One undoubtedly was that the depression did not yield easily: the national income for 1934, after almost two years of the New Deal, was only a little more than half of the 1929 figure, and there were still almost ten million unemployed. More radical action was needed. Secondly, business men had grown critical of various items in the New Deal, and Roosevelt was by no means unwilling to take up their challenge. Thirdly, he was worried by extremists who were winning considerable popular interest. One of them was Huey Long, the brutal but gifted senator from Louisiana, with his 'Share Our Wealth' movement; another, less sinister but more appealing, was Dr. Francis Townsend with his pensions plan for providing everybody over 60 years of age with $200 a month on condition that they did no paid work and spent the entire $200

[1] The word 'professor' still seems to suggest an absent-minded, short-sighted old gentleman. This is an illusion; generally in England, certainly in America.

in the U.S.A. within the month. The best way to undermine quack remedies for the depression was to make the genuine ones effective. Lastly, and perhaps most important, Roosevelt had not yet satisfied the trade unions, as a series of strikes in 1934 indicated. All these things tended to propel Roosevelt to the left after his first two years in office, and thus to bring more far-reaching reforms.

The chief details of the New Deal as a whole may be summarised as follows:

a. Banking and Finance. With every bank in the land shut when Roosevelt came to office, his first task was to get the national financial system working again. He did this by giving the people confidence in their banks once more. Within a week of entering office he got Congress to pass an Emergency Banking Act, giving him control over the banks and power to re-open those which he considered solvent. In the first 'fireside chat,' eight days after entering office, he convinced the people that all was well with the country's finances. Confidence was restored; banks were re-opened; and the people deposited their money in them again. He followed up this emergency action by other important laws. The Banking Act (1933) established stricter government control of the banks; in order to prevent fraud, separated banks which simply did banking business; and —most important—set up a Federal Deposit Insurance Corporation which insured deposits in banks and thus safeguarded depositors against losing their money because of a 'run' on the bank in a time of panic. The Securities Act (1933) attempted to stop the formation of fraudulent companies. It ordered all companies to state the facts about themselves clearly and accurately on any prospectus which they issued to the public. Another act, in 1934, set up the Securities Exchange Commission. This was a special body to make sure that companies carried out the act of 1933, and to investigate all dishonest and dubious practices on the stock exchanges. Finally, Roosevelt tried in many ways to use finance to assist the recovery of industry. He did so mainly by encouraging banks to lend money at lower rates of interest, and for this purpose he made use of the Federal Reserve Banking System created by Wilson.

b. The Farmers. American farmers had gained little from the prosperity years, and had suffered in common with the rest of the people during the depression. Their difficulties were many, and the chief of them was the low price which most farm products were fetching. This low price was mainly the result of the fact that the farmers, unable to sell their crops overseas, were growing more than the American people could consume. The depression made their plight worse by making Americans able to pay still less for farm produce. Roosevelt's main object, therefore, was to raise prices. His government, indeed, did many other things to help farmers. It lent them money to save them from being evicted from their farms, and to help those whose farms were on poor land to start again in more fertile areas. But the only satisfactory cure for the farmers' ills would be to make sure that they got a good price for their produce. So in 1933 the Farmers' Relief Act was passed. This created the Agricultural Adjustment Administration (A.A.A.). The A.A.A. encouraged co-operative marketing of some farm products. Much more important, for all the important products in which American farmers had lost some of their overseas trade—for example, cotton, tobacco, rice, wheat, pigs—it devised a scheme for cutting down the amount grown by the farmers. Farmers who wished to do so could sign agreements with the A.A.A., promising to reduce, for example, the amount of corn they grew and the number of pigs they bred. This meant destroying some of their crops and animals in the first year,[1] and planning to grow and breed less in the following years. The government paid the farmers to do this, arguing that fewer crops meant higher prices. The money which went to the farmers was provided by 'processing taxes.' Examples of these were taxes on cotton-spinning to be used to withdraw poor cotton lands from cultivation, and taxes on flour-milling to give similar help to wheat farmers. Nature helped the scheme: there were severe droughts in 1934 and 1936. But in 1936 the Supreme Court ruled that the A.A.A. was unconstitutional: it took particular exception to the processing taxes. The government replied with a Soil Conservation Act, which did much the same as the A.A.A., raising the money by a different method and leasing poor land from the farmers.

This act also paid attention to the problem of saving American soil from wastage caused by reckless farming and drought. Much land had been ruined in the South and in the 'Dust Bowl,' the western part of the Plains, from which great dust-storms blew tons of soil into the Middle West.[2] Roosevelt's government undertook research into methods of beating drought and dust. Thus it tried to prevent great areas of the U.S.A. from going the way of parts of Iraq and North Africa, which were once fertile land but are now sandy waste and desert. All these attempts to help the farmer produced one clear sign of improvement. The total income of American farmers was almost doubled between 1932 and 1937.

c. The Civilian Conservation Corps (C.C.C.). One of the worst features of the depression was that it threw so many young men out of work. Roosevelt tried to do something to solve this problem by creating in 1933 the Civilian Conservation Corps. Under this scheme unemployed, unmarried men between the ages of 18 and 25 were given the chance of joining for six months government camps set up chiefly in mountain or forest areas. There they did various jobs of benefit to the community; they learnt forestry, built dams, fought forest fires, floods, and dust-storms,

[1] They were not wholly destroyed: many were bought by the government and fed to the hungry poor in the great cities.

[2] There is an American tall story of a Kansas farmer who one day went to see his bank manager, to ask whether the latter would lend him money on the security of his farm. The bank manager said he would have to come out and see the farm, in order to value it. 'You needn't bother,' said the farmer, pointing to a great cloud of dust which was coming down the road. 'Here it comes now.'

constructed tracks and telephone lines through remote areas. Each member of the C.C.C. was paid $30 a month, of which $25 had to be sent home to his family. The scheme began with 300,000 men; before 1940 over 2,000,000 had passed through it. Many of these rejoined after their six months were up. But the number of those rejoining grew less; employers became anxious to take on C.C.C. men, because the training in the camps made them fit and alert and gave them technical skill.

d. P.W.A. and N.R.A. The central feature of Roosevelt's plan for the recovery of America from the depression was the National Industrial Recovery Act (1933). His chief aim was to put people back to work; once in work and earning wages again, they would be able to buy more; the factories would produce more; and national recovery would be under way. He also aimed at reforming the conditions under which men worked, by raising wages and lowering hours, by getting rid of child labour, and by making trade unions legal. The act had three important features. First, it set up a Public Works Administration (P.W.A.). This organisation encouraged the building of public works of all kinds. The Federal government itself employed many men on building dams, aerodromes, warships, post offices, and various government offices. It both gave and lent money to states and cities for public works; these included roads, bridges, hospitals, schools and slum clearance schemes. In sum, P.W.A. provided work for millions of men. Secondly, the act set up a National Recovery Administration which was to make rules, or 'codes' to govern industries. These codes were usually first drawn up by the industries themselves, and approved by the N.R.A. They abolished child labour, lowered hours, fixed a minimum wage, and stopped unfair competition. Within one year 500 codes had been approved. But they took time to draw up, and Roosevelt wanted quick action. So in July, 1933, he first drew up a 'blanket code,' to be applied to any industry that wanted it. This abolished child labour, established an eight-hour day, and gave a minimum wage of $12.50 a week. Over 2,000,000 employers asked for it, and it eventually covered 16,000,000 workmen. All employers who accepted it were given the privilege of displaying a Blue Eagle on their goods, and the government encouraged the public to deal with firms showing the Blue Eagle. A third feature of the act was a section which gave workmen the legal right to bargain with their employers through trade unions.

e. Poor Relief, C.W.A., and W.P.A. The C.C.C. was only one means of tackling part of the huge unemployment problem. Roosevelt used the Reconstruction Finance Corporation, which Hoover had set up, to lend money to those states which needed it to give immediate cash help to the poor. In 1933 he set up the Federal Emergency Relief Administration; under this the Federal government itself gave direct cash relief to the poor throughout the country, as well as assisting local charitable schemes. Such 'doles' were essential for the time; yet it was clearly not satisfactory to go on paying money to keep the poor in idleness, and Roosevelt determined to provide work instead. To do this he created in 1933 the Civil Works Administration which provided work for about 4,000,000 unemployed. A good deal of this work was rather useless, and the scheme was scrapped in 1934. In 1935 the government created another and much more satisfactory organisation—the Works Progress Administration (W.P.A.). Under the W.P.A. millions of men and women were employed on many jobs of value to the community; the government paid them wages enough to keep them alive, though not as large as those they would have earned in ordinary employment. The W.P.A. built roads, dams, airports, schools, hospitals, community centres, playgrounds and swimming pools. Its activities covered every part of the country. Moreover, it gave work to out-of-work actors, musicians, writers, and artists; the Federal Theatre Project, for example, sent travelling companies who performed plays in the big cities, while artists were employed in decorating post offices and other public buildings. The W.P.A. was costly, but it saved millions of people from wasting in idleness, and most of its work was of permanent value to the U.S.A. Taken as a whole, the W.P.A. was a bold and notable achievement.

f. Social Security. The U.S.A. had, before 1933, no national scheme of unemployment or health insurance, or of old age pensions. The world's richest country was very backward; Germany had had Old Age Pensions since 1889, Great Britain since 1909. One American state alone, Wisconsin, had an unemployment insurance scheme before 1935. So one of the most important of all the New Deal laws was the Social Security Act (1935). This established a scheme of old age pensions, run by the Federal government, and paid for by contributions from both employers and employed; created a plan of unemployment insurance, under which the separate states were to make their own detailed schemes; and provided Federal government grants to states for such problems as help to the blind and children's health. The whole scheme aimed to provide social security —safety against old age or unemployment—for millions of Americans.

g. Trade Unions. The National Industrial Recovery Act also included a section which gave workmen the legal right to bargain with their employers through trade unions. This, though beneficial to workmen, proved difficult to enforce, and was in effect replaced by the Wagner Act (1935), which was very much the achievement of Senator Robert Wagner of New York rather than of Roosevelt. This act compelled employers to recognise the union to which the majority of their workmen belonged, and to bargain with it in any dispute over hours and wages. It also forbade employers to interfere with their workmen's freedom to join unions, and set up a National Labor Relations Board (N.L.R.B.) to which workmen could complain and which had power to punish employers. Further, the Fair Labor Standards Act (1938) improved standards in many poorly-paid occupations by fixing maximum hours and minimum wages. The New Deal gave immense encouragement to trade unionism: whereas in 1933 only

7·8 per cent. of American workers were organised in unions, by 1938 the proportion was 21·9 per cent. One notable feature of this development was the start of a huge new union, the Committee for Industrial Organisation, (later the Congress of Industrial Organisations). The C.I.O. was founded in 1935 when a group of leaders of the A.F. of L., headed by John L. Lewis, seceded from that body and set out to organise the unskilled workmen in mass industry. They were remarkably successful: by 1938 the C.I.O. had almost 4,000,000 members, about the same number as the A.F. of L. itself. In 1937 it had won strikes against two of the biggest American corporations, General Motors and United States Steel—although it failed against another group of steel companies, in a strike marked by bloodshed when police killed ten strikers in the 'Memorial Day Massacre' at Chicago.

  h. The Tennessee Valley Authority. During the First World War the government had built at Muscle Shoals on the Tennessee River a dam to provide power, and a nitrate factory. Twice Senator Norris of Nebraska had got through Congress bills which would have enabled the Federal government to use the Muscle Shoals dam for the benefit of the inhabitants of the Tennessee Valley. But Coolidge and Hoover had vetoed them. Roosevelt took up Norris' scheme and extended it. In 1933 the Tennessee Valley Authority (T.V.A.) was created. Through this the government undertook a great experiment in planning the welfare of the whole Tennessee Valley, a region of 41,000 square miles covering parts of seven states, the largest planned area outside the U.S.S.R. The T.V.A. took over the Muscle Shoals dam, and built others. It set up hydro-electric stations and sold electricity direct to industry and farmers, at rates well below those charged by private companies. It undertook schemes of flood control; built navigation channels in the Tennessee River; helped to stop soil erosion in the valley by planting trees; aided farmers by developing new fertilisers; and built model villages. Cheap electricity brought great changes in the lives of the farmers in the valley. It also attracted industry. T.V.A. meant something more than the fact that the government had gone into the business of selling electricity. The government had also begun to replan the whole life of the valley by using its natural resources for the benefit of its inhabitants.

  i. Other Details. The laws and schemes described above were the principal features of the New Deal. There were many others. The Home Owners Loan Corporation, originally set up by Hoover, greatly extended its work, and helped to save the homes of many Americans from being sold up because of non-payment of loans and mortgages. A Pure Food and Drugs Act tried to save the public from fraudulent advertisements for patent medicines and similar articles. The Federal Housing Authority (1937) encouraged the clearance of slums and the building of sound, healthy flats and houses at low rentals, by lending money to cities and counties. A national electricity scheme was established in 1938. The National Resources Board (1934) made a survey of the natural wealth of the

PUNCH OR THE LONDON CHARIVARI.—March 5, 1919.

A HOME FROM HOME.

President Wilson (*quitting America in his Fourteen-League-of-Nations Boots*). "IT'S TIME I WAS GETTING BACK TO A HEMISPHERE
WHERE I REALLY AM APPRECIATED."

Woodrow Wilson, President during the First World War (1914-18)

The second Roosevelt—Franklin, author of the New Deal, President 1933-45

country; Franklin Roosevelt, like Theodore Roosevelt, was particularly anxious to check the wastage of American minerals, timber and land. The Taylor Grazing Act (1934) forbade the sale of those lands (just over 160 million acres) still owned by the Federal government. They were to be kept by the government either as parks and game reserves or as grazing lands. In its taxation the government strove to place higher taxes on the incomes of the rich. An excess profits tax (1939) was among its devices. In 1938 Roosevelt attempted to tackle the trusts by anti-trust laws. Finally, Cordell Hull, Roosevelt's Secretary of State, made a series of trade agreements with many foreign countries. These attempted to improve American foreign trade, by reducing American tariffs in return for similar tariff reduction by the other country making the treaty.

Inevitably cases were brought before the Supreme Court to decide whether or not the New Deal laws were valid under the Constitution. The Supreme Court before 1937 was a very conservative body. Seven of its nine members had been appointed by Republican Presidents, and one, Justice Van Devanter, as far back as 1911. Roosevelt was unlucky in his first term of office; he was unable to appoint any new member of the Court, since none of the nine died or retired. Between 1933 and 1936 it ruled that numerous New Deal measures were unconstitutional. The most important decisions condemned N.R.A. (1935) and A.A.A. (1936). The decision against N.R.A. was unanimous; most of the others were by a five to four majority only. The older and more conservative judges of the Supreme Court were holding up the New Deal. So in 1937 Roosevelt proposed a plan of reform for the Supreme Court. He suggested that if any judge of the Supreme Court declined to retire when he reached the age of seventy, the President, with the approval of the Senate, should appoint an extra judge; but that the total number of judges should not exceed fifteen. This proposal provoked widespread protests, and Congress rejected it. During Roosevelt's second term of office, however, the attitude of the Court changed, and it upheld, instead of condemning, New Deal laws. Moreover, Roosevelt was able to appoint five new judges in place of members of the Court who died or resigned.

The quarrel with the Supreme Court, at the beginning of Roosevelt's second term as President, is something of a landmark in the history of the New Deal. Inevitably his policies had, even before this, aroused opposition. Much of it centred upon one main point—the extent of government control which the New Deal involved. Roosevelt was denounced as a dictator, and his methods were called socialism. Big business opposed him, because of his labour laws, his taxes, and the work of T.V.A. The cost of the New Deal was very great, and the national debt rose well beyond previous levels. Men of conservative opinions, in his own Democratic party as well as among the Republicans, assailed him; so staunch a Democrat as Al Smith strongly attacked the New Deal. But Congress supported him strongly during his first term, passing his main measures with handsome majorities—not only in the 'first hundred days' of crisis in 1933, but also in 1934–5. And American people, as voters, made their opinion plain. In the election of 1936 the Republicans put up as their presidential candidate Alf Landon, the Governor of Kansas. Big business and most of the press backed him. But 'F.D.R.' won a massive victory, carrying every state but two; and the Democrats increased their majorities in Congress. The political barometer seemed to be set fair for the New Deal.

In fact precisely the opposite turned out to be true. It ran into storms, and by 1938 it had virtually come to a halt. Partly through his quarrel with the Supreme Court, Roosevelt lost his hold upon Congress, which rejected his main proposals for new laws. There were serious labour troubles, with 'sit-down strikes' in the works of General Motors and other automobile firms. The slow recovery of industry stopped: unemployment almost doubled between the autumn of 1937 and the summer of 1938, reaching over 9,500,000 at that time. In 1938 Roosevelt made what was for him an unusual tactical blunder in politics: he did his best in the mid-term congressional elections to get his main conservative opponents in the Democratic party defeated—and failed. Finally, by 1938, the main emphasis in politics was moving to foreign affairs—to the problems created by the rise of Hitler and the prospect of a European war. In effect, there were no significant additions to the New Deal after 1938—although Roosevelt held office for six more years.

How much did the New Deal achieve? Some of its experiments clearly failed: thus, many Americans welcomed the Supreme Court's decision against N.R.A. because N.R.A. was already in much difficulty. Others were only partially successful. The laws to help farmers, for example, improved the lot of the farmers themselves, but made that of agricultural labourers and sharecroppers worse. The banking reforms were not invariably effective; the labour laws seemed to encourage strikes. The New Deal, moreover, did not lift America clear of depression. The public works programme, backed by government spending, stimulated industry; but when, in 1937–8, the government spent less, industry produced less. American industry never worked at full capacity between the beginning of the depression and the entry of the United States into the Second World War. Even in September, 1940 the number of unemployed was nearly 7,000,000. More broadly, many Americans—even among those who sympathised with Roosevelt's aims—maintained that too much government control interfered with the liberties of Americans; and some thought that it would sap and destroy the enterprise and independence which Americans traditionally regarded as characteristic of themselves.

On the other side of the balance, it is clear that in its early days the New Deal saved the jobs, the farms, the homes, even the lives of countless Americans caught up in a desperate and unexpected economic catastrophe. On a longer view, certain features of the New Deal were clearly successful. C.C.C. was in many ways of great value to American youth. Both W.P.A.

and P.W.A. provided the country with much of lasting value, from roads and bridges to schools, hospitals and works of art. T.V.A. transformed a great region, returning millions of acres to cultivation and making possible the establishment of many prosperous industries. The Social Security Act did much to remedy American backwardness in providing old age pensions and unemployment insurance. Yet perhaps the greatest achievement of Roosevelt and his fellow New Dealers was to change the outlook of many millions of Americans. Many of the ideas the New Deal put into practice—collective bargaining between employers and workmen, the regulation of the Stock Exchange, the control of the output of crops, the restriction of hours of work—are now accepted as a part of the normal pattern of American life. Above all, Roosevelt made his fellow citizens recognise a new role for government in American life. He made them realise that the vast resources of the United States should be used by means of national planning for the benefit of all its people and not merely for the private profit of a few; that it is the proper task of the Federal Government, representing all the people, to look after the unemployed and the poor; that the people can look to the Federal government as a means of securing for everybody fair and decent conditions of life. Yet Roosevelt could also maintain that this had been achieved without the introduction of the socialism for which his conservative critics condemned him. In 1936 he could claim that his administration had 'saved the system of private profit and free enterprise after it had been dragged to the brink of ruin.'

24   The United States and the
Second World War

1. ROOSEVELT'S FOREIGN POLICY, 1933–41

Franklin Roosevelt at first continued American foreign policy along the lines laid down in the past. The Monroe Doctrine, the neutrality of the U.S.A. during periods of war, the Open Door in China—all these familiar items appeared. In certain details, too, Roosevelt followed the example of his immediate predecessors. Thus he carried the unofficial American co-operation with the League of Nations a stage further by joining the International Labour Organisation in 1934. In his first inaugural speech in 1933 he promised that he 'would dedicate this Nation to the policy of the good neighbor—the neighbor who respects his obligations and respects the sanctity of his agreements in and with a world of neighbors.' In practice this meant two things. First, the U.S.A. tried to win more friendship in Latin America. Secondly, members of the American government, and notably Roosevelt himself, made frequent speeches condemning those countries in the world which were bad neighbours.

Hoover had already adopted a more neighbourly attitude towards Latin America, and had officially dropped the policy of Theodore Roosevelt which justified the interference of the United States in the affairs of the Caribbean Republics. Franklin Roosevelt went further. In 1934 he withdrew American troops from Haiti; in the same year he announced that the United States would no longer insist upon the special rights which the Platt Amendment (1903) gave to her in Cuba. He was sincerely anxious to remove the suspicions left behind by such events as the war with Mexico and the seizure of the Panama Canal Zone. During the 20th century the movement for Pan-Americanism, which James G. Blaine had advocated in the 19th century, grew stronger. Periodic conferences were held between the various American republics, and three notable ones—at Montevideo (1933), Buenos Aires (1936), and Lima (1938)—took place in Roosevelt's presidency. At them the U.S.A. agreed that no American republic should intervene in the affairs of another, even to collect debts. The republics agreed to consult together in the event of any threat to any part of America. In 1936 Roosevelt himself visited South America. Many of the South American states have in recent years been ruled by some kind of dictatorship, and Roosevelt felt it necessary to recognise the rule of such men as President Vargas of Brazil, in spite of his condemnation of dictatorship in Europe. In the Caribbean 'dollar diplomacy' was veiled, though the extent of American investments in that area remained great. Thus the pursuit of the 'good neighbour' policy brought criticism. Nevertheless, it was sincerely pursued both by Roosevelt and by his Secretary of State, Cordell Hull.

In the Far East it was not so easy to be a 'good neighbour.' The Nine-Power Treaty of 1922 meant only a temporary halt in Japan's advance in east Asia. In 1931 she attacked the Chinese territory of Manchuria, and in the following year set up the puppet kingdom of Manchukuo under her domination. The United States declined to recognise these proceedings, and Henry L. Stimson, Secretary of State under Hoover, proposed joining with Britain and the League of Nations to impose economic sanctions upon Japan. But Hoover refused to take action which might lead to war, and Stimson had to be content with issuing a strong verbal condemnation of Japan. In the face of this Japanese advance the U.S.A., in 1933, at last gave official recognition to the Soviet Union. The fear of Japanese advance did not stop Congress from passing in 1934 the Philippine Independence Act, promising independence to the Philippine Islands in 1945.[1] After that time, however, the Roosevelt government found itself in increasing difficulty in the Far East. Japan had walked out of the League of Nations in

---

[1] In 1938 the Filipino-American Joint Committee recommended full independence on July 4, 1946, but the continuance of 'mutually beneficial economic arrangements' until 1964.

1933 and next year gave notice that she no longer considered herself bound by the London Naval Treaty of 1930, which had drawn up a ratio of naval building between the great naval powers. Another London Naval Conference in 1935 failed to agree, and Japan and the U.S.A. began a naval armaments race. Then in 1937 Japan launched another attack on China and overran great areas of the country. In that same year Japanese aeroplanes bombed the American gunboat *Panay* while it was lying in a Chinese river; this incident, in spite of Japan's apologies and cash compensation of £443,000, strengthened American hostility to Japan. The reports of American missionaries and traders, describing the activities of the Japanese in China, won the support of many Americans for the Chinese. The American government was committed to defence of the 'Open Door' for all nations in China, but the Japanese were fast closing it to all but themselves. Yet Roosevelt's government moved slowly, being anxious to avoid any steps which might lead to war in the Pacific, and American help to China took the form of large-scale loans. Meanwhile the U.S.A. went ahead with a naval rearmament programme.

Two facts dominated the policy of Roosevelt's government towards Europe. The first was the traditional desire of the American people to avoid what Jefferson had once called 'entangling alliances' with European powers. The second was the growth of dictatorship in Europe, and the increasing possibility of another European war. Hitler, as well as Roosevelt, came to power in 1933. As his dictatorship and that of Mussolini in Italy grew stronger and more aggressive, and as it became clear that the war of 1914–18 had not made the world 'safe for democracy,' so the American people became more concerned to safeguard their neutrality.

The first step in this direction was the Johnson Act (1934). Hoover left behind him the old problem of War Debts. By 1933 it was clear that no European power—except Finland, which paid in full—was going to pay. Therefore Congress passed the Johnson Act, which forbade all American loans to countries which had not paid their War Debts. This was followed in 1935 by the Neutrality Act, which attempted to prevent the U.S.A. from becoming involved in a second war in the same way as in the war of 1914–18. It forbade American exports of arms to either side in any war and forbade American ships to carry goods for either side. It also stated that American citizens could only travel on ships of belligerent powers at their own risk. In this way it was hoped to avoid incidents like the torpedoing of American ships which had helped to bring the United States into the war of 1914–18; and also to stop Americans from becoming interested, for financial reasons, in the victory of one side in a war. The act was immediately applied in the war between Italy and Abyssinia (1935–6). This Neutrality Act was revised in 1937, and was put into force in the Spanish Civil War. This neutrality legislation benefited the aggressors, who were armed already, and injured their victims, who were not.

From 1937 to 1939 tension grew swiftly in Europe. German and Italian forces helped General Franco destroy the Republican government of Spain. In the spring of 1938 Hitler occupied Austria; in the autumn after threatening war, he persuaded the governments of Britain and France to sign the Munich Pact which gave him the Sudetenland area of Czechoslovakia and left the remainder of that country defenceless; and in the spring of 1939 he swallowed it up, entering Prague in brutal triumph, while Mussolini took the opportunity to seize Albania. The great majority of Americans disapproved of these things, and hated the German Nazis' persecution of the Jews; but they had no wish to get involved in any European war.

In September 1939 the German invasion of Poland brought war between England and France and Germany. Roosevelt, in accordance with the Neutrality Acts of 1935 and 1937, immediately forbade the exports of arms and the supply of loans to either side. In some ways the situation was the same as in 1914, and the principal object of the U.S.A. was to keep out of the war. But Americans as a whole were far more hostile to Hitler's Germany than their fathers had been to the Kaiser's Germany. This was partly because Japan and Germany were on friendly terms, but mainly because the Nazi outlook and way of life were so obviously opposed to everything for which the U.S.A. stood. Roosevelt, while standing for American neutrality in action, did not ask Americans to be neutral in thought. He asked Congress to alter the Neutrality Act in order to enable Britain and France—who had command of the seas—to buy arms and munitions in the U.S.A. Congress passed in November 1939 a new Neutrality Act which permitted countries at war to buy arms and munitions in the U.S.A. on a 'cash-and-carry' basis. This meant that goods sold to powers at war had to be paid for before leaving the U.S.A., and had to be taken away in foreign ships. American ships and American citizens were forbidden to travel in 'combat zones.'

The object of this act was clear—to keep the United States out of the war. Exclusion of Americans from the 'combat zones' might stop incidents which could bring her into it. 'Cash and carry' would give the European democracies war materials with which they could defeat the Germans without calling upon American forces. Yet it marked a step away from strict neutrality, and from then onwards Roosevelt's government was to move further away still. But the process was slow. The fact that nothing happened on the western front during the first six months of the war made Americans less interested in it. Moreover, the Russian attack upon Finland in November 1939 provided another issue. American public opinion was overwhelmingly in favour of the Finns, especially when Russia refused an offer of mediation from the U.S.A., and the Americans loaned £4,000,000 to Finland.

Then in the spring of 1940 the German invasion and conquest of Denmark, Norway, Holland and Belgium, followed by the collapse of France in June, transformed the position. The spectre of a Nazi-dominated

Europe appeared with its threat to the freedom and future of the United States. On June 10 Roosevelt, proclaiming that 'victory for the gods of force and hate would endanger the institutions of democracy in the Western World,' committed the United States to 'two obvious and simultaneous courses.' 'We will,' he said 'extend to the opponents of force the material resources of this nation and, at the same time, we will harness and speed up the use of those resources in order that we ourselves in the Americas may have equipment and training equal to the task of any emergency and every defense.' In July, the American republics, in conference at Havana, agreed that, if necessary, they might take temporary control of any European possessions in America which seemed likely to change hands. In August the Ogdensburg Agreement between Roosevelt and the Canadian Prime Minister, Mackenzie King, provided for joint defence of their two countries. In September Congress passed a Conscription Act, the first known in peace-time. That same month Roosevelt obtained from Britain the right to fortify a series of naval bases on British territory extending from British Guiana and Trinidad to Newfoundland. In return, he handed to Britain fifty over-age destroyers, desperately needed to fight Hitler's submarines. This 'destroyers-for-bases' deal was generally approved in the U.S.A. as a wise bargain in terms of national defence. But it was another step away from neutrality. Roosevelt's foreign policy at this time was the subject of bitter debate. Some, like the Committee to Defend America by Aiding the Allies, maintained that only by giving all possible help to Britain could the United States hope to survive. Others, led by the America First Committee, denounced Roosevelt and his government for a policy which was leading to an unnecessary war.

In November, 1940 another presidential election was due. In 1796 Washington had refused to accept a third term as President, and never since then had the Americans elected a President for a third term. But the Democrats nominated Roosevelt again. His programme in foreign policy was to keep America out of the war, but to give all aid 'short of war' to Britain and her allies. The Republicans nominated a dark horse, Wendell Willkie. In foreign policy he took much the same line as Roosevelt. But in home affairs he was a vigorous and eloquent opponent of the New Deal; he was the president of a company which had suffered greatly from the competition of the Tennessee Valley Authority. As in 1936, big business and the wealthy supported the Republican candidate, and Roosevelt was charged with wishing to make himself a dictator. Once again the people chose Roosevelt, although Willkie was a powerful rival, capturing more votes than either Hoover in 1932 or Landon in 1936. The 'third-term' tradition, which had lasted since the birth of the republic, was broken by his re-election.

Once re-elected, Roosevelt adopted a more war-like policy. In a 'fireside chat' in December, 1940 he spoke of the United States as 'the great arsenal of democracy,' and in the following month he laid before Congress proposals to make the supplies from the arsenal more easily available to Britain and other American allies despite the obstacles of the Neutrality Acts. These 'Lease-Lend' proposals, finally passed by Congress in March, 1941 after bitter debates, empowered the President to 'sell . . . exchange, lease, lend, or otherwise dispose of' defence materials to the government of any country 'whose defense the President deems vital to the defense of the United States,' and they made possible a vast programme of assistance during the next few years. It was extended to Soviet Russia after Hitler's attack upon her in June. Henry Stimson, the Secretary of War, described 'Lease-Lend' as 'a declaration of economic war,' and it could be only a matter of time before Germany and the United States were in armed conflict with one another. In his annual message to Congress that January Roosevelt declared that men should look forward 'to a world founded upon four essential human freedoms'—of speech, of worship, from want, and from fear: and these 'Four Freedoms' were to serve in some measure as a statement of the values for which millions of Americans and their allies believed themselves to be fighting in the Second World War. Soon after 'Lease-Lend' became law the government seized all German and Italian shipping in American ports, and this was followed in the summer by the closing of their consulates and the freezing of their financial assets in the U.S.A. Meanwhile American forces took over Greenland in April and Icelandic bases in July, and the American navy began to patrol the western Atlantic sea lanes and to take over convoy duties there. A brush between the U.S. destroyer *Greer* and a German submarine early in September marked the beginning of American naval fighting in the Second World War, and further clashes followed in the next few weeks. But this was still undeclared war; the formal declaration in Europe came only after far more remarkable events in the Far East.

By 1941 American relations with Japan had reached a crisis. The Japanese, conquerors of great areas of China (though not of the Chinese government under Chiang Kai-shek, which had withdrawn to Chungking, far up the Yang-tse River), had plans for supremacy in East Asia, over Indonesia, Malaya and the Philippines. The European events of 1940 had encouraged the extremists among them, and led to the Tripartite Pact of Germany, Italy and Japan that September. The prospects of snapping up British, French and Dutch colonies in East Asia looked excellent. The only obstacle was the United States, which in 1940 based its main fleet at Pearl Harbor in Hawaii as a deterrent. In the spring of 1941 the two countries began diplomatic discussions in Washington, and it soon became clear that their views were far apart: the Americans wanted the Japanese to leave China, the Japanese wanted the Americans to stop helping Chiang Kai-shek. But the talks went on, for the Japanese were reluctant to go to war if there were any chance of achieving their aims without it. That summer they occupied French Indo-China, and the U.S. retaliated by freezing Japanese financial assets. What seems to have brought Japan to the point of making war was the recognition that she might be cut off from essential supplies of oil and other vital materials, e.g. from the Dutch East Indies, by American embargo. On December 7, 1941, even while Japanese diplomats were still negotiating in Washington, she launched a large-scale carrier-based air attack on the American base at Pearl Harbor. The Americans were taken by surprise. 2403 people (over 2000 of them naval personnel) were killed and over 1000 injured in less than two hours; nearly 150 aeroplanes were destroyed; six battleships were sunk or severely damaged. Next day Roosevelt, calling December 7 a 'date which will live in infamy,' asked Congress to declare that a state of war existed with Japan. Three days later Germany, as an ally of Japan, formally declared war on the United States, followed by Italy.

2. THE UNITED STATES AT WAR

The United States took part in the Second World War as a member of a world-wide alliance. Its leaders, besides the U.S.A., were Great Britain and Soviet Russia: their partners included China, the self-governing dominions of the British Commonwealth, Brazil and other Latin American states, and many free governments whose lands were in enemy occupation. The first purpose of the alliance was of course the military defeat of the Axis powers, Germany, Italy and Japan. Its further objectives, at least in the eyes of Britain and the United States, had been stated in the Atlantic Charter, drawn up in August, 1941 at a secret meeting between President Roosevelt and the British Prime Minister, Winston Churchill, held on the cruiser *Prince of Wales* off the Newfoundland coast. Among other points, the Charter spoke of 'the right of all peoples to choose the form of government under which they will live' and of the establishment of 'a peace which will afford to all nations the means of dwelling in safety within their own boundaries'; and it looked forward to 'a wider and permanent system of general security.' It was in some ways an echo of Wilson's Fourteen Points nearly a quarter of a century before, in that First World War which had failed to make the world safe for democracy. Franklin Roosevelt had served as Assistant Secretary of the Navy in that war, and was a great admirer of Wilson. Mindful of the tragic failure of Wilson to get the United States to join the League of Nations, Roosevelt took care to have the phrase 'international organisation' cut out of the draft of the Charter, lest it prejudice American opinion this time.

There were other similarities to the previous war: Germany was once more the chief foe and the submarine her chief weapon at sea, the United States once more the main source of supplies for her allies. But the differences were far more important than the similarities, so far as the American war effort was concerned. In scale and range of operations and in the degree to which the United States was involved, it was an immensely greater war; and for her it was both more costly in lives and in resources and more significant in results. In the Second World War the United States not only shared with Britain the main burden of naval and air warfare against the submarines in the Atlantic. She placed huge armies in the field against the Germans and Italians, first in Africa and then in the invasions of Europe through Sicily in 1943 and Normandy in 1944; provided most of the troops and nearly all the equipment for the Pacific Ocean war against the Japanese; was by far the greatest supplier of weapons and war materials of every kind for all the allies: and developed out of her resources in the course of the years 1941–5 the most terrible weapon known to man, the atomic bomb used against the Japanese in 1945. Such commitment in war, as both Roosevelt and those who had opposed his pre-war policy foresaw, would mean that this time the Americans could not withdraw into isolation afterwards. The Second World War inevitably brought the United States to world leadership, and out of the war itself grew problems and challenges unrealised at the time of Pearl Harbor.

More than fifteen million Americans served in the armed forces, and nearly eleven and a half million of them went overseas. The U.S.A. suffered well over a million casualties in battle, and some 304,000 Americans were killed in action. American forces took part in some of the most severe and brutal fighting of the war, as at Guadalcanal in the Solomon Islands and on Okinawa in the Ryukyus. On the other hand, the United States was the one major power in the war which endured neither armed invasion nor air bombardment. German submarines sank dozens of ships virtually within sight of American shores during the first half of 1942; this was the nearest the actual fighting came to the United States itself. Nor was there hardship or serious shortage. Some foodstuffs were rationed, but civilian food consumption reached a record in 1944; for American agriculture, thanks to mechanisation, better planning and good weather in the war years, could cope comfortably with the demands made on it by armed forces, allies and civilians alike. Petrol and tyres were also rationed, for Japanese conquests in the Far East cut sharply into the world's supplies of oil and rubber; yet many Americans kept their cars going. Prices of many goods were controlled, with fair success despite a good deal of 'black market' activity. Wages rose, though not steeply. Jobs were plentiful. The 7,000,000 unemployed of 1940 had practically vanished by the end of 1942; great numbers of teenagers, married women, and retired people took temporary jobs; and people worked longer hours. As a result there was plenty of money about, and the American people were prosperous. Nor were they without goods and services to spend their money on. It has been reckoned that only about half of the vast industrial production of these war years consisted of government purchases or of war materials for the American or allied forces; the other half consisted of civilian goods.

The output of 'the arsenal of democracy' had not risen very fast before Pearl Harbor, but the impact on Americans of that event, together with more effective government planning once the country was at war, brought great changes from 1942 onwards. In that year Roosevelt fixed a target of 60,000 military aircraft a year; this was thought to be impossible, for in the eighteen months from June, 1940 to December, 1941 the country had produced only 23,000. In fact nearly 86,000 were built in 1943 and over 96,000 in 1944. In the peak year 1944 29,000 naval vessels were built, compared with 8000 in 1942. Guns, tanks and ammunition; ships, vehicles, tyres; medical drugs, wheat, canned and packaged foods, cotton clothes, petroleum—these and many other commodities poured out from the United States, across the Atlantic to Britain, by Murmansk or Archangel to Russia, by devious routes to China, to Australians fighting in the jungles of New Guinea, to Frenchmen and Danes in the resistance movements of Europe. Much of the vast export was under the 'Lease-Lend' scheme, by which Britain obtained over $30,000,000 worth of goods and Russia over $11,000,000 worth. The arsenal did not function without difficulties. Although there were proportionately fewer strikes than in war-time Britain, there was some trouble with organised labour, which did not invariably accept the views of the National War Labor Board set up by the government. In 1943 the Secretary of the Interior took over the coal-mines because of the threat of a strike by John L. Lewis's United Mine Workers. There was also some trouble with the management side of industry: in 1944 the government placed the celebrated mail-order house of Montgomery Ward and Company under the control of the army after a dispute about wages. Yet these episodes were very much the exception, and in general the co-operation of the American people, whether managers or workers, with the purposes of the government was impressive. No doubt wartime prosperity helped greatly to make this achievement possible. So too did the taxation policy of the government. In financial terms the Second World War cost the United States between eleven and twelve times as much as the First World War, a total sum bigger than the combined expenditure of Britain and Soviet Russia. Rather more than half of this was met by borrowing, and by 1945 the American national debt had risen to over $250,000 million. A special 5 per cent. 'Victory Tax' was imposed, and the more wealthy were heavily taxed in a variety of ways; but the tax burden of the average American was substantially lower than that of the contemporary British citizen.

Inevitably the Federal government extended its authority in countless ways during the war. The President was given special powers by a War Powers Act at the start, and in 1943 the Office of War Mobilisation was created to co-ordinate the running of the war at home. The most glaring abuse of governmental authority was the removal in 1942 of some 112,000 Japanese, two-thirds of whom were American citizens, from the west coast to 'relocation' centres inland. The conscription laws allowed for exemption on conscientious grounds; there were perhaps 100,000 objectors, and although many went to prison, declining alternative service, there was no general hostility towards them. The Supreme Court in a number of cases vindicated the citizen's rights of free speech. Congress kept a watchful eye on the President's use of his powers. For example, a special committee, whose chairman was Senator Harry S. Truman of Missouri, scrutinised defence expenditure and the activities of the armed forces in connection with war production. But this did not mean any lack of unity behind Roosevelt, nor any serious doubts about his capacity as a war leader. His strength lay in his ability to inspire public opinion and to win the support both of American and foreign diplomats and officers; and in his perpetual optimism about the future. He was supported by a strong team of advisers. The United States was well served in the Second World War by such able men as Harry Hopkins, the former social worker who had been Federal Relief Administrator during the New Deal and who became both head of the Lease-Lend administration and Roosevelt's most intimate adviser; General George Marshall, the Virginian who was Chief of Staff to the Army; and Henry M. Stimson, the former Republican whom Roosevelt appointed Secretary of War. By 1944 Roosevelt's energies were beginning to flag, but it was in the circumstances of the war impossible for the Democrats not to nominate him for the presidential election of that year. The Republicans named Thomas E. Dewey, Governor of New York. The election was vigorous but its issue was never in doubt. Roosevelt carried 36 of the 48 states and got 3,500,000 votes more than Dewey, and thus moved on into his fourth term, with Harry Truman as his Vicepresident. He served in fact a little under three months, long enough to see the pattern of victory in Europe emerge; for he died suddenly in April, 1945.

3. THE WAR IN EUROPE

The American war effort was made in very close collaboration with that of Britain. The chiefs of staff of both countries had met together in secret in the spring of 1941, and from this meeting there grew the organisation known as the Combined Chiefs of Staff which, so far as Britain and America were concerned, ran the war, holding periodic meetings under the leadership of Churchill and Roosevelt. This alliance took at once a major strategic decision which was to determine the course of the war—namely, to concentrate first on the defeat of Germany. It was clear that Germany was the more dangerous foe; if she were allowed to conquer Russia she might become impossible to defeat—and at the end of 1941 German armies were hammering at the gates of Moscow; moreover, the longer the defeat of Hitler was delayed, the greater the chance that brilliant German scientists might produce some devastating new weapons of destruction. The swift Japanese conquests which followed Pearl Harbor did not cause this decision to be altered, although they did affect the way in which it was carried out. The despatch of substantial reinforcements to the Pacific to save Australia meant so many fewer troops and supplies available for direct attack on Europe. The American commanders were anxious to launch in 1942 some kind of large-scale emergency onslaught upon German-occupied Europe, in order to relieve the tremendous pressure upon the Russians. The British, on the other hand, feared the risks of launching a cross-Channel attack too early, and proposed instead an attack upon French North Africa. This would remove the Italian and German threat to Egypt and the Suez Canal; in the summer of 1942 the German commander Rommel and his Afrika Korps captured the fortress of Tobruk and were thrusting eastwards to the borders of Egypt. Moreover it would open the way to an attack upon Europe from the south. Roosevelt backed the British plan, and so preparations began for the first great offensive by the western powers in the Second World War.

Yet in a sense the biggest issue of 1942 was what came to be called the Battle of the Atlantic, the fight against the German U-boats. If this were lost—if links between Britain and the U.S.A. were severed, or so weakened that huge supplies of food, munitions and troops could not be securely carried across the ocean—then the war would be lost. The entire prospect of any assault upon Hitler's Europe depended upon maintaining the Atlantic lifeline. During the first half of 1942 the submarines, hunting in packs, did great damage to shipping, especially in the coastal waters off the eastern U.S.A., and losses exceeded new construction of ships; and later in the year they met with almost equal success in the Caribbean and off Brazil. Only gradually was the menace overcome—or very largely so—by the use of a variety of devices. These included the extension of the convoy system; the development of long-range bombers and of teams of ships and carrier-based aircraft; highly-specialised training of anti-submarine personnel; and a range of new scientific techniques, including the use of radar, sonar gear, and magnetic equipment. It was a harsh, long conflict: the Germans retaliated with their own scientific advances, such as acoustic torpedoes, and developed new and faster types of submarines, many of which were still in use at the end of the war. By the summer of 1943, however, it may be said that the Battle of the Atlantic had been decided in favour of the allies. The sea-lanes were open, even if they were not entirely free from obstructions.

A second aspect of the European war to which the United States devoted early and vigorous attention was the use of air-power as a means of contributing to the destruction of Hitler's Germany. The American Eighth Air Force established itself in England in the summer of 1942 and launched its first raid that August. Whereas British aircraft concentrated upon night bombing, the Americans developed the technique of high-level daylight raids. These were costly, particularly until the development of an improved system of fighter escorts in 1944. Their targets ranged from submarine pens to oil installations, and from ball-bearing factories to marshalling yards; in the latter stages of the war they joined with the R.A.F. in preparations for the invasion of Europe and in highly destructive raids on German cities.

In October, 1942 General Montgomery, in command of the British Eighth Army on the borders of Egypt, launched an attack upon the Germans which won the decisive victory of El Alamein, turned the tide of battle in Africa and early in 1943 drove the Axis forces out of Libya and Tripoli. In November, 1942 an Anglo-American invasion force landed at three points in French North Africa—Casablanca, Oran and Algiers. Its commander was the American, Dwight D. Eisenhower, and about four-fifths of its 110,000 troops were American. This Operation Torch, as it was called, which had been prepared in four months, was initially successful; there was little opposition from the French forces, and the Germans were taken by surprise. Part of the success at least resulted from a much-criticised agreement which Eisenhower made at Algiers with Admiral Darlan, the second in command of the Vichy government which had ruled the unoccupied southern part of France since the collapse of 1940. Darlan issued a cease-fire to the French forces in North Africa, which saved much possible bloodshed. But the Germans reacted strongly, occupying the rest of France and flying in a powerful force within a few days to occupy the critical area of Tunisia, lying opposite the toe of Italy. Six months' bitter struggle followed, with Montgomery's forces moving up from the south to join the Americans in cornering the Axis troops round the cities of Tunis and Bizerta. Both fell in May, 1943, and 275,000 enemy troops surrendered.

Suez was safe, North Africa was clear, and the way was open for the invasion of Italy. The decision to make this the next step had been taken by Roosevelt, Churchill and the Combined Chiefs of Staff at a conference at Casablanca in January, 1943.[1] It was not reached without opposition from the Americans, who wanted to halt advance in the Mediterranean in order to prepare for a massive cross-Channel invasion (for which the Russians also, not surprisingly, were pressing) and who also wanted to build up an onslaught upon the Japanese. The great Russian victory at Stalingrad at the end of 1942, the turning-point of the war in eastern Europe, stimulated the Soviet demand for a 'Second Front' in Europe in 1943. The Casablanca Conference also had one other feature which may have had great consequences upon the later development of the war. In his broadcast report on the conference Roosevelt declared that 'the only terms on which we shall deal with an Axis government or any Axis factions are the terms proclaimed at Casablanca: "Unconditional Surrender".' Roosevelt insisted upon this famous phrase, first used by Grant in the American Civil War, because he wanted to make it clear—to the Russians as well as to the Germans and Italians—that there would be no compromise with Nazism or Fascism, and because of the criticism that had arisen over the deal with Darlan. Many people at the time believed that this statement would encourage desperate resistance and thus needlessly prolong the war; and some have maintained that it did in fact enable Hitler to make the

[1] This was the first time any American President had left his country in war-time.

The Second World War: Europe and North Africa

Germans fight on to the bitter end after the war was hopelessly lost.

In July, 1943 a quarter of a million British and American troops landed in Sicily in an immense amphibious operation, and within just over five weeks the island was conquered—though most of the German forces there escaped to the Italian mainland with their equipment. One consequence of this was the fall of Mussolini from power. But after this resounding start the Italian operation did not go well for the allies. Delays in arranging the capitulation of the new Italian government gave the Germans a chance to strengthen their hold, especially in northern Italy. In September allied armies landed in the south. The American Fifth Army, which went ashore at Salerno, met with stiff German opposition, but managed to fight its way into Naples in early October. Thereafter it took eight months of hard fighting to reach Rome. German military engineers took full advantage of the mountainous countryside; and two allied divisions (one American, one British) which landed at Anzio, south of Rome, in January, 1944, instead of becoming the starting-point of an advance on the capital, found themselves besieged by the Germans. A defensive line through Monte Cassino, site of the famous Benedictine monastery, held up allied advance for three months until it fell in May, and not until June, when the German army fell back to prepared positions further north, did American and British forces enter Rome, which escaped destruction because the Germans decided not to defend it.

While the soldiers were struggling in Italy in the last months of 1943 the leaders of the allied nations were taking important decisions at a series of conferences. At Moscow in October the foreign secretaries of the U.S.A., Britain and the Soviet Union agreed upon the rapid establishment of a 'Second Front' in western Europe, and, with a representative of China, signed a pact pledging their countries to the formation of an international organisation to maintain peace and security in the world. In November Roosevelt and Churchill met Chiang Kai-shek, the Chinese leader, at Cairo, and agreed on measures against Japan. From there they went on to meet Stalin, the Russian leader, at Teheran. Here with their military advisers they concerted detailed plans for the western invasion of Europe in 1944.

Thus by the time Rome was liberated Europe was on the eve of greater events. The final campaign in the west was about to begin. The cross-Channel invasion, Operation Overlord, planned in detail since early in 1943, was launched on D-Day, June 6, 1944. Its success was made possible by a vast range of contributory factors. Among them were the complete air superiority which the allies had achieved over the Channel and northern France; the pressure exerted upon German resources of men and materials by the great Russian armies, which at this time were starting to drive the enemy out of their homeland; the success of the steps taken to persuade the Germans that the attack would come not upon the beaches of Normandy but upon those of the Pas de Calais further north; the discontents among

German generals; the bold technical devices used, notably the 'Mulberry' artificial harbours; and, far from least, the courage of those who took part in what, for all the individual soldier knew, might have been one of the great failures of human history. To separate the American part from that of the British is difficult and indeed in one way most misleading: one of the underlying reasons for the triumph of so complicated an example of that very difficult military operation, an amphibious landing upon a coast strongly held by the enemy, was undoubtedly the astonishing co-operation of the people and leaders of two distinct nations. The supreme commander was the American Dwight D. Eisenhower, and two of the most prominent subordinate commanders were Omar Bradley, in charge of the American First Army in the landings, and George S. Patton, who led the American forces which later broke out from the beachheads and overran France. Some 60,000 Americans formed the actual assault forces on the two most westerly—nicknamed Utah and Omaha—of the five beaches where landings were made, and American airborne troops had preceded them into action.

Within a week of the landings the joint forces held some seventy miles of the Normandy coast to a depth varying from five to fifteen miles, and over 300,000 troops had been put ashore. Cherbourg fell to the Americans on June 26. A month later the battle for Normandy had been won, and the allied forces were ready to break out into the plains of France. While British forces under Montgomery swung northwards along the coast towards the Belgian frontier and Antwerp, which they took early in September, the American columns, headed by tanks, moved west to Brittany, south to the Loire, and east to Paris and the German border, with the enemy armies in full retreat. The French capital, its citizens in revolt, was liberated by French and American troops of the allied army on August 25. Ten days earlier fresh American forces had landed in the south; they seized Toulon and Marseilles, moved easily up the Rhône valley, and by mid-September linked up with part of Patton's forces which had turned south-east to meet them. At the same time other American forces which had pushed on north-east had crossed the German border near Aachen. The success of Overlord had surpassed expectations. Within some seven weeks of the break-out from Normandy most of France had been cleared of Germans, Luxembourg had been liberated, Belgium entered, and Germany invaded. Meanwhile the Russians had made vast advances in the east in their summer offensive, driving into the Ukraine and Poland, removing the Germans from Roumania, and overrunning much of the Balkans; and in Italy the Germans had fallen back upon their last ditch, the line of the River Po. 1944 had indeed been a year of victories.

But the war was not won. The unexpected rapidity of the success in the west brought its own problems: supplies, not least of petrol, could not keep pace with the victorious tanks, which were thereby brought to a halt at the time when the Germans were turning to defend their own frontier. The great port of Antwerp was useless until the stubborn German defenders lower down the Scheldt could be removed. The British airborne landings to secure a bridgehead at Arnhem on the Rhine in Holland in September were a costly failure. There was much severe fighting in October and November—on the lower Scheldt, in and around Aachen, in Alsace, in Lorraine; American casualties in the last three of these areas were heavy. Then, in mid-December, came an unexpected German counter-offensive in the Ardennes, ordered by Hitler himself with the objective of splitting allied forces in two and driving through to the Channel once more. The 'Battle of the Bulge' (as it was called from its effect upon the allied line) which resulted, centred round the Belgian town of Bastogne, where an American airborne division resisted with great heroism; it lasted about a month, until Patton's forces from the south restored the situation. It was the last desperate throw of the German armies. Even while it was taking place the Russians had launched a winter offensive on a scale substantially greater than that of the western allies, and poured into Germany on a wide front as well as into Hungary and Czechoslovakia. In late January 1945 Eisenhower gave the order for the final advance in the west. His armies cleared German forces from the lands west of the Rhine, and on March 7 began to cross the great river, seizing at Remagen a railway bridge just as the Germans were in the act of blowing it up. By mid-April they had encircled the Ruhr, the greatest industrial region of Europe, capturing over 300,000 prisoners, and were driving into the heart of the shattered Nazi empire, British forces in the north, Americans in the centre and south. On April 25 American and Russian soldiers met at Thorgau. On April 30, two days after Italian partisans had killed Mussolini, Hitler committed suicide in his bomb-proof shelter in the ruins of Berlin. On May 5 the Germans in Italy surrendered, and on May 7 the German General Jodl signed before Eisenhower at Rheims a preliminary surrender of the German forces. The final act came the next day, when at Russia's request Marshal Keitel as head of the German representatives signed in Berlin a formal surrender of all German armies. Military victory in Europe was complete.

4. THE WAR AGAINST JAPAN

The Japanese attack on Pearl Harbor was the signal for the most extraordinary series of conquests in modern history. Pearl Harbor was attacked on December 7, 1941. Within six months the Japanese were masters of a vast arc of land and water from Burma and Thailand to the Solomon and the Gilbert Islands. The British and Dutch empires in South-East Asia and the western Pacific had toppled and the Philippines too were gone. The time-table of conquest was remarkable. By the end of December Thailand had surrendered and the Japanese were fighting their way relentlessly southward in Malaya; Hong Kong, British North Borneo, the Gilbert Islands, had fallen; so had the American outposts, Wake and Guam. In the Philippines, invaded on December 10, the capital, Manila, had been abandoned and American forces under General Douglas MacArthur were withdrawing to the Bataan Peninsula. In January, 1942 Rabaul in New Britain, chief port of the Australian mandated territory of New Guinea and possessing a superb natural harbour, was captured. Other Japanese forces were pressing their onslaught on the rich Dutch East Indies. In February Singapore surrendered. In April, after MacArthur had been ordered by Roosevelt to return to Australia to assume future command, 70,000 American and Filipino troops surrendered on Bataan: many of them died on the 'Death March' which followed to prison camps. The last stronghold on the Philippines, the island of Corregidor with its 11,000 defenders, yielded in May. That same month the Japanese took both Java and Rangoon. Over an immense area of land and ocean their plans had triumphed beyond expectations.

The allies faced a threefold task in the war against Japan. They had first to hold the Japanese advance, to prevent them making further conquests: in the summer of 1942 there was a clear threat to India and to Australia. Secondly they had to recover the ground they had lost—or at least sufficient of it to enable them to undertake the third part of their task. This was to carry the war to Japan itself and there compel the enemy to surrender; for it was accepted from the start that the mere reconquest of lost territory would not be enough. This formidable task was undertaken in conditions utterly different from those of the war in Europe. Tropical jungles, coral islands, and above all the endless spaces of the ocean provided the battlefields of the war against Japan. The land fighting was peculiarly bitter—partly because geographical conditions often made it a hand-to-hand conflict, partly also because traditions of the Japanese made them unwilling to yield as prisoners. The basic key to success lay in naval warfare, yet naval warfare of a novel kind, in which the vital elements were the great carriers and their aircraft. Perhaps the most important single feature of the attack on Pearl Harbor was the fact that the three aircraft carriers normally based there were away at the time. The four battleships which were sunk mattered far less in the balance of sea-power in this war. Certainly two great naval battles in the summer of 1942 halted the Japanese advance. The first, the Battle of the Coral Sea in May—the first naval battle in which surface craft did not fire at one another—was a confused affair in which each fleet suffered substantial losses, but which turned back a Japanese attempt to take Port Moresby on the southern shore of New Guinea. They went no further in the south-western Pacific, and the threat to Australia receded. The second battle, fought in June some 2700 miles away to the north-east, was the result of a Japanese attempt to capture Midway Island. The Battle of Midway was a decisive American victory, in which the Japanese lost four aircraft carriers. Midway and also Hawaii, 1100 miles away to the east, were henceforth safe. If any single battle

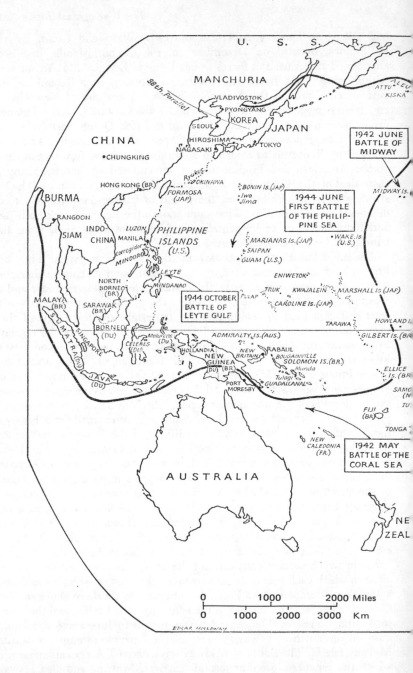

The Second World War: The Far East and the Pacific

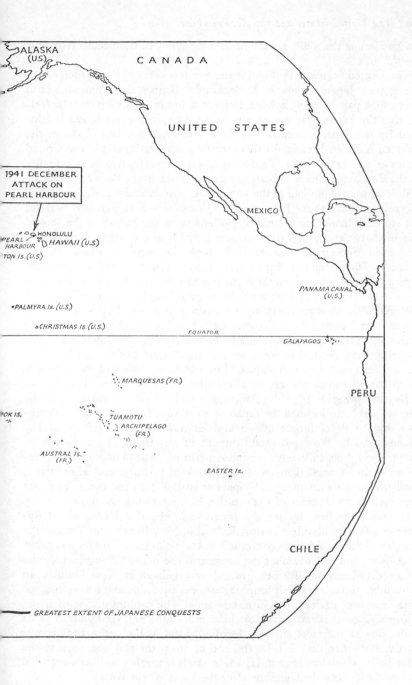

ALASKA (US.)

CANADA

UNITED STATES

MEXICO

1941 DECEMBER
ATTACK ON
PEARL HARBOUR

HONOLULU
PEARL
HARBOUR
TON Is. (U.S.)
HAWAII (U.S.)

PANAMA CANAL
(U.S.)

PALMYRA Is. (U.S.)

CHRISTMAS Is. (U.S.)

EQUATOR

GALAPAGOS

PERU

MARQUESAS (FR.)

OK IS.

TUAMOTU
ARCHIPELAGO
(FR.)

AUSTRAL Is.
(FR.)

EASTER Is.

CHILE

GREATEST EXTENT OF JAPANESE CONQUESTS

can be seen as the most important turning-point in the Pacific War, this was the one.

The United States carried by far the greatest share of the burden of the war against Japan, although, for example, British and Commonwealth troops took part in heavy fighting in Burma and in New Guinea. The feeling that the Pacific war was peculiarly an American concern was heightened by the Japanese capture in June, 1942 of Attu and Kiska in the Western Aleutian Islands, for this formed a potential threat to the United States as well as to Alaska. There was always powerful American pressure on the Combined Chiefs of Staff to step up action in the Pacific; and in the middle of 1942 about half of the 500,000 American soldiers who were then overseas were facing the Japanese. The decision to beat Germany first did not stop the launching of an allied offensive in the Pacific in the second half of that year, though its scale was limited, as the name given to it— Operation Shoestring—indicated. It took the form of attacks in the Solomon Islands and in Papua (Australian New Guinea), to drive the Japanese out of areas which they had recently taken and were preparing to use as bases for further conquests. In August American marines landed on the Solomons, thus precipitating a tremendous series of battles, by land, sea and air, centred on the island of Guadalcanal, which the Japanese eventually left in American hands in February, 1943. Meanwhile a mixed American and Australian force under MacArthur pushed the Japanese out of Buna and Gona in Papua. The combined effect of these bloody campaigns was to clear a way for allied advance in the western Pacific.

By the spring of 1943 the Americans had seized the initiative in the Pacific, and henceforward the Japanese were kept constantly on the defensive, by the development of sea and air-power, by the seizure of key islands, and by the rapid establishment of air-strips. The technique of 'leapfrogging' began to emerge: the Americans, instead of allowing themselves to be compelled to the endless task of taking island after island, used sea and air supremacy to by-pass or seal off Japanese bases. This was first used in the summer of 1943 in the Aleutians when the more westerly Attu was taken first, forcing the Japanese to abandon Kiska, and it was later employed with effect against Rabaul in New Britain and Truk in the Caroline Islands. Advance continued in the Solomons: Munda was taken in August, and in November the biggest of the islands, Bougainville, was attacked. Meanwhile further ground was gained in New Guinea. In November too a large-scale amphibious operation, involving over 100,000 men, was sent against the Gilbert Islands. The capture of one of them, Tarawa, a coral island less than three miles long and six hundred yards wide, one of the most strongly fortified posts in the entire Pacific, was costly. But when they fell, by the end of 1943, the way was open to the Marshalls, which had been in Japanese hands since they had been acquired as mandates from the Germans after the First World War.

By the beginning of 1944 two broad lines of advance towards Japan were emerging. The first, the more westerly, under the command of MacArthur, lay through New Guinea and the recovery of the Philippines. The second, across the central Pacific, under the broad control of Admiral Chester W. Nimitz, was by way of the Marshalls and the Mariana Islands to the Ryukyus, the long string of islands which linked Japan to Formosa. The Japanese capture of American air bases in China during the spring of 1944 put paid to the earlier plan of launching the final attack on Japan from the Chinese mainland. The year 1944 saw the remarkably successful unrolling of this pattern of advance, accompanied, and made possible, by the continuous and heavy losses of Japanese ships and aeroplanes. In January and February Kwajalein and Eniwetok in the Marshalls were taken; and the occupation of this group, together with a huge carrier-based air raid, compelled the Japanese to withdraw their ships from Truk, the big naval base in the Carolines, 800 miles to the west. On the other line of advance, MacArthur's forces took the Admiralty Islands in March and Hollandia in Dutch New Guinea in April, and thereafter extended their control of this area and of the Moluccas in preparation for an attack on the Philippines, now coming within bombing distance. In June the central Pacific forces took up the tale by landing on Saipan in the Marianas. Saipan was within bombing distance of southern Japan for the newly-developed B29 American bombers. The invasion of the Marianas, over 1000 miles from Eniwetok in the Marshalls and some 3500 from Pearl Harbor, involved over 125,000 troops—in the same month as the invasion of Normandy. It provoked violent reaction from the Japanese navy: but in the First Battle of the Philippine Sea (June, 1944) they were driven off with the loss of 475 planes to the Americans' loss of 130. By early August the Marianas, including the American possession of Guam, were firmly in American hands. Their conquest was a clear sign that the Japanese had effectively lost the war, and it was not long before raids by B29 bombers on Japanese cities were bringing this home to them. But another year's fighting lay ahead, and the worst horrors of the entire war were yet to come.

The two lines of American advance united for the next stage, the attack on the Philippines, which began with a landing on the island of Leyte in October, 1944. The Japanese committed their main fleet to action in the Battle of Leyte Gulf (sometimes called the Second Battle of the Philippine Sea), the last and greatest naval action of this war. The result, at one point in grave doubt, was an immense American victory, giving them immediate control of the sea round the Philippines; more important, the Japanese Navy never again put up a serious challenge after this battle, in which their losses included four carriers and three battleships. It took the Americans two months to take Leyte. Of the other islands, Mindoro was invaded in December and Luzon, the main island, in January, 1945. Manila, the capital, was retaken early in March, though fighting continued in the Philippines right on to the end of the war. In this same spring British forces recaptured Burma, entering Rangoon in May. Meanwhile the advance towards the Japanese mainland was intensified. The islet of Iwo Jima, half-way between the Marianas and Japan, less than five miles long and, at widest, two and a half across, yet fit for an air base, was taken by March 14 after a month's fighting in which nearly 7000 Americans died. Okinawa in the Ryukyus, only a little over 300 miles from the Japanese mainland, was captured by the end of June after three months' bitter fighting, marked by suicidal Japanese attacks. Off Okinawa the U.S. navy suffered extremely severe losses, not because of Japanese naval resistance but from the Kamikaze, or organised suicide attacks of pilots specially trained to crash-dive their loaded bombers on to enemy ships, especially carriers.[1] Okinawa was intended to provide the final stepping-stone for invasion of Japan.

Such an attack, it was apparent, would not be long delayed, now that Germany had surrendered. It had been agreed by Roosevelt, Churchill and Stalin at the Yalta Conference in February, 1945 that 'in two or three months after Germany has surrendered' the Soviet Union would join in the war against Japan—and the Japanese knew that this was probable. By late May the American military chiefs were planning an invasion for November. Yet it was plain that such an invasion would be fanatically resisted, would lead to immense loss of American lives, and might involve years of warfare. There were many who hoped that aerial bombardment, together with the loss of supplies of vital materials like oil, might convince the Japanese of the wisdom of surrender. Throughout the spring and summer of 1945 Japanese cities, densely populated and built largely of wood, were subjected to savage air attacks, many of them with incendiaries. A single incendiary raid on Tokyo in March burned a quarter of the city, killed some 83,000 people and made a million homeless; and Tokyo was only one of sixty cities so attacked. A new Japanese government which had taken office in April was aware that defeat was inevitable, yet hoped that somehow the demand for unconditional surrender might be modified, if only to secure the position of the Emperor, who in the eyes of the Japanese was sacred. As the American government, which had broken the Japanese diplomatic code, knew, the Japanese government was seeking Russian mediation as a means of securing peace.

On July 26, 1945 the American President (now, since Roosevelt's death in April, Harry S. Truman) and the British Prime Minister (still Winston Churchill) issued from Potsdam an ultimatum calling for complete surrender by Japan. The alternative was 'prompt and utter destruction.' Behind this statement lay the possession of the atomic bomb, a weapon immensely more destructive than anything hitherto known to man. Its development was much the most significant scientific consequence of the Second World War. The German Einstein and the Italian Fermi, scientists

[1] The name 'Kamikaze' meant 'Divine Wind,' and referred to the typhoon which according to Japanese story had saved their Emperor from a Mongol armada in 1281.

of outstanding distinction who were refugees from their totalitarian governments, had warned Roosevelt of the possibility of German development of atomic fission. In 1941 Roosevelt had placed the development of nuclear energy under the control of the Office of Scientific Research and Development. Research had proceeded under conditions of great secrecy despite the millions of dollars involved, and, after 1943, under military control. During 1944–5 at a special laboratory in Los Alamos in remote New Mexico, under the direction of John R. Oppenheimer, the first atomic bomb was made. It was successfully exploded on July 16, 1945. Before this elaborate preparations in the training of pilots and modification of aircraft were made for its military use. Some of the scientists involved advocated that its effect should be demonstrated to the world on a desert island; but most of President Truman's civilian and scientific advisers supported its use against Japan without warning. On July 28 the Japanese Prime Minister informed the Japanese press that his government would ignore the Potsdam ultimatum—although it was known to the American government that the Japanese in fact were seriously seeking peace. On August 2 Truman took the terrible decision to use the bomb, and on August 6 it was dropped on the Japanese city of Hiroshima. It is hard to believe that the same political objective, the surrender of Japan, could not have been achieved by dropping it on open ground. Four square miles of Hiroshima, hitherto unattacked, were obliterated, and over 60,000 people were killed—apart from those who died later from the results of atomic radiation. Three days later, some hours after the Russians had declared war on Japan, a second atomic bomb was dropped on Nagasaki, killing some 36,000 people. In face of this appalling power, the Japanese, led by the Emperor, Hirohito, surrendered. In his message to his people announcing the decision he said, 'Should we continue to fight, it would not only result in an ultimate collapse and obliteration of the Japanese people, but also it would lead to the total extinction of human civilisation.' The formal surrender of Japan took place before General MacArthur on the American battleship *Missouri* in Tokyo Bay on September 2.

25   The United States and World Affairs, 1945–73

I. THE PRESIDENTS

Franklin Roosevelt's twelve years in office considerably increased the importance of the presidency, partly because he was himself a strong personality, mainly because they were years of crisis and danger in which the American people called for strong leadership. By 1945 the power and the responsibilities of the President of the United States were far greater than ever before. When Vice-President Harry S. Truman heard the news of Roosevelt's death that April he said to the journalists: 'I feel as though the moon and all the stars and all the planets have fallen on me.' To succeed Roosevelt at any time would not have been easy. To inherit the most important office on earth during the greatest of wars, with immense decisions to be made which would determine perhaps for generations the peace and happiness of all mankind, and to do so at the very dawn of the nuclear age, when scientists had given to men—and particularly to the American nation—powers of destruction far beyond previous knowledge: this was the fate of Harry Truman. He regarded himself as a very ordinary man. Born in Missouri in 1884, he had as a young man worked in various jobs including those of haberdasher and farmer; fought with modest distinction in the First World War; and sat as a Democrat in the U.S. Senate since 1934. By no means an outstanding senator, he had shown steady party loyalty and voted consistently for the New Deal. Friendly, outspoken, thoroughly honest, Truman rose to the challenge of his task. He made, as he himself later admitted, serious mistakes, and he never won the confidence of the American people as his great predecessor had done. Nevertheless by hard work, courage and a certain breezy individualism he earned world-wide respect. In particular he displayed what Churchill called 'an obvious power of decision' in facing up to the tremendous international problems of the time. He held office until 1953, being re-elected in his own right in 1948.

His successor was Dwight D. Eisenhower, the commander of the victorious North African and Normandy landings. Born in Texas in 1890 and spending his boyhood in the 'cow town' of Abilene, Kansas, Eisenhower had entered West Point at the age of 21 and had spent nearly all his adult career as a professional soldier. The first Republican President since 1933, he was elected on his record as a war hero, rather than as a Republican, winning massive popular majorities over his Democratic opponent, Adlai Stevenson, in the contests of 1952 and 1956. A man of conservative views, he disliked politics and thought the President should be not so much a political leader as a symbol of national unity. He organised his staff on somewhat military lines with the object of delegating as much responsibility as possible. In addition, he played a good deal of golf, he liked to withdraw to the farm he bought at Gettysburg, and he was three times seriously ill. As a result considerable authority fell into the hands of his subordinates, while Eisenhower himself remained ignorant of much that he should have known, a situation made worse because he did not often read the newspapers. His relations with Congress were hampered by the fact that for the last six of his eight years in office the Democrats had a majority in both the Senate and the House of Representatives.

Yet so great was his popularity with the voters that there can be little doubt that Eisenhower could have had a third term had the law permitted it. But the 22nd Amendment to the Constitution (1951), a belated protest against the dead Roosevelt, now forbade anyone to be elected to the office of President more than twice. So for the election of 1960 the Republicans nominated Eisenhower's Vice-President, Richard Nixon, while the Democrats chose Senator John Fitzgerald Kennedy of Massachusetts. The contest was the closest in popular votes for seventy years: in a total poll of over 68 millions Kennedy won by only 112,000, a margin of 0.2 per cent. In several ways the new president was notably different from his immediate predecessors: he was young (43) and extremely wealthy, and he was the first Roman Catholic to be elected President. He had fought bravely in the war, had an unusually beautiful wife, and had performed very skilfully on television in the election campaign. Kennedy also captured the imagination of the American people by summoning them to meet the challenge of what he called 'the New Frontier' of the second half of the 20th century, and his popularity grew substantially during his term in office. That term was tragically cut short on November 22, 1963, when he was shot dead by an assassin while riding in an open car during a visit to Dallas, in Texas.

Ironically, his successor, the Vice-President Lyndon Baynes Johnson, was a Texan. Born in 1908, he had as a young man been an ardent supporter of the New Deal; served five terms in the House of Representatives; been three times elected Senator for Texas; and since 1955 led the Democratic majority in the Senate. Hard-working and tough, highly-experienced in handling Congress, a liberal-minded Southerner,[1] 'LBJ' brought to the presidency abilities at least as great as those of the more glamorous Kennedy, whose New Frontier policies he pledged himself to continue.

Johnson won a mighty victory for the Democrats in the presidential election of 1964, taking the biggest percentage (61) of the popular vote any candidate had ever obtained. Under his guidance and prodding Congress carried through important domestic reforms, notably in the field of Civil Rights. Abroad the United States maintained its role of world responsibility; in particular, there was a significant easing of tension in relations with Soviet Russia. But Johnson's period of office was increasingly darkened by American involvement in a costly and unpopular war in Vietnam, and early in 1968 he announced his intention of not standing in the presidential election of that year. Instead the Democrats nominated the Vice-President, Hubert Humphrey, while the Republicans chose the man whom Kennedy had so narrowly beaten eight years before, Richard M. Nixon. This time it was Nixon who won by a slender margin, taking 43·4 per cent. of the electorate against Humphrey's 42·7 per cent.; a third-party candidate, Governor Wallace of Alabama,

[1] Johnson was the first genuinely Southern President since the Civil War. Woodrow Wilson had been born in Virginia, but spent all his adult life in the North

whose main policy was 'white supremacy', got ten million votes. In party terms the election of 1968 seems a turning-point. Defeat split and demoralised the Democratic leadership, and four years later Nixon won a landslide victory for the Republicans, winning 60·7 per cent. of the popular vote and carrying 49 of the 50 states, to secure himself a second term. Yet it should be noted that in 1972 as in 1968 the Democrats won majorities both in the Senate and in the House of Representatives. Very large numbers of Americans were not voting on straight party lines. Moreover, of 140 million Americans eligible to vote, 63 millions did not even go to the polls.

2. WORLD LEADERSHIP, 1945–73

The Second World War thrust world leadership upon the United States. Most Americans recognised that they had, for the sake of their own security, to accept that leadership; yet many also believed it their duty to do so, in view of the sharp contrast in 1945 between the desperate needs of millions whose way of life had been wrecked by the war, and the prosperity of the people of the United States, the only great country whose material wealth had been virtually undamaged. It was leadership in a world profoundly different from that of 1939, when Hitler's soldiers had fired the war's first shots against the Poles. The long supremacy of western Europe among mankind was finally over: the peoples of her greatest nations— Britain, France and Germany—were in dire need of American help, either to save them from near starvation or to get their economic life back to normal working.[1] There were now only two great powers, capitalist America and Communist Russia. Although they had fought as allies, even during the war there had been signs of deep disagreement; and the post-war politics of all human beings were to be dominated by the rivalry between these giants, their lives haunted by the fear that out of this 'Cold War' there would arise a Third World War. Moreover the flame of revolution was sweeping the non-white world: in China the Communists were destroying Chiang Kai-shek's régime, in India Britain's hold was slackening, in the colonial territories of Asia and Africa the forces of native nationalism were gathering for victory. The old political scene had vanished forever. And overshadowing everything else in the new post-war world was the terrible force which the Americans themselves had conjured up, nuclear power. For a short while only could they hope to be its sole possessors. Thereafter the risks and stakes of American policy would be the survival not only of the United States, but of all mankind.

The most obvious, and encouraging, sign of American acceptance of

[1] Immediate relief, to the millions in many countries made homeless or near-starving, had of course begun while the war was still going on: U.N.R.R.A. (the United Nations Relief and Rehabilitation Administration) had started work in 1943, largely with American funds.

world leadership lay in the part the U.S.A. played in the formation of the new international organisation. The United Nations grew out of the war-time alliance, with powerful encouragement from Franklin Roosevelt. The San Francisco Conference of fifty nations, meeting in the month of his death (April, 1945) drafted the Charter, with its realistic provision for a veto by permanent members of the Security Council. The American Senate which twenty-six years earlier had rejected Wilson's League of Nations accepted American membership of U.N. with only two negative votes. Many prominent Americans who had hitherto been isolationists, like Senator Arthur Vandenberg of Michigan who had strongly opposed Lease-Lend, had now changed to support of internationalist policies. It was symbolic of American commitment to the new organisation that it made its headquarters in New York, in the exciting new building erected beside the East River. With U.N. there were created a number of special agencies, like U.N.E.S.C.O. (the United Nations Educational, Scientific, and Cultural Organisation), the International Labour Organisation, and the World Health Organisation, in which the United States played a full part—indeed, in terms of financial contribution, considerably more than its full part.

It fell to Truman to preside over the final stages of the Second World War and over the beginnings of the establishment of peace, and it was here, particularly in connection with the settlement of Germany and of eastern Europe, that the rift between Soviet Russia and the United States first became clear and serious. In February, 1945 Roosevelt, Churchill and Stalin had met for the second and last time at Yalta in the Crimea, and there had reached a series of agreements. Stalin agreed to enter the war against Japan and to support the organisation proposed for the United Nations; Churchill and Roosevelt accepted the westward extension of the Russian border well into what had been pre-war Poland, with provision for Polish compensation at the expense of Germany, and it was agreed that a new Polish government should be set up 'pledged to the holding of free and unfettered elections.' It was out of these last items that disagreement soon arose, for both in Poland and in other lands released that summer from the Nazi yoke the Russians soon made it clear they would tolerate none but Communist-dominated régimes subservient to themselves. In May Truman sent Harry Hopkins to Moscow to protest against Russian policies, but without real effect. In July, as we have noted in connection with the war against Japan, Truman, Churchill and Stalin met at Potsdam and agreed upon the occupation of Germany by the four powers: Britain, Russia, the U.S.A. and France, each controlling a separate zone[1] with Berlin to be jointly occupied by the four; Poland was to extend its frontiers westward to a line along the rivers Oder and Neisse. Each power was to belong to the Allied Control Council which would decide questions affecting Germany as a whole. These arrangements, intended to be temporary until the signing

---

[1] The American zone was in the south, and included Bavaria and Hesse.

of a definite peace treaty, became permanent as the gulf between Russia and the western allies widened. It soon became evident that the Russians intended to make their zone a Communist-dominated state, and the Poles proceeded to expel millions of Germans from the land they had 'temporarily' acquired. Behind the formation of the rift lay western fear of Communist expansion, and Russian fear that a reunification of Germany might lead to the revival of militarism.

In some ways the wartime allies continued to collaborate. They joined, for example, in organising the Nuremberg Trials (November, 1945 to October, 1946) of leading Nazis as war criminals; and after long negotiations they signed treaties of peace (December, 1946) with Italy, Hungary, Rumania, Bulgaria and Finland, all of whom had fought on the German side during the war. But the gulf between east and west widened; in the famous words of Churchill's speech at Fulton in Missouri, in March, 1946, 'an iron curtain' descended across Europe. Nor was the disagreement confined to Europe: there were disputes about Iran, about Russian help to the Communists against Chiang Kai-shek in China, about Communist activities in promoting revolution in North Korea, Indo-China, Burma, and Indonesia. For their part the Russians deeply distrusted the motives which led the Americans to maintain bases in Germany, Turkey, Japan and elsewhere which seemed clearly to threaten the Soviet Union. Most dangerously of all, the deadlock extended to atomic power. In June, 1946 the Russians rejected at the United Nations an American plan, based upon international inspection, for the establishment of an International Atomic Authority, on the ground that inspection would be contrary to national sovereign rights. The Americans—at this stage the sole possessors of atomic bombs—for their part turned down a Russian proposal for the immediate destruction of all such weapons and the future prohibition of their manufacture.

In March, 1947 Truman put forward a clear statement of what was coming to be known as the policy of 'containment' of Russian activities. At this time there was much Communist activity in Greece, while the Russian government was apparently threatening the independence of Turkey. Britain, traditionally the champion of these countries against the Russians, was no longer strong enough to continue in this role. So Truman, in one of the notable decisions which he took in these years, asked Congress to grant $400 million economic and military aid to Greece and Turkey, saying 'I believe that it must be the policy of the United States to support free peoples who are resisting attempted subjugation by armed minorities or by outside pressures.' Nor was this Truman Doctrine the only notable American initiative of that year; a second and greater one, far wider in its implications yet put forward with the same underlying motive, was the Marshall Plan. In June, 1947 the American Secretary of State, George C. Marshall, called upon the nations of Europe to draw up a plan for economic recovery and submit it to the United States, who would respond by large-scale financial aid. This was timely, for the countries of Europe, not least Britain, France and Italy, were experiencing great difficulties in re-establishing their trade and industry after the war. The sudden ending of Lease-Lend in August, 1945 had been a blow to them, and even substantial American help in the form of loans and supplies of goods (amounting to $11 billion since the end of the war in Europe) had produced only temporary recovery. Sixteen nations eventually responded to—and benefited from—the American invitation; none of the Communist states was among the number, though there had at first been hopes that they might take part. After vigorous debate in Congress—for there were many in the U.S.A. who thought it burdensome and hazardous—the plan was approved, and the first instalment of what eventually amounted to some $12 billion of foreign aid was voted in the spring of 1948. Its passage was sharply stimulated by the Communist coup which took over Czechoslovakia that March. The plan, carried out in Europe by O.E.E.C. (the Organisation for European Economic Co-operation) was highly successful in promoting European economic recovery: within three years the countries concerned had lifted their industrial output to almost 40 per cent. above the 1938 level.

The year 1948 also brought a sharp crisis, perhaps the most dangerous up to that time, in Germany, where in February the three western powers (the U.S.A., Britain and France) had united their zones to make western Germany a single working unit, though not yet an independent state. In June, with the purpose of forcing the western powers out of Berlin, the Russians cut all road, rail and water routes from the west into the city. The allies replied with an airlift of supplies, which built up to an average of nearly 5,000 tons a day, rather above the amount needed to keep the 2,000,000 inhabitants of the city's western sectors alive. Eventually, in May, 1949, the Russians called off the blockade. The episode, which brought the world near to war, emphasised the American intention to stand firm in Europe; it also gave Berlin great symbolic importance in the east–west conflict. Moreover, it led on to a notable step in American foreign policy, the formation in April, 1949 of the North Atlantic Treaty Organisation. This N.A.T.O. treaty added military guarantees to the economic help provided under the Marshall Plan. It stated that all the members (the U.S.A., Canada, Britain and nine other west European countries) would regard 'an armed attack against one or more of them in Europe or North America' as an attack against them all. The Senate ratified the treaty by a big majority, despite its complete departure from the American tradition of no 'entangling alliances.' In 1950 General Eisenhower was appointed supreme commander of N.A.T.O. forces. The Federal Republic of Germany, consisting of the three western zones, was established as an independent state in May, 1949. Both this step and the formation of N.A.T.O. were a clear challenge to Russia. Her scientists enabled her to make a formidable counter-stroke. In September, 1949

Truman informed the American people that the Russians had exploded an atomic bomb. The brief period of American nuclear monopoly was over; and the widely-held view that the Russians were incapable of the highest scientific and technological achievements was shown to be nonsense. In January, 1950 Truman ordered American atomic scientists to go ahead with the production of an even more horrible weapon of mass destruction, the hydrogen bomb.

In 1950 American attention was sharply turned to the Far East, where great changes had taken place since the end of the Pacific War. In Japan itself the occupation which followed victory, with its de-militarisation, trials of war criminals, economic aid and establishment of a new democratic constitution (1946), was on the whole quite astonishingly successful. In contrast with reconstruction in Germany, it was an all-American affair, conducted under the Supreme Commander for the Allied Powers, General Douglas MacArthur. One feature of the Constitution came to cause its American authors some embarrassment: this was Article 9, which forbade the Japanese to have any armed forces, and which had been very widely approved in Japan. Towards the end of the 1940's, events elsewhere in the Far East led the Americans to want all possible help against the Communists, and in 1950 they began the creation of a well-equipped Japanese army. This change of front caused disillusionment among the Japanese, and helped to make them less enthusiastic about the occupation in its closing stages. A peace treaty was signed—but not by the Russians—with the Japanese in 1951, and the occupation ended the following year. By this date the United States had been embroiled for nearly two years in a savage war in Korea. The background of this lay partly in Korea itself, where at the end of the war Russian troops were in occupation north of the 38th parallel and Americans south of that line. As in Germany a temporary military frontier had begun to harden; the Russians had set up a Communist Republic in North Korea, the Americans backed a very reactionary régime in the Republic of South Korea; neither side was willing to recognise the claims of the other. What made this potentially a very perilous situation, for the United States and for world peace, was the Communist Revolution which had taken place in China since the war. Here Communist armies, aided by the Soviet Union, had destroyed the corrupt and hated régime of Chiang Kai-shek. By the end of 1949 the Communists ruled mainland China; Chiang held only the island of Formosa—and the Chinese seat in U.N. The Americans had poured large sums of money, and a good deal of direct military aid, into China in vain attempts to save the old régime. A mission under General Marshall gave up in 1947 its efforts to persuade the two sides to cease fighting and form a coalition government. Later critics were to attack the Truman administration bitterly for its failure to withstand the Communist advance in China; yet it seems clear that the Chiang Kai-shek régime was fundamentally rotten and that only a full-scale war against the Communists, which few

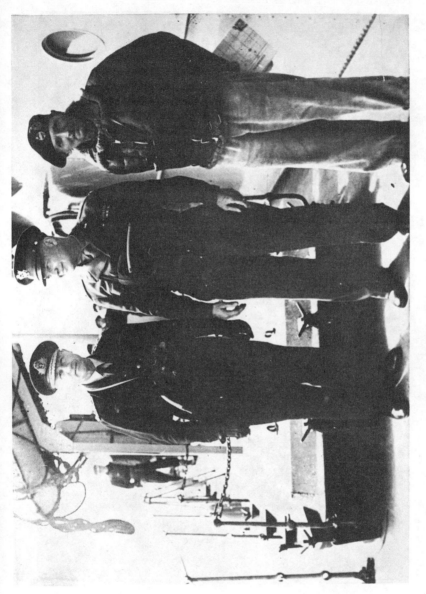

General Eisenhower during the invasion of Normandy, 1944

Martin Luther King addresses his supporters in Alabama, 1965

Americans were ready to accept at that time, could have halted them. But the consequences of the change—perhaps the most significant of all post-war political developments—whereby the world's largest nation became Communist, were certain to be immense.

And they were felt almost at once. In June, 1950 the Republic of North Korea launched an attack on South Korea, and within three days took its capital, Seoul. Truman responded as firmly as he had done to the blockade of Berlin. He sent American troops to the assistance of South Korea, and the U.N.—in the absence of Russia, who was temporarily boycotting the Security Council—condemned the North Korean attack as aggression. By October U.N. forces—predominantly American and under the command of General MacArthur, but including British, Turkish and other contingents—had driven the North Koreans back to the 38th parallel. Despite a warning from the Chinese Communist government, they then pushed on into North Korea, taking the northern capital, Pyongyang. MacArthur, arrogantly confident, told Truman that the whole thing would be over by Christmas, that the Chinese would not dare to attack, and that if they did 'there would be the greatest slaughter.' In November 750,000 Chinese troops entered North Korea and hurled MacArthur's army southwards across the 38th parallel. Seoul was lost again, though it was soon regained. By the spring of 1950 fighting was going on just south of the parallel. The conduct of MacArthur himself added confusion to the situation. He publicly advocated a full-scale war against China, with bombardment, blockade, and invasion of the mainland. Truman's government realised that this would mean Russian intervention and the start of a Third World War; and after further public statements from MacArthur criticising the policy of the government he was serving as a soldier, Truman dismissed him, a move which provoked a congressional investigation and widespread public debate of American policies. Meanwhile the Korean War went on—bitterly fought, in harsh country, with cruel treatment of prisoners, and with little change, after the spring of 1951, in the ground held by the two sides. That summer the Russians at the U.N. proposed an armistice, with both sides to withdraw behind the parallel. But it took two years, with more fighting, to reach even a temporary settlement. In July, 1953 a truce was signed, with the frontier to run where it was at that time, i.e. a little north of the 38th parallel. To achieve this, over 50,000 American soldiers had died and twice that number had been wounded; Korean and Chinese casualties ran into millions, and the country itself lay in ruins. On the one hand, it could be claimed that the United States, and the United Nations, had successfully resisted aggression. On the other, the Korean War, as we shall see, had some unhappy consequences inside the United States.

By the time of the truce, Truman had ceased to be President. He could, despite all the criticism that was made of his policy towards China, claim to have 'contained' Communism over the world as a whole, and to have taken a series of notable decisions which laid the foundations of American policy for years to come. One of them had produced its result late in 1952, when the U.S.A. exploded the first hydrogen bomb on Eniwetok in the Marshall Islands; the Russians followed suit in the summer of 1953. This development, immeasurably expanding mankind's potential for self-destruction and raising at once the problems of the radio-active poisoning of the earth's atmosphere caused by the testing of these new bombs, laid a heavy burden of responsibility upon the new President, Eisenhower. His administration set out to pursue a new and tougher line in foreign policy. It was perhaps encouraged in this by the death of Stalin in March 1953 and by a hope that the new Russian government might be more disposed to compromise. The architect of the new policy was the Secretary of State, John Foster Dulles, an experienced diplomat and the strong man of the cabinet, upon whom Eisenhower relied completely. Dulles believed that 'containment,' which implied 'coexistence' with the Communist world, was not enough; he wanted more 'dynamism' in American policy, aiming at the 'liberation' of those peoples who had been subjected to Communist control. The obvious risk of this policy, that the Russians would react by threatening the use of nuclear force, must be faced. It must be met on the American side by what Dulles in January, 1954 called the 'deterrent of massive retaliatory power.' The United States must be ready to 'go to the brink' of war. Dulles was one of the most notable of all American Secretaries of State. He was a man of high principle and courage, who suffered much pain from cancer in his last three years in office (he died in May, 1959, a month after resigning); he did not spare himself, travelling well over half a million miles on official missions. His policy was narrow as well as tough, for he failed to recognise that men in backward lands such as Indo-China might positively want Communist rule in the hope of putting an end to the poverty and hunger they had hitherto endured. His tactless speeches offended America's allies, and his 'brinkmanship' frightened them; and his policy failed badly in some areas. Yet in his defence it must be said that world peace was in fact maintained throughout the six years (1953-9) when he was by far the most important figure in western diplomacy.

During 1953-4 two dangerous disputes arose in Asia. The first was a consequence of the American commitment to Chiang Kai-shek, now merely master of Formosa (Taiwan) by courtesy of the U.S. fleet. He garrisoned several islands (Quemoy and Matsu being the best known) close to the coast of China as bases for raids on the mainland. Not surprisingly, the Communist government forces bombarded them and showed signs of intending to invade. Should the Americans go to war for the 'offshore islands'? On this point, Dulles resisted pressure from those who believed that now was the time to confront China, and Eisenhower made it clear that the U.S.A. would defend Formosa, but not Quemoy and Matsu by themselves. The problem remained, and flared up several times during the 1950's whenever either Chiang's Nationalists or Communist

China chose to stir up trouble. The second Asiatic problem reached a climax in 1954. For eight years the French had been fighting a losing war in Indo-China against the Communist-led national movement, the Vietminh, and in March of 1954 the Vietminh laid siege to a large French army in the fortress of Dien Bien Phu. Its fall would mean the end of French Indo-China. Should the Americans intervene with military force? Again Dulles and Eisenhower declined to act. The fortress fell, and negotiations followed at Geneva—in which the United States took no part—whereby Vietnam was divided into two parts at the 17th parallel, with provision for later unification after free elections. In fact the country remained divided, and its problems returned to plague the Americans and disturb the whole world. By the 1960's the government of South Vietnam, despite considerable American support, faced a widespread revolutionary movement backed by guerrilla forces from Communist North Vietnam. The formation in September, 1954 of the South-East Asia Treaty Organisation, a military alliance (including the U.S.A., Britain, France, Australia and New Zealand, together with Thailand, the Philippines and Pakistan) on the lines of N.A.T.O. was Dulles' reply to events in Vietnam. But several countries of Asia, notably India and Indonesia, refused to join; moreover, many critics said that a military alliance like S.E.A.T.O. was the wrong sort of answer to a problem whose real roots lay in the poverty and hunger which gave the Communists their opportunity.

During 1955 the skies brightened a little over Europe, despite the admission the previous October of the German Federal Republic (i.e. western Germany) to N.A.T.O., a move which alarmed the Soviet Union. There were signs that the new Russian leaders were beginning on their side to appreciate the perils involved in blundering into a nuclear war, and to think at least of the possibility of 'peaceful coexistence' between the capitalist and Communist areas of the world. It was certainly clear that they now attached far more importance to spreading Communist doctrines among the undeveloped peoples of Asia, Africa, and Latin America by relatively peaceful means—like the spread of propaganda about the superior merits of Communism, the support of nationalist movements, and the supply of technical experts and economic assistance—than to the use of military force. In May, 1955 the Russians at last agreed to the signature of a treaty ending the four-power occupation of Austria. This encouraged the holding at Geneva in July of a 'summit' meeting attended by Eisenhower and the chief statesmen of Russia, Britain and France. They met amicably enough, and spoke fair words, like Eisenhower's remark that 'the American people want to be friends with the Soviet peoples'; and the mere fact of meeting did a little to relax tension. But nothing definite emerged, and the Russians flatly rejected Eisenhower's 'Open Skies' proposal to allow both sides complete freedom to take aerial photographs of each other's military and other installations. So the cold war went on.

Indeed, from this time onwards until the end of Eisenhower's presidency, it might be said that things went from bad to worse for American foreign policy. October, 1956 produced—a few days before the presidential election—two simultaneous crises which in quite different ways damaged American pride and influence. On October 24 the Hungarians rose in revolt against their Communist-dominated government; the Soviet Union, now headed by Nikita Krushchev, sent in tanks and many thousands of troops to suppress them. On October 31 British and French armies attacked Egypt, whose ruler, Colonel Nasser had that summer nationalised the Suez Canal. The United States did nothing to help the Hungarians. This was inevitable, for nothing could be done, short of nuclear war, but it made the earlier talk of 'liberation' from Communism a sour memory, and it was a cruel blow to Americans as champions of freedom. In the Suez Crisis the U.S.A. found itself in the odd situation of joining with Soviet Russia in the U.N. to condemn the aggressive activities of its own chief allies; and within a week Britain and France climbed down and withdrew their forces. Dulles' action over Suez was wholly justified, for Britain and France were defying the U.N. Charter by their resort to force in this wretched adventure. But the episode did real, though temporary, harm to the western alliance. Moreover, Dulles himself had contributed to the crisis, by his abrupt withdrawal earlier in the year of an American offer to finance the proposed new Aswan Dam in Egypt. And there were many who said that the real reason why the United States was so prompt to condemn her allies was the vague threat which the Russians made at the time to use long-range missiles against the aggressors.

The production of such missiles was one part of a development which was increasingly alarming the Americans—and which no Secretary of State could do anything about: namely, the remarkable scientific and technological progress of Soviet Russia. The two countries were beginning to enter the 'race for space,' and the first successful satellite, the Sputnik launched in October, 1957, represented a tremendous triumph for the Russians in its early stages. Although the Americans were not far behind in the race and soon put up their own satellites, the Russian lead was a great blow to their national pride; and the lead seemed to be maintained in 1959 when the Russians fired a rocket to the moon. Another, and more immediately ominous, sign of Russian technical progress was the increasing frequency of hydrogen bomb testing. This was paralleled by similar American testing, and the increased fall-out of radioactive materials which occurred, with its long-term menace to human health and to the survival of the human race, aroused widespread concern everywhere in the world. Although negotiations between the U.S.A., the Soviet Union and Britain to reach a 'test-ban' agreement dragged on for years with no result, there were suspensions of testing by both sides at different times in 1958. Undoubtedly this was one of the factors which contributed to something of a thaw in the cold war in 1959. Another one may have been the early beginnings of disagreement between Russia and China. The Chinese Communists had no belief in the idea of 'peaceful coexistence,' and Krushchev may therefore have been the more anxious to make it succeed.

In 1959 he paid a visit to the United States, toured some parts of the country, and had friendly discussions with Eisenhower at Camp David in Maryland. A summit meeting was arranged for May 16, 1960 in Paris. But on May 5 Krushchev announced that an American aeroplane had been shot down over Russia four days before. The United States government stated that it was a weather plane which had strayed off course. Krushchev replied on May 7 that it was in fact an American U2 reconnaissance plane engaged in 'intelligence' on a flight from Turkey to Norway, that the Russians had captured the pilot, and that he had owned up to being a spy. This affair—or Krushchev's decision to exploit it—wrecked the 'summit', and mankind's cautiously high hopes of it. The American government admitted its breach of international law, but claimed it was justified; Eisenhower accepted responsibility, but declined to apologise at the 'summit' meeting in Paris. Krushchev, recognising that there would soon be a change of president, indicated that he could place no more trust in Eisenhower. Nor was this the only blow to American hopes in 1960. It was humiliating when in June the Japanese government, after an outburst of anti-American rioting in Tokyo, asked Eisenhower to cancel a visit he had arranged to pay to Japan. It was far more serious in American eyes when trouble arose over the establishment of what looked like a Communist state in Latin America.

Hostility to the United States had grown in many parts of Latin America since the ending of the Second World War. This was partly because the U.S.A. had relatively neglected that area in its distribution of overseas aid; there had in fact been quite substantial grants and loans to Latin American countries, but they had been on a far smaller scale than those to the rest of the world. There had been nothing like the Marshall Plan in the American hemisphere. More seriously, the United States government had shown considerable friendship to various dictators in the Latin American republics. The one notable intervention of this period had taken place in 1954, when Dulles sent arms to help overthrow a Guatemalan government sympathetic to Communism; the move had not been popular in Latin America. In 1958 rioting had greeted Vice-President Nixon in Peru and Venezuela when he visited those countries on a goodwill tour. The climax came in Cuba. Here a revolution in 1958–9 organised by a young student leader, Fidel Castro, had overthrown the long-established and long-hated régime of the dictator Batista. At first the United States welcomed Castro. He was greeted by cheering crowds in the U.S.A. in 1959, and in Washington he was promised economic aid. But on his return home he quickly revealed both dictatorial methods and Communist sympathies, carrying out radical—and necessary—social reforms, putting banks and plantations under government control, and imprisoning many of his opponents and of his early supporters. Despite these measures—indeed, because of some of them—Castro won considerable popularity among the poor and the intellectuals in the rest of Latin America. American protests encouraged him to turn to Russia for financial and technical aid in 1960. It became evident that he was creating something like a Soviet satellite state in the Americas, and one which was alarmingly close to the United States. Eisenhower broke off American diplomatic relations with Cuba just before his term of office ended. The Cuban problem was a difficult legacy to his successor.

There were high hopes of a fresh start in foreign relations when President Kennedy was inaugurated in January, 1961, even though few Americans had any illusions about Russia's readiness to compromise on any major issue. He laid down the broad line of his approach in his inaugural address, saying 'Let us never negotiate out of fear. But let us never fear to negotiate.' These hopes remained unfulfilled in the period of less than three years for which he held office. Yet the forward-looking idealism which was part of his character found expression in several plans which he launched. One of these was the Peace Corps (1961), a project whereby young American men and women were to be trained to serve in various ways—in teaching, in public health, in village development, in providing technical advice in farming—for periods of two or three years in under-developed countries. Another, more political and on a greater scale, was the Alliance for Progress (1961), a scheme to provide massive aid in order to promote the economic and social development of Latin American countries—an attempt to regain the ground, and the good will, lost by his predecessor. A third, of very different kind, was his appeal for nuclear disarmament (1961), addressed to the United Nations in a speech whose opening para-graph pointed out that 'Every man, woman and child lives under a nuclear sword of Damocles, hanging by the slenderest of threads, capable of being cut at any moment by accident or miscalculation or by madness.' The appeal met with no immediate response from the Russians, who were at that time re-starting after a two-year interval the atmospheric testing of great hydrogen bombs; and in March, 1962 the United States resumed the testing of these weapons. The 'race for space' also continued: in 1961 two Russian astronauts circled the globe, in 1962 the first American, John Glenn, followed hard upon their heels.

The toughness which was also part of Kennedy's character found scope in a succession of crises. Among them was a dispute (1960-2) arising from the prolonged civil war in the kingdom of Laos, formerly part of French Indo-China, where there was at one stage a distinct possibility of an open clash between the U.S.A. and the Soviet Union; here Kennedy's government dropped a policy which in previous years had spent countless dollars in the hope of establishing a pro-American régime, and instead helped to set up in 1962 a system of government representing all groups—pro-western, pro-Communist, and neutral—in the small country. There was, too, a further crisis over the status of Berlin when Krushchev, at a meeting with Kennedy in Vienna in June, 1961, proposed the ending of four-power control of the city, and threatened to sign a peace treaty with the Communist state of East Germany under which western access to Berlin would be stopped. Kennedy stood firm in opposition, saying that an attack upon Berlin would be regarded 'as an attack upon us all,' and taking steps to strengthen the American armed forces. The Communist response was to build a heavily-defended concrete wall separating the eastern and western parts of the city.

Yet, perhaps inevitably in the light of earlier events, the biggest issue in foreign policy during Kennedy's presidency was Cuba. Here he made a disastrous start. In April, 1961, with the full knowledge of the president,[1] some 1200 Cuban exiles, preceded by bombers from Florida, set out from Guatemala and from Florida to invade their native land. They landed in the Bahia de Cochinas (Bay of Pigs) on the southern coast, where Castro's forces destroyed or captured nearly all of them. This sorry episode enabled Cuba and Russia to portray the U.S.A. as an aggressor before U.N., increased Cuban support for Castro, and tarnished Kennedy's image in the United States and before the world. Kennedy accepted full responsibility, and cut off all trade between Cuba and the U.S.A. The real crisis was yet to come. Castro strengthened his ties with the Communist countries, especially after Cuba was in January, 1962 excluded from the Organisation of American States—the Latin American international organisation for economic and social development—on the ground that the country was being used as a base for communist infiltration of other Latin American states. That summer it became plain from aerial reconnaissance that the Russians were not only sending jet aircraft and other military equipment into Cuba, but were also establishing missile bases in the island. There was a brief but very tense crisis that October, when Kennedy ordered the United States navy to prevent the delivery of any further military material to Cuba, and demanded that Russia dismantle and remove the bases. In November Krushchev yielded, demolished the bases, and withdrew the aircraft. The world breathed again.

Mankind had been closer to nuclear war than on any previous occasion. It was recognition of this fact that brought about, in June, 1963, the installation of the so-called 'hot-line' for instant communication between the heads of state in Washington and Moscow. More important, this was followed in August by the 'test-ban' treaty, in which the United States, Russia and Britain agreed not to test nuclear weapons above ground. This proved to be an important turning-point in the Cold War, inaugurating a period of better Russo–American relations. Deep rivalry and tension remained, particularly in the race to develop intercontinental ballistic missiles and early warning systems, and the improvement was slow and

[1] The invasion was to have taken place in the late autumn of 1960, but Eisenhower had called it off after consulting Kennedy, by that time president-elect.

modest. It was shown in relatively minor matters, like exchanges of cultural and meteorological materials and information, sales of American wheat to the U.S.S.R., and the mutual release of captured spies. In 1964 the American government cut down its forces in Europe; in 1966 it relaxed restrictions on travel to Communist countries. Much more significantly, in the later 1960's there were continuing negotiations with the Russians on nuclear disarmament. They seemed to achieve little; but it was immensely important that they took place at all. One reason why they did so was certainly the recognition on both sides of the appalling hazards involved in a nuclear arms race. But a most powerful stimulus to Russo–American agreement lay in the renaissance during the 1960's of China, as a major Communist state under Mao Tse-tung. Both the U.S.A. and the U.S.S.R., for different reasons, were hostile to the new China; and both were profoundly fearful of China as a nuclear power, the more because the range of her material resources was so largely unknown. For their part the Chinese made no attempt to disguise their hostility to all the manifestations of American capitalism, and throughout the 1960's there were periodic alarms in the U.S.A. about the possibility of a war with China.

The role of the United States as leader of the non-Communist world involved heavy defence expenditure, with considerable forces stationed in western Europe and elsewhere overseas; it also involved a continuing measure of compulsory military service for America's young men, under a conscription law of 1963. This military outlay had its parallel in the many millions of dollars provided by the American taxpayer for technical and economic assistance to a wide range of countries, most notably in Asia (e.g. to India, Ceylon and Indonesia), and to Latin America under the Alliance for Progress. The motives behind this vast programme of civilian aid, on a scale never before equalled in human history, were very mixed indeed. They range from a direct and sincere humanitarianism, very strong among many thousands of younger Americans, right across to an equally direct and sincere form of political insurance against the spread of Communism, backed by Russia or by China, into the lands where the aid went. Whatever its motive, this outpouring of dollars and services seemingly did little to win friends for the United States. Anti-Americanism, actively encouraged by the Communist countries, was a powerful political force in the 1960's: the appearance of American statesmen, from the President downwards, in foreign capitals from Japan to Peru was often a signal for demonstrations and riots. Such episodes seemed most disturbing in the Caribbean lands or in South America, where United States nerves were specially sensitive. Cuba, under Fidel Castro, became and remained defiantly Communist, a seedbed of anti-American propaganda. In 1965 Johnson, fearing the effect of this propaganda, sent U.S. forces to intervene in the civil war which had broken out in the Dominican Republic—action which evoked widespread protests both in Latin America and inside the U.S.A. itself.

One field in which there was continuous rivalry during the 1960's between Russians and Americans was 'the race for space.' On a long view of human history those events of this decade which culminated in man's first landing on the moon make contemporary political developments seem trivial. The scientific and technological achievement, based in both the super-powers on colossal expenditure and an extraordinary concentration of resources, dwarfed all other material advances of this period. On the American side, the progress was a clear response to the challenge first thrown down by the Russian *sputnik* of the 1950's and persistently maintained ever since. At its heart there was the Apollo Project, set going by President Kennedy in 1961, to put men on the moon by 1970; around this, an immensely complicated programme of satellite launchings and planetary investigation. Thorough planning and massive preliminary work laid foundations in the early 1960's, and from 1964 onwards remarkable results began to appear, starting with the moon-shots of that year, Ranger VI hitting the moon in January and Ranger VII crash-landing and sending back photographs in July. In 1965 the satellite Mariner IV recorded close-up photographs of the planet Mars; in 1966 an American satellite was in orbit round the moon. These were immense achievements, far beyond any earlier technology. Yet they were overshadowed in the same years by the development of manned space-flights and the beginnings of space-walks and dockings, tests of manœuverability in preparation for the final stages of Apollo. All this was made the more astonishing by the control of rockets and satellites exerted over vast distances of space from the ground headquarters at Houston and the launching-site at Cape Canaveral (renamed Cape Kennedy) and also by the extent to which television made it possible for ordinary mortals to see and thus in a way to share in these wonders as they were actually happening.

The planned climax came in 1969. In December, 1968, the manned space-ship Apollo 8 had successfully orbited the moon and returned to earth. Now, on July 21, 1969, the astronauts Neil Armstrong and Edward Aldrin in Apollo 11 became the first human beings to set foot on the moon. Their landing and triumphant return were seen by countless millions on television screens. The same November Apollo 12 followed suit. In all, by the completion of the Apollo programme in December, 1972, there were six successful landings on the moon (one space-ship only had failed, and that was brought safely back), as well as a long series of investigations in the early 1970's of the planets Venus and Mars. The long-term value to the United States and to mankind of the programme can only be guessed at, not measured. Its expense, in the use of materials and of the resources of brilliant scientists and engineers was enormous, and there were many critics who maintained that the money and the effort would have been better spent on tackling the huge problems of poverty and violence which afflicted contemporary American society. Yet three comments may fairly be made. The successful completion of so vast a programme was an unparalleled feat of applied science and technology; the extension of man's knowledge of his universe was quite unprecedented; and the bravery of the astronauts was immense.

Unhappily, these triumphs in space came to be overshadowed by American involvement in an unsuccessful war in Vietnam. The roots of this tragic episode, which cost the lives of some 50,000 Americans and did incalculable damage to the image of the United States in the eyes of the world, lay in the collapse of the French Empire in Indo-China.[1] The French surrender in 1954 of the fortress of Dien Bien Phu had been followed by the Geneva Agreement recognising a group of independent states including Cambodia, Laos, North Vietnam and South Vietnam. As in Korea ten years earlier, so in Vietnam: the North, with its capital at Hanoi and led by the veteran nationalist hero of the fight against the French, Ho Chi Minh, was a Communist state, while South Vietnam, governed from Saigon, was non-Communist and backed by the western powers. The Saigon government was unpopular, oppressive and corrupt in policy, notably severe to its many Buddhist subjects, and in 1960 a vigorous revolutionary movement, the National Liberation Front (Viet Cong), was started in the South by the Communists. Backed and guided by the North Vietnam government, preaching freedom and land reform to the poverty-stricken and backward peasants, it demanded the unification of all Vietnam and conducted widespread and successful guerrilla warfare. Here was a clear threat to the Geneva Settlement and to the separate existence of South Vietnam. The Eisenhower and Kennedy administrations viewed developments in Vietnam with grave concern. This was scarcely surprising in view of the role of the United States in the 'cold war.' Communism must be resisted or contained in Asia as firmly as in Europe. In particular, there was widespread American belief in what came to be known as the 'domino theory' of the anti-Communist position in South-East Asia. The collapse of one state to Communist pressure would bring the collapse of others in turn: if South Vietnam went, Laos would go, then Thailand, and then Burma. The moral was plain: Communist advance must be checked early, before it gathered irresistible strength.

It was President Kennedy who took the first steps towards armed American intervention in Vietnam: by 1963 there were 16,000 American servicemen in the South, mostly military advisers, helicopter pilots and supply troops rather than ground combat forces. But it fell to Johnson to make the decisive moves. In 1964 his government guaranteed economic and military aid to South Vietnam, proclaiming 'South Vietnam is a test case for the new Communist strategy.' The future of South-East Asia must be seen as a whole: what was going on in Vietnam was not just a 'jungle war' but part of a world-wide struggle for freedom against the Communist threat. That August North Vietnamese gunboats attacked American warships in the Gulf of Tonkin. The United States retaliated

[1] See above, p. 243.

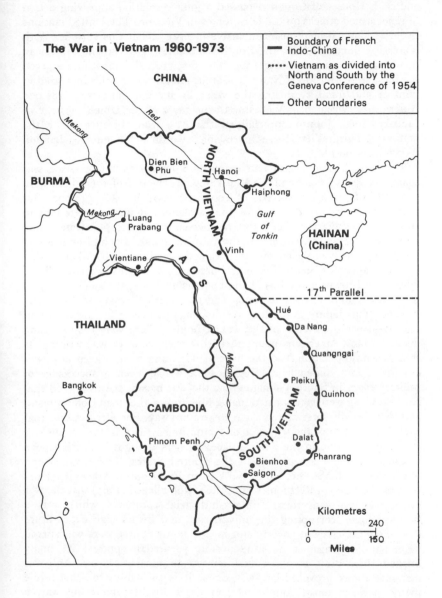

The War in Vietnam 1960-1973

—— Boundary of French Indo-China

***** Vietnam as divided into North and South by the Geneva Conference of 1954

—— Other boundaries

CHINA

Mekong

Red

BURMA

Dien Bien Phu

NORTH VIETNAM

Hanoi

Haiphong

Mekong

Luang Prabang

LAOS

Gulf of Tonkin

HAINAN (China)

Vientiane

Vinh

THAILAND

17th Parallel

Hué

Da Nang

Quangngai

Mekong

Pleiku

Bangkok

Quinhon

CAMBODIA

SOUTH VIETNAM

Dalat

Phnom Penh

Bienhoa

Phanrang

Saigon

Kilometres

0 _____ 240

0 _____ 150

Miles

by bombing torpedo-boat bases and oil storage depots in North Vietnam, and both Houses of Congress passed a joint resolution approving action to repel armed attacks on the U.S. forces in Vietnam. The United Nations Security Council held an inconclusive meeting about this episode. With increasing demands from the South Vietnamese government, American involvement escalated during 1965. The first ground combat forces (3500 marines) were sent to Da Nang in March; American air-raids increased in number and intensity during the year; by its end there were 181,000 American servicemen in Vietnam. In his State of the Union message of January, 1966, Johnson proclaimed the American objective to be the halting of North Vietnamese aggression: 'we do not intend to abandon Asia to conquest.'

Thus the United States had committed herself to a large-scale war against North Vietnam and the Viet Cong. By the end of 1966 there were 389,000 U.S. troops involved; of 1967, 453,000; of 1968, 540,000. But there was no victory to show for the escalation. It was a war fought in conditions peculiarly difficult for the mechanised and sophisticated warfare of the 'advanced' powers: the terrain was harsh, much of it steaming jungle, and many of the enemy were trained guerrillas, sheltered and aided by the peasants of South Vietnam. There was widespread destruction, of villages and towns as well as of military installations; the gains, in terms of territory, went to the Viet Cong and the North Vietnamese, especially in 1968. This failure to produce results was one reason for the early and rapidly-growing criticism of the war at home. There were others, going deeper. Many Americans maintained that their country was wasting its treasure, its reputation, and the lives of its young men to keep in power a corrupt and undemocratic régime; there had been a succession of military *coups* in South Vietnam since the war began. It was argued that the Viet Cong were genuine nationalist liberators rather than Communists; and that the villagers wanted them to win anyway. Some critics said that such a war was not the way to halt Communism: it was 'the wrong war at the wrong time in the wrong place.' Others thought it was having a disastrous effect upon politics in the United States. There was strong opposition in the Senate, led by J. William Fulbright of Arkansas, chairman of the Foreign Relations Committee, who alleged (1967) that the war had created a dangerous 'military-industrial complex,' which was a political force 'corrupting the universities' and by its high expenditure deepening the crisis of poverty and race at home. There were widespread demonstrations against it. Students in particular opposed it: many burned their draft cards or fled abroad to escape call-up. Anti-war demonstrations provoked pro-war ones; it is probably true that while many, perhaps most, Americans had grave doubts about the war, a majority backed the government's policy out of simple loyalty. A good deal of the opposition concentrated not on the war itself but on the way in which it was being conducted. In particular there was much disapproval

The American envoy Dr. Henry Kissinger meets the Chinese leader Mao Tse-tung (1973)

American space craft on the moon: Apollo 15's pilot and lunar rover

of the use of napalm bombs and of other devices for defoliation, to clear the jungle growth which gave shelter to the guerrillas. Abroad there was widespread condemnation of American actions, seen daily by millions on the television screen with its pictures of burning huts and terror-stricken Vietnamese women and children. This, if somewhat easy to indulge in, did at any rate express much feeling in the western world that this was not the way in which to answer Communism. And there was much scepticism of American motives, particularly when the fighting spilled over, as it almost inevitably did, into the neighbouring states of Laos and Cambodia.

In 1968 the total of U.S. troops in Vietnam rose to over half a million. But by this time the forces of doubt about the whole affair had gained much ground. Peace negotiations opened in Paris that March: they proceeded at snail's pace for years, ceasing altogether for months on end when the strategic situation seemed to suit one side or the other. In March too Johnson, always sensitive to public opinion, announced that he would not be a candidate for re-election in November, and there can be little doubt that the consequences of Vietnam influenced his decision. In October the United States temporarily suspended its bombing of North Vietnam. Although this brought no effective response from Hanoi and bombing was later resumed, the readiness of the U.S. government to take such action both revealed American concern about world criticism and suggested that the heart of the nation was not in this war. The time was ripe for a change of approach, and the Republican Richard Nixon's succession to Johnson at the White House in January, 1969, provided the opportunity.

The change was not sudden or dramatic; and Nixon's policy in Vietnam must be seen in the context of his foreign policy as a whole. His central aim was to reduce tension among the powers. In particular, he wanted to put an end to the Cold War by negotiating agreements with Soviet Russia; to improve relations with Communist China; and to reduce the burden of the Vietnam war by the gradual reduction of American involvement, if possible to the point of total withdrawal. It was arguable that the achievement of the first two items hinged upon the successful accomplishment of the third. So in 1969 Nixon's government moved clearly yet cautiously in the direction of scaling down American participation in the war: withdrawing a number of ground combat forces, putting up detailed peace plans, establishing direct contact with the North Vietnamese leader Ho Chi Minh, and—perhaps most important of all—publicly committing himself (April) to a withdrawal of 150,000 more troops within the next two years. During 1970–71 the scale of fighting greatly diminished, and, particularly in 1971, the number of Americans engaged fell sharply, so that in May, 1972, Nixon could announce a ceiling of 69,000 American troops compared with the 549,500 involved when he took office rather over three years before.

It was not easy to put the machinery of war into reverse. There was resistance from the South Vietnamese government and vociferous opposition from patriotic and right-wing quarters at home. The North Vietnamese were naturally not at all unwilling to drive home their advantage and did not hurry peace negotiations. Nixon's government was ready to use spells of strategic bombing to accelerate the talks. There were problems over the involvement of Cambodia, and complex difficulties in the mutual exchange of prisoners of war. Not until January, 1973, was an agreement reached in Paris between the United States, North and South Vietnam, and the Viet Cong, providing for the ending of the fighting and the restoration of peace. The cease-fire itself was to prove difficult to establish, even with the aid of a small United Nations force, and the details of the peace complicated to sort out. At home there was general welcome for the peace, sweetened as it was by the simultaneous ending of conscription. The long conflict had been the most unsuccessful of all America's wars: it had cost the lives of over 50,000 Americans and wounded six times that number; contributed to a great wave of anti-American feeling in the world; and caused bitter divisions among Americans at home, not least between students and older people.

It is impossible to measure how much the Vietnam war did to check the advance of Communism in South-East Asia. Certainly from 1969 onwards Nixon's government did much in other directions to display the American wish for peace in general, and for agreement with the Communist world in particular. The President himself was a persistent traveller, touring the globe from Dublin to Bucarest, from Rome and Bonn to Moscow and Peking. He made significant statements of policy, like the United States renunciation of all methods of biological warfare (November, 1969). In 1969 he negotiated agreements with Rumania, and began the important SALT (Strategic Arms Limitation Talks) discussions with the Soviet government. In May, 1972, the United States signed with Russia agreements for joint limitations on Anti-Ballistic Missile Systems, and for joint space flights in 1975. Yet the most interesting development of Nixon's diplomacy was a reversal of policy towards China, with whom the U.S.A. had been on bad terms since the Communists had seized power there in 1949. After a gradual relaxation of trade and travel restrictions, some ambassadorial talks and a little 'diplomacy by pingpong,'[1] Nixon was cordially received by the Chinese leaders in Peking. The Chinese Communist government took its seat on the Security Council of the United Nations, replacing the hitherto American-backed Taiwan where Chiang Kai-Shek still claimed to be the legitimate ruler of all China. How significant this change of front really was remained to be seen; there was still grave alarm about the Chinese move into the ranks of that small group of powers which had produced hydrogen bombs. Yet at least the short-term trend of Nixon's policy was plain.

[1] American table tennis teams were permitted to visit China in 1971 to play against the native experts.

26   The United States at Home, 1945-73

I. DOMESTIC POLICY

President Truman's administration carried through with remarkable smoothness the change-over from war to peace. Nearly 12,000,000 servicemen were efficiently demobilised; industry turned back to the production of civilian goods, aided by the public's demand for things they had been unable to buy during the war; farmers found ready markets for their produce abroad, thanks to the American money poured into U.N.R.R.A. and other organisations which were helping to deal with post-war distress in Europe. Under the 'G.I. Bill of Rights,' originally passed in 1944, millions of ex-servicemen obtained higher education and training at government expense. In 1947 the Presidential Succession Act laid down that in the event of the President's death in office the succession should go first to the Vice-President, then to the Speaker of the House of Representatives, and next to the President of the Senate. The number of government departments and agencies, which had multiplied under Roosevelt, was substantially reduced. But, for the rest, Truman's first term in the White House, so far as domestic affairs were concerned, was a record of frustration. His 'Fair Deal' proposals, first put forward in 1945, for such extensions of, or additions to, the New Deal as health insurance, laws to maintain farm prices, and the development of housing, met with little welcome. The important measures passed by Congress, like the Taft–Hartley Act (1947),[1] were ones of which the President disapproved.

This limited achievement was partly Truman's own fault: he made some bad appointments, he gave offence by rash words and actions, he offended liberal-minded men by getting rid of leading New Dealers from office, his vigorous championship of Civil Rights for Negroes lost him white support in the South.[2] He was also heavily preoccupied with the great problems of foreign affairs in these years. The ending of wartime price controls in 1946 brought a sharp rise in prices, and contributed to a Republican victory in the mid-term elections to Congress that autumn, the first time they had won both houses since 1928. Truman indeed won the presidential election of 1948, after a remarkable personal campaign in

[1] See below, p. 263.   [2] See below, p. 265.

which he defeated not only his Republican opponent, Thomas E. Dewey, and a breakaway 'Dixiecrat' white supremacy candidate who carried four normally Democratic states in the South, but also the Gallup Poll, which had firmly predicted a win for Dewey; and the Democrats regained control of Congress. But even this triumph was of little use to him. Some parts of the Fair Deal—e.g. a housing act, wider social security benefits, a higher minimum wage—did become law. But his main proposals for reform were still blocked by the alliance in Congress of southern Democrats and conservative Republicans. More serious, he ran headlong into the problem of 'McCarthyism.'

The Cold War provoked in the United States a morbid fear and suspicion of spies and 'subversive activities.' Events early in 1949—the year which brought the final Communist triumph in China and the first Russian atomic bomb—heightened these feelings. Alger Hiss, a former official of the State Department (the U.S. foreign office), who had been with Roosevelt at Yalta, was imprisoned for perjury in denying accusations that he had passed secret documents to the Russians; shortly afterwards Klaus Fuchs, a brilliant British scientist of German origin who had worked with Oppenheimer on the American A-bomb, was found to have been supplying the Russians with vital atomic information. In 1950 came the Korean War, intensifying anti-Communist hatred and arousing in many Americans a frenzied nationalism; its failures, and the stalemate which set in, stimulated a feeling of betrayal and a hunt for scapegoats. Against this background emerged the figure of Senator Joseph McCarthy of Wisconsin, an unscrupulous and skilful demagogue who from 1949 to 1954 led a cruel campaign against all those whom he could label as Communist or 'un-American.' His methods included the outrageous bullying of witnesses before Senate committees, malicious smears in public statements, cries of treachery and appeals to nationalist prejudice against any politicians who opposed him, and large-scale lying. Unhappily, vast numbers of Americans accepted his lead, and under the guise of a search for traitors there was a widespread attack upon freedom of opinion. The civil service was combed for those who could be regarded as 'disloyal' or as 'security risks,' often because of membership of left-wing movements in the 1930's; many cities and states demanded 'loyalty oaths' of their teachers or university staffs; suspicion was widely thrown on pacifists, artists, eminent scholars, members of liberal organisations and others who did not appear to hold orthodox views; distinguished public officials were branded as 'friends of Moscow.' In 1950 Congress passed—over Truman's veto—the McCarran Internal Security Act, banning the entry to the country of anyone who had ever been a member of any totalitarian organisation.

The performance continued for two years after Eisenhower's accession to the presidency in 1953, partly because Eisenhower was, in his own words, unwilling to 'get in the gutter with that guy' and because Secretary of State Dulles was willing to accept McCarthy's support. But in 1954 McCarthy got involved in a quarrel with the army, whose chiefs resisted his interference. The points at issue were investigated by the Senate in a series of hearings lasting over a month. These were televised, and public opinion—now that the Korean War was over—turned sharply against McCarthy, mainly perhaps because millions of Americans saw for the first time on their screens what sort of man he was. The Senate censured him by a large majority, and he was an ineffectual figure thenceforward until his death in 1957. It had been a lamentable episode in the history of a great nation. 'McCarthyism' blanketed that free expression of opinion which Americans traditionally claimed as one of the values upon which the United States was built; and the amount of personal unhappiness it caused to countless innocent people in these years is immeasurable.

Eisenhower liked to see himself as a President above party differences, nor did he regard it as the President's task to give a vigorous lead in domestic policy. But his appointments gave a clear enough indication of his general attitude. His first cabinet, it was said, consisted of 'eight millionaires and a plumber'; the plumber resigned after eight months.[1] Thoroughly conservative in outlook, Eisenhower thought highly of businessmen, and the aims of his government were those acceptable to business— a reduction of government activity and spending, a balanced budget, and increased scope for private enterprise. More extreme Republicans wanted to scrap the New Deal reforms and the welfare state they had created. Eisenhower recognised the impossibility of such steps, and talked genially of 'dynamic conservatism' and of 'middle of the road' policies. In a few directions he did much to satisfy his business supporters. For example, he cut spending on the Tennessee Valley Authority and sharply reduced its staff; handed over to private enterprise the site of a dam on the Snake River in Idaho; put under the control of private companies the operation of two atomic energy plants which had been built by the government; and did harm to some independent government agencies, such as the Federal Power Commission, by appointing to their boards opponents of regulation. He contrived to reduce certain taxes, mostly those which were burdensome to companies. But in general he completely failed to reduce either the size or the spending of the Federal government. For most of his eight years in office the budget was not balanced and in 1959 the deficit was the highest recorded. The reason for this, of course, was that it was felt to be impossible to reduce military expenditure, which accounted for some two-thirds of the total, in this period of nuclear competition with the Soviet Union. Yet the Eisenhower government spent great sums of money in tackling the problems of farm incomes, which were falling in the 1950's despite—or because of—more successful production and increased yields. The Department of Agriculture adopted the so-called 'soil bank' plan

[1] He was the Secretary of Labour, who was a leader of the Plumbers Union and a prominent trade unionist.

which involved paying farmers to take land entirely out of crop production, and by 1958 its expenditure was six times what it had been in 1952—without really benefiting the numerous poorer farmers who needed assistance most of all.

The Republicans were no longer the popular party, and Eisenhower could not make them so. The exceptional circumstances created by the Korean War had worked out to their profit in 1952, but they could not hold their advantage. They lost all three Congressional elections of the years 1954–8. That of 1956 throws an interesting light on the working of the American system. While 35,500,000 citizens—the largest number ever before 1964—were voting for Eisenhower and giving him a popular majority of 9,500,000 over his Democratic rival Adlai Stevenson, these same citizens were also voting to maintain the Democrats' majority in the Senate and to increase it in the House of Representatives. Eisenhower's second term (1957–61) was not an easy one, and other circumstances added to his difficulties. Unemployment increased in 1957–8, and again in 1960–1. He lost the two men who had carried much of the burden of government for him: Sherman Adams resigned in 1958 after a congressional investigation had revealed that he had accepted presents from a shady business man who wanted government assistance, and Dulles died in 1959. Perhaps the most interesting developments of these years were the establishment of a National Aeronautics and Space Administration to direct space research; the admission of Hawaii and Alaska as states of the union; and the setting-up of a Civil Rights Commission to investigate the denial of the vote and other rights to members of minority groups. This last item was one of a series of events which indicated growing tension over the Negro problem.[1]

Eisenhower's successor, the young and able John Fitzgerald Kennedy, held office for only two years and ten months before his murder in 1963, and inevitably the record of this short term bears the mark of promise unfulfilled. Many of his supporters shared the outlook he had expressed in his speech to the Democratic Convention at Los Angeles when he was nominated in July, 1960, saying 'We stand to-day on the edge of a New Frontier . . . Woodrow Wilson's New Freedom promised our nation a new political and economic framework. Franklin Roosevelt's New Deal promised security and succor to those in need. But the New Frontier of which I speak is not a set of promises—it is a set of challenges.' There were lively young men among his appointments to office, and he drew heavily upon universities for his advisers. Yet in substance he achieved little in home affairs. Like both his predecessors he came up against the coalition in Congress between southern Democrats and the conservative Republicans, which defeated some of his more striking reform proposals, including those for Civil Rights for Negroes and for the creation of some national system of medical provision for the old. The Kennedy administration did

[1] See below, pp. 264–8, for details.

make notable progress on the Negro question, but, as we shall see, this was through direct executive action, not by legislation. Proposals which Kennedy made for the increase of Federal aid to education failed because of opposition from leaders of his own Roman Catholic community; they wanted the aid extended to church schools, whereas the President took the view that it should properly go only to the state-provided ones.

Lyndon Johnson was a more successful reformer than Kennedy: he was in the White House almost twice as long, he was more adroit in handling Congress, and he was a man of the South, the section most affected by the reforms. Calling on Americans to set course toward 'The Great Society' which 'rests on abundance and liberty for all' and 'demands an end to poverty and racial injustice' Johnson persuaded Congress to accept some major reforms. The Negro benefited substantially from the Civil Rights Act of 1964, which forbade racial discrimination in hotels and restaurants, public facilities (e.g. libraries and golf courses), Federally-aided programmes (e.g. in housing and public building), and employment. It was fiercely contested in the Senate: the debate of 736 hours on 83 days was the longest in history, and contained the longest recorded filibuster. Congress passed another Civil Rights Act in 1968, which tried to prevent discrimination in housing and to protect other civil rights of the Negro; and also the Voting Rights Act of 1965, which outlawed literacy tests in elections and provided that Federal officials would register *bona fide* voters if state officials declined. With these must be grouped the 24th Amendment to the Constitution, ratified in 1964, which abolished the poll tax as a condition of voting in presidential elections.[1] Important measures of the Johnson years aimed at poverty included the Economic Opportunity Act (1964) providing, on a scale never before envisaged, nationally organised opportunities for training for employment; the Appalachian Regional Development Act (1965), making possible special help for one of the nation's most poverty-stricken areas; and the creation of a new Federal Department of Housing and Urban Development. Also in 1965 the Elementary and Secondary Education Act was largely concerned with financial assistance to special education programmes in poor areas; and the Social Security Act, passed only after a considerable struggle against the powerful medical lobby, broke new ground in the United States by providing medical benefits ('medicare') for the first time, to people over 65. 'LBJ's' work as a reformer was not spectacular; yet it was firmly in the tradition of the New Deal, in which he had served his political apprenticeship.

Under the Republican Nixon the Federal Government was less committed to change at home. Moreover he had to face a Democratic majority in both Houses of Congress, and growing economic and financial difficulties.

---

[1] Another Amendment, the 25th, ratified in 1967, enables the Vice-President to act as President when the latter is unfit to do so; and empowers the President to nominate a Vice-President should that office become vacant.

Unemployment rose quite sharply, reaching in 1971 5·9 per cent. of the 'employable' population, the highest rate for ten years; and, inevitably, withdrawal from Vietnam could not in the short run make this situation better. There was a financial crisis in that year, the product of the inflation which afflicted the United States as it afflicted all the 'advanced' countries: the Federal Government cut its own expenditure, declared a wage and price freeze, and accepted some devaluation of the dollar. On the positive side, there was some development of the social security programme, and in particular the scope of medicare was extended. Nixon's decisive victory in the presidential election of 1972 seemed possibly to herald a more successful second term. The prospect was quickly blighted by the Watergate Affair. In January, 1973, the month of his second inauguration, seven men were charged with breaking into the offices of the national committee of the Democratic Party in the Watergate Building at Washington in June 1972, and tapping telephones, planting electronic devices, and abstracting and photocopying documents. The trail quickly led to the heart of the Republican Party and to leading members of Nixon's White House staff. A select committee of the Senate was set up to conduct a public investigation of the whole affair. There were resignations, confessions, allegations, rumours; above all, general discussion of the possible implication of the President himself.

Nixon's reluctance to provide evidence seemed evasive, and public opinion polls showed widespread distrust of his word. Congressmen talked seriously of the possibility of impeachment, and many Americans called on him to resign. His position was complicated by the resignation of the Vice-President, Spiro Agnew, when faced by criminal charges involving large-scale bribery. Agnew's successor, nominated by the President under the 25th Amendment and approved by Congress in December 1973, was Gerald Ford, a well-respected Republican politician. But as 1973 moved towards its close a grave doubt hung over Nixon's personality and regime.

2. THE PROBLEMS OF CHANGE

However great and terrifying the risk of nuclear war, it did not diminish the confidence of the American people in their own way of life. One sign of this was the growth of population in these years. American parents were giving hostages to fortune in large numbers. The population of the U.S.A., which had been 132 millions in 1940, had risen to over 203 millions by 1970. Part of this steep rise resulted from a decline in the death-rate; thanks to improved medical skill, more public health services and better diet, Americans were living longer. But much of it came about because the birth-rate went up from 16·9 per 1000 in 1935 to 25 per 1000 in 1957. Moreover, during the period 1950–70 the gates of the United

States opened more widely to immigrants than at any time in the previous thirty years; some 5,800,000 entered during those twenty years. Some of these were European displaced persons deprived of their homes by the war, others were political refugees like those from Hungary after the rising of 1956; yet most of them came from other parts of the Americas, notably Mexicans who went to work on the land in the south-west and Puerto Ricans who settled by the thousand in New York City. Nevertheless by 1970 the foreign-born inhabitants of the U.S.A. numbered only under 5 per cent. of the population, by contrast with the 14·5 per cent. of sixty years earlier. An immigration Act of 1965 abolished the National Origins quota in force since 1924;[1] henceforward skills and family relationships were to be the main qualifications for admission.

Americans have always been ready to uproot themselves and move to another part of the country to live. The Second World War encouraged this process, and it continued after 1945. Three particular sorts and directions of movement were of special importance. First, large numbers of people, most of them comfortably off and many of them retired, moved from the cities and towns of the north-east to the more attractive climate of the south and west, notably to California and Florida. Florida's population rose from under 2 millions in 1940 to over 6,700,000 in 1970, while California, outpacing New York, had become by that date the biggest state in the Union in population. Secondly, Negroes, hitherto mainly concentrated in the south-east, in the old Confederacy of the Civil War years, moved northwards and westwards in vast numbers, especially to the big cities like New York, Chicago and Philadelphia; a change of balance which had important political consequences. Thirdly, the cities themselves underwent notable population changes. Despite the influx of Negroes into some of them, and despite the fact that during these same years an increasing number of Americans ceased to live in the countryside and shifted into urban areas, the old-established big American cities were steadily losing population. Their inhabitants were moving away from the centres, leaving behind the decayed buildings and the squalid streets, and occupying instead the rapidly-expanding suburbs on the outskirts. By 1960 over a quarter of the entire population were living in suburbia —a move which meant for millions of Americans a manner of living very different from that in which they had grown up in the tenement blocks of the cities.

Many things helped bring about these population changes. One was improvement in transport. The American railroads, already in financial trouble before the war, fell further into decline as the automobile and the aeroplane captured the traffic. While 26,000 miles of railroad went out of use between 1940 and 1970, great new motor highways were carved across the continent, and every city got its airport; so more and more Americans commuted ever greater distances, from suburban home to city office or

[1] See p. 197, above.

from one urban area to another. A second element in the changes was a substantial increase in the amount of leisure time available to Americans. Many could live farther away from their work because the working day was growing shorter; many others retired younger, and departed from Boston or Detroit to the sunshine of California. The development of automation, strikingly evident in the vast automobile industry, became clearer every year, and for a growing number of Americans the working week fell to thirty hours. A third, more fundamental, cause of the population changes was that these post-war years were, on the whole, a period of great prosperity for most people in the United States. The output of industrial goods rose, real incomes rose; and so Americans could afford to commute farther, to pay high prices for houses in Florida—and to increase the size of their families. This rise in the material standard of living showed itself in countless ways. To take examples from two familiar kinds of mid-20th-century expenditure: the number of motor cars in use rose from 47 millions in 1955 to 83 millions in 1973, and the 'two-car family' was normal in suburbia; while only 4 per cent. of American households had no television set in 1970. This prosperity was, in general, more equally shared out among Americans than before the Second World War. A rise in real wages was the principal reason for this, for it meant that a far wider range of goods and services—clothes, foodstuffs, electrical appliances, holidays, and so on—was within the reach not merely of the wealthy but of the average American citizen.

The United States continued to hold its place as the richest land in man's history. American industrial and trading enterprises continued to be the strongest in the capitalist world, and those at their head continued to be extraordinarily rich, even if they no longer commanded such power over their fellow men as the first Rockefeller and Carnegie had in earlier days. About one-quarter of all American wealth was in the hands of 1 per cent. of the population. The great corporations which dominated American industry grew bigger than ever: the post-war years saw the growth of many giant mergers, like General Motors in the automobile industry. In a sense, these were matched by the growth of giant trade unions. In 1940 there were less than 9,000,000 trade unionists in the U.S.A. When in 1955 the two great unions, the A.F. of L. and the C.I.O., patched up their differences and joined together in a single vast combine, the A.F.L.–C.I.O., it contained 17,000,000 members. By 1970 there were nearly 21,000,000 trade unionists all told. Moreover unions secured great advances for their members in these post-war years, not merely substantial wage increases to keep up with the cost of living, but also numerous 'fringe benefits,' such as longer holidays, health insurance schemes, pensions and the like. Nevertheless these were far from easy years for the unions. Public opinion was hostile for various reasons: they had antagonised people by strikes during and immediately after the war, some of their leaders like John L. Lewis seemed aggressive and selfish men, some unions suffered from Communist leadership. So the Taft-Hartley Act, passed in 1947 over President Truman's veto, restricted them in several ways: it declared the 'closed shop' illegal, it forbade them to spend money on Federal elections, it provided for a sixty days' 'cooling-off' period before they could come out on strike, it made them liable for the actions of their officials, whether they had authorised these or not. Some scandalous cases of corruption by union officials, notably in the big Teamsters' Union, lowered all unions in public esteem. And in some ways their future was a little uncertain. They had met with relatively little success in the South, and—more significantly—among 'white collar' workers; and an increasing proportion of Americans were becoming 'white collar' workers as automation spread in manufacturing industry.

The standard of living of most Americans was far above that of the vast majority of human beings in these years. But the developments which made this state of affairs possible also brought problems which worried thoughtful Americans. Some of these were obvious material ones, like the immense social consequences of the automobile—the death and accident roll, the congestion and rush-hour 'snarl-ups,' the fumes, the parking problems. Others, in various ways, went far deeper. For example, many Americans wondered whether the vast growth of advertising which seemed to be a necessary accompaniment of prosperity was entirely desirable. It often looked as though Madison Avenue, the New York centre of the advertising industry (on which in the late 1950's the Americans were spending three times as much as upon higher education) devoted much of its energy to persuading Americans to buy things they neither needed nor really wanted—and that its 'hidden persuaders' enjoyed powers which might be highly dangerous to individual freedom. Some features of economic development also caused alarm. Would not automation put millions of men out of work altogether? And would not industry itself therefore collapse for lack of customers? Machines might be better than men at making mass-produced goods, but they would not buy them when they were made. And was there not something very odd about the growing practice of 'built-in obsolescence'? This meant that manufacturers had to be certain that the goods they produced were not too sturdily made; for if they did not become obsolete within a limited time, the factories would have either to limit their sales or to close down altogether for lack of new orders.

Millions of Americans still alive had bitter personal memories of the sudden collapse of prosperity in the years after 1929, and nobody could be wholly sure that the same thing might not happen again. And the prosperity of the years after 1945 certainly had its limits. Some decaying industrial areas, like parts of New England or the coalfield of West Virginia, got less than their fair share of it; so did the members of some minority groups in the country, especially the Negroes and the Puerto

Ricans, who tended to get the badly-paid jobs; so did the slum-dwellers in the big cities; and so too did an alarmingly high proportion—perhaps one in every three—of Americans over sixty-five, who for one reason or another got little in the way of pensions either from public or from private schemes. Nor was this post-war period without its own economic ups and downs, even if these were small movements compared with the catastrophe of the previous generation. Jobs now depended on the Federal government far more than ever before in American history: partly because it directly employed huge numbers of Americans (the figure by the 1960's was 10 per cent. of the total labour force), partly because of military expenditure in these days of N.A.T.O., wars in Korea and Vietnam, and nuclear weapons. Thus the ending of the Korean War, with a sharp fall in military spending, brought something of what economists now call a 'recession' in industry, and a rise in unemployment. When Kennedy took office in 1961 nearly 5,500,000 Americans were unemployed; ten years later there was another alarming rise. Prosperity was neither complete nor certain, even if many Americans seemed to assume that it was both.

To many thoughtful Americans, the most dangerous of the problems which the changes of the mid-20th century brought to the United States was that of the Negro. To many English people, too, it seemed the most important of all American issues, partly because at bottom it was the same colour problem which in different ways confronted men in other parts of the world, from South Africa to Smethwick and Notting Hill, and partly because it sometimes seemed that the world reputation of the United States depended on its solution. By 1970 the 22,500,000 American Negroes formed over 11 per cent. of the country's population; more than half the inhabitants of the national capital, Washington, were coloured. Could a country which denied them equal political and civil rights honestly call itself a democracy in the 20th-century world? It was not a new problem, but during the years after 1945 Americans became increasingly sensitive to world criticism about it, and concerned about the image they presented to the rest of mankind. This was of real political importance. The Soviet Union made full use, for example, of the denial of voting and other rights to Negroes in the southern states of the U.S.A., as a weapon of anti-American propaganda in dealing with the new African nations.

Other circumstances gave the Negro problem an entirely new urgency in the years after the Second World War, and strengthened the coloured man's chances of securing complete equality. Some were the legacy of the war itself—a war fought against a German Nazi government which preached and practised odious doctrines of racial supremacy. Great numbers of Negroes had served in the armed forces; many had gone overseas, and had been welcomed in homes, bars, theatres, hospitals, trains and elsewhere on the same terms as their white comrades. They were scarcely likely to take kindly to the old ways of segregation when they returned to the land they had fought to defend. Moreover, there was by 1945 a strongly established

Negro middle class, many of whom had obtained their education in the schools and colleges of the North. Out of its ranks—from among lawyers, clergy, professors, business men and journalists—came a group of new Negro leaders, working both inside and outside the N.A.A.C.P., which was the strongest organisation fighting for Negro rights. Both tougher and more flexible than their forerunners, adroit and tireless in organising propaganda and demonstrations, they showed no trace of 'Booker T-ism,' as readiness to accept inferiority was sometimes called.[1] Their target was complete equality—in voting, in education, in housing, in American life as a whole. Communist propaganda won astonishingly few adherents among them. The loyalty of Negroes to the United States was very great; their aim was to become full American citizens, for they knew no other homeland.

Their basic weapon was the vote, not so much yet in the South, but in the cities and industrial areas of the North and West to which they moved in great numbers during and after the war. In 1940 77 per cent. of Negroes lived in the South and only 23 per cent. in the North and West; by 1970 the proportions had changed to 53 and 47 per cent. respectively. In cities like New York, Chicago, Philadelphia, Detroit and Baltimore their votes could be decisive in elections. Traditionally Negroes had supported the Republicans, for the Democrats had been the party of white supremacy in the South, but in the 1940's they moved into the Democratic column. This change had begun under Roosevelt and the New Deal, when Eleanor Roosevelt had been a prominent champion of the coloured people. Harry Truman came out strongly for civil rights for Negroes, setting up a committee which issued a report, *To Secure These Rights* (1947), calling for radical action by Federal and state governments to get rid of discrimination against Negroes in voting, employment, schools and protection under the law. Congress made no effective response to the President's appeal to pass new laws. Truman, however, did much by executive action, i.e. by measures which lay within the President's own powers. He made sure that Negroes received their fair share of Federal jobs, and, despite opposition from some trade unions, he refused defence contracts to firms which would not employ coloured people. Under his order of 1948 segregation was to end in the armed forces—in camps and canteens, in the fighting line, in chances of promotion; by 1954 there were no separate Negro units in the U.S. armed forces.

New and highly important developments in the Negro problem took place during Eisenhower's presidency (1953–61). His government itself did not show great vigour about the issue, although it managed to get two Civil Rights Acts through Congress in 1957 and 1960, despite southern opposition. The earlier of these, the first Civil Rights Act for eighty years, set up a Commission on Civil Rights to investigate denial of voting rights,

---

[1] A reference to the policy of an earlier Negro leader: see above, p. 146. It is also called 'Uncle Tom-ism,' from the attitude of the hero of *Uncle Tom's Cabin*.

and the later one provided for Federal referees to help Negroes to register as voters. But the most significant single event of these years was a Supreme Court decision. The N.A.A.C.P., using able Negro lawyers, had devoted much energy to securing Negro rights through the courts, and had won important Supreme Court decisions requiring the inclusion of Negroes on juries and declaring illegal some of the methods by which coloured people were excluded from the polls in the South. The Supreme Court had clearly become favourable to Negro claims, and a climax of this development came in 1954 in a case concerning segregation in schools, *Brown* v. *Board of Education of Topeka*. The Court on this occasion reversed its decision in *Plessy* v. *Ferguson*.[1] It handed down a unanimous verdict against segregation, declaring that 'separate educational facilities are inherently unequal.' Next year it followed this decision up with a ruling that the desegregation of schools must proceed 'with all deliberate speed.' It was one thing to declare the law; it was quite another to get it carried out. In the eyes of white southerners this was a revolution. They formed White Citizens' Councils of protest, and they proceeded to employ every possible legal device to prevent the mixing of white and coloured children in their schools. There was also some violence, with mobs in some areas preventing coloured children from attending desegregated schools. In 1957 the governor of Arkansas, an outspoken champion of white supremacy, .called out the state National Guard to prevent Negro children attending the high school at Little Rock. Eisenhower eventually sent a detachment of Federal troops to Little Rock, and the Negro children entered school—although the governor continued his efforts in the courts, with some success in delaying the issue. The whole situation, not merely at Little Rock, was a delicate one, for education was under the Constitution the responsibility of the states. Nor could any President seriously contemplate the wholesale use of armed force to coerce the South on such a matter. The deliberate southern defiance of the law was not unsuccessful. By 1960 only a fraction of southern schools were 'integrated.' In five states in the South not a single school contained both white and coloured children.

By this time the Negroes themselves had developed new forms of protest. Perhaps appropriately, students were prominent in them. In 1955–6 Martin Luther King, a coloured Baptist minister who became the most celebrated Negro leader, led a successful non-violent boycott of the buses in Montgomery, the capital of Alabama, to compel them to abandon segregated seating. In 1960 a group of students in a town in North Carolina staged a 'sit-in' demonstration against a café proprietor's refusal to serve four Negro students. This touched off a 'sit-in' movement through the South which, backed by the threat of a widespread Negro boycott, did much to destroy discrimination against coloured people in stores and city

1 See above, p. 146.

shopping centres. Next year there began the 'Freedom Riders' movement, of Negroes and white sympathisers, an attempt to challenge by non-violent means the practice of segregation in public transport in the South; it was backed by the Congress of Racial Equality (C.O.R.E.), a body which believed N.A.A.C.P. was too cautious in its methods of action.

The 1960's were a critical period in the story of American Negroes, marked by two related but very different lines of development. On the one hand there was a rapid growth of Negro militancy, inspired by the astonishing multiplication of independent states in Black Africa at this time, as well as by conditions inside the U.S.A. itself. This took various forms, among them a crop of Negro organisations, such as the Black Muslims and the Black Panthers, which talked, and to some extent practised, violence in support of their cause. Prominent among their leaders was Stokely Carmichael, advocating the slogan of 'Black Power,' which emphasised self-help, racial unity, and, at its extreme, retaliatory violence against whites. Perhaps luckily for the forces of law and order, the Negro groups were much divided among themselves. Their mere existence led during the later 1960's to a hardening of attitudes on the colour problem. But the most immediately alarming events of the period were the succession of riots which occurred in the poorer quarters of American cities during these years. Usually occurring in the heat of the summer, these involved arson, looting, murders and beatings-up; they provoked brutal retaliation by the police; nor were those taking part only Negroes. During the 1960's they ranged from Harlem (the Negro ghetto of New York City) to Detroit, and from Chicago to the smaller cities of the South. The worst of all took place in Watts, a business area of the Californian city of Los Angeles, in the heat wave of August, 1965: 34 people were killed, several hundreds injured, nearly 4000 arrested, and some 35 million dollars' worth of damage done to property.

The second strand of development in these years was more hopeful. Presidents, Congress, and Supreme Court did much of potential benefit to the Negro, in a variety of ways. Kennedy and Johnson symbolised their attitude to the whole issue by giving important official posts to Negroes: Kennedy appointed the first Negro ambassador and the first Negro commander of a U.S. warship, Johnson appointed the first Negro Supreme Court Justice (Thurgood Marshall in 1967) and named five Negroes to the nine-member council which ran the local government of Washington, D.C. (1967); and between 1967 and 1970 there was a marked increase in the number of Negroes appointed to posts in the public service. Congress —despite embattled 'white supremacy' opposition—passed some epoch-making measures, especially in the field of Civil Rights.[1] The Supreme Court continued to follow the liberal line which it had shown in the 1950's.[2] In 1964 its judges unanimously declared the Civil Rights Act of that year to be constitutional. In 1968 they decreed that all racial discrimination in

[1] See above, p. 259.   [2] See above, p. 266.

the sale and rental of property was illegal. In 1969 they ruled that de-segregation in the public schools—which had gone forward only spasmodically against white opposition in the South—should take place 'at once'; a clear step beyond their decision of 1955 which had demanded only 'with all deliberate speed.' These were major decisions. If effectively carried out they would transform the status of the coloured people of America and open a new future to them: for they dealt with the three central issues of voting, housing and education. But they could be effect-ively carried out only with the full backing of public opinion in the various parts of a great land of over 200 million people. Hostility was strongest in the Deep South, in such states as Mississippi and Alabama; in other southern states like Texas and Louisiana the cause of racial equality made considerable progress during these years. Yet opposition was not confined to the South, as the nationwide controversy over 'bussing' revealed in the early 1970's.[1] There were no easy or quick solutions in the race problem.

The riots of the 1960's drew public attention to the growing amount of violence in American life. They were merely one example of it, even if a terrifying one; and race was only one cause of violence, although a peculi-arly stimulating one. Between 1960 and 1967, while the population increased by about 10 per cent. the volume of crime had risen by 89 per cent. The statistics of murder and crimes of violence in particular had shown an alarming rise, notably in the great cities and most notably in their ghettoes and poorest areas: there were increasing areas of great cities, among them Washington as well as New York, where it was no longer safe for respectable citizens to walk at night. The place of violence in American life had been thrown into sharp relief by the assassination of three outstanding American citizens within five years—of President John F. Kennedy at Dallas in Texas (November, 1963), of the coloured leader Dr. Martin Luther King at Memphis in Tennessee (April, 1968), and of Senator Robert Kennedy, younger brother of the dead president, at Los Angeles in California (June, 1968). Even the widespread horror aroused by these shootings had failed to get Congress to pass in 1968 anything more than a very limited Gun Control Act to curb the traditional claim of every American to be able to carry a gun in 'self-defence'. A further aspect of violence in American society which aroused concern in these years was the strong-arm methods used by some state and local police to deal not only with genuine riots but also with peaceful demon-strations and with political meetings: this had been brutally illustrated by the techniques used by the Chicago authorities in handling demonstra-

[1] To prevent neighbourhood schools being virtually confined to children of one race, many school authorities had adopted the policy of transferring large numbers of children by bus daily to schools in other neighbourhoods, thus securing de-segregated schools. For obvious reasons this device aroused high feelings and much protest from parents, even though the Supreme Court in 1971 ruled that 'bussing' was constitution-ally legal.

tors at the Democratic Party Convention when it was held in that city in 1968.

There were other serious problems in American society in the 1960's and early 1970's, like the industrial pollution which was destroying the land's natural resources and fouling its atmosphere, or the sharp increase in drug addiction which was starting to kill more of the nation's young people. In the shadow of all these ills and of Vietnam, many thoughtful Americans came to believe that their country, once so confident of itself, had somehow lost its way—even though it was clear that most of the problems were by no means uniquely American and that many of them were not entirely new. Among the sceptics were many students, members of an age-group (the 18–21 year-olds) of which by 1970 about 50 per cent. were in full-time higher education, a proportion far bigger than in the United Kingdom. One of the most striking characteristics of American life in these years after 1960 was the conflict of opinion between old and young—a conflict exemplified not merely by the groups of hippies wandering around to the distaste and alarm of suburbia, or by the burning of draft cards but, perhaps more significantly, by the clashes at many universities and colleges between students and authorities. These clashes took place all over the country—from Berkeley in California to Columbia University in New York City, from Kent State College in Ohio to several campuses in the Deep South. They were set off by extremely varied issues—the colour bar, the programme of lectures, Vietnam, what the university was spending its money on or using its buildings for, real or alleged interference with free speech. Behind these lay fundamental doubts about the American way of life and some of its features—among them the power of the state as reflected, for example, in the Pentagon, the military nerve-centre of Washington; the wealth and strength of the great industrial corporations; the traditional patterns and purposes of high school and college. It may be doubted how far American students of this era were revolutionaries of the kind they had been taught to believe that their 18th-century ancestors were. But at no period in the entire history of the United States had differences of belief and attitude between old and young been so sharp, the 'generation gap' so wide. In view of this, it may well be that the most significant single event of the most recent years of American history has been the 26th Amendment, ratified in 1972, which lowered the minimum age for voting in presidential elections to 18.

The American States, with Dates of Admission to the Union

I. THE ORIGINAL THIRTEEN STATES

Virginia
Massachusetts
Connecticut
Delaware
Maryland
New Hampshire
New Jersey

New York
North Carolina
South Carolina
Pennsylvania
Rhode Island
Georgia

2. STATES FORMED AND ADMITTED AFTER THE CREATION OF THE UNION

1791	Vermont	1859	Oregon
1792	Kentucky	1861	Kansas
1796	Tennessee	1863	West Virginia
1803	Ohio	1864	Nevada
1812	Louisiana	1867	Nebraska
1816	Indiana	1876	Colorado
1817	Mississippi	1889	Montana
1818	Illinois	1889	North Dakota
1819	Alabama	1889	South Dakota
1820	Maine	1889	Washington
1821	Missouri	1890	Idaho
1836	Arkansas	1890	Wyoming
1837	Michigan	1896	Utah
1845	Florida	1907	Oklahoma
1845	Texas	1912	Arizona
1846	Iowa	1912	New Mexico
1848	Wisconsin	1959	Alaska
1850	California	1959	Hawaii
1858	Minnesota		

The Presidents of the U.S.A.

1789–97	George Washington	Virginia	—
1797–1801	John Adams	Massachusetts	Federalist
1801–9	Thomas Jefferson	Virginia	Republican (1)
1809–17	James Madison	Virginia	Republican (1)
1817–25	James Monroe	Virginia	Republican (1)
1825–9	John Quincy Adams	Massachusetts	National Republican (1)
1829–37	Andrew Jackson	Tennessee	Democrat
1837–41	Martin van Buren	New York	Democrat
1841	William H. Harrison	Ohio	Whig
1841–5	John Tyler (2)	Virginia	Whig
1845–9	James Knox Polk	Tennessee	Democrat
1849–50	Zachary Taylor	Louisiana	Whig
1850–3	Millard Fillmore (2)	New York	Whig
1853–7	Franklin Pierce	New Hampshire	Democrat
1857–61	James Buchanan	Pennsylvania	Democrat
1861–5	Abraham Lincoln	Illinois	Republican
1865–9	Andrew Johnson (2)	Tennessee	Republican
1869–77	Ulysses S. Grant	Illinois	Republican
1877–81	Rutherford B. Hayes	Ohio	Republican
1881	James A. Garfield	Ohio	Republican
1881–5	Chester A. Arthur (2)	New York	Republican
1885–9	Grover Cleveland	New York	Democrat
1889–93	Benjamin Harrison	Indiana	Republican
1893–7	Grover Cleveland	New York	Democrat
1897–1901	William McKinley	Ohio	Republican
1901–9	Theodore Roosevelt (2)	New York	Republican
1909–13	William H. Taft	Ohio	Republican
1913–21	Woodrow Wilson	New Jersey	Democrat
1921–3	Warren Harding	Ohio	Republican
1923–9	Calvin Coolidge (2)	Massachusetts	Republican
1929–33	Herbert Hoover	California	Republican
1933–45	Franklin D. Roosevelt	New York	Democrat
1945–53	Harry S. Truman (2)	Missouri	Democrat
1953–61	Dwight D. Eisenhower	New York and Pennsylvania	Republican
1961–3	John F. Kennedy	Massachusetts	Democrat
1963–9	Lyndon B. Johnson (2)	Texas	Democrat
1969–	Richard M. Nixon	California	Republican

Notes. (1) 'Republican' was the name which the members of Jefferson's party gave to it: their opponents called them Democrats, and after 1829 they themselves adopted that name. Thus Jefferson, Madison, Monroe, and John Quincy Adams were members of the same party as Andrew Jackson and all the later Democrat Presidents. But in 1824–5 this Republican Party divided into two groups: that led by Adams became known as the National Republicans, and the Jacksonians were called the Democratic Republicans.

(2) These Presidents were originally elected as Vice-Presidents and became Presidents because their predecessors died in office.

The names of states given are those in which the Presidents had lived and in which they had therefore passed their political career; they are not necessarily the same as those in which the Presidents were born. Thus Woodrow Wilson was born in Virginia, but spent most of his life in New Jersey, and made his political reputation as Governor of New Jersey: Calvin Coolidge, born in Vermont, had lived in Massachusetts and became its Governor.

APPENDIX 3

Political Parties in the U.S.A.

1. THE MAIN PARTIES

A. The Federalists. Arose about 1792, and flourished from then until about 1815. By 1825 they were practically extinct. One President, John Adams (1797–1801), was a Federalist, and Alexander Hamilton was the earliest leader of the party.

B. The Democrats. Also arose about 1792, and have remained in continuous existence ever since. Originally called Republicans or Republican-Democrats: adopted the name Democrat about 1829. Jefferson was the founder of the party.

C. The Whigs. Arose during the 1830's as an opposition to Andrew Jackson: remained in existence until the 1850's, when they split up over slavery, and were superseded by the new Republican party.

D. The Republicans. Founded in 1854, and have remained in continuous existence ever since. Lincoln was the first Republican President.

2. THE MINOR PARTIES

There have been many of these. Most came into being over issues of local or temporary importance, and did not survive long. Among them were the Liberty Party (see p. 101), the Anti-Masons (p. 81), and the Know-Nothings (p. 106). From about 1890 onwards there have arisen several minor parties whose general object has been social reform. These have included the Populists (p. 148), the Roosevelt Progressives (p. 166), the LaFollette Progressives (p. 181), and the Socialists. None of the minor parties has ever produced a President, although Theodore Roosevelt in 1912 and Robert LaFollette in 1924, standing as Progressives, each polled over 4,000,000 votes. No purely Socialist candidate has ever polled a million votes, although there has been a Socialist candidate of some kind at every presidential election since 1892. At almost every presidential election during the last hundred years there have been more than two candidates, and considerably more than two at those of the 20th century. In each of the years 1900, 1908, 1924, and 1928 there were eight. But the real contest has almost invariably been between two candidates, those of the two chief parties at the time.

Thus in 1932 there was a candidate from each of the following parties: Democrat, Republican, Socialist, Socialist Labour, Communist, Liberty, Prohibition, and Farm-Labour. The real contest lay between the Democrat, Roosevelt, and the Republican, Hoover: the six others got only 3·1 per cent. of the popular vote between them.

3. WHAT THE PARTIES STAND FOR

It is easy enough to say what the minor parties have stood for: often it is for a single reform, like that of the Prohibition Party, or against some easy target for abuse, like the Masons whom the Anti-Masons opposed. The major parties are much harder to understand. It is very misleading to think of them as resembling in every way British political parties. Great Britain is a small and compact country. The U.S.A. is much more like a continent, in its size and in the great variety of people which it contains. One result of this, as we have seen, has been the growth of sectional feeling. The inhabitants of each of the sections have stood fairly firmly together on important issues: the supreme example of this came in 1861, when the people of the South stood firmly for extending slavery, and those of the North stood as firmly against it. This sectionalism has not, except perhaps at the time of the Civil War, been anything like as strong as the nationalism which has divided Europe into so many different countries. Equally, however, it has been far stronger than any widely-held local feeling in Great Britain. The U.S.A. is neither a compact nation like Britain, nor a continent of nations like Europe, but something in between the two. Thus it contains not only separate states with interests of their own, but also these large areas, the sections, also with interests of their own.

The existence of this sectional feeling has had a curious effect upon parties in the U.S.A. In Britain political parties have been formed either by groups of people sharing the same ideas—like the Liberal and Conservative Parties in the nineteenth century: or by groups of people of the same class— thus in the 20th century the Labour Party has been a working-class party, while the Conservative Party has contained the great majority of the middle and upper classes. But in the U.S.A. sectional feeling has made the major parties much more like alliances between people of the different sections. They are indeed in some ways far more like alliances between different European states than like the British political parties. Thus the Democratic party under Andrew Jackson (1829–37) drew much of its voting strength from an alliance between the farmers of the West, the working-men of Eastern cities, and the cotton-growers of the South against the bankers and manufacturers of the North. The Republican party of Lincoln's day, on the other hand, was based on an alliance between the manufacturing North and the farming West against the cotton-growing and slave-owning South. Further, each major party has usually had one great section as its core. The Democrats, for example, were mainly a western party under Jackson. But after the Civil War and Reconstruction they were primarily a southern party: and for long after Reconstruction was over, almost every white man in the South voted Democrat, because the Republicans had been responsible for Reconstruction. Hence came the phrase 'the solid South.' It was so solid in fact that six southern states (Alabama, Arkansas, South Carolina, Georgia, Louisiana, and Mississippi) always voted Democrat in presidential elections for nearly a century after the Civil War. The Republicans, on the other hand, began as a northern party, and their main strength has remained in the North, Pennsylvania and most of New England having been Republican strongholds.

Another consequence of sectionalism has been important, and seems strange to British ways of thinking. Since parties are not associations of men with similar ideas, each major party includes men of very different and frequently of contrary ideas. There are liberal Democrats and conservative Democrats, conservative Republicans and liberal Republicans. The New Deal proposals, put forward by Roosevelt, a Democrat, emphasised this fact. Conservative Democrats joined conservative Republicans in Congress in voting against the New Deal, while liberal Republicans joined liberal Democrats in voting for it. Yet the conservative Democrats still remain Democrats, the liberal Republicans still remain Republicans; they do not change their party, and their party does not turn them out. This could not happen in the British political parties.

Thus it is not possible to say that American parties stand or have stood for any definite ideas. Yet some general statements can be made about those two parties which have dominated the American political scene since just before the Civil War. The Republicans have, on the whole, been the party of the North. Most big business men have supported them, and the party has stood for a high tariff. Generally the party has been the more conservative of the two. The Democrats have drawn most of their votes from 'the solid South' (until recently) and from the foreign-born people of New York and other great cities. Negroes, who used to vote Republican, have since the New Deal voted Democrat. Most Irishmen have voted Democrat. Their policy has on the whole been more progressive in domestic affairs than that of the Republicans. The most progressive Presidents of the 20th century, Woodrow Wilson and Franklin D. Roosevelt, Truman, Kennedy and Lyndon Johnson have also been the Democratic Presidents of the century.

4. THE PARTY 'MACHINE'

The principal object of each major party has been to put its members into office. This means a very great deal more than winning the presidency and a majority of seats in the Senate and the House. It means winning State governorships and majorities in the legislatures in the 50 states: it means winning control of cities and counties all over the U.S.A. It means, more-over, getting its candidates elected to the many offices like those of State judges, sheriffs, public prosecutors and others, which in the U.S.A. are elective offices. Further, victory in elections carries with it the right to appoint party members to vast numbers of civil posts. There are numerous Federal government jobs, and very many State, city, and county ones. A large number of these are filled not by competitive examination but by appointment by the victorious party in Federal, State, or local elections. They are the 'spoils' of office, the reward to party members for faithful service, and the means of capturing votes.

The existence of such spoils means that the parties are very efficiently organised. Each party goes to a great deal of trouble to make sure that the people vote in the very large number of elections, and to make sure that they vote the right way. The party leaders or 'bosses' in cities and counties are influential persons, controlling many votes. Here in particular corruption has crept into American politics, and some of the local party 'machines' have been notoriously dishonest. Tammany Hall, the Democratic party organisation in New York, which has been very powerful since the days of Aaron Burr, acquired a very unsavoury reputation.

The centre of the national organisation of each party is the Convention, whose main purpose is to choose a presidential candidate. The presidential election is held in November, every fourth year,[1] and the parties hold their conventions in the preceding summer. The convention is attended by delegates from every state. These delegates are themselves elected by the party members in the states in what are known as 'primary' elections, and they are frequently instructed to support particular candidates at the convention. At the national convention the delegates decide on the party candidate for the presidential election: the possible candidates make speeches and the party leaders weigh up the power of different sections of the party, and decide on the most suitable candidate. One result of this method of choice is that the final candidate is very often not the ablest man in the party, but someone with a comparatively undistinguished record. Sometimes the two ablest candidates will cancel one another out, and a third, less able but less offensive to some powerful group in the party, will be chosen as a kind of compromise candidate. Thus in 1920 the Republicans nominated Harding in preference to two far more able possibilities.

[1] All elections in the U.S.A. are held on fixed dates at regular intervals. Thus the President is elected on the first Tuesday after the first Monday in November in every fourth year: and there are similar fixed dates for other elections—usually, of course, the same date for a great variety of elections, Federal, state, and local.

Index